"Are We Nearly There Yet, Dad?"

One Family's 30,000-Mile Road Trip Across
Europe, Asia And Around Australia

By

Graham Naismith

Printed in the United Kingdom

First Edition 2019

ISBN 978-1-9993761-1-6

Hen Publishing

Tunbridge Wells

website: www.drive-to-oz.com

email: info@drive-to-oz.com

twitter: @grahamnaismith

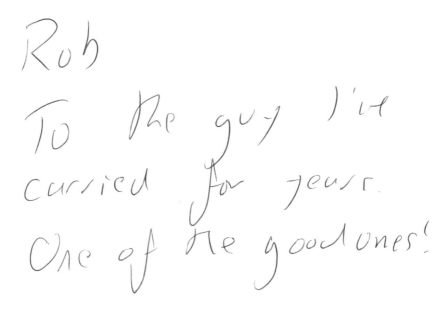

Rob

To the guy I've carried for years.
One of the good ones!

For Eirene for always tolerating me.

For Hannah, Emily and Abigail for embracing it all.

You are the journey I'm most proud of.

Thanks for all your support.

Keep in touch

"Twenty years from now you will be more disappointed by the things you didn't do than by the ones you did do."

Mark Twain

CONTENTS

FOREWORD

This is the bit where you thank people and therefore possibly the scariest bit of the lot in case I forget anyone. I want to thank the people that believed in us. Sara Harrison, a friend of a work mate, heard about the trip and gave up lots of time helping us with PR. I spent ages contacting sponsors, 125 in total with a positive return rate of 12% (15 companies), but those that responded really believed, helped and were interested in what we were doing, and I'm indebted to you for that. You're all in Appendix H. My cousin Fiona Trowbridge inherited my notes, proofread them and provided much historical context to the places I visited. A painful but fruitful process. And Nicola Withers Editorial Services for proof-reading my proof-reading.

Stu Sibbick and Chris Martin who gave up a day to come and help me look at a Land Rover miles away that I never bought!

The RAC had a guy called Paul Gowen who took care of all the Carnet de Passage. But he was much more than that. One of those old fashioned, specialised guys who knew his job inside out and took great pride in it. He was so helpful, bent over backwards for you and knew everyone who was travelling. They got rid of him in the end, but I can understand why he has been thanked in so many books.

Lesley Ashmall at BBC Radio 5 live for picking the story up before them all and following it through right to the end.

My parents taught me to reach for the stars and go for it as they did and never be scared of failing. A tremendous gift if there ever was one.

My brother is my hero and the first person I told. His reaction made it all worthwhile.

And (almost) last but not least. Shameen Koleejan who I trust implicitly and has been a loyal friend for many years. Brilliant and efficient. Thank you for everything you did.

But actually, it's the cynics that I'd really like to thank. The people that criticise, scoff and mock are the ones that drive you on and make you more determined. Their jealousy, ignorance and fear are fuel when the tank is empty. Destructive and cynical as it is, it really is something that kept me going when times were tough.

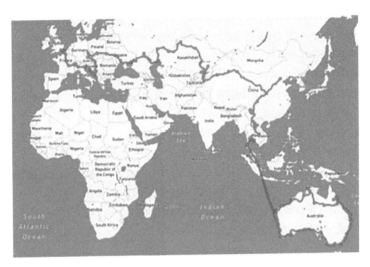

CHAPTER 1.

THE FIRST WEEK

January to April 2008, Warlingham, Surrey, UK

A restless sleep had left me knotted in my duvet. My mouth felt as though a small furry creature had passed away in it during the night. And my stomach yearned for something fried as minor explosions ricocheted inside my skull. As I picked out familiar voices in the distance, my vision and mind were unfocused from the "one" celebratory drink I'd had with my mates Andy and Paul the previous evening. The voices sounded happy and excited. I shivered when I realised that it wasn't a normal work day and I pulled the duvet up around me; not because it was cold, but as a barrier. Outside was the start of something new and I was terrified.

An accumulation of arbitrary decisions had led to this predicament although major influencers were moving from Scotland to England with my parents, then to South Africa with my dad's job and inter-railing through Europe in my gap year; but it was that one statement from my wife, Eirene, as we drove back from dropping my parents off at the airport after Christmas that was the catalyst which had led directly to this situation.

"I've always fancied taking a year out and spending a month in a different place all round the world," Eirene had dreamily suggested. We were renting, having fortuitously sold our house the previous summer a few months before the recession officially started, and decided to bide her time looking for the right place. So we would have no concerns about covering a mortgage or renting out a house.

Finally, on Thursday 1st May 2008, after four months of preparation, frustrating phone calls and unanswered emails to embassies, tourist boards and other government departments (the paperwork, the posting of original passports for visas and anxious waiting for them to be returned, before sending them off again for another visa, and the almost weekly visits to the surgery for painful inoculations against Rabies, Tuberculosis, Japanese Encephalitis and Hepatitis A-Z), we made it to the start of our biggest family adventure ever - a drive across Europe, Asia and Australasia in a Toyota Land Cruiser.

The preparation had been immense. A family of five, with only one bloke, needs a container load of stuff for a trip of nine months but that was nothing compared to the luggage the Land Cruiser needed.

We had roof racks, bull bars, winches, all-terrain tyres, wheels and two spares, a roof box, additional roof and driving lights and protective grills, raised suspension to increase ground clearance, sand-ladders, tinted windows to protect from prying eyes, a hidden safe, long-range fuel tank, shortwave radio, walkie talkies, jerry cans of fuel, plastic cans of water , hi-lift jack, bottle jack, a compressor to inflate tyres, snorkels and under body protection – yes, all just for the car.

We bought camping and cooking equipment, enough dried food to last us 14 days, a satellite phone and an emergency beacon, maps for every country that had them and a cartography kit for those that didn't, first aid kits, satellite navigation systems, electronic maps, digital cameras, a laptop, phrase books and travel guides. I became an expert in what water filter to buy and which cooker could boil water in less than a minute using only sticks as fuel.

We had training from Paul at Footloose 4x4 on every aspect of the car and seemingly had enough spares to build a second one. We learnt to grease the driveshaft nipples without giggling, and remove, repair and replace a punctured tyre. We studied Russian and had every embassy number and worldwide Toyota dealer on speed dial.

We had a card that gave us access to 60 minutes of on-the-phone specialised medical advice, 24 hours a day, in the event of snake bite, shark bite, tropical disease, serious accident or other major trauma. Although nothing was said about what happened if you came to the end of the 60 minutes and you were at the second stage of a four-step lifesaving procedure.

I read books and studied maps until my head nearly exploded. We queued in Belgravia from 6am for visas and were thoroughly interviewed/interrogated by embassy staff. We had a stack of paperwork and an insurance policy that covered our car being stolen or set on fire in any country in the world except Antarctica. It was intense, but I loved every minute of it. It gave me hope and inspiration, a world away from my everyday job in IT. Occasionally I pondered that the simplicity of just climbing into the car with a credit card, passports and change of clothes was all that was required but the guilt of failing to prepare if something bad happened soon assuaged that.

Departure day had arrived and I still had loads of little things to do on the car when Zulf, a friend from work, turned up with a camera, tripod and a teddy called Scrappy to look after.

"Scrappy has been round Cape Horn," he announced enthusiastically, "he'll bring you good luck." Superstitious clap-trap I thought, but little did I know that I would end up swinging between praying to and throttling that Taiwanese teddy over the next nine months.

Eirene had agreed to the trip on the condition that she would drive as she felt she would be safer. I took my position in the passenger seat and began to do some filming. There was a euphoric atmosphere in the car. I looked at Eirene excitedly and filmed the kids buzzing with delight. I had hoped they would be excited at heading off on a road trip that was going to be a talking point for the rest of their lives and the mother of all geography and history lessons. But it was not to be. They were elated because they finally had their hands on their game consoles and were already immersed in a Disney film. A small group of friends had gathered to wave us off and were barely afforded a passing glance from the absorbed trio as we pulled out of Eirene's parents' Surrey drive.

I tried to figure out how to turn Eirene's voicemail off, a costly service to have activated while travelling. As we headed to the motorway, I attempted five times to listen to the recorded message telling me how to deactivate it but each time it reached a crucial point, someone squealed, shouted or announced above the noise of everyone else that that they needed to go to the toilet. Emotions were starting to run high and less than 10 miles from our starting point, barely at Clacket Lane services, the first cracks began to emerge in our idyllic vision as the battle for power within the confines of the car began.

At the Eurotunnel terminal entrance, we all jumped out of the car to take snaps next to the big Eurotunnel sign before heading into the departure area. The expansion tank holding the anti-freeze had been giving me some concern, so once we were on the train and set off under the sea, I opened the bonnet of the car to check the level of the tank. Like the iron you turn around to check on, it was predictably fine. However, I tried to shut the bonnet and it wasn't fine and wouldn't close. I once read that the definition of a psychopath is someone who keeps on repeatedly trying the same thing and expecting a different result. On my psychopathic seventh attempt, I looked around in exasperation and noticed the "Do not take cooking gas canisters onto the Eurotunnel train" sign on the wall. I immediately recalled the three cooking gas canisters in the back of the car, sat back down and silently steeled myself for the remainder of the journey for the destruction of the channel tunnel.

Calais thankfully arrived in a blink and we drove out tentatively and ultimately successfully, listening as Wendy, the sultry Home Counties lady who lived inside our satellite navigation system, disappointed us immediately by insisting for 20 minutes that we were still in Folkestone. A quick delve into the settings to change country and it was off in the direction of Hardecourt aux Bois.

The remainder of our journey was a bit of an anti-climax with little in the way of tears or threats of domestic violence, and we arrived at our destination with "Are we there yet, dad?" resounding in our ears. No matter how witty, self-mocking, satirical, clever or whatever the children make out it is; it infuriates me and they never tired of it for the whole nine months.

I had cunningly booked our first night's accommodation in advance in an attempt to take one less stress out of the day. I had tried to book a place at a guesthouse by the Somme but the English landlady said it was full and offered us two double rooms at another place in the village. I had emailed her a few times but she wouldn't give me the address of the other place, insisting we come to her first and pay her direct - so she could take her slice from her French neighbour it transpired.

We arrived, via the English slice taker, at a textbook French farmhouse with ivy covered brick walls. In the grounds, a blossoming orchard and neat grass filled the south facing view while in contrast an untended old barn with tall, once blue doors and dull brass fittings formed one side of an enclosure. An ancient, vine-clad wall and the back of the farmhouse formed the other two sides and Hannah and Emily waited patiently at the fence while the occupants of the enclosure, Anna the donkey and Susie the sheep made their way over to be petted. Four nameless cats made random stealthy appearances to check on proceedings but stayed well out of arms reach. I was slowly and painfully told the cats' names but I chose not to remember them.

We drove into Perron for dinner at 5pm but eating in France is a late affair, and we found ourselves an hour or so and several overpriced paninis later, back where we started. In typically British fashion we were so sycophantically grateful to the moustached owner for our €37 paninis, I think if we were mugged we would have expressed our thanks for their time and apologised for the low takings.

The transaction with the moustacheless panini waitress was not without incident. Hannah has a strong allergy to milk, the manifestation of which is intense itchiness and rashes and some swelling of the tongue. Fortunately, although we carried an EpiPen with us, it was rarely more severe than that and hadn't to date had any impact on her breathing. However, Eirene tried to head the issue off at the pass with, "mes fils adorent le beurre," before popping in an unmistakeable milking action. Ten minutes later our over-priced paninis arrived with butter dripping from the sides. We later discovered that we should have said, "Ma fille est allergique au beurre," and what she had in fact told them, according to our French farmhouse owner who speaks much better English than we do French, was that, "our son loves butter.".

Apart from that, it had been a good first day overall, so we pushed our luck by deciding to put up Abigail's new travel cot, kindly provided by Bush Baby. It was one of those contraptions that sprung into shape with the erection instructions taking up no more than a line, but those to put it away again involved 10 pages of diagrams and notes coupled with a link to an instructional video on YouTube. Shrewdly Eirene suggested that I film her putting it up on the digital camera so we knew how to put it back in its little bag. It was a decent camera that captured 60 frames per second but it popped up so quickly that later analysis revealed that we had only three frames of film to work with. Despite this it proved brilliant and preferable, in Abigail's eyes, to a proper cot or bed.

Breakfast the next morning was a somewhat nervy affair. Any parent with young children knows the gut wrenching fear of being invited to a home of elderly friends or relatives, whose youngsters have long since fled the nest and who are now wholly oblivious to the ways of the little people. An almost deliberately enticing set of ornaments, glasses, hot drinks and low-level curios will be put on display to tease your children as the hosts perform a well-rehearsed breathless double act to distract you from any form of control of your now wide-eyed and exploratory darlings. When the accident inevitably occurs, there is much scurrying and apologising by both parties preceding a hasty departure before a hushed but venomous spew of wrath descends on both sides of the door.

But this place was something else. It must have taken the delightful sexagenarians (not being rude, look it up) virtually half a life time to set up this baby. The dining room walls were richly adorned with a variety of kiddy height weaponry including swords, muskets, daggers and revolvers. It was clear the continental breakfast would only absorb them for so long but, not for the first time, they surprised us by not grabbing the opportunity with both hands that they still had, failing to stroke blades and grab swords. I may have been mistaken but the landlady looked almost disappointed when she returned with more croissants to see our angelic three sitting politely at the table eating her wares. "Filles – you must come and see Pierre's collection of 250,000 dominoes he has set up in his study in preparation for his French record attempt later this month. He has been preparing for years," I envisaged her saying but she remained pensive. Despite the distractions and perhaps subconsciously as some sort of reckless envelope pushing challenge, we elected to stay another night at this child-friendly establishment, so enamoured were the girls with the animals and us with the lack of stress. We even saved €25 by paying the farmhouse owner directly and, out of some sort of perverse sense of loyalty, I yielded not to the temptation to grass on her English referrer.

We visited the Thiepval Memorial where I texted my dad to see where his dad fought on the Somme as I thought it would be good to visit and pay my respects. He replied promptly with "he lost his left leg there".

I knew this and pondered whether he was hinting that I should be looking for it. The construction was an impressive symmetrical tower of interlocking arches standing nearly 50m above the adjoining cemetery and the largest British battle memorial in the world. The main tower was supported by four red Accrington brick arched legs, themselves comprised of four complex archways and the names of nearly 73,000 officers and soldiers beautifully inscribed at the foot of each structure - and that was just those who were missing, presumed dead. What with it being 90 years since the conflict, they were not taking too many risks with the "presumed" label but I unusually kept the observation to myself. It was a deeply moving place though and my poignant reflection was only interrupted by the vibration of my Nokia secreted in my back pocket – "might have been his right leg".

The children showed their own inimitable reverence to the immaculate lawns but they did no damage, and in some ways I think the fallen would have wanted innocent children to be playing in such a carefree fashion upon this ground they surrendered their lives for - although I drew the line at Emily literally dancing on the grave of one young Shropshire corporal.

With the sun almost at its zenith, we stopped at several other smaller memorials before coming across the Ulster Memorial. The kids were becoming mass cemeteried out, so I popped up to the Mill Road one myself and then walked across a field to the back of the Ulster Memorial where I pottered around and discovered tunnels hidden by some debris. I'd taken a walkie talkie and was impressed at how patiently the family were waiting for me, but I later discovered the flat battery on Eirene's radio was due some of the credit.

Lunch in Albert followed and then a stop at the Newfoundland Memorial with its near intact trenches where we all had a more sombre walk. Going there was one of the things I was most looking forward to and one that least appealed to Eirene. I sensed her reticence at history appreciation as early as 8.30am that morning when she tried to start a clothes wash. "We need to keep on top of it," she said without any hint of awareness that we had left England less than 48 hours previously. Within a couple of hours, she was pushing for a haircut for Hannah and I smelt a rat. A woman resembling Davina McCall cut her hair at panini prices in the afternoon and a picnic followed, which became our newly emerging pattern, as little was open at 5pm.

Eirene, who worryingly mentioned late in the afternoon that she felt ready to go home to England, had an unsuccessful attempt at a school lesson with Hannah and Emily whilst, unconnected I'm sure, I was equally unsuccessful in trying to repeatedly slam the bonnet shut a few feet away.

We woke the next morning to a bright cloudless sky having had a comparatively good night's sleep despite the small hard beds and a nightmare where I was being repeatedly hit by a small child. Hannah had a similar one where a 17-stone daddy kept on rolling over and squashing her. We had breakfast with the shotguns and a chat with the landlady's son who was curious about our trip. We told him we had been learning Russian and he earnestly offered the opinion that he thought it would not be of much use in France. Nevertheless, they were a delightful family who offered us pancakes in the evening, maps the following morning, bin bags for the car and bottles of water for the kids.

A few mechanical tweaks had started to emerge and there was a slight problem with the inverter which kept switching off when I tried to charge the laptop. But Wendy had begun to gain our trust once more as she took us on to Reims.

We made Reims by mid-afternoon, a delightful place with a magnificent Gothic cathedral, the site of which has been of importance since Roman times when the Roman Baths were replaced by this cathedral in around 400AD. Records show that the cathedral was destroyed by fire in 1210 but rebuilt soon after, substantially larger and grander, probably to accommodate all the people who attended the coronations of which there were 33 over the following years.

After Reims and the cathedral were liberated from the English during the 100 Year War in 1429 by Joan of Arc, Charles VII was crowned there and as such set the precedence for a long list of other royals to be crowned at Reims Cathedral. It was used as a hospital during World War I but required intensive care itself after suffering severe damage from German bombs. Ironically, Reims was also the sight of the formal German capitulation in World War II when the first German Instrument of Surrender was signed on 7th May 1945. Hitler had rather symbolically insisted that the French signed their surrender at the start of World War II in Compiègne Forest in the same rail carriage where the Germans had been compelled to sign the 1918 armistice at the end of World War I. I pondered whether this location carried a similar degree of symbolism – bringing the Germans to the scene of some of their most overt devastation.

I marvelled at the architectural detail in this incredible structure before me and I was tempted to start counting the statues of which our guidebook said there were more than 2,300 but the family persuaded me to leave the cathedral and sample one of the town's famous biscuits. It would seem that when the people of Reims were not renovating cathedrals or signing important war documents, they were doing a bit of baking. In fact, Reims claims to be the place where the biscuit was invented in 1671, in particular the Biscuit Rose de Reims. I wondered if the Germans were offered any in the early hours of that May morning.

The town is probably better known as a short break destination for visitors in search of a great meal, a case of bubbly and a tour of a champagne house and since our previous landlady had a cousin in Reims and there was talk of accommodation, we thought we'd accept their hospitality. However, the cousin very kindly called about the accommodation and said, "You've got to be kidding me, it's a bank holiday here and everyone booked up months ago.". I paraphrase but that was the gist of it.

The tourist information offered us two rooms at Mister Bed for €42. You just know by the name what sort of place it was going to be; a bit like the Quality Hotel when you know it will be anything but. Mister Bed was just as I had expected with one additional unexpected disappointment - the reception shut between 12 and 5pm at weekends of course.

With increasing confidence, we used one of Wendy's fangled features and asked her to "take us to the nearest attractions in Reims.". I'd paid extra for this when buying the software but my smugness was short-lived when she apparently translated our instruction to "Take us to all the gypsy camps in Reims.". After three unsuccessful sojourns we came back to sit and wait in the car park until reception opened.

Once squashed into the cells Mister Bed provided, the blood dispersal pattern adjacent to Hannah's head by the top bunk could only keep my former police detective mind absorbed for so long. I escaped the confines of the bastille and spent three hours in the car park calling up farmhouses in Burgundy looking for a week's accommodation while I witnessed from afar the girls' faces occasionally flashing past the window, at a variety of angles, as they ascended and rapidly descended their mountainous bunkbeds.

Accommodation secured, we explored the area in search of dinner and distractions and pitifully ended up in McDonald's. I overtly declared that it wouldn't have been our first choice to entertain these corporate pimps and the stuff they call food, but they serve it all day, have free wireless, clean toilets and an indoor play centre. Covertly, I yearned for a quarter pounder with cheese.

Back in our lockup and over the sound of the alarm bell at the end of the corridor that had been ringing since our arrival, Eirene again nonchalantly remarked, "I'm quite looking forward to getting home.". This, I hoped, was in reference to our plan to fly back from Prague, in June, for some visas but it sparked my own internal alarm bell. She grabbed the laptop and made strides to post her homesick thoughts on our trip forum board but it was like watching my dad trying to programme the video and she quickly gave up.

Our constant sudden proximity was always going to be precarious. I wasn't naïve and I'd recognised that this human element was likely to be the biggest challenge. What surprised me was how soon cracks were starting to appear, anticipating an initial holiday period before issues would begin to emerge. Group harmony was clearly going to be critical to the success of the trip and I'd decided before we left that any time there was a dispute or argument with Eirene then I would apologise, regardless of whether I was right or wrong. In fairness it would do little to balance out the amount of apologies Eirene had unjustifiably given me in our relationship. But the storm clouds were gathering. I could feel them over Eirene's head and they were drifting closer to Hannah and Emily.

I tackled it, with limited success, by putting forward visions of what countries to come would be like. "A nice beach, pool for the kids, great food," I promised when it was actually this form of conventional civilisation that I was keen to avoid.

"So, what's wrong?" I ventured.

"I'm pissed off. I feel like a mobile cleaner," she responded. We had met at University but, after a spell in law and insurance after graduating, she had turned to teaching before giving it up when Hannah popped out.

"That's what you were before but I've added the mobility angle. A bit of glamour," I proffered, foolishly signalling around our cell as an indication of how far she'd come.

"Yesterday I told you to go to the shops," I continued, "have some time on your own, have a coffee, and I would take care of the girls but you never went. Why not?"

"Because what I was doing would still need doing when I got back."

I was holding out hope for a perfect place in Burgundy the next day, but it was the burgundy on the walls of Mister Bed that focused my mind that evening.

The next day we set off for the Loire Valley, and arrived at the rustic and remote old bakery in Perreux near Roanne. It appeared grand in the English sense but the French would probably call it petit. The old bakery had been tastefully modernised to blend sympathetically with the adjoining, original blue-shuttered house, although the difference between them was still stark. It did, however, have a lovely closed pool in an enclosed courtyard which was a perfect base for us from where we could explore and immerse ourselves in the French culture over the following few days.

Hannah confidently wandered off to explore her new surroundings, striding away without even glancing back. Emily skipped along loyally after her big sister and Abigail watched happily and attempted a few experimental steps as though to follow her sisters but quickly returned to the safety of her mother.

Wendy had done us proud and, as we had not ticked the "Avoid off road" option, had been having good fun. Painfully though, this resulted in Eirene, who was at the wheel, acting like the stunt driver from the set of *Driving Miss Daisy* but it provided us with some excellent views of the French countryside which we otherwise wouldn't have seen. As I enthused to the children about some of the amazing features and astonishing sights we were driving by, like the golden field of rape that flowed towards the winding river which in turn snaked around the base of a distant chateau with intricately detailed towering spires, I was greeted with an instant "Wow" in unison, in reply.

Looking round at them, expecting to see wide innocent eyes, wild with amazement and excitement, I instead found myself looking at the crowns of Hannah's and Emily's heads, their eyes firmly fixed on their consoles and I started to realise that they had not seen anything of the surrounding landscape.

We were very strict with time in front of the screens but allowed them on long car journeys, which was always counterbalanced with activities and cultural experiences when we arrived at a place.

There was a bigger problem though with the girls, particularly Emily who was adopting a Beelzebub like stance in the face of Hannah's undeniably great goading prowess. She had been exercising some top-rated teasing of Emily throughout the day and topped it off with a 4pm display of unwarranted petulance. Emily then became temporarily possessed and we sent them both off to bed early.

But then they played the toilet card, visiting as many as six times because they knew we could never turn them down for this. They incisively recognised this as our Achilles Heel and exploited it to the hilt. The principle has now been amended to 'we can never turn them down from going to the toilet except when they have the hump and are taking the piss and want to go six times in an hour.'

As the light fell, those precious couple of hours when it was just the two of us together arrived and we started to relax and share a glass of wine with conspiratorial whispers.

"I really seem to be getting the eye of the Frenchmen," Eirene said. "They really look me up and down."

"You never know, it might just be because they think you're attractive," I playfully offered.

She un-playfully scowled at me and we continued to enjoy the rest of the evening listening to the cicadas clicking in the darkness and the distant voices and lights of the summer festivities in the Loire valley. It might have been the French wine but as I looked over at Eirene, I was starting to see what the French stares had been about. The sun and the outside life certainly suited her.

We put our faith in Wendy again and asked her to take us to some local attractions. Le Parc de la Plage, she came back with. We weren't sure that she'd understood our request but we dutifully followed her directions until we arrived at Lac de Villerest, a beautiful beach park with water slides, rowing boats, trampolines, floats and a giant ball park (the square footage of the park, not the ball size itself). It was like one of those dreams that you have as a kid where you visit an amusement park and it turns out there's no one else there and you ride all the attractions with no queues. Well, it happened! Villerest Lake was the location of the dream come true. I chased the girls as they ran from one water contraption to another then into the pools then onto the trampolines. Even Abigail had a go on a mini trampoline with the help of mum.

The next day we visited Châteaux de la Roche, a glorious castle near Neulise. The castle is situated on an island in the middle of the River Loire formed by Villerest Dam, the same dam that was almost responsible for the drowning of the castle as it was being constructed because the castle didn't fit in with the developers' plans. Luckily it was bought by a group of local people for one franc and has been loving restored to its original gothic style with coned turrets, ramparts, drawbridge and of course, a moat. On the north bank, a pleasant meandering path followed the river on either side of the castle and on the opposite bank, steep wooded cliffs protected the castle from attack. Over the years, the castle has seen more attacks from flooding than human invaders and even with the construction of the dam, the castle was flooded in 2003 and 2008. The only thing scaling the castle walls when we visited were the yellow trumpet vines and wild thorny roses that were just coming into bloom.

Hannah sulkily said she didn't want to go to a boring castle, then conceded on arrival it was awesome, before drawing a big picture of it, including the bird and mermaid crest above the door, as part of her homework. She finished her piece and rounded it off with a whopping sulk, closure perhaps on the initially interrupted one.

We found a suitable spot on a hill in the afternoon for a picnic overlooking the castle and its reflection in the still River Loire where the girls could run around on the grass while we relaxed in the sun. I realised that, for the first time, I truly felt that I was in a different country. We finished off the day with a visit to a park where Emily was fixated with the deer and Hannah showed her strength on the climbing ropes before we all negotiated the supermarket run and let the kids wreak terror on the trolleys.

We were living and spending like it was a holiday or busy weekend and I was unsure if this was a good or bad thing. I felt we should be immersing ourselves in the country and culture to a much greater degree rather than frequenting theme and play parks. But then that is part of the country and it was in these familiar environments that the differences became more noticeable. The concern was minor, the happiness of us all was a more prominent thought and everyone seemed to be happy.

We decided on a BBQ as the heady weather continued and embarked on a long walk armed with water and two carrots to feed the local donkey who was perpetually in a state of arousal. It was the elephant in the room, almost literally, but any hint of awkwardness evaporated when Emily shouted, "God, look at his winkle!" and feverishly pointed at it. Our walk turned into one of those educational segments covering so many interesting topics drawn from what they were seeing and hearing, we must have covered nearly every subject on the national curriculum.

We watched silk worms crossing the road; one of the few survivors from a once thriving silk industry in France, I told them, until several silkworm diseases wiped them out in the early 20th century.

We counted the rings in a felled oak tree and calculated that it was more than 150 years old. A short-tailed eagle hovered in the air, scanning the ground for reptiles, but he missed the green lizards making a dash for a hole in the wall as we patiently stalked our environment.

The girls pointed out the snow on the distant mountains.

"That's Mont Blanc, the highest peak in the Alps and the highest mountain range in Europe," Eirene told them.

"And it's where we'll be heading in a few days," I added.

"What, to the highest mountain in Europe?" questioned Hannah excitedly.

"No! To Switzerland!" I said.

She beamed expectantly and Emily followed suit.

I was enjoying this as much as the children. I felt free from all the modern-day constrictions and expectations. I was living the life most only dreamt about and I felt like my heart was going to burst with love for the children.

I was feeling closer and closer to my family as each day passed and Abigail was gradually moving out from underneath her mother's wing. We were out and about, running around, eating local fruit, BBQs in the evening, living in a chateau and we felt so alive.

We sorted out a chalet in Switzerland for €400 for a week which was good news. When I say 'we', patently I mean Shameen, my long-standing work mate and top egg, serving as the UK HQ and all that goes with it with nothing in return save for patronising praise from me. I chose her as she has a calm head under pressure, completely trustworthy, meticulously thorough, highly intelligent and has the strong character that we might have to call on at some point. And also, I reckon, she was the only one that would have done it.

We decided to spend a second day at Lac de Villerest and again we had the whole place to ourselves until two other kids, a French boy Emily's age and his sister who was Hannah's age, turned up and crowded the place out. They were both very keen to be friends with Hannah who appears to have an aura that attracts people to her company. Maybe it's because she's the oldest or because she feigns disinterest but it's something Emily didn't possess yet.

Back at the old bakery, our neighbour Francois invited Hannah over with his son and daughter to the pool across the road from him, owned by another English bloke. Francois was exceedingly neighbourly and, if I was a lady, a handsome French bloke who had given Hannah an inflatable beach ball with the French flag on it when she was having a tantrum yesterday.

Emily couldn't go as the pool was too deep for her. Up until we had left England, she had religiously attended weekly swimming lessons on a Monday and near weekly swimming pool visits with me on a Sunday morning. She had a towel so covered in swimming badges the colour was almost impossible to discern. It was a product of the parental need for recognition for their darling child no matter how minute the progress and makes a happy bed fellow with the fiscal aspirations of most swimming schools. There was even one for managing to put your costume on. To the untrained eye, you'd think she had achieved a channel swim, an illusion only shattered when you saw her in the water floundering and flailing.

She was unhappy at not being able to go with Hannah, so we procured some chocolates (a rare treat) for her instead, as Hannah happily scurried off across the road with a man we had nodded to twice, on the way to the home of a man I had spoken to once. So much for our 'never let them out of our sight' philosophy that we had laid down back home. I quickly pushed the chocolate down Emily's throat and took her round there, ostensibly to drop off the beach ball.

Brian, the English owner and aspiring property developer, passionately imparted his knowledge of architecture to a nodding me. Together with a French couple, who were his business partners on this project, he shared with me every intimate detail of his house's growth which admittedly would not have been out of place on *Grand Designs*. As Emily paddled in the shallow end, Brian continued to dominate the conversation with his self-absorbed renovation ramblings at the expense of my self-absorbed trip ramblings.

It had been a great start. We both recognised that this was the easy bit and when we were in a shithole in Kazakhstan with everyone staring at us and we were alternating shifts in the toilet after a day when the satnav failed to deliver, then things would be different. Still, don't dread a Monday when you're only halfway through a Saturday.

CHAPTER 2.

SWITZERLAND, ITALY, CROATIA

Monday 12 May 2008

Day 12 - Veysonnaz, The Alps, Switzerland - 1,224 miles

As we entered Switzerland, the scenery became increasingly striking, with snow-topped peaks dropping steeply before merging with vibrant green meadows and picturesque waterfalls. Isolated chalets could just be made out on the lower regions of the mountains as the road snaked through the valleys. It was Heidi stuff, rich with clichéd picture book images.

Our early departure for Switzerland was a surprisingly excellent drive until I made what proved to be a disastrous decision. Frustrated at the kids' artificial "wows" and their permanent torpor, I rashly (and without consultation with any party) ordered the confiscation of their iPods. My endless list of useless facts and superfluous descriptions of the voluptuous landscape cut no ice and anarchy ensued as they were quickly anaesthetised to the wonder of the views. This, coupled with two lots of directions that we'd received, both of which turned out to be wrong, presented near perfect conditions for an explosion. And as the last dregs of our energy escaped us, it came.

"Stop telling me to turn left when we've been down that road twice already!" I raged.

"No, we haven't! That's the one over there!" Eirene fumed, pointing to the actual road we'd been down twice.

But of course, to back down at this point, right or wrong, would have been absurd. I live my life by that. So, I did what any normal man would have done - accelerated rapidly with a squeal of the tyres for no justifiable reason before breaking sharply a few yards later in dramatic fashion at the end of the dead-end road. The kids had a look of consternation on their faces; Eirene adopted a more fearful look, but I felt I'd made my point.

It took two hours for us to find the chalet, which of course turned out to be down a road that said, "Access Forbidden". But by then, I'd been ultimately reduced to the unedifying spectacle of asking another man for directions.

The view of the snow-capped mountains from the veranda was to die for, which Eirene took even further by requesting that her ashes were to be scattered there. She wasted most of her time scanning the landscape and paid scant regard to the electronic remote-controlled shutters on the underground car park and the most impressive electronic programmable toaster I had ever seen.

We were in Veysonnaz, a mountain village overlooking Sion and the Rhone valley where, despite year-round tourism, they still managed to maintain an authentic way of life. Cow bells resonated in the hills, identifying their location more accurately than a GPS, and the lively chatter of the herders echoed for miles across the valley as they encouraged their languishing livestock up the steep paths. From our west facing balcony we had panoramic views of the Rhone Valley. Flecks of coloured Gortex peppered the mountains as day walkers, hikers, climbers and mountaineers embraced their respective challenges. Brilliant white snow iced the top third of the spiky summits, the jagged peaks almost at eye level with our lofty position on the opposite side of the valley, forming a colourful horizontal triad from sky to valley floor of sapphire, quartz and jade.

The following day, we found a Swiss swimming pool; the only thing distinguishing it from an English swimming pool was the suspicious looking moustached swimming attendant wearing what appeared to be the Speedos of a five-year-old boy. Despite that, the swimming was good and I had all three kids wanting to be with Daddy. Eirene wasn't too chuffed at my newly acquired popularity until I pointed out that it was a drowning thing, not a favourite thing.

We later discovered, after much searching, that I'd left the kids' super sun hats in the locker at the swimming pool. I returned to the pool where they told me they didn't have them, so a heated debate ensued followed by their production of a swim cap. What followed was more arguing, the vaulting of a barrier by me, a plea from them to take my shoes off and me arriving at the empty locker with no hats before realising all three hats were in the locker next to it. I marked my victory with a glorious strut, hats aloft as I headed for the exit and walked straight into the wrong barrier, nearly cutting myself in half. A victory for a little Englander nonetheless.

Our itinerary for the next day was "The Greatest Underwater Caves in Europe." I put it in quotes as it was in quotes in the leaflet and by putting such a subjective opinion in quotes prevents any form of legal recourse as they are merely stating someone's opinion and not an incontestable fact. That someone, it transpired, "was undoubtedly the manager." However, by "greatest" it turned out they meant largest at 60,000 square metres and by "underwater", they actually meant underground (although without undertaking a full dive survey, I couldn't verify that the caves didn't also continue underwater). So, there we were at St Leonard, Europe's largest underground lake, which until the earthquake of 1946 was no more than a flooded cavern. It was after the earthquake that the water level subsided to a tourist attraction level; three years later, the clever Swiss saw it as a great money-making scheme, so installed some subtle lighting and invited the public to visit this spectacle by providing guided rowing boat tours through the ominously reinforced gypsum-roofed cave. Surprisingly, there was even an altar in the cave where weddings could be held and I read that it was quite popular for conferences too.

"A few fish have been introduced for quality control purposes," added our guide reassuringly. "If they die, the lake will be closed and water tests will be carried out."

Initially reassured, I began to question the statement as we paddled deeper into the darkness.

"The fish must eventually die through other means," I thought to myself, "and then what – a post-mortem?"

Despite my initial reservations it turned out to be an enjoyable experience with that perfect level of fear and excitement that the kids welcomed. We finished about 2pm thinking, where now? I put my faith in Wendy and under the attractions menu, she spat out, "Happyland 2 km."

We turned up at Happyland with the teacup ride in a spin as we pulled in. That was the highlight though and it was tiny with many of the rides closed and/or inoperable, which failed to be reflected in the overpriced admission. Hannah quite eloquently observed that "it should be called Glumland."

Like some desperate punter trawling the backstreets of the wrong side of town, I turned back to Wendy for more. She gave me Le Plage; something I wasn't expecting being more than 300 miles from the nearest beach.

Winding roads and whinging kids followed before we eventually ended up at a delightful lake with its own beach and grassy area for relaxing. But relaxing wasn't on Hannah and Emily's itinerary and after they'd dabbled on the swings for a while, the lure of the adventure playground with zip wires and tree top crossings drew them in. I reluctantly agreed to spend a bit extra on them to go on the baby jungle course. A few harnesses and hard hats later and they were zip sliding from tree to tree, their delightful squeals resonating through the idyllic woodland - although that was perhaps not how the conservative Swiss would have described the noise pollution. Emily proved to be really systematic with her karabiner transfer routine whilst Hannah opted for a speedier and riskier ascent and descent. Exercise, confidence, creative thinking, team bonding and more, all mixed into one. A real winner compared to Glumland.

The next day, we hiked down our Heidi hill to explore the medieval town of Sion, but not before Eirene prepared and delivered some inspiring lessons for the kids whilst I attempted to look useful with some tinkerings on the car, complete with overalls and a large spanner. Sion is one of the oldest towns in Switzerland with a history dating back 7000 years. It is recognisable from a great distance by the two towers of Castle Tourbillon and Valère rising from the glacier carved Rhône valley, and is situated in the very important wine growing region of Valais. It's a small town, with a mild climate, great for exploring on foot and sheltered in a valley with numerous piazzas for alfresco dining. The main draw was the pedestrian-friendly streets, lined with whimsical buildings with colourful wooden shutters, balconies with potted geraniums, and ornate ironwork on the wall-mounted street lighting. The stalls sold fresh, local produce and winding alleyways meandered to the mountains and vineyards beyond.

The Valais region is also famous for its amazing irrigation channels, known as bisses. Unfortunately, over the years, many of them were allowed to fall into disrepair but more recently these ancient waterways and incredible feats of engineering have been restored and make great walking routes. Just north of Sion is the 15 km Bisse de Sion which has some spectacular features like the wooden aqueduct that crosses the Lourantse torrent, and a scary path where the channel passes over a chasm with a 200m plunge. I was keen to visit the bisse but thought about the combination of three small children with a 200m vertical drop and decided to visit Castle Valère instead.

Our ascent to the castle on wide, cobbled lanes winding past old and characterful houses was steep but the kids bombed up it with bounding enthusiasm and even the normally lethargic Hannah sprinted to the top, outpowering the enthusiast waddling of Abigail in the final stretch. Castle Valère is more like a fortified church. Built between 1100 and 1130 AD, it has one of the oldest functioning pipe organs in the world, installed in 1435, which almost appears to be suspended on the wall of the west side of the Valère basilica. The organ pipes form the outline of the church, the larger pipes representing the towers and the smaller ones, the church roof. Quite a construction.

We left Sion the following day and travelled to Arolla, which felt like we were driving through a scene from a sci-fi meets Middle Earth fantasy film. We arrived having travelled through dug out tunnels, glaciers, mountains with platforms of snow seemingly teetering on the verge of an avalanche, and waterfalls that plummeted in to white foam. Only a few wizards, ogres and monsters were missing.

We had gone a bit over the top and booked a once in a lifetime flight over the Matterhorn in one of those little Cessna planes that you always see upside down in news bulletins. Unfortunately, after waking up to clear blue skies and not a hint of a breeze, I received a text to say our plane flight was cancelled due to bad weather. I actually received the text as I was looking down from our chalet towards Sion airport, watching a Cessna take off. I have a feeling our pilot had been out on the juice the night before which, if that was the case, was just as valid reason as to why I shouldn't push it.

So I turned to the other woman in my life, Wendy, and asked her to take us to the nearest leisure location which turned out to be a great pool. After years of children who always wanted their mother above anyone else, victory was within my grasp. First the kids wanted to hold onto me in the pool, and then I had them all playing football outside afterwards. In the on-going war between husband and wife, where the goal is to win the children over to your side whilst slowly dismantling your rival's self-esteem, it was first blood to me I'd say. Of course, I don't view it like that, that would be shallow, but I was chuffed to bits. I made a mental note to buy them all a set of boxing gloves and gum-guards the next time we stopped at a bigger town. Later on, after I had done more fun dad stuff with them, Eirene took Hannah and Emily off for a good hour of shouting and crying all under the wrapper of teaching.

We headed off to see Claire, a former workmate of Eirene's from her post-Uni Canary Wharf days. Claire moved out to Switzerland six years previously with her husband Ben and they have fully immersed themselves in the culture, language and life. It's tempting, I imagine, as a Brit to seek out English people, food, schools and experiences like an injury prone northerner who has just been signed by Lazio. They, however, serve as the antithesis of this; their French is so good that their English, if I can carry on the football analogy, is almost Bartonesque.

Our visit wasn't without its memories. Hannah played a little too well with Jamie, their eight-year-old, for my liking, ignoring the family charter of "All Boys are Bad". Emily *may* have been behind the breaking of a large pane of glass covering a collage in Harry's room - although witness testimony later indicated it was a case of spontaneous combustion. Abigail commenced a lone wolf mission and was caught on two occasions attempting to climb into a petrified guinea pig's cage. Despite these happenings, Claire and Ben's hospitality was boundless, serving beer, the FA Cup Final and fondue which was disappointingly not served via a 1970s serving hatch onto a hostess trolley. The Swiss, they assured us, are actually a friendly bunch if you put the time and effort in and respect their ways.

"The first four years are the hardest," Ben said without a hint of a smile.

Our next stop was Gimmelwald where we, and probably all the other guests, had a rather disturbed night caused by Abigail, Emily and Hannah in that order. We spent most of our first hour apologising profusely to any other resident we bumped into, including our next-door neighbours from Washington State. I didn't feel the need to apologise to them too much as, despite signs about a maximum of three minutes hot water being available per person, one of them elected to have a 35-minute shower. This followed a six-minute spell of noisy key turning in the lock but perhaps that was all they could muster to drown out the noise of our kids.

After clearing up a broken glass at breakfast, we were greeted outside by a chap from Texas with a one-year-old who apologised for the noise his baby made during the night. Too late to withdraw our apologies to the other guests.

But enough of the domestic anarchy. Gimmelwald is the most enticing and enchanted, fairy tale-like Swiss village, located high above the Lauterbrunnen Valley. Farming traditions still hold strong in the village, which was evident in the fact that they have more cows than letter boxes. I am taking this statistic, which I read in the information leaflet, as truthful as I didn't actually count every cow and letter box. The place would have been completely perfect had it not been mentioned numerous times in *Lonely Planet* and by a variety of American authors. As a result, it contained a guestbook almost wholly authored by US citizens with too frequent use of the words "swell" and "awesome."

Gimmelweld is traffic free and the only way to reach it was either by hiking or cable car, neither of which featured on Eirene's bucket list. There wasn't really much choice though, as at a height of nearly 1500m and with three small children, we felt the only viable course was to take the James Bond option. This proved somewhat stressful for Eirene, however; my jovial comment to a nervous Californian tourist that they'd cleaned up their act considerably since the 2003 and 2007 incidents induced a minor panic attack as we dangled above steep ravines. Adopting the mantra "laughter is the best medicine" in order to counter Eirene's growing queasiness, I attempted to rhythmically and comedically sway the cable car with barely perceptible movements of my upper body. Didn't help though. If anything, it made it worse.

The weather, though, was calm and the air almost silent apart from the gentle whirr of the cable cars' driving gear, children's laughter and cow bells. I noticed many of the rooftops weighed down for protection by large, flat stones so I guessed it must be a different story in winter when violent winds sweep through the valley.

The Gimmelwald cable car proved to be a walk in the park compared to the journey up to Schilthorn, another cable car trip of 32 minutes (she counted). On this part of the trip, I was more nervous about Hannah being discovered as the almost seven-year-old she was and not the five-year-old we pretended she would be in an effort to save a disproportionate amount of Euros. I needn't have worried as she insisted on only communicating via a meow and refusing to let go of either Duckie (her stuffed toy duck) or Blankie (her blanket). She has a rigid naming convention that she refuses to deviate from.

We had anticipated one long trip which would have perhaps been easier for Eirene to cope with. Unfortunately, she needed to pluck up the courage for five sections as we had to change at every stop as the cable car zigzagged its way up the mountain.

On the penultimate leg we broke through the duvet of clouds to witness Schilthorn and the Piz Gloria restaurant slowly revolving on an isolated mountain top, encompassed by the north face of the Eiger, Jungfrau and Mönch.

Those names conjured up images of death and despair in my mind, predominantly the Eiger. I had recently watched *The Beckoning Silence*, a woeful story of Toni Kurz and his fellow climbers who perished under the most horrific circumstances during an attempt at this mountain in the mid-1930s. As I stole a glimpse of the ground, thousands of feet below our now stationary but rocking cable car, I attempted to distract Eirene with a brief synopsis of the documentary. Again, no help at all.

Thick cloud and a film crew hung outside our swinging cable car. They precariously cleaned the outside windows, almost oblivious to the fatally long drop below, which made us think that perhaps they themselves were part of a Royal Society for the Prevention of Accidents training video.

"Wait until we get moving," I gently reassured her as we swayed together in the claustrophobic confines of the stationary cable car.

At the top, the five of us trudged up to a round viewing room beneath the restaurant called the Touristorama. It contained a number of chairs and a big red button on the wall. I beat the kids to the big red button which triggered the descent of the all window shutters in unison, together with the emergence of a screen. A documentary flickered onto the screen with much focus on the James Bond filming of *On Her Majesty's Secret Service* that took place here in 1968.

We then climbed slowly up to the viewing platform itself where I witnessed the most amazing spectacle I've ever seen in my life to date. At almost 10,000 feet, I was presented with the vertical mountain face of blackness of the Eiger, ripping through the soft, bouncy, white cloud below, rising up seemingly to the heavens, 1,000 metres above. The mild symptoms of altitude sickness I experienced put paid to any hidden aspirations I may have had about climbing such mountains one day. That, along with my fitness, vertigo, inability to climb, lack of opportunity, zero experience, bad knees and lack of any real desire to do it.

As I studied the smooth and innocuous face of the Eiger in my alpine appropriate clothing, I concluded that this was a place for madmen and wondered how on earth Jemima Morrell, a Victorian lady from Selby, managed such a journey in 1863, when at the age of 31 she joined Thomas Cook on his first tour group of the Alps. She would have had little in the way of suitable clothing, no waterproof and breathable jackets or lightweight walking boots. Instead, according to her diary which was published in 1963, Jemima carried an umbrella, wore a long crinoline petticoat under an enormous Victorian skirt, lace-up leather boots and a corset, all of which she wore the entire trip. She did not have the luxury of a cable car or an overpriced mountain top restaurant. A fact evident in her diary entry which read, "At last the mountain ridge is reached. Oh! thanks for that shade, rest and wild strawberries."

It was a poignant and truly humbling moment amongst these powerful and ancient peaks as I contemplated all who had come before – but that was brought to an abrupt end when Hannah thrust some fresh snow down the back of my trousers.

"Daddy, how much pocket money do I have?" she rhythmically enquired, and barely pausing for a response, "I want to go to the gift shop."

Like cascading dominoes, Emily was in with, "Can I go to the gift shop please dad? Pleeeeease?" she said giving me her baby browns.

"I want the git shop," Abigail quickly demanded, knowing she was on the verge of missing out on something but knew neither exactly what it was or how to pronounce it. Eirene, safely ensconced at least 10 metres this side of the nearest barrier, approached us with some trepidation, due to our relative close proximity to the edge, before scolding me, "Don't let them go to the gift shop. It will be too expensive." Without pause she delivered her assumption of guilt: "How much have you given them to go to the gift shop?"

"I haven't given them any money, and no one is going to the gift shop," I protested.

Hannah offered a submission straight from my own dialogue. "Surely someone is going to the gift shop, Dad, even if it is not us? And you did give us some money yesterday." Six years old. I had created a monster. Her pedantry was drowned out by Emily and Abigail's unoriginal but nonetheless compelling chant of "Gift shop, gift shop," as they sensed the cracks and confusion in the parental unit.

I bid a lamentable farewell to the remarkable mountaintop spectacle and began our descent in the cable car. We were packed between Japanese tourists who, within seconds, managed to elicit Hannah's actual age from her which she loudly announced in the presence of the inspector, making what had merely been a physically uncomfortable journey a socially uncomfortable one too. Back in our packed car, we were grateful for the space and privacy, and promptly began driving down a waterfall-filled mountainous gorge that Eirene conceded was better than the Cheddar Gorge she had visited in 1983.

I elected to trust my 2001 AA Road Map of Europe and ignore Wendy, opting for a more direct route to Lake Como in Northern Italy. We found ourselves heading down the most scenic road I had ever driven, going from Meiringen to Gletcsh. We were presented with amazing views of the Rhone glacier, a river of blue ice halted in its tracks, hairpin bends that fringed gushing alpine gorges and enormous limestone ravines. And not another vehicle on the road. We liked it so much we did it twice, turning around when the road eventually ended after 60 miles at the unbuilt remainder of it. I thought the dotted lines on my map would have been transformed into a proper road by now but progress was slow in this part of Europe, so I reluctantly turned Wendy back on.

It really did warrant an exasperated expletive but I contemplated Hannah's ability to pick up on my least likeable characteristics. You can tell kids to say "thank-you" 1,000 times but you only need to say "shit" once for them to remember it, so I had to elicit something much milder. "Oh no!" I proclaimed, ever so briefly jolting my daughters from their devices, as Eirene glowered and silently mouthed a "for fuck's sake".

After a journey that seemed to spend more time underground than over it, including an 11-mile tunnel that felt like some endless *Star Wars* Death Star attack loop, we arrived at our four-star hotel. It had appealed to me on the net as it guaranteed private parking right outside your room and included free condiments. Well, it turned out that the private parking was purely to ensure "visitors' discretion" and "condiments" wasn't translated as well as perhaps it should have been. When I checked it out, the four heart-shaped mirrors on the ceiling gave me an inkling that our family would be spending their first night in Italy in an upmarket brothel. Even the shower, with an array of water jets that covered every angle into every orifice, had a red light in it. The kids loved the "disco" lights that bordered the curtains, door and ceiling mirrors but were a bit put out that the telly didn't work (it did but we'd discovered, whilst they were exploring, that it was showing *Dora the Blower)*. None of the additional beds we requested were there which made for an uncomfortable request with the bloke at reception for some bedding for children. He was more surprised when I asked what time breakfast was and I formed the impression that we might be the first ones to ever actually have breakfast there. With hindsight his "you're here for the whole night?" query should have had the alarms bells ringing from the outset. It didn't have internet access as I'd hoped but then I guess a place like that is sort of in competition with the internet. For those single travellers wishing to definitely avoid it, the establishment was called The Dream Hotel (again another clue there) and is on the Via Vignetta in Appiano Gentile between Milan and Lake Como. Clearly signposted and lots of parking.

After checking in, we departed for an Italian restaurant down the road and had a good run in with *Point It* which Eirene's friend Beverley gave us. The nifty, pocket-sized, low-tech book is nothing more than a series of pictures of apparently every object in the world that assists with communication where language is a barrier. The food section is reasonably big and rapidly became our menu. Hannah picked up the book when Eirene visited the ladies' room and performed a priceless impression of Eirene ordering food with it.

"Can I have," her face contorted in a theatrical smile, pointed index figure at the ready, "one, one, one of these, please." She carefully mouthed loudly and clearly, followed by a rapid and rhythmic tapping of a picture in the book and a sharp turning of the head in the direction of a non-existent waiter. Perhaps unsurprisingly, when our order arrived, we ended up with massive portions topped with numerous misunderstandings.

We only spent one night at The Dream Hotel and you can say what you like about Italian brothels, but they did a great breakfast and the staff would have done anything for us. Although Emily enquired about the unusual neon lights outside our room I think we managed to pull it off and departed smugly with her innocence still intact.

Our destination the next day was The Venetian Hotel which had, its website told us, a top pool, Wi-Fi, a well-rated restaurant, laundry facilities and beds for all of us.

It was a long drive and it rained as soon as we arrived. En route, we'd lost power in the iPods, the seriousness of which I cannot over-emphasise. The consequences of mixing the volatile combination of a bored Hannah and a minding-her-own-business Emily quickly came to fruition. Hannah had a clear aim and that was to leave Emily sobbing. Absorbed with driving and navigation we didn't nip her antics in the bud quickly enough and a violent confrontation ensued. Hannah launched what she later claimed was a pre-emptive strike, the old book slap across the face chestnut. My passive Emily, despite the barrier of her younger sibling's car seat, countered with a straight jab which Hannah managed to avoid but only by placing herself in the path of Emily's follow-up uppercut which arrived shortly after. The temporary pain they both experienced was little in comparison to the demented verbal assault which we laid on them, primarily focussing on Hannah who, under the onslaught, failed to cement her role as the wide-eyed, vulnerable victim.

We arrived at the place and realised that we would have been closer to Venice if Ryanair had flown us. The hotel had sounded good on paper but it was based more on hope than fact. They had a pool but we couldn't use it till Saturday. They had Wi-Fi but no password and they claimed not to have it. They had beds but didn't receive notification that we were bringing kids. They had a restaurant but it wasn't open and they had a laundry but not for customer use.

The bad day continued to deteriorate as we finished it off with a three-hour search for a place to eat with numerous false leads thrown in. We arrived back at the room two hours past their bed time with a quick put to bed and a large bottle of San Miguel to look forward to. The former was compromised by the accidental smashing of the latter by Eirene. Such was the devastation that resulted, we were drawn to ask the less than approachable staff for help. They were nothing if not consistent and refused to help clean up but did provide a mop. Eirene spent a forensic amount of time clearing up the glass, so much so that I decided if I was ever to murder anyone, Eirene would be my Harvey "The Wolf" Keitel, the "clean-up" man from *Pulp Fiction*, on condition that the police promised not to arrive at the scene for at least three hours.

The following day was, we hoped, to be a fresh start. We ditched the car and caught a bus to Venice with lovely affectionate, verging on sycophantic, children. We ambled around its canalled corridors and finished off on a waterbus tour, taking in the architecture in glorious sunshine. A unique city and one that the children got. I stood in St Mark's Square reflecting on when I came here as an 18-year-old with two school friends, Nick and Jeff, interrailing on the tightest of budgets. It was part of my gap year before leaving for Leicester to study law with a bit of computer science. I met Eirene five months after dropping in on Venice, on my first day at uni in our first lecture, although it took us until the following summer to get it together so my first year wasn't entirely wasted. I relished every moment at university, safe in the knowledge that it was unlikely I would ever experience such a carefree time again. It contrasted starkly with school and was, in many ways, the best time of my life to date. And now I was back in Venice with that girl I'd met a short time after, and three wide-eyed and pensive kids who couldn't take in enough, embarking on another journey that would hopefully rival that year out and first year at uni.

The girls were amazed when they saw a beautiful bride carrying a bouquet, resplendent in her immaculate white dress with the aura of unparalleled happiness when a lifelong plan comes together. It literally made the children stop in their tracks and watch in awe as the princess that they always wanted to be gracefully floated by them. We were all glowing on our return to the hotel and the kids played happily on the lawn until Emily misplaced a worthless toy somewhere in the gardens which, once lost, naturally became priceless. I was more elated than perhaps was healthy when my systematic fingertip search of the prescribed area came up with a result. I didn't think I could be happier until John Terry missed a penalty later that evening in the Champions League Final in Moscow, giving the trophy to Man United.

CHAPTER 3.

CROATIA, BOSNIA, HUNGARY, CZECH REPUBLIC AND BACK TO ENGLAND FOR A WEEK

Thursday 22 May 2008

Day 22 - Venice, Italy - 2,130 miles

I felt despondent as my aspirations to be on the road by 7am for a 330-mile trip to a place near Zedar in Croatia failed to materialise. What did transpire was a 9.20am departure, following numerous interspersed toilet trips, and then a five mph journey along Venice's equivalent of the M25. The fact that I had booked the Croatian place we were going to through the same website that gave us the brothel and the Italian "hotel" unnerved me a little. Unusually I was driving and in terms of directions, both Wendy and Eirene were starting to become more vague as we moved into their lesser knowledgeable areas of south central Europe and map reading respectively. We barely stopped although Slovenia was marked by the sudden and imminent onset of the Leon Trotsky's for me, resulting in a hasty stop at a roadside café. In my panicked state, I'd made it halfway across the car park, seconds away from a potential Code Brown incident, when one of my most feared creatures, an Alsatian dog, came bounding from behind an outhouse towards me. It did little to help calm my volatile bowels, having been badly mauled by one in the UK when I was six. Ever since, I've always been terrified of dogs and this breed in particular. In the police, one dog handler even suggested that their general aggression towards me, including that of his "Tyson", was because I always turned my groin away from them. Apparently not letting them sniff your clangers can be viewed as aggressive behaviour. Even now I can wake up in a sweat with the vivid image of the moment I realise that the police dog behind me has lost sight of the fleeing criminal in front of me and is now focussed on my pumping, currently un-bandaged, right arm.

So, with these memories vying for prominence inside my head, on the outside I had Cujo sprinting towards me as a different type of hell threatened to break loose from within me. I was in No Man's Land, between the car and the café, and I decided to go with momentum and carry on running. The Gods carried me and I made the steel door of the toilet relieved to be relieved and unmarked so far. However, a return journey beckoned but I played a waiting (and wiping) game before going for a surprise dash back to the car before he had barely time to stir. Hannah and Emily, who have my dog fearing gene, were very much kept amused by the sight of the undignified sprint of their once heroic father.

"They were absolutely besides themselves with anticipation of you coming back," Eirene enthusiastically regaled as if this in some way would sooth my exasperation at her failure to drive just a bit closer to the café for my return leg.

A six-hour drive, diarrhoea and canine carnage were all put to one side when we finally arrived at our Croatian destination of Vinjerac. Our accommodation afforded us superb sea views of a tranquil fishing village protected by the Velebit mountains where pastel coloured buildings with terracotta roofs huddled around the harbour. We relaxed with a delightful paddle in the clear waters by our apartment until hysterical tears at a lost shell that was going to make Hannah her fortune ensued. The water was freezing but in I went and claimed the shell from deep water. Or at any rate, a shell that looked very like the one she had lost. We then made our way into town and explored the narrow streets and old buildings. The rendering on the buildings showed signs of wear, not from the ravages of war that had blighted this country 20 years previously, but from the bura, a cold northerly salty wind that blows in from the Adriatic Sea. When the bura arrives, it can feel very cold, even on a sunny day we were told, but it's vitally important in the drying of pršut, the local cured ham. That day the bura rested and we had a delicious meal outside in one of the side streets and decided to stay a bit longer.

We'd barely been there 24 hours and our running tally of breakages stood at two with an early dropped glass at breakfast (Emily) and a later fumbled encounter with a bottle in the room (Emily). We took a run out to a nearby island called Pag and I felt positively slim next to my German counterparts. Although famous for its lace and Pag cheese made from sheep's milk which is naturally salty from that bura wind, we didn't have time to sample either of them. Instead, Eirene rumbled me discreetly passing a brief glance over a topless girl on the beach and appointed accusatorily, "you were ogling!"

"No, I was looking at that sand," I quickly and pathetically responded.

The kids were behaving brilliantly and played really well together after we introduced a carrot and stick points system. I took Abigail out during Hannah and Emily's lesson time and we dangled our feet off the end of the harbour wall for what seemed like ages. She looked at me and, for a fleeting moment, I saw someone so much older and wiser. Immediately she tried to vault into the water below and I realised it was just a trap, so I took her for an orange juice in humble recognition of her superior mind tricks.

The view from our apartment was so compelling that we all watched the sunset every night. We were facing due west, straight across the harbour, which started six feet from our window. The view stretched out to the distant horizon which gave us incredibly vibrant rays as the sun and watery landscape merged. Clouds of orange and pink wisped towards us from the glowing, fiery horizon and in the distance, lights twinkled on hilly, black silhouettes of the opposite shore. All of it was topped by a sky with a palette of blue hues. Magical stuff certainly helped by the local wine.

The local restaurant was manned by one person, an exceedingly sociable and bubbly girl with excellent English and two very annoying habits. One was to pour half my bottle of lager straight into the glass (so that my dry and begging throat had to fight through four inches of foam) before she then departed with the remaining half in the bottle. Her second annoying habit was to say, "thank you" numerous times when I paid the bill at the end, no matter how much change I was owed. The first one was certainly the most annoying whilst the second one wasn't so much a habit as it was simply theft. She had a monopoly as it was the only place that sold food locally, so I ended up ordering things that we didn't want to make sure that our bill came to exactly the size of notes that I had. Inevitably I ended up 1 kuna over hence a bigger note and a total loss to me. Eventually I made my feelings known in the only way I knew - with a number of sighs and humphs.

After two or three days, we left Vinerjac and headed for Klek. 240 miles on a near empty motorway made the trip reminiscent of the opening scenes from *Vanilla Sky*. There were signs of life like signposts, bridges and houses by the roadside with parked cars in their drives but just no life itself. It felt very strange.

We took the direct route, as opposed to the scenic route, as Eirene and I were the only ones who looked out the window and it halved the travel time. We stopped for supplies, relieved to see some people at last, and arrived at our new abode having followed a series of cryptic directions that wouldn't have looked out of place on a pirate's treasure map.

It was always hard to know what we were going to find when we looked at a place on the internet. "The Dream Hotel" near Milan didn't mention that it was a knocking shop on its website and the hotel in Venice failed to point out that it wasn't really a hotel. The place we were heading that day looked superb in the online snaps with a view out over the sea, three bedrooms and a BBQ. On arrival, we quickly realised that the internet failed again to describe the place accurately. Only this time it was for all the opposite reasons.

Svebor, the owner, was elated to see us arrive. There were no superlatives to do justice to the view from our covered veranda, which looked out over a large inlet towards a small island with a lighthouse converted to a church about three quarters of a mile away. We settled in and explored our own very small beach, two very big paces away, and began to spend our waking hours snorkelling.

Unlike her sister, the abundance of badges on Hannah's swim towel did not mislead. Her tentative first few strokes were replaced by more confident ones and she began to revel in her growing ability. Emily relished wearing flippers and clinging to my back. Her small fingers gripped my shoulders tightly and occasionally she pointed a finger towards the shallow seabed, an unspoken order for me to collect a particular shell. She paddled patiently on the surface, awaiting my return as I dived below to collect her latest target. Abigail adopted a more observing role, fascinated with the antics of her siblings but natural caution prevented her from indulging in a more active role.

There was a large beach and restaurant about 200 metres away along the little coastal path and the house was basic but clean with everything we needed. As I stood at the end of the private jetty just next to our mini-beach, watching the sun set over the shadowy hills on the other side of the inlet, I contemplated the tranquillity of the moment. Emily was, as always, nearby, absorbed with the patterns her dangling feet made on the surface of the water. I realised that it was perfect for what we needed right then, notwithstanding the excellent price and balmy weather. I decided to call my mum and tell her just how deeply happy I was. I took my Nokia from my shirt pocket, fumbled, and dropped it through the faded wooden jetty slats. I watched forlornly as it briefly chicaned through the struts below before arriving at its watery grave. Emily pointed at it,

39

ordering me to collect it. "Oh, for fuck's sake!" I said under my breath.

Each morning a local fisherman putt-putted into the bay, his little boat low in the water with his early morning load, and woke everyone up with his singing, his sign for a good catch. Eirene decided to indulge the quaint custom but, strangely, returned with some squid.

While Eirene worked with Hannah and Abigail on some lessons, I decided to swim to the island with Emily on my back, carefully following the shoreline. She was insistent on persistently playing the comedy "hands round throat", "pulling at goggles" and "finger in top of snorkel" routine. All three were, to her at least, timeless crowd pleasers although I tried to explain to her that these triplets of comedy genius could be compared to a man sawing the branch he is sitting on. Didn't change a thing.

There was larger beach about 10 metres from our house, regrettably covered in a wide array of man-made rubbish that Eirene was keen to pick up. Under the surface, snorkelling revealed a massive dumping ground of cans, bottles, tyres and rubble and I felt a sense of future shame that subsequent visitors would see this and pass blame onto predecessors. We cleaned up the beach as much as we could and, wary as I am of sounding like Hannah whose diary was fast becoming nothing short of a series of dated menus, we had a great lunch of local produce.

By the time of our evening BBQ, the kids were still suspiciously on best behaviour, having even applied themselves to the day's lessons with more than a modicum of enthusiasm and rigour but the barbecued squid wasn't a triumph. Hannah, who normally eats like a horse, had a face like a horse and politely declined a second helping.

We decided we were here for a good few days and familiarised ourselves with the local supermarket. On one visit (and they were numerous, often twice a day, for my wife was a person who always indulged in what I term "goldfish shopping"

– literally only buying those items that you think you'll need for the forthcoming five seconds) we bumped into a young French couple at the supermarket who I established, from my Del Boy French and his excellent English, were cycling to Iran from France. They rode recumbent bicycles and looked so vulnerable when they pedalled off. What pleased me though was that she took about an hour pottering around with her basket inside the air-conditioned shop as he stood outside in the boiling hot car park guarding the bikes. This waiting for women to shop appears universal and wholly independent of means of transports, storage capacity and culture.

We celebrated Eirene's birthday in Klek, although Eirene doesn't really like her birthday. The kids wanted her to have the top party they always have but she's just not big on them and it often signals the onset of a mini 24 hour depression. "Always a build up as to what they should be," she shared, but inevitably anticlimactic. She told me that her best birthday ever was her 12th when she spent most of the day inside before visiting Westminster Cathedral to see the Pope wave from the balcony. And that was the best one! Personally, I think I may be to blame. I've always asked her what she wanted but never organised the big bash that I think she privately desired. As planned, the kids attempted to make a surprise breakfast but, despite her discreet briefing the previous night, she emerged during on-going operations and refused to move from the breakfast table, much to their disappointment.

We took a day trip over the border to Neum in Bosnia, which was approximately 300 metres away from our place in Croatia. The Bosnian/Croatian border was a strange experience; the staring blank faces of the border guards gave little indication as to whether we should stop or go. Sometimes they checked our passports and other times they didn't. Neum, just inside Bosnia, is the country's only coastal resort and has only about 5 km of coastline for which there is a silent agreement from residents, tourists and the local authorities to fill it with as much rubbish as possible.

We stopped off at a supermarket before our Adriatic water excursion on a pedalo that I'd planned for Eirene's birthday, but even the presence of two bars on the unsecured Wi-Fi connection at the supermarket car park failed to raise her spirits.

I knew the pedalo excursion wasn't on a par with a weekend in Monte Carlo but then again, neither was it a day inside and a train ride to see the Pope waving briefly. Unfortunately, Eirene decided to refrain from the excursion. I thought she might like some time on her own, so I headed out to sea with three kids on my own with all the chaos and naïve excitement of the opening scenes from an episode of *Casualty*. However, we made it back safely and, despite the break, I was still receiving strong signals on my melancholy detector from Eirene. My quest for her to have an inactive day for a change was proving ineffectual and our later attempts at a cake proved futile too. Her birthday climaxed with me dropping Emily on her head in a hastily put together acrobatic routine. Not even a smile.

The day after Eirene's birthday, I suggested we all go to Dubrovnik but Eirene's post-birthday blues kicked in and she wasn't keen. I decided to go anyway and one by one her disloyal kids joined me and eventually she cracked. She ate her hat and swallowed her words when we arrived at the ancient walled city overlooking the Adriatic. It was a city paved with gold-coloured limestone and multi-coloured roofs with an abundance of cafes and restaurants hidden down narrow alleyways. The alleys spread out like a maze from Strada, the main pedestrianised thoroughfare which itself was guarded by two enormous arched gates named Pile and Ploče, marking the entrances to the city from the east and west.

Like many countries, Dubrovnik had suffered numerous battles in its lifetime from the Slav invasion in the 7th century to attacks and subsequent rule from Venice in the 11th and 12th centuries. However, during the 16th century it was extremely wealthy and boasted one of the largest merchant naval fleets in the world. To defend itself from these invasions, a fortified city wall was built and thickened to a depth of six metres on the land side and three metres on the sea side.

Although the city suffered severe damage during the Serb invasion in 1991, it was quickly, substantially and sympathetically restored. New terracotta roof tiles where bombs hit the buildings shine brightly beside their older counterparts, a sight best viewed from high up on the city wall.

As we took a walk along the sturdy medieval fortifications, I relished the amount of time we were spending together outdoors in the sunshine. It was a surprisingly hot day and the little cool breeze from the blue opalescence of the Adriatic did little to refresh us, so we bought the kids some ice creams.

Svebor (or Webbie, Sweater and Bernie as Eirene alternated between) had promised us a free trip on his 95-year-old sailing ship which he filled up with tourists a couple of times a week. The kids had been beside themselves with excitement about it ever since they'd seen his boat chugging around the peninsula, laden surreally with a choir of children singing powerfully and beautifully to all in their range. We were due to leave at 9am the following morning but I rose early and decided to go and buy some beers for Svebor as a token of our appreciation. Unfortunately, it took longer than I thought and I turned the bend by our house at 9.03am to see the boat heading out to sea. I screamed out a desperate "No!" like I was about to lose one of my children, both arms outstretched towards the boat and a look of despair and anguish on my face. It was like the closing scene of Platoon as the helicopter pulled away. Eirene was really good about it and Emily was lovely but Hannah was really upset. She was sitting down by the sea on her own, all dressed up for the trip in her best dress, in tears. They were all packed and had been buzzing about the whole trip. It felt so horrible. There's something about disappointing people for the very first time, people who have or had such faith

43

in you, that really cuts to the bone. As minor an incident as it sounded, it was to stick with me for a long time.

As a poor substitute, we decided to visit Trstenik on the Peljesac Peninsula and were greeted by an empty sandy beach at the base of the Peljesac hills with clear blue water rich in marine life. Agave and salt cedar tress provided welcome shade and we found a perch on a bench where we were joined by three fat blokes who chose to sit right next to us. Nevertheless, we had a top time swimming, particularly Abigail who loved the "daddy taxi". This involved her attaching herself to my back as I swam around snorkelling and her putting her finger occasionally into the top of my snorkel. I am not sure where she learnt that from but she didn't hold on as tightly as she should and had all the confidence of someone whose head had never been accidentally or forcibly submerged in water.

Abigail's affection was almost wholly reserved for Eirene although she found a little perch on a drainpipe by the BBQ that she sat on at night when I was cooking. She commenced the ritual by hopping onto the pipe and asking, "Are you cooking a Barber Queue, Daddy?"

"Yes, my little chicken," I'd respond, before playfully giving her a tweak with the currently clean BBQ tongs. She then started asking beautifully inane questions, literally a monologue from an almost two-year-old girl that was a window into her mind.

"Daddy, what's that?" she enquired pointing into the alcove of the brick-built BBQ.

"That's a fire, mate," I said, as I opened a can of local beer.

"Daddy, is that your beer?" she enquired.

"Yes mate, it is."

"Daddy, are you going to drink it?" she followed up.

"Yes mate, I am."

And then she cutely proffered, "Although you comfort yourself with the fact that it is the only internal organ capable of the natural regeneration of lost tissue, you really still need to consider the impact prolonged exposure to alcohol has on your liver." And then she smiled that all too familiar, coy, knowing smile.

Ok, so I exaggerated a little, but I certainly sensed from her line of questioning, an unspoken condemnation of my level of alcohol consumption.

To make up for our missed boat trip, Svebor took Hannah, Emily and me for an hour's shimmy in his mini boat up the coast on our final evening, which proved to be a great opportunity to learn first-hand about Croatian culture and the area. The Croatians, he shared, had started building a 2 km long, 300 metre high bridge just so the part of Croatia containing Dubrovnik didn't become completely isolated and dependent on the road border crossing at Neum. The Bosnians requested that it could be constructed to accommodate ships at least 56 metres high, but work on the bridge stopped almost immediately with lack of funds being given as the official reason, with politics and corruption unofficially sitting firmly beneath it.

Svebor used to be a master mariner, sailing large cargo ships around the world; his parents were teachers and his father a very well recognised twitcher in the area. His brother was an archaeologist and Svebor had a degree in maritime engineering from Dubrovnik. There appeared, however, to be considerable corruption throughout Croatia and he described the building of a single shower on the beach at Klek as the only testimony of a £60k income from tourist tax the previous year. Low incomes ensured that multiple jobs were not only common but essential. I'd been to the shower and it was indeed a nice shower.

Before she had their son, his wife was on €350 a month in a full-time job and although supermarket prices were cheaper than the UK, it wasn't by much. Svebor had an orchard and rented out his property in the nearby town for much of the year, living in a couple of small rooms underneath the property which we had temporarily acquired. In the summer he took tourists on trips on his old boat and caught fish that he sold when he could.

Everything was a constant effort for money, just to keep the family afloat, but they appeared really content and it seemed like an idyllic upbringing for their Gabrielle who was one-and-a-half at the time. As we neared his jetty he asked, "So what are you escaping from? You have it all in England." I was injected with a sharp dose of perspective that was also surprisingly still tinged with jealousy at the simplicity of their living and the environment they lived in.

After the boat trip he invited us both down for wine. We took an opened one litre £1.50 bottle but were humbled when he insisted that we take from his £12 bottle. He cut some submerged oysters from the side of his small harbour wall which I consumed enthusiastically while encouraging Eirene to do the same. She politely declined the freshly plucked delicacy and I was sick all night.

The next day was Emily's 5th birthday and despite Hannah's complete lack of discretion and dreadful attempts at subtlety, we managed to purchase some presents from the supermarket and a booking at the glamorous sounding Hotel Hollywood in Sarajevo, which came complete with a large water park. We woke her up with a procession of presents and a mouth-watering cake which she was over the moon about, but Eirene wasn't too keen on the birthday present I had bought; a pirate copy of an MTV Unplugged CD, which the vendor didn't even have the decency to lie about when I queried him about its originality. It had Bryan Adams' *Summer of '69* on it which the kids loved and Eirene hated, and which resulted in a growing sense of unease from Eirene that Emily might use her birthday to earn repeated plays of it on the drive to Sarajevo.

Before we left for Sarajevo, we documented our damages which turned out to be six items. We packed, cleaned, hugged goodbye, departed and returned shortly after for Eirene's money belt containing $800 and three passports cunningly secreted behind the egg-cups in the crockery cupboard. When we were finally on our way it was virtually a physical battle with the steering wheel to prevent Eirene from pulling into the first garage we came across to fill up our already three quarter full tank. Further enquiries revealed this to be a throwback to her childhood when her dad's fuel gauge never climbed above the red bit and there were plenty of free-wheeling into forecourt incidents. I made a mental note to re-examine my conduct with the children and undertake a "future mental scar" analysis exercise if it wasn't already too late.

I was driving as near tragedy had almost struck the household when Eirene pulled out of our drive (after the return for the money belt and passports) just as a blue Volkswagen Polo came storming around the corner. Unfortunately, like the proverbial rabbit caught in the headlights, she decided to stop right in the middle of his path in a moment of indecision. When my fear of imminent death had passed, embarrassment took over at the realisation that, with our right-hand drive car, the Polo driver thought I was driving. A stranger I was unlikely to ever see again, I nevertheless felt it important to communicate this fact to him by the medium of sign language but I don't think he understood. His sign language though was very clear, the signal for "wanker" seemingly being a universal insult. I made the most of my time behind the wheel as we headed towards the border, screaming "It's time to die," followed by maniacal laughter on every overtake.

We headed for the Bosnian border at a different crossing, with a degree of confidence having passed through it numerous times over the previous week on entering Neum. You have preconceptions of certain countries and for Bosnia it was a war-torn country full of cold faces and staring eyes, topped up with a healthy level of corruption. And so it was to be.

We were stopped at the border by a mumbling, smoking (these two often went hand in hand I noticed) policeman who wanted to see our passports which, this being our first time of asking on our trip so far, we excitedly handed over. He then asked for our Green Card which wasn't acceptable and he said that I would have to buy insurance. Despite my protestations and double playing of both the kids and the charity angle, he sent me off to buy some insurance. With Euros, Croatian Kuna and Bosnian KM all playing a part in the grunting agent's figures, the price changed from £14 to £16 to £18 for five days with the wrong change returned in Bosnian KM. Arithmetic obviously wasn't his strong point but I was indignant as a consumer when I read that the certificate effectively had £12 written on it as the price I paid. Had there been a Bosnian insurance ombudsman, I would certainly have sent him a sternly worded letter to express my indignance as a consumer.

He was also very vague on my questions about any associated benefits such as legal assistance, windscreen cover or breakdown service. We departed with our mood lessened and Svebor's warnings about corrupt police officers and strict speeding enforcement coming to the fore. As we drove to Mostar, many of the buildings still carried the bullet holes and shrapnel of a war that had only ended 13 years previously. In Dubrovnik it was almost unnoticeable, but it was a UNESCO World Heritage Site and had had the benefit of considerable international funding. Mostar had shells of buildings on most corners and bullet-ridden fascias on the remainder. We were attracting a great deal of attention from the locals, some of it felt rather threatening and the staring was just downright uncomfortable. Were it not for Abigail's decision to eat our Serb Croat language guide and notes a few weeks earlier in Italy, I may have been inclined to engage these starers with a firm handshake and some fancy dialogue.

The drive to Sarajevo was a long one on the basis of the frequent imposition of 40kph speed limits on long straight stretches of isolated road. They also never told you when it returned to the normal speed limit which was infuriating. Police and speed traps were far too frequent but we were lucky to be stopped only once for not having our main headlights on, naively opting, in the bright sunlight, for our sidelights instead.

When we entered Sarajevo it felt like the furthest away from home we had been. That feeling was partly based on the fact that it was. Also, there were damaged buildings everywhere and little difference in many ways from some of the news footage of the early nineties. The famous Holiday Inn, where the world's media stayed during the conflict, was easily recognisable and had been restored to its former glory, if that's the right phrase for any Holiday Inn.

We found Hotel Hollywood whose nomenclature appeared to be wholly based on a picture of James Dean in the foyer. The triple room cost €107 a night (our most expensive yet by a long stretch) and consisted of a double bed and a camp bed. The air conditioning switch lit a panel on the unit but that was it and there was a very inconveniently placed speaker right outside the door pumping out James Blunt numbers for most of the night. I contacted reception and they sent an oversized incompetent cartoon character who tried unsuccessfully to fix our air conditioning with a hammer and a large spanner.

The guy running the swimming pool had the face of someone who'd just had a kid crap in his shallow end again and an attitude to match. I had specifically chosen the place as they also had a massive water park with slides and tubes but that turned out to be slightly misleading and derived through the cunning use of a telephoto lens and a nearby water park that had nothing to do with them. On asking at reception about the price, directions and opening hours of the water park that featured as the main picture on their website, the receptionist replied "No."

It had not been a great introduction to Bosnia, but I realised I was probably and unfairly seeking England in another country which isn't travelling. I had ignorantly expected happy and inquisitive people, grateful for the tourism and enamoured with our manners and those of our delightful children. But it was a country that had been raped, and raped on our watch and under our eye. There was rawness to it, coupled with a bitter cynicism borne of sights and experiences that I could only ever read about. And then we sent them James Blunt in a tank and then, shortly after, on a CD.

The scars that Bosnia carries were never more in evidence than when I counted at least a dozen wheelchair-bound people in the restaurant the following morning. We later discovered that the hotel was in fact holding a wheelchair sales conference with a diverse array on display in the foyer. However, we tried to educate our children on the events that took place during the 90s by visiting the Sarajevo Tunnel Museum where the infamous tunnel under the airport runway had ended and brought much needed supplies and weaponry to the people of Sarajevo during the bitter three-year siege. A helpful policeman bid us to follow his car to an old shuttered-up house on a deserted small road. The insignificant battle-scarred and pale-faced house concealed the tunnel entrance and on entering we discovered we were the only visitors. We were shown a powerful but thankfully gore-free 20-minute video as the kids bombarded us with questions.

"How did they get rid of the water that filled up the tunnel when it rained?" asked Hannah and, "Why didn't the tunnel go up to the sky?" questioned Emily.

Unlike many sites of interest in the UK, there was freedom to look and touch anything and go anywhere, an alien concept to us and one that appeared not to have been abused. They had a plethora of memorabilia and weaponry out on display with the only warning message being not to try to tune the telly where the 20-minute video played in a loop. The tunnel felt claustrophobic and the sheer authenticity of the place was as inspiring as it was moving. A galaxy of stars, famous people, respected leaders and Paddy Ashdown appeared in pictures on the walls and the visitors book. Emily, Hannah and I added our comments to the visitors' book, nervous as to how best to sum up this quite profound experience. I opted for the clichéd "Lest we forget." Hannah, "Thank you for having me in your home." And Emily, "Emily."

So a somewhat reserved Naismith family headed back to the hotel for the pre-dinner fight with the kids but frankly our hearts weren't in it. And perhaps it was Stockholm Syndrome but that evening the waiter seemed a dash charming.

We left for Hungary grateful for the experience of Bosnia but more thankful that we were leaving it. We had become oblivious to our surroundings and the bullet holes in the building masonry had become as second nature to us as the "Mine Sweeping" Land Cruisers of the UN that were there in great numbers. Their elevation and blacked-out windows perhaps sparing them the shocking sight of four-year-old kids begging at the major road junctions.

When we arrived in Hungary we headed for the famous spa town of Harkany, entering through a border point manned by about 20 guards, half of whom looked only slightly older than Hannah.

We decided to take some money out and then eat but discovered that our debit card had again been "efficiently" blocked. I was starting to not be as enamoured as I originally was with my bank who would block my card in a town, happily agree to unblock it and then block it at the next transaction 10 minutes later. They'd agreed to sponsor us with free cash point and sales transactions so that might explain their enthusiasm. I opted instead for a different bank card. I won't name them, but they're a dark horse and wouldn't seem to mind if you were paying £10,000 to an African prince in different countries on a daily basis, so it was one that could be relied upon.

The restaurant owner proved to be as accommodating as a Bosnian waiter. We sat down in our cramped spot in the outside seating area of the empty restaurant and Eirene nipped to the shops for something and left me to take the helm. As soon as Eirene left the restaurant, Hannah knocked over a glass of apple juice and I didn't grab Emily quickly enough to stop her falling off her chair as she reacted to the breakage. The food arrived within minutes of the order which, when you have hungry kids, is unheard of and was subsequently covered in water as the heavens suddenly opened. While I tried to exert some control and reclaim my self-respect as a parent capable of looking after their children on their own, Eirene returned to a post-apocalyptic scene. We departed as quickly as possible, leaving what resembled a murder scene (Abigail had spaghetti bolognese). We watched the waiter survey it with one old J-cloth in his hand and as we sheepishly disappeared, we saw him attempt to convey the scene of disgust to someone at the end of his mobile phone, presumably a dodgy-looking problem solving, Winston Wolf-type character.

Harkany is basically a large spa complex surrounded by restaurants and guest houses. The construction of the spa started around the mid 1820s after the accidental discovery of the mineral rich, healing waters. However, Harkany dates back much earlier than that with archaeological and written evidence of its existence since 1323. It has a very small permanent population of just over 3000 but during the summer months this increases to over one million visitors who go there looking to relax and benefit from the relaxing and therapeutic mud and spring waters. When we arrived, the old and fat abounded and I felt quite at home. Summer was here and the pools were bustling. Our non-swimming Abigail was prohibited from entering the baby pool by the newspaper reading lifeguard as she was over one year old and was directed to the much deeper pool nearby. No doubt a tick on a clipboard and a good day's work by him.

Our prospective landlady was called Madame Jo Jo which hinted at Dream Hotel-like living quarters. She met us in town and showed us our house which, with mild horror, we realised was hers and she headed off to the room on the side. Other than pool attendants, we found the Hungarians to be really amiable people who loved the kids. In return, the kids worked it. A simple purchase of peas in the supermarket, with much smiling and fluttering eyelashes from them, resulted in a big bag of free cherries. The market stall holders were attentive without the intense selling that is the downfall, from a Western perspective at least, of some other cultures.

Friendly as they are, they are a trifle forgetful, confusingly thinking it was Sunday and not Friday. On finding a parking place in the street, numerous passers-by that I asked told me not to bother with a parking ticket, but their kind-hearted forgetfulness resulted in us receiving a parking ticket on our return. Restaurant owners employed an on-going wheeze when we looked in their window; they offered us a menu and when I told them we were not hungry, they kept on showing me the English translation saying, "This is not Hungary, this is English one." It was timeless and they never tired of it.

However, one bizarre aspect that we noticed in all our travels up to that point was that if a waitress asked us what we wanted to drink and I replied, "Coca Cola," the most commonly known drink, nay word, in the world, they looked mightily confused. I then repeated it, sometimes up to 10 times, before pointing it out in their fridge, on their fridge, over their fridge and over the doorway we came through at which point, with a dawning realisation, they declared, "Ah Cocah Colaah" with some almost imperceptible inflection on it. I wouldn't have minded so much had it not been that when I'm working in London I am repeatedly asked directions to the usual attractions, like "Backinghon Palickee" or "Round Eye of the London" yet I still furnish the goods. Rest assured though, on my return, things will change. "The House of Parliament you say pal? Haven't got a clue. Literally never heard of the place. Are you sure it is the House of Parliament?"

On the morning we were leaving Harkany, we mobilised our troops in a timely two and a half hours and said goodbye to Madame Jo Jo who had kindly offered us her washing machine on arrival but charged us £10 for the privilege on departure. It was still raining when we left but it was a cracking three-hour drive to Siofok, in so far as many of the lay-bys on the road were frequented by a number of barely dressed ladies waving at the traffic, particularly the lorry drivers.

We arrived at Siofok, on the banks of Lake Balaton, around lunchtime and decided on a shimmy into Budapest. Our accommodation, in a house in the garden of a bigger house with access to two pools, was delightful.

Wendy was back to her best, partly, the kids suspected, as I changed her to a Texan named Chuck for a while. On a Sunday, in one of the most culturally rich cities in the world and with the kids in tow, I could think of no better place to go than the former Hungarian secret police headquarters. The lift down to the cell area was slow and we were a captive audience as a former executioner nonchalantly explained his routine on a DVD. He finished as his victim died and the lift doors opened to complete blackness. It was neither gimmicky nor gory, just overwhelmingly disturbing. The horrors that took place there are not for these pages, but the experience was profound and shocking. The methods employed in general to control the masses serve as a valiant attempt to knock Orwell's *1984* off the fiction shelves. A deeply impressive museum, despite having little in the way of any English explanations.

We ended up, to our eternal shame, going to a TGI Friday's and paying London prices for American food from a Polish lady. She was very efficient and cordial, wearing the customary worldwide zany TGI uniform of badge adorned braces and back to front hat, but debatably overdid the tip routine. She presented the bill with the words "SERVICE CHARGE IS NOT INCLUDED" stamped four times across it. In case I had trouble with the uppercase red font as she handed it to me she said, "Service charge is not included. In Hungary 10% is standard."

After lunch we found ourselves on a little island on the river and we hired a human-powered rickshaw for the five of us. The human power was to come from us. Hannah and Emily sat in the front with little more than a fairground chain across their laps and Eirene and I sat behind with Abigail. It was a four-wheeled vehicle with two sets of pedals and one steering wheel and we spent the afternoon scooting around the island, watching dancers and eating ice-cream as we took it in turns pedalling and driving. I am not sure if it was up there with the waving Pope but Eirene isolated the rickshaw ride as being the best time she had had on the trip so far. Whatever her reasoning, it was good to see her so buoyant.

We departed with us all waving goodbye to the landlady as, unbeknownst to us, Emily's teddies, Poley and Monkey, sat idly basking in the morning sunlight on the swing. We were well on the way to Austria before we realised we had a catastrophe of cataclysmic proportions on our hands. Poley is the Paddington Bear of Teddies, having been left on his own on numerous occasions, including a four-night stint at the London Hilton, coincidentally by Paddington Station. But Monkey should have known better. The very efficient landlady kindly agreed to have them deported back to the UK for us if we transferred some money over.

It was a long journey to Cesky Krumlov in the Czech Republic taking 330 miles, seven and a half hours, nine viewings of the same two Peppa Pigs by Abigail and 12 "Are we there yet"s. We travelled via the outskirts of Vienna (I venture that we could now say we've "done Vienna') and stayed in the same loft apartment in Cesky that I had stayed at the previous year for my mate Neil's stag do. It had a high view out to the river from a small balcony and narrow banister-less stairs to the loft's loft where the kids were staying. What had seemed ideal on a stag do now appeared to be a house of health and safety horror for a family with three children under eight.

We made it through the morning unscathed though and visited the imposing Cesky Krumlov castle. Standing on a rock promontory reached via a large bridge over the river Vltavaand, it is constructed of 40 buildings and palaces, including a flamboyant tower all built in different eras throughout history. The original castle was built in 1240 by the Wiliganen family, the main branch of the influential Bohemian Rosenberg family who played an important role in Czech Medieval history. Entry to each of those sections was priced separately and would have required a good portion of the day to explore. The painted courtyard walls and multi-storeyed archways connecting the sections were enticing; but with the children it was always a balance of choosing an enforced and prolonged cultural education versus garnering some knowledge but having more fun. Basically, Pol Pot v Ronald Reagan and the aging actor won as we had a good time running around chasing each other in the Rococo Gardens which were free.

We left Cesky the following day and headed to Prague where we met up with my mate Neil and his family. Prague was a bit of a mixed pot. Some fascinating architecture in the centre which was encompassed by grey, cold war tenement blocks in districts numbered in Orwellian fashion – Prague 2, Prague 3, Prague 4 etc. Prague Castle towered over the city, a jigsaw of architectural styles from the Romanesque-style buildings from the 10th century through to the Gothic modifications of the 14th century. Major renovations took place during the time of the First Republic between 1914 and 1938 and still continued, making it a complex architectural timepiece with cobblestone lanes and hidden alleys.

Neil had settled there and to my untrained ear appeared to know the lingo. With the recent arrival of their daughter Anna, Neil was left in charge of Joseph, their first born, and he gave us an insider's guide to his home city. Our kids were fascinated by where he lived, what he did and his children in particular. Neil took us for a trip to the market for the usual things like clothes, a quick look at the brothel and some pepper spray for our onward journey, before visiting a nearby park where the kids and Neil released some energy playing in the climbing web. That night Neil kindly gave up his time to drive two hours to his farm outside Prague where I left the Land Cruiser for the duration of our planned trip back to the UK.

It was nearing the end of June and, as planned, we flew back to England to sort out some visas and innumerable other things. It was a welcome return for both of us - Eirene had really missed her mum and I was desperate for a curry. On arrival, we discovered that Emily's teddies hadn't yet arrived from Hungary. She was distraught but numerous emails and finally a phone call to the landlady assured us that they would be with us before we departed again. I started work on our 40-strong list of things to do and buy, which ranged from checking whether the kids were allergic to penicillin (much of our medicine is penicillin-based) to the crucial purchase of one of those special demisting cloths for the inside of the windscreen. Eirene's brother Simon and family arrived the day after us from Australia for 10 days and the days became a myriad of tasks, trips, to-dos and list ticking. I did what I needed but realised that I had lost the kids to friends, family and my own industry, and I missed them desperately.

I was glad we came back but glad we left again at the week's end. Emily was sobbing as we departed. The teddies hadn't arrived.

CHAPTER 4.

STAGE 2: EASTERN EUROPE INTO ASIA

Wednesday 25 June 2008

Day 56 - Prague, Czech Republic - 4,069 miles

We arrived back in Prague to discover the UK pound had weakened so much that the basic hotel we had booked into, with no telly or air conditioning, turned out to be the most expensive of the trip so far.

After spending another day with my friend Neil in Prague, we left for Oswiecim in Poland, home of one of the largest killing factories in history.

Eirene was not what she was before we left and I don't think it was the thought of all the people that died as a consequence of the "Final Solution" that was affecting her. She was really happy in England and I witnessed her and her mum come together in a few mutually tearful moments on a number of occasions in our week or so back. I was worried that her happiness in the weeks leading up to the time we flew back to England was just that – happiness at the countdown. I was having the best time of my life and I now reluctantly include my first year at university in that statement. For Eirene, I think it had been something to endure to make me happy so that she could eventually go back to the happiest time of her life which is bringing up children and being near her mother. She warned me before we left, "This is it though, no more trips."

In terms of our marriage, my primary grievance, issue, anger or whatever you would call it was that she never seemed to be happy with her lot, something that I was ironically just as guilty of. So I threw money at it, ensuring that whilst her friends returned to work she never had to. We had a new car, someone who ironed, someone who cleaned the house, someone who came and valeted the car and an elastic budget. As a contractor I earned a decent amount and saved little, but she rarely took advantage of the finer things that were on offer to her. Her bank statement read like a supermarket sweep with the occasional Pizza Express treat. No weekends away or manicures for her. I concluded that I might have been doing this journey to find out what I didn't know I wanted - and I think Eirene realised she had what she wanted but she didn't know.

The atmosphere was sullen and her responses were curt.

"When will we get there?" she demanded.

"About six hours?" I suggested, scanning the map and vigorously tapping Wendy.

"Why are we going there again?" she rapidly retorted.

"I thought the kids would like to see where millions of men, women and children were gassed," I answered, safe as always in the knowledge that sarcasm is as good a calmer of people as it is a lifter of moods.

A heavy cloud of emotions hung over us. In the nine days we were back, Hannah and Emily had a great time playing with their cousins, being doted over by everyone and popping into school for a day for a hero's welcome. Even they seemed on the melancholy side. I was starting to think that if the trip itself was a bad idea then, having embarked on it, all of us coming back to the UK after six weeks was an even worse idea.

I was on a high but the weight of dragging my family eastwards inevitably turned me moody. Europe had been easy – people spoke English, Wendy knew where she was going and we had five bar phone reception virtually everywhere with a flight home to look forward to. Now, as we pushed eastwards, it was the antithesis of that and I felt the burden of the family's gloom on me. I sensed from Eirene a "let's get this over and done with quickly" feeling and something similar though less well formed from the kids. Still, we had Auschwitz Concentration Camp to cheer us all up.

"No children under the age of 14 advised." Not a rule, just a wholly understandable request based, one would submit, on the potentially profound impact of the experience on the young child who manages to grasp what the place is all about. And the potentially profound impact of the experience on the adults around them when the child doesn't grasp it and decides to run around screaming, crying, having a tantrum and blowing raspberries.

Birkenau, however, was a little different as it was not a museum as such but a massive camp. Having read much about both these concentration camps, both in first and third hand accounts, I was excited to see it all, and I know how crass that sounds.

Time was against us so this was an extravagance for both our timetable and for me personally and it certainly wasn't up there with Euro Disney on the kids' list. We stayed in a very swanky, albeit probably not appropriate, hotel, exactly opposite the entrance to Auschwitz itself. Surprisingly the hotel's website failed to mention this fact or even Auschwitz. Eirene very kindly took the kids off to the park late in the afternoon, departing with the words, "Enjoy yourself," and I quickly nipped across the road weaving through abusive parties of European school children, on their mandated visits, towards the entrance. Regrettably I missed the renowned 15-minute introductory film and the guided tour I had been keen to join. But with everyone else on the tour, I was left with the place pretty much to myself and an atmosphere that literally stood the hairs up on the back of my neck.

Seeing the famous entrance, with "Arbeit macht frei" ("Work brings Freedom") above it, and a half open barrier, in colour on a clear and still day, seemed more hard hitting than anytime I'd seen it in black and white prior to my visit. Entry was free, the exhibitions profound and the atmosphere suffocating. I tentatively edged around, looking at mountains of shoes and hair and combs and suitcases. Each hut housed an exhibition to specific groups who were subjected to the genocide attempts. The wall against which they were shot; the hooks on which they were hung with their arms high above their backs, painfully dislocated; the hanging frames; the guard towers; the exact fences; the framed beds. The scale of the atrocities is beyond my comprehension but it was the recency of it that I found more disturbing. There is something about the passage of time that provides safety and comfort but this was too close. Some of the people who did this are still alive.

I offered a tissue to a blonde lady in her mid-twenties who was crying at a small glass-covered table containing a broken doll and a few items of baby and toddler clothing. Possibly more than anything else, exhibits like that resonate the loudest and clearest to parents.

My moment and the atmosphere were cut short by an audible Morse code spelling of SMS. Embarrassed, I checked my phone and saw a cryptic text from Eirene – "H BANKED HER DEAD ON THE POUND A LOT." A discreet call simultaneously established both the flaws in Nokia's then primitive autocorrect capabilities and that Hannah had banged her head on the roundabout. Having been contemplating her death in another world just a few seconds before, my elation at her having a small cut on the back of her head may have seemed confusing to Eirene.

I hastily departed and caught up with them at the hotel. Her cut proved to be a tad worse than I anticipated but I hid my relief that it hadn't happened on my shift. It transpired that she had been on some sort of floorless roundabout and had been enthusiastically pushing when she decided to stop suddenly, only to be surprisingly (only to her) clobbered by the section coming behind her. How it hit her on her head I'm not quite sure but the blood-stained hair confirmed it had. It had stopped bleeding and it was too small to stitch but, fresh from her remote expedition first aid course, Eirene was keen to put superglue on it, based on the fact that it was allegedly invented to deal with

61

severe lacerations in the Vietnam War. I managed to lever the tube from her enthusiastic grip and we tended to it as I anxiously checked my watch eager to return to Auschwitz, knowing that I'd probably never have the opportunity to visit again. Eirene, however, was keen to show me the scene of the crime so I agreed to drive there. Unfortunately, in my haste to depart, I inadvertently flattened one of those trendy little two-foot-high light posts that hotels like to have. Within seconds the mandatory dungaree-suited handyman appeared and, despite Hannah hamming up her injury to almost Premier League standards, coordinated our payment for the damage with reception.

It was on this note that we departed for a drive past the offending roundabout and onto nearby Auschwitz II – Birkenau. There is something about that moment when, having seen a picture of something so many times, you feel you know it when you finally lay eyes upon it (and I'm not referring to the roundabout). I had seen the infamous railway entrance archway many times on print and celluloid but never the surrounding area. So when we turned round a bend and there it was, I was completely caught by surprise. The size of the camp itself cannot adequately be portrayed without seeing it with your own eyes. Auschwitz has the notoriety but Birkenau was where most of the killing was undertaken, three quarters of the passengers coming straight off the train and straight into the gas chambers.

Before going in we gave the kids "The talk" but it wasn't necessary. They didn't understand the numbers but they understood they were big. They paid it the respect it deserved and asked who, when, where, what and how; and then they asked why until we didn't, quite rightly, have an answer. I saw the blonde lady again in there - she looked much older than I remembered.

———————————————

Who attempts border travel on a Sunday?

We had the luxury of time to contemplate that question as we spent ages going through a load of seemingly different borders in our attempts to leave Poland and enter Ukraine. Handing over photocopied vehicle documents didn't go down well and neither did not having car insurance. Rain, our traditional gift from a new country, kept the guards and border police in their little boxes, while we were given a load of forms (in Russian) to complete which we half managed to do although that half proved to be wrong. It was slow, painful and for a family travelling with nothing to hide, surprisingly nerve-racking. I used to get excited going through borders or being stopped by the police, safe in the confidence that I had done nothing wrong. But there, it terrified me and I didn't know why. Perhaps it was the hidden pepper spray and thousands of dollars secreted in various alcoves throughout the car and perhaps I've answered my own question. I was worried both if I did declare the money and if I didn't. I suggested to Eirene that I should perhaps re-count the hidden dollars in the car so that after the border I could establish if they had taken any. She tentatively and respectfully asked me what I would do if I found out some or all of it was missing. Good point!

When we finally made it through the border, we drove past two miles of stationary lorries waiting on the other side. We navigated successfully to Lviv and then resorted to using the Holy Trilogy – Garmin Wendy, *Lonely Planet* and a map, as we began optimistically looking around for signs of our target, Hotel Sputnik. For all I could fathom, it could've actually been, as its name suggested, on another planet.

Wendy was clearly out of her depth and her offerings of a compass, calculator and five minutes of reading from *Charlie and the Chocolate Factory* were starting to become tedious. I called the hotel but they either didn't know themselves or did know and couldn't speak English. I realised there was a third option but put my paranoia to one side for the moment. I decided to swallow my pride and ask for directions. When that failed, I offered a taxi driver money to take us to our hotel; a scenario, I soon found out, I was to repeat frequently as our trip went on. Of course, one of the key benefits of taking your own vehicle when travelling is that you should never need to pay for taxis.

We followed him through cobbled streets, renaissance architecture, quaint arches and into an area of colourless and tired looking 1970s tower blocks of the same style that the UK is at pains to demolish arguably with no reciprocal replacement plans. The taxi driver appeared to do a few orbits of the Hotel itself before finally pulling up outside a modern building but in the same insipid colourings as its predecessors. The only indication that we'd arrived at something special was the manicured grass, vibrant green hedge and looming fir trees.

I'd obtained a price from the hotel when I booked it in advance but this was clearly only the opening move of the drawn-out game to come. With all the intended confusion of an illusionist changing two £20 notes, I ended up well and truly shafted, paying twice that price. It was late and Eirene and kids were tired. They stood there with all the bags looking as though all the fight had gone from them so I agreed to the deal I was being offered. Once the robbery was amicably completed, I was then able to wallow in the discovery that I'd in fact negotiated more money for fewer rooms of a lesser standard. Things didn't help when the hotel cash point failed to give me money against my cards and the main debit one was turned down by their machine. I was just beginning a second attempt when my bank called me on my mobile. The format of such a call is that you then pay 50p per min + VAT to receive their call to give them a brief autobiography focussed around my wife's maiden name, where my mother was born, my first dog's star sign and my memorable date, which if anyone is interested was Anne-Marie and we went to the Fulcrum in Slough. The minutiae of this detailed security check was all performed in the privacy of the busy hotel lobby. Our stay there wasn't all bad though – the Germans lost Euro 2008 and Eirene found the breakfast, and I quote, "satisfactory."

With a bad taste in our mouths (though not from the "satisfactory" breakfast), we elected to move on from Lviv the following morning on gradually deteriorating roads. Ukraine looked exactly like we thought it would. Ladas passing horses carrying bundles of twigs; isolated houses; a multitude of headscarves; flat fields with no apparent boundaries; fat policemen; beautiful girls; 80s fashion; and an inhumane amount of Celine Dion on the radio. What I didn't bank on were the large number of immaculate and seemingly brand-new petrol stations. What Ukraine lacked on the "Best Kept Village" front, it more than made up for with its petrol stops with fully stocked shelves. Most of them had cafes and restaurants as an integral part and others had great parks for the kids. I reckoned most of the people that used them didn't even bother with the petrol. And the toilets. The toilets! What can I say? An absolute pleasure. Where toilets do exist at UK petrol stations, you can be sure of three things. First, there will just be one of them for everyone regardless of gender. Second, that one seat will be covered in piss. Third, there will be a scratched Perspex sign with a picture of a penis engraved on it and a paper insert somewhere on the door detailing non-existent cleanliness checks with a note directing you to a member of staff if your surroundings are in any way unsatisfactory. In the Ukraine, the toilets lacked all of these basic UK ingredients.

Despite their excellent public conveniences, the people of Ukraine weren't too smiley. We ordered a meal one evening using our *Point It* book, supplemented with Eirene's hand and body gestures. I deliberately asked for chicken for Eirene's impression alone, but there wasn't even a flicker of a smile from the waiter.

They do, however, have a culture and a code which we sorely lack in England. A truck in front of us pulled in heavily to the right without any indication. Naturally my instinct was to emulate the sign language I picked up from the near-death Croatian Polo incident. Fortuitously I realised in the nick of time that he had stopped for a procession of cross bearing people on either side of a horse-drawn carriage with a huddle of head-scarved elderly ladies struggling to keep up behind. We followed, turned off the engine and savoured their exquisite singing as they solemnly struggled up the hill and passed us while mourning the departure of a loved one.

After our experience at the Hotel Sputnik, we had made no arrangements for accommodation and aimed to arrive at Uman as early as possible. To this end I encouraged Eirene to overtake an old Lada in front of us which, with some coaxing, she eventually did. She is not big on overtaking is Eirene and this was probably only the second time I'd ever witnessed it first hand from her. However, she left this one in her wake, telling Hannah to turn down her Nintendo in the process. Except Hannah wasn't playing her Nintendo and the siren-like noise we thought was emanating from it was coming from the Lada. By the time these simple facts had been ascertained we were some way ahead and I was astonished when Eirene, completely out of character and in a *Dukes of Hazard*-type moment, put her foot down.

We pulled off at the first junction we came to, fate taking us into the car park of a large hotel. The place had finely mowed lawns and air conditioning units outside every room and we were chuffed to bits that our efforts to outrun the police had led us to such a haven. We parked up and I'm not sure if it was the big blue Police sign over the entrance or the old Lada with the siren pulling in behind us that I clocked first, but I realised that we're weren't as lucky as we had initially hoped. Much like when you walk into an unfamiliar pub for the first time and realise it is as rough as hell, you somehow believe that turning around and immediately leaving will be worse than staying. Seamlessly, I ordered the metaphorical half a lager and walked up to the front door of the station to stare studiously at a notice in Russian. I walked back, straight into the hairy eyeball of three armed 18-year-olds emerging from their car. I decided to go into the attack and delivered a pre-emptive "directions request" strike. The driver jumped out, cigarette in hand and started gesticulating.

He played with the button on his holster as I pulled out my phrasebook and, after having a cloud of smoke blown in my face, he told me to stay in my car and wait.

"What's going on?" asked Eirene.

As I sidled in I gave her a knowing nod and then confessed that I had no idea. Lada man drove off, giving me the horn as he did, and we obediently followed. Gamekeeper had turned poacher as we struggled to keep up with him through amber lights and cutting across lanes willy-nilly before arriving outside a very glamorous looking hotel. During the day, Eirene had come up with the idea of us finding a great and cheap hotel with comfy rooms and secure parking where they spoke English. There would be a great and cheap restaurant nearby, the kids could swim in the pool and air their hair afterwards, running around a lovely, big garden. While I was not entirely sure she was embracing the entire concept of travel and different cultures, I was confident that this wouldn't happen. But this, as it turned out, was precisely what the police led us to. From the outside, the hotel wouldn't have looked out of place in Beverly Hills. A long, tree-lined drive led up to the pillared entrance. An elegant cream and white brick façade was carpeted with a green roof and balconied suites ran along the top floor. Eirene was almost verging on jubilant. Ker-ching was all I could think.

Suitably refreshed and placated, our next stop the next day was Mykolayiv, the road to which consisted of a great motorway to Odessa and then a crap road after that. One criticism of Ewan McGregor and Charley Boorman's brilliant 2004 "Long Way Round" documentary was that turned into a monologue on road surfaces and petrol stations. But I was starting to get it.

Aesthetically we were treated to very flat countryside which was not too dissimilar to England except instead of fields of flowering brassicas, there were fields of poppies and sunflowers all pointing in the same direction.

While exploring Mykolayiv, we discovered a park which looked like it was used by everyone in the community. There were giant inflatable slides and colourful exercise equipment and there was even a pool with mini hovercrafts for the kids to drive. A serious game of chess was being played out on a nearby table, which was being observed by a group of old men and then Hannah. She was curious and wandered over to watch for a while but the men were so engrossed in the game, they didn't even cast a glance at this little British girl staring intently.

We met a half Canadian/half Ukrainian girl at the park with whom we were terrifically unsuccessful in soliciting any useful information whatsoever about either the town or Ukraine. What she did tell us, though, was a very thorough account of her life. I've found that people who offer their life stories to strangers generally have little to tell and she was no exception.

Hungry from our listening endeavours, we headed to a restaurant who said they had a power cut and all they could give us was Chicken Shashlick. We ordered five of them but it took 15 minutes before she returned to say the Chicken Shashlick was off and strangely questioned whether we wanted anything else. We left and wandered in the direction of town and came across a "British Pub", wrong I know but we were hungry. We weren't expecting chicken in a basket, £3.50 pints, a game of darts and a piss in a lidless toilet but we did expect something remotely British. Our request for chips was greeted by two bowls of crisps 30 minutes later and the remainder of the menu was a mystery. The beer was right though because, like a typical British pub, they only had foreign stuff on draught, and the toilets were breathtakingly appalling so they were heading in the right direction.

In Mariupol, I had my daily £5 chat with my bank who had an established cycle of cancelling a card before a complete stranger called up to verify who I was with a series of personal questions. They would then unblock the card, make a note of where we were travelling to next and cancel it the following day.

Most of Europe insisted on employing someone to fill up our tank for a small tip whilst we stood and watched them try to put the wrong amount of the wrong stuff into the wrong tank (we had two). It had been rather quaint at first but it was starting to annoy; and they all seemed to have scruffy, black hair and be clad in denim dungarees, white t-shirt and a neck scarf. Apart from the variation in physical size, each one could have been gainfully employed as a lookalike from the 1980s band, *Dexys Midnight Runners*. Petrol pump attendants in the UK were dropped in the 1970s as it was labour intensive, created queues and stopped the punter going into the shop to spend more money. Moreover, filling up your car is one of the last things a man has left to cling on to that he can call his own and it shouldn't be taken away from him without very careful consideration. My dad, like many dads of his era, would even be known to arise from his dedicated armchair between televised games on a Sunday in order to undertake a special journey specifically for this task.

It came as a bit of a surprise then when, on the road to Mariupol, we had a female pump attendant. It took eight minutes for her to put the pump in the car then she wanted to know how much to put in but had apparently never had a customer who wanted it filled to the top. Eventually we settled on 1,000 litres and she looked surprised when she only managed to squeeze in a fraction of that. The paying bit was even more painful as I had to almost limbo dance down to pass money through a low window that was open no more than 5° and the petrol pump attendant almost totally blocked me. All and sundry emerged to witness me squeezing my hand through the gap in the window and enter my PIN number. I could only assume that their entire lack of subtlety meant that they weren't of a criminal nature or were cunningly double bluffing.

We found a place in Mariupol on the Black Sea that looked great but then so it should for an initial quote of £600 for an apartment per night and then, compromising slightly, £240 for two double rooms. We dragged ourselves off the floor and tried the hotel next door. Their price dropped so we carried on along the road until we came across a rundown looking place that was closed. The hotels were all owned by a steelworks company who offered discounted holidays as a benefit to their employees, a common thing in the former Soviet Union. All were allowed the benefit of the company hotel but in an "Animal Farm" sense some hotels were better than others. It was clear that the one you stayed in was dependent on your status in the company.

When the closed hotel opened later that day it emerged that it was £80 for the deluxe apartment which, after considerable haggling, came to £80 for the deluxe apartment. Everything was black and white, especially pricing. If you were staying for one night it cost £80, for three nights £240. It was an ingenious marketing ploy but they had done a good job of embracing capitalism. Washing clothes cost 66p per item so we did essential items. Eirene unfortunately left a sock in a sleeve so that came back pristine at a cost of 66p. Car parking cost an extra £1 but there was some ongoing discussion of an additional charge due to the size of my car even though it fitted in one of their spaces. They did have internet at a price but if you were using an internet terminal and not your own laptop, the first 20 minutes was almost wholly devoted to trying to change the keyboard to English.

A television holiday show presenter described the place as, "This lively Black Sea resort has an intimate communication network and a unique vista and is ideal for the casual paddler. The town has a variety of cuisines on offer at competitive prices, laid back locals and all the facilities you would expect of a place like this."

I was dubious about his colourful description of the place which led me to believe that he was once an estate agent. The "intimate communication network" meant that trains ran along the beach. The "unique vista" was of factories with plumes of acrid smoke pumping out on either side of the beach and I worried that if the "casual paddler" spent longer than five minutes in that water, they'd be glowing like a full moon; "all the facilities you would expect" turned out to be one public toilet that charged admission and would not have been out of place on the set of *Hellraiser*. One mother emerged from said set, shook her head and warned us against using it. She pointed to a nearby bush instead.

We decided there was nothing to keep us in Mariupol and so we headed to the Russian border.

Chapter 5.

Russia

Friday 4 July 2008

Day 65 - Rostov, Russia - 5,626 miles

Our arrival at the Russian border did not conform to the impression I had of it, which granted was based on Elton John's *Nikita* video, complete with pouting blonde guards, flirtingly fingering my documentation. However, if my memory of the video serves me right, I am sure there wasn't a fat man with a gun shouting at someone for 20 minutes as I experienced. I drew the verbal abuse to a close by calling Anna, our gorgeous and helpful Russian teacher who had offered her number if we had any problems. She talked to the man for five minutes, told me it was all fine and I then watched as the man filled out all my forms for me, the 2,000 miles apparently no barrier for her to work her magic. He also assured me that I didn't need a declaration form for any dollars I was carrying, and I was fine up to $3,000 (at the time £1 = $1.50). On exiting the border post a guard, 20 yards from the customs man, asked me where my form was for my dollars. Mysteriously he also asked if I had a machine gun, leaving me unsure if he was suggesting I should have one. As we finally drove the first few yards into Russia, Hannah looked up from her iPod.

"Are we there?" she said, casting the briefest of glances out of the window.

"Yes, we are," her mum replied, prompting an excited Emily to declare, "We're in Australia!"

For some reason, only my name was put on the temporary insurance certificate that we were compelled to buy on entry. As a result, I took the wheel for the first time proper and was stopped by the police twice in 30 minutes. Naturally I was to blame for this. The first time was for my headlights not being on but thankfully I wasn't fined anything. However, the second time was just total corruption. He wanted paperwork but didn't know what. Then he asked me to sound my horn and followed that with a considerable amount of time spent staring at the engine but not checking VIN or chassis numbers. He then started flicking his throat with his finger which we later learned was a request for a bottle of something alcoholic. I gave him 100 roubles (£1 = 41 roubles) but that wasn't good enough. He then wanted schnapps and then stickers for his kids and balloons and, even though he knew we had only been in the country for 30 minutes with our kids and were doing a charity drive for cancer, he was not happy till we left with a bad taste in our mouth.

There are two schools of thought on the bribing front. Many Westerners expect to be asked for a bribe so they pay it, so the police know Westerners pay bribes so they ask for it and it's all a bit self-perpetuating. The other side is that you unwaveringly refuse to pay even the smallest amount as the chances are they really won't do anything and it helps spread a message. I had been so looking forward to going to Russia and this first half hour in the country caught me off guard. We talked about it afterwards and concluded that next time we would just plead ignorant and pretend we didn't have a clue what they were after. And if that didn't work then we'd pay them the bribe. "You don't have to pay a policeman daddy," Hannah helpfully advised, "they help you for free."

We arrived in Rostov-on-Don, the largest city in Southern Russia, without any further repugnant corruption other than some small-scale robbery from a couple of taxi drivers we employed to take us to a couple of hotels.

The city is a major transport hub and it appeared that all the transport was out on the streets for our arrival. Like most major cities, it had numerous buildings of cultural interest but our stay there was brief although memorable due to Eirene's gymnastic flexibility in the boot of our car. It all began when the two hotel receptionists shimmied in on the robbery act by dramatically increasing the previously agreed room prices on our arrival. The more attractive of the tag team lost her command of English when I began probing her inconsistencies but it quickly came back when I decided to swallow my pride and accept it. With a need for the toilet all of sudden becoming number one priority for the girls now that their electronic devices had been turned off, we rushed to retrieve our bags from the car only to find the boot was locked from the inside. A pantomime routine then followed whereby, in the style of a Victorian chimney sweep, we pushed the urchin Emily over the top of the boot/backseat netting into the jam-packed boot. "Use Abigail, she's smaller." Emily disloyally muffled, quickly selling out on the weakest member of the pack. As we pushed her deeper into the dark recesses in order for her to flick the boot switch from the inside, she unfortunately became stuck and panicked, bellowing that she was "costaerobic" so we dragged her out and wedged Hannah in. She made a great entry which was ultimately marred by her inability to pull the big lever right in front of her eyes. And so it was left to the elder of the pack (Eirene) to slither boa-like over the netting into the boot, leaving her dignity firmly in the front of the car. She opened the door though and we all grabbed legs to drag her back out the way she went in.

We made the long trip to Volgograd reasonably quickly with only two stops by the police who didn't actually drive along and pull us over, but instead opted for numerous permanent roadside checkpoints. At one of these the officer watched me stop at a stop sign, waved me forward, signalled for me to step out of the car and then took me back to look at the stop sign telling me that I should have stopped and stayed still. No bribes were requested nor proffered and the 40 recently purchased emergency Marlboroughs remained untouched.

Volgograd, formerly Stalingrad, is a large city dominated by a massive statue of Mother Russia. We started accommodation enquiries at the posh hotel and ended up at the Hotel Volgograd in two rooms, a considerable distance apart, for £80. Despite our protestations and provision of our own bedding we were forbidden from sharing a room in any of the hotels.

With its high ceilings, noisy old lift and once grandiose but now faded decor, it fitted my stereotype of an old eastern bloc hotel perfectly. I turned on a light in Eirene's room and it literally exploded, sending a flame through the lamp shade onto my hand. I fared little better with her air conditioning, which outwardly showed all the signs of working whilst failing to produce any cold air at all, and we had to promise the kids a bubble bath after we saw the murky brown water that came from the taps. The bubbles proved effective cover in masking what lurked beneath.

Eirene was so hot that she elected to open her window and let in the noise from the bars below that closed at 6am when breakfast started. I, on the other hand, had a very enjoyable evening with Emily in my room, playing "Football Manager" (very realistic - Leicester had just been relegated) and reading Joe Calzaghe's autobiography over a couple of beers.

Concern grew about Hannah who appeared to be coming down with something terrible. Her only symptom was that she had refused to eat all day, but this was coming from the girl whose diary of the trip had completed its metamorphosis into an international menu.

An increasingly hot, clear morning saw us set off for Mother Russia at the Hill of Mamai the next day. Mother Russia, also known as The Motherland Calls, is an amazing feat of engineering. We could see her from the car park, standing stoically at the top of the hill overlooking Volgograd, the epicentre of the battle of Stalingrad. The statue portrayed a powerful, sword wielding woman draped in a flowing robe; her head turned away, towards her outstretched, beckoning left arm with her mouth open as though calling her people to follow her. When it was completed in 1967, it was the tallest sculpture in the world, with the sword alone measuring 33m and the total height of the statue, 85m. It is still one of the biggest statues in the world today and is not too much shorter than Big Ben.

I was at once struck by the size of her breasts, barely able to avert my gaze when paying an old man 50 roubles for secure parking in the free public space at the bottom of the steps.

As we followed the sloping path towards her, we passed a relatively small statue of Father Russia and a walled approach with carvings of Russian soldiers and authentic recordings of machine gun fire on either side - at least we hoped it was a recording. The path snaked around her as we respectfully climbed to the summit and rested at her feet. As is normal, views from a high point are always a crowd pleaser but it was worth remembering that one and a half million people died there in less than a year.

"Not as many as Auschwitz," Hannah remarked almost competitively to her middle sister and I was conscious again of perhaps how meaningless the numbers were for the kids. However, the girls proved their worth and looked silently in awe at the tens of thousands of names that adorned the walls of a very well-crafted underground cenotaph with a flame and rigid, sweating soldiers on either side, resplendent in their immaculate uniforms and thick winter trench coats which they regrettably lacked in that bitter cold winter of 1942.

I took Abigail and Emily for a walk while Hannah and Eirene opted for a lie down in the hotel. We came across a funfair, electric cars and bouncy castles and, after lunch, returned to tell Hannah. The passing of this information coincided with a remarkable recovery and we all headed back down there late afternoon with the promise of a couple of rides. It was a ticket-only affair and I queued for some time at the ticket office and requested six tickets for the kids. No amount of polite finger raising, signalling or use of the *Point It* book could convey that we wanted to give her money to go on the funfair rides. I was convinced that this wasn't the first time she had been asked for tickets, but we had to leave empty handed with our devastated children. Only an ice-cream and a shot on the nearby electric cars ensured a remission of Hannah's mysterious illness.

Later that evening, a £75 bill for an admittedly appetizing one course meal confirmed my fiscal concerns about us living like we were on a permanent holiday.

The next morning, a pleasant breakfast was brought to a rapid conclusion when Hannah chundered all over the *Point It* book, much to the understandable disdain of fellow guests. With this event in mind we debated whether we should stay there another day. Eirene rationally submitted that as it may well be something at the hotel that was causing Hannah problems, we should move on. We drove to Astrakhan and found a hotel on the river, with ongoing "work in progress" but their prices sign had been finished first.

We settled in Astrakhan for a couple of nights so I caught up on some emails and received an upsetting text from my friend Tristan. His wife Nikki had given birth to their first child, Sophia, just under four months ago. The text was to tell me Nikki had died of cancer. We were both stunned and even more grateful for the extraordinary experience we were having. This tragic event occupied much of our talks and thoughts for the remainder of the trip and beyond.

I started on some serious car tinkering early doors. However, it was not as early as I had hoped as I made the mistake of using the lift in this unfinished hotel and became trapped for just short of an hour. I'm not normally the sort of person who gets scared by the prospect of being trapped in the pitch black with nothing but a thin, possibly "work in progress" wire holding me from my maker, but I was after that experience, I can tell you. Eventually the door was wedged open a fraction and needed the strength of two men to allow me to pull myself out. Unfortunately I didn't have that and had to utilise the engineer's arm strength to pull me out.

The next three hours produced the following conclusions:

My "working on the car" boiler suit was too small for me, specifically my testicles;

Having been stuck under the car for so long in such heat and with my face in such close proximity to the underside of my engine, I felt I had a pretty good idea of what the tenth circle of *Dante's Inferno* would be like;

Greasing the nipples on a driveshaft is as frustrating as counting granules of sand unless you have an inspection pit or platform and/or someone to help you;

I brought every spanner there is up to 21mm only to find that the filler on the transfer box was 22mm;

I could not find the filler on the front diff box;

The workshop manual I bought for my car is not, in fact, a workshop manual for my car.

Having spent the morning pottering around we decided to go to a nearby restaurant for lunch, which featured a slide and bouncy castle for the kids. We were sent the "'English speaking" waitress and commenced the standard routine. We asked her what food they had as we could not read the 20 items a page on the eight-page menu. She asked us what food we wanted. We mentioned six general things and she said no to all of them. An uncomfortable silence reigned which I broke by asking her what food was on the two pages of 20 items in front of her, and she said "pizza." Our faces lit up and we started ordering different topped pizzas. She stopped us and said that they only do one type of pizza. I ordered it, still curious as to what the other 39 items were. Following the arrival of the partly frozen mushroom and olive pizza (how did they know I hated both mushrooms and olives), I left early as I felt a bit ill, feeling and acting like the typical Englishman abroad. I managed to make it back to the hotel in a taxi but was beginning to feel a bit desperate following 20 minutes of ominous southern rumblings. I scrabbled around for the room key as I contemplated the stairs to our seventh-floor room and realised that I'd left it in the room. I asked at reception if they could let me in. The three members of staff, on being told I had locked the key in the room, had an absolutely wonderful time playing a game of, "Your family has the key?", "You want to buy another key?", "You want another room?", "You can unlock your door?" finished off with a cracking, "Why did you lock it in your room? You need it to get in." It was a masterful and unmistakably well-rehearsed script of which a young John Cleese would have been proud. I too would have been hooting if I hadn't been on the verge of crapping on the lobby floor.

Surprisingly, breakfast passed without any vomiting and we met an English couple travelling to Uzbekistan by train with their teenage daughters. They were the first English people we'd met since we left and after the traditional British cautious glances culminating in a nod, the floodgates opened and we all talked quickly and excitedly about where we had come from and where we were going to. No details exchanged, for that would be preposterous, and we set off on the 400 km trip to the Russian/Kazakhstan border.

We crammed the kids and bags into the car and set off before I realised that Eirene was map-reading from a map so minute in scale that it had the UK on it. One of those miniature globe pencil sharpeners would have been more useful. A search for the Kazakhstan map proved fruitless so we headed back to the hotel as I remembered leaving it on the bonnet. We searched the car park to no avail before Eirene asked the girl on reception, showing her another fold up map by way of demonstration, but she said that nothing had been handed in. Eirene pointed to the folded-up map of Kazakhstan that her right hand was resting on, which she reluctantly handed over without a hint of embarrassment or shame.

We set off again, following signs to our destination and headed in totally the wrong direction. Two hours later and we felt like we were lost in the world's largest maize maze. Large, major multi-lane roads quickly became small unmade roads and signs were at odds with our compass. We asked a couple of policemen, one of whom was very cooperative and provided us with the simple pointing that we needed. The second policeman spent an inordinate amount of time pointing in different directions, talking and creating great confusion when what he actually wanted to do was point to the road behind him, which took us straight to the border. At the border, no one asked to check our now lost immigration departure cards which was bizarrely frustrating! The final guard, a Gary Barlow lookalike (early Take That days), was very chirpy and helpful by which I mean he smiled and sent us on our way 10 km down the road towards the Kazak border. So off we trotted, at one stage driving over a 500m stretch of crunchy dark road which, it transpired, was in fact a popular locust crossing. Minutes later, Eirene, scrunching of shells still vividly reverberating around my head, managed to catch me out on the comedy "locust on your neck" routine that, after jamming on the brakes and doing a funny sit-down dance, I begrudgingly gave her due credit for.

The Kazak border had a small chatty corporal and a less chatty sergeant. The chatty one initially seemed very receptive but became a bit more sinister as time passed. Being a Muslim country, he was quite taken by Eirene's lack of yashmak but lacked training in the art of the subtle look.

Working as a guard at one of these borders can be a breeding ground for megalomania which, combined with boredom, isolation and lack of women, makes for a dangerous combination. This little man had us jumping through lots of his little hoops for an hour until he became bored and let us through his gate. We then attended numerous different windows and gates in order to obtain entry cards, get our passports stamped and purchase worthless third-party insurance and temporary import forms for the vehicle (that thing that we paid a load of money for in England called a Carnet de Passage which wasn't accepted there). We became separated and Eirene took the three kids off on her own while I sorted the vehicle, only to have to return on realising that they had not stamped her immigration cards. Finally, after three hours, we drove off only to be stopped by Napoleon from the first guard house who had me empty most of the back of the car. The purpose of this primarily appeared to be to repeatedly use his "Is this Viagra?" gag whilst going through the medicine box. However, I'll leave it there as I do recognise the hypocrisy of me levelling criticism at an individual for repeated use of the same joke whilst still expecting a laugh.

We entered Kazakhstan with half the boxes in the boot emptied out into the car and drove like the wind on pretty much the worst roads yet. The roads contrasted with the terrain which was extremely flat whilst the desert, of which we were on the southern stretch, was reasonably green - which isn't desert in my book but I know factually, and only factually, I'm wrong about. Our route took us across a rickety old bridge that lay just above, and I mean just above, the Buzan River. It was used by every traveller, local and goods vehicle travelling through Kazakhstan and was so close to the water that it looked like a vehicle one gram heavier than ours would be driving through the river. We slowed down to return the stares of a group of wild camels at the side of the road while further on, a herd of wild horses cantered across the road in front of us. That, a lack of petrol stations and even fewer policemen, were the key features that initially marked it out as being different from Russia.

As I started to warm up my Borat impression, something I knew I would have to ration over the next four weeks, we felt like we were travelling in its true sense where the true sense consists of an air-conditioned Land Cruiser, four iPods and two Nintendos. Ornate mud huts lined the side of the road and what appeared to be isolated cemeteries acted as lone markings in the surrounding landscape. Shanty towns, factories and isolated thrusting oil pumps came into view as we drove closer to Atyrau, a harbour city on the Caspian Sea. Groups of ostensibly friendly kids waved excitedly as we drove through the outskirts of their town.

Traditionally we spent one to two hours finding accommodation in a new city which, as usual, started off with the confidence that we could find a place ourselves. We drove around in circles for the first half hour or so before stopping to look at one of the guide books. The failure to find any of them took us past the hour and we filled the redundant time by shouting at each other. We then emerged into the now familiar routine of paying and following taxis to take us to the expensive places and then gradually moving down the star ratings until we arrived at the ones we'd grown to know and love so well, the starless ones.

With time ticking on as a result of our late exit from Astrakhan and the three-and-a-half-hour border crossing, we knew we would have problems. However, we came upon the big square that featured on the postage stamp map that is synonymous with *Lonely Planet* city maps. We immediately noticed a three-star place that had a sign proclaiming the presence of a sauna and a pool. Post check-in we discovered that this meant a sauna pool, also known as a sauna, which was out of order. One hearty meal of horse and camel later and we settled down in our £70 air-conditioned room having decided to stay for another night in a town that the ever optimistic *Lonely* "you have to go and see this unmissable museum/statue/rock/fossilised piece of excrement" *Planet* uncharacteristically advised visitors to leave and leave quickly. We also swiftly realised that distances between towns were pretty substantial which wasn't surprising I guess, considering the country is bigger than Western Europe. In some instances, they were a gut-wrenchingly two to three times an iPod's battery life apart.

Atyrau is a modern, bustling town with a European and Asian influence. Islam and Christianity sit side by side as the dominant religions of the city, with both the opulent Russian Orthodox church and the lapis-domed Mangali Mosque receiving an equal number of worshippers. During a late morning stroll round Atyrau, we popped into the five-star

Renaissance Hotel for a £4 glass of freshly squeezed orange juice and use of their Wi-Fi. It was a case of "let's see what we could've won" and I sensed the family were becoming restless. This place had a proper swimming pool and we asked if we could pay to use it as non-guests.

"Certainly," the man said, and produced the membership list, the cheapest of which started at just over £2,000 each for six months membership. We said we were only going to be there for a day so, after the briefest of ponderings, he came up with a three-month deal at just short of £1,000 including joining fee. At least their pricing policy was consistent with their Russian counterpart's "1 rouble for 1, 10 roubles for 10" approach to bulk discounts. As I turned to head downstairs with my forlorn family in tow, all obediently following their breadwinner of a father who had completely failed to provide them with water, the man called out.

"Maybe I speak to manager about the joining fee," he charitably offered with a wink. To cut a long story short he came up with a weekend deal which worked out at about £85 for all of us which we snapped up. He put me on the phone to reservations who took me through a painful autobiography before telling me it would cost £200. Thankfully Irena, the kind receptionist with the familiar sounding name, sorted it out. After we purloined the internet for a quick video Skype call to the mother-in-law, we all left happy in the knowledge that we all would be paddling the next day and we duly did.

As any local will tell you, a visit to Atyrau would not be complete without popping into an English themed pub. We found *Guns and Roses,* which its own literature described as having "a phone box, number plates attached to the wall and other things impossible to describe". Perhaps it is a unique gift I have but I found I could describe them with ease. The "other things impossible to describe" were guitars, posters, stage props, tickets and LPs. Keen as I was to immerse myself in local culture and the people, I recognised we all had to take small steps. We trotted out the pub refreshed, though not convinced at all that this was the local pub of the LA band by the same name. Outside it was 40° heat and we all scurried for the air-conditioned car. The contrast between the Western oil worker refuge we left, to the poverty of the old town we then drove through, was stark to say the least and exceeded anything we'd witnessed so far. Malnourished kids littered open sewers and improvised lopsided shacks dominated the streets. Our kids were shocked into silence, their windows temporarily replaced their screens, as, mouths open, they returned the residents' empty stares. We returned to our posh hotel in embarrassed silence.

It was Friday 11th July 2008, and it was also Abigail's birthday. She had a cake and a few presents and was delighted with the events of the day.

We received word from fellow overlanders, Nessie's Adventures [1], about grave concerns they had over some of our forthcoming roads. They painted a picture of something akin to the Somme and I was concerned we would be driving over submerged cars. I decided to nip down for a drink at the hotel bar, hoping to chance across some ex-pats and oil workers who could shed some light on what was and wasn't passable. Unfortunately, on engaging with them, it became apparent that their zone of knowledge didn't extend beyond any of the town's bars or brothels. Like many ex-pats they had a wealth of anecdotal evidence to call on and cite as fact but there was little of substance, albeit they were very sociable and drunkenly offered their business cards in case of an emergency, which I gratefully took.

I took a moment to contemplate our achievements so far and concluded that I was thoroughly enjoying the trip. Whilst recognising that we weren't fully embracing the cultural diversity whilst simultaneously going through money like it was going out of fashion, I appreciated that this would come and harmony would best be achieved by gradual immersion. We'd covered

---

[1] www.nessiesadventures.com

6,548 miles in total and I had no stress. My worries that I had before, my dissatisfaction with life, my hatred of office work, the mind and sometimes body numbing pain of commuting, my endless list of things I had to do, the quick weekends and the slow weeks had all evaporated. I could rarely recall the day of the week and the day boiled down to the very simple – what to eat, where to stay and where to go. My mind was clear and I was happy. Yes, I was concerned about the length of time the kids spent in the car, with their Nanos and Nintendos, neither of which gave them an appreciation of their surroundings, nor quality family time. However, Hannah demonstrated that her imagination had not been affected by the time spent in front of a screen when, on being greeted with a dead Nano battery and a Nintendo with a selection of games she was bored with, she embarked on a verbose description of her ideal house.

"It will have a slide from my room into a pool. The one from my husband's house will join up with it in the middle." It lasted nigh on two hours and was a remarkable insight into her values and dreams. What emerged was that her husband's house will be next door and there's going to be unlimited food and toys and that the toys will be edible.

Eirene missed her mum like mad. That was very clear. In truth I was jealous of their closeness. We had a blog and I was emailing my mum and dad and they replied religiously and enthusiastically, but they'd moved to Spain shortly after Hannah was born and our contact was primarily electronic. And I'm a boy and boys don't telephone their parents! Eirene and her mum spoke and/or Skyped almost every day. Eirene was understandably unsettled and told me that I'd taken her outside her comfort zone but conceded, which I recognised, that her comfort zone had increased. She wanted the big house near all her friends and most of all near her mum. This was not her and she seemed reluctant to ever agree she was enjoying it even when it was apparent she was. I worried that she would let the time pass and then bemoan her lack of appreciation. She suggested the trip but we both knew that was not the reality of it. I certainly didn't think she appreciated the repercussions of that January when she suggested, "let's drive to Australia," but I will forever love her for bringing it up and, above all, for following it up.

I can see that the life Eirene had back home, surrounded by her children, her mum and her friends, was everything that she ever wanted. She liked, as I did, telling people about her forthcoming adventure and recognised that, with property prices still dropping like crazy, it wasn't the time to buy a house. She was having the time of her life as it was and she gave it all up. I didn't know if we were closer but we were together all the time and I had no yearning for a break and neither, she assured me, did she. We occasionally snapped at each other but I was happy with her company and we knew each other inside out so I didn't have to try and kid her. I liked doing little things that made her happy and enjoyed much of the car time as it was effectively just the two of us and we talked about things that TV, telephone and computers had prohibited back home. It concerned me though that we were not experiencing and embracing countries as much as we should. It might have been because we were with kids and virtually in bed by 7pm, or it might have been because we were in hotels and not experiencing the closeness that comes with camping, hostels and living with families.

When I went inter-railing with Nick and Jeff as a teenager, everyone talked to us and I returned with an address book full of names and numbers. That wasn't this experience. In shopping centres and amusement arcades you sometimes have those spaceship-like rides that jiggle around on the hydraulics and make a bit of noise but don't actually go anywhere. Inside it's an illusion of travel, you feel like you're travelling and looking out of the windows it appears you are, but you're not. And we would regret it. That was my fear.

I recognise that I've stopped saying that the kids were behaving like horrors which is my way of saying that they were behaving great. Perhaps it's the last traces of the Glaswegian in me (I left Scotland when I was ten) that sometimes drew me to greet the good with silence and the bad with words of condemnation. The greatest compliment a Glaswegian can pay is when he says something is "no bad." Well I'll say it now. The trip, the kids and the wife were definitely "no bad."

It was a challenging drive to Oral or Uralsk as it is sometimes known. An ambitious road development programme was underway in Kazakhstan, which meant there were hundreds of miles of roadworks with hundreds of miles of potholed mud tracks adjacent to them. One day they will be great but not for a very long time as virtually no-one seemed to be actually working on them. The tracks were a combination of the old road, tracks created by lorries and diggers (always immobile when we saw them) and random paths through fields that frustrated drivers had adopted. There was a strong argument for being able to undertake our journey without the need for a four-wheel drive but it would have meant avoiding this country. I had never seen road conditions like it and, as more vehicles dug them up and more rain came, they were only going to worsen. Eirene did an admirable job with the driving but a glance at any time in the rear-view mirror would always see three kids, iPods in hands, doing some sort of synchronised head-bobbing-from-side-to-side routine in time to the continuous rocking of the car. These road conditions marked most of our time in Kazakhstan which, although initially good fun, became painfully tedious after a while and the mutually shared elation at hitting the occasional bit of tarmac would have seemed grossly overstated to someone who hadn't experienced it.

We had three police stops on our way to Oral all of whom looked at our cramped, tightly packed boot and said "Ok," presumably daunted at the prospect of going through it. When being stopped we had established a set routine – stop the car, glasses off to reduce the potential intimidation factor and appear more humble, Buffwear bandana off so we didn't look like drug carrying hippy tourists, air-con off just to save on the additional petrol, hazards on, all windows down, music off, earphones off the kids coupled with the issuing of "look cute" commands and a final practice of their "Zdra stuyve te", Russian for "Hello." Nessie's Adventures had warned us not to stop at all and that they were all pigs but we unashamedly had the kids up our sleeve and, so far, it had been fine. The second time we were stopped, a US/Kazakhstan student came over to help translate. We're still not sure what he said but the policeman posed for a picture and insisted we autographed a couple of our business cards for him.

On arrival, we settled on the Park Hotel which was a simple, cosy hotel with a real pool that wasn't also a sauna or just a sauna. It was situated in a park by a river and, by all accounts, a great place for nature watching - but nothing wild hung around when my brood appeared with the stealth-like qualities of a brass band. I nipped off to find an additional pillow from the cleaners for Abigail. They seemed startled and then very happy when I asked them for a "bolshoi babushka," accompanied with associated sign language. It turned out I should have said "bolshoi padushka," my initial submission translating as "a large old lady." Well, that was my bed made, so to speak, and much flirting from the aged staff followed.

The hotel restaurant was set out to the most decadent of standards, mainly because they were preparing for a wedding and we were subsequently put in a side room. Having been brought up with only a brother, I assumed most childhoods involved guns, soldiers, mock executions and climbing and I seem to have missed out on what it is girls like about weddings. It appears to be their lifelong aim, somehow bred into them from birth and before. Our three were never happier than when they were dressing up as princesses and staging a mock wedding. If I'd known how important it all was to girls, I'd have put a bit more thought into my own engagement and wedding. Even Christmas couldn't compete with how excited my flock were, and I include my wife in that, at the arrival of the bride. She kept us hanging on for some time, which only increased their appetite to see her, but when she finally appeared, she held them all transfixed.

Even I surprised myself when I was drawn to comment on the sequined dress and the ambitious nature of her sleeves. They were an absolute triumph.

The next day we drove to Aktobe, a key location in the 1918 Russian Revolution, and found the people there to be delightfully affable. At one point a restaurant owner took the trouble of phoning his son to translate the menu for us. We later discovered his son was in America and he probably underestimated the fiscal implications of waiting for Eirene to decide what she wanted, even off a one item menu. A friend of the waitress gave us her home and mobile number in the event of an emergency translating requirement. After, our children transcended cultural barriers at a local funfair park and we engaged with another mother who spoke reasonable English. Progress.

There were a few notable features about driving in Aktobe. You have to stop in the middle of a roundabout to allow oncoming traffic on to it and a road map in Cyrillic would be preferable to English to save time on the slow translation between the Cyrillic alphabet and ours. It also transpired that the requirement for UK car alarms to sound for two minutes and then stop hadn't reached this region, as we discovered when an electrical storm at about 4am set off 30-odd car alarms in the car park below our hotel window. We just managed to doze off with alarms ringing in our ears when Hannah woke us up and asked, "Is it morning time?" before promptly going back to sleep.

A 490-mile journey awaited on what we knew for a fact were top roads. The fact was based on word from the friend of the waitress who called a girl who had a friend who told us the roads were fine. We bought it and the initially resplendent dual carriageway (and I'm not sure those words have ever been put together before) confirmed our expectation. There were even some very smart petrol stations; but we quickly moved to single track and then to single track without tarmac. It turned into an off-road course with descents down steep verges and much deep wading through water. Eirene was on the wheel and the bumpiness of the drive meant I had to leave Leicester in a tricky position (Norwich and Watford away with Ian Hume still injured) and close the laptop to *Championship Manager*. Some countries eh?

After four hours of driving, three hours from the nearest town and two hours from the last petrol station, we drove past a Land Rover Discovery and another Toyota bearing British plates. I persuaded Eirene to spin it round and we met a bunch of blokes undertaking the Mongolian Rally, an annual charity drive from London to Mongolia. We started chatting. The Land Rover was experiencing some problems with its head gasket and in the principle of six degrees of separation, it turned out we were only one degree away from a mutual chum, Neil Patel. This served as considerably more of a surprise to me than coming across a Land Rover with a head gasket problem.

We did what we could, which transpired to be nothing, and headed off with Eirene and I both strangely euphoric for some time at the chance meeting. The roads impressively, in one sense, deteriorated further and, at one point, we came across a couple of teenagers and a man whom we assumed to be their father. We asked them how much longer before we hit tarmac and one of the wits replied, "Russia." They were excited to see us and we gave them a pack of our "bribe cigarettes" which we were confident we wouldn't need anymore. That kept the kids busy but proved to be the incentive for their father to thrust his head through my passenger window and go for the handshake to end all handshakes. As his vodka breath set to work on slowly intoxicating me and his eyes settled lecherously on the females in the car, we enthusiastically commenced our attempt on the world's longest handshake. I felt I was having a stroke down my right side, such was the vice-like nature of his grip and as it continued, his smile became as glazed as his eyes. By this stage he had levered himself half into my window, feet off the ground and the atmosphere had clearly changed. We talked and gesticulated for some time and, in typical British fashion when in the midst of a potential robbery/hijacking or worse, I announced that "we really must be on our way. An absolute pleasure to meet you." Unsurprisingly this cut little ice as he spat out an incomprehensible barrage of words that I blindly guessed were at best an anti-smoking message. Through gritted teeth and an etched-on grimace, I told Eirene to start to drive off which she glacially commenced. This made his attempt to clamber into our car even more of a personal mission and I started to push him out whilst telling Eirene to just put her foot down complete with welcoming smile on my face. The situation was rapidly deteriorating but Eirene insisted on maintaining her hearse-like progress. I escalated my one arm wrestling routine before turning to Eirene and, with big beaming grimace, said "Put your fucking foot flat down now." I concede I didn't check whether all the kids had their mp3 earphones in when I let slip the Anglo-Saxon, but it did inspire Eirene to increase the speed ever so slightly and I managed to lever him out. The ruts and holes of the road were suddenly their most welcome feature as we left a cloud of dust behind us. I was angry at Eirene's initial lack of initiative and subsequent lack of action but appreciated that as far as she was concerned she might be killing him. It made us realise that despite all our prep and good fortune so far, we needed clear guidelines for what to do in a similar situation again. I had visions of us surrounded by a baying mob with a reluctant Eirene attempting to ease her way through them as they set about smashing our windows, trying to drag us out.

With our thoughts to ourselves we settled down once again to the appalling roads which inevitably began to take their toll. A disturbing rattle emerged from one of the front wheels and I prayed it wasn't a bearing or a vodka-fuelled Kazakhstan man wrapped around the axle. Kazakhstan has a freakishly large number of vehicle inspection ramps throughout the country, thick concrete walls with 45° inclines that allow you ease of access under your vehicle. Where we have laybys with overflowing bins, a burger van smelling of last year's cooked fat and a group of doggers surrounding a Mark 2 Escort, they will have an inspection ramp. Typically, now that we were after one, there was none to be seen. Eventually we came across a garage and I popped into the workshop to offer them a few Tenge in return for popping the car on the ramp. I was greeted by a garage full of physically disabled people, none of whom I recognised from the Sarajevo Ironside convention. However, they let us use the ramp and helped find a loose nut on the shock absorber, but they wouldn't take any money at all from the "Westerners in their big car" and we left with a feeling of genuine warmth, our hackles now firmly down but our windows still firmly up. The British equivalent would be a family saloon on EU plates pulling into the car park of a Kwik Fit Fitters with brake pads grinding, like an injured gazelle on the plains of the Serengeti.

After eight hours we finally made Kostanay, which was originally known as Nikolayevsk until 1895 and then Kustanay until 1997 when the then and still now Kazakhstan president, Nursultan Nazarbayev, decreed a spelling change. Kostanay is a small town north of Rudny, which has an unusual selection of monuments embracing modern technology. A giant concrete keyboard sits in front of the university, the keys of which are often used as benches. A bronze sculpture of a girl with a mobile phone to her ear stands near some fountains on a pedestrianised thoroughfare. Another one, a bronze of a student with a laptop sitting on a bench, has seemingly caused some comments about her unbuttoned top button exposing her ample bosom, but it has not discouraged people from sitting beside her for a photo. There is even a landmark bronze statue of Charlie Chaplin, which was unveiled just months before we arrived.

We were delighted to find a hotel without the aid of a taxi driver and I involved myself in an international game of Chinese whispers by speaking Afrikaans to a French/Dutch girl who spoke to a German girl who could speak to the Kazakhstan girl behind the desk. We ended up with something close to what we asked for, although we didn't specifically request a toilet with blocked drains that smelt like a cow-shed. We strolled around the town for a good 45 minutes looking for a restaurant that was open before finally being directed back to the hotel restaurant. The food was fine, but we did have to endure a very badly and loudly sung *Tears in Heaven* which would've had Clapton turning in his grave if he was dead. The singer's killing of other well-known 80s and 90s pop songs was almost enhanced by a rare and unsolicited tantrum from Abigail.

There were unprecedented levels of restraint and professionalism from the family the following day as we managed to be on the road for 6.50am, despite me having had a disturbed night sharing a room with a thrashing five-year-old and 35° heat. I had been woken by Emily with a headbutt followed by an unconventional uppercut and straight right combo.

A mere 10 hours of my anecdotes later and we found ourselves approaching the outskirts of Astana, one of the most visually extravagant cities I've ever been to. Just a mile or two outside the city, Kazakhstan's now capital, there was virtually third world poverty on display for all to see while in the city itself, we were greeted with decadence on an unprecedented level. The buildings and monuments were so grandiose, many designed by Norman Foster, the famous British architect who had seemingly been given a blank canvas stapled to a blank cheque. There were pyramids, futuristic slanting skyscrapers, arches, golden monuments, cavernous mosques, multi-coloured buildings with big holes through them and hedonistic hotels all built on a site that didn't even have proper roads 10 miles away. Judging by their natural gas resources and presidential ambition it was probably still in its infancy. Nevertheless, the inconsistency in the distribution of wealth was hard to reconcile with the opulence of the presidential palace in a country where so many of its population live below the poverty line. Kazakhstan is a country where roads are optional and there is little in the way of any public service; that, and the fact that the president is regarded as one of the richest men in the world, did leave us thinking it was more Ceausescu than Evita.

Arriving there in a car that had the appearance of being completely spray painted with mud made us stand out more than we had before; there seemed to be city cars and rural cars and never the twain met. The commencement of our stage one accommodation finding process was delayed as we spent an hour and a half driving around in awe at our unexpected surroundings. It had distracted us from our hunger and weariness but as the kids' bickering escalated, the atmosphere became ripe for a punch-up. And so it came.

I had been stewing, in my inimitable way, about a remark Eirene had made during the day to the effect that she was just driving to see her mum. It had left me with a feeling that I was doing everything – navigating, sorting out the car every day, sorting out all the accommodation, speaking to the taxi drivers and policemen for directions, sorting out all the money, doing the diary and the emails and the website and the forum, charging everything and ensuring that phones, iPods and Nintendos were all working. Despite this she wasn't enjoying it and would rather be with her mum than me. My growing contempt was exasperated by a rubbish night's sleep, a massive day of driving and whingey kids. The catalyst though was Eirene who, in the navigating seat but devoid of any form of map whatsoever, uttered, "I have a *feeling* it's a right turn here."

I snapped and let loose with my frustrations.

"Where in God's name does this feeling come from? A great feeling would be based on looking at a bloody map and then looking up at some road signs," I spat venomously. "The quicker you check the map the quicker you will be getting away from this God forsaken trip and all these expensive hotels that you've had to put up with and back home to your nice comfortable life style!" I shouted.

With hindsight, what perhaps might have been a good idea would have been to have navigated by myself and kept my counsel for a quiet chat over a glass of wine later that evening. Instead I went on strike and sulkily left a lone female to speak, somewhat unsuccessfully, to taxi drivers and hotels. I caved in and went and spoke to one further down the road. He had wanted 1,000 Tenge (£1 = 240 Tenge) and I, midway through the aforementioned sulk, immediately refused knowing he was taking the piss, whilst failing to fully appreciate the weakness of my position. Thankfully, he didn't appreciate the weakness of my position either and halved his price to under £2. We followed him to a three-bedroomed apartment in a socially deprived part of the city. A ten-inch-thick steel front door opened into a grandiose, spacious apartment that the kids loved. We hastily dumped our bags and headed to an overpriced Turkish restaurant and filled ourselves whilst the kids played in the park. The waiter, obviously sensing our parched state, followed the adhered to Worldwide Waiter's Code of leaving our two pints on the bar for about 10 minutes whilst he wandered around doing very unimportant things very slowly.

The following day in Astana was brilliant but, compared to the previous day, one spent bathing in camel shit would have topped it. We started by persevering with the home schooling aspect of the trip with Emily moving onto the computer-based training aspect of her educational obligations, which roughly meant she pottered around on the laptop playing a pirate maths-type game called *Fraction Island*.

We decided to reward the kids' (let's call it) stoicism on the long journeys with an outing to a large water park. We were the only visitors and appeared to shock the girl on reception when we asked to come in. The lack of clientele and apparently abandoned rides made it feel like a Chernobyl funfair. Without a hint of irony, my female changing room attendant told me that I couldn't bring any of my daughters into the changing room. The male employee in Eirene's changing room had the same message about boys. Outside we bumped into two Kazakhstani doctors (one a PhD and the other a medical doctor) visiting with their two sons who had spent time in the UK and recognised that we had British plates on the car. I remarked on how impressive their city was and he agreed. I asked where he had been in England and he replied Sheffield. We eventually made it through the uncomfortable silence.

We had expensive spaghetti for lunch at a very modern shopping mall where the waiter cunningly, on arrival, placed an ashtray in front of Abigail which she immediately discarded on the floor, smashing it into a thousand fragments. On departure we were charged £2 for the ashtray but I was unsuccessful in retrieving the remaining pieces of it back. Actually it's right. Why should a restaurant foot the bill for kids' clumsiness? Potentially it's a British thing but something I think they certainly shouldn't profit on.

We continued our day with a visit to a place called Duman, an entertainment centre with an aquarium and activities aimed at children. It was an echoey, cavernous hall with the double whammy of both poor music and poor quality music. However, on entering we spotted a bucking bronco which Hannah immediately elected to try. She was just over the minimum age of seven by four weeks and I had my doubts as to whether she would like it, but she insisted and I relented. I paid for it promptly before she could change her mind which she wanted to do after witnessing another customer being violently flung from the horns, onto the floor. As a token of international cooperation, the operator agreed to throw in an extra minute free of charge, but Hannah didn't seem as elated as me at this and in fact didn't seem keen to let go of my arm at all. Prising her gorgeous little nails out of my forearm, I plonked her atop the mechanical beast, popped out the camera and then watched as the bearded operator engaged warp factor 10. The lens had barely finished extending when she landed at my feet. "Still got two minutes 50 seconds left, pet," I assured her before popping her back on and re-focussing the camera.

We then explored the aquarium with its apparently famous 70-metre glass tunnel through a shark pool. It's the only oceanarium in the world that is more than 3000 km from the sea

96

and probably as close as most Astana residents will ever get to seeing life in the ocean. There were various tanks with freshwater fish from South America and another with carnivorous inhabitants. Bottom feeders and clown fish swam among the rocks while the coral community played host to seahorses and sea anemones and an assortment of fish named after other animals or inanimate objects like: pipefish, cowfish, Japanese boxfish, foxface fish and dogfish. It wasn't SeaWorld but for £8 for the five of us it was excellent value for money putting to one side the ethical questions and transportation queries.

We had a stopover near Lake Balkhash where we found a solitary motel and were unable to cram all units into the same room so had to elect for two. The following morning, I was woken to the sound of bat-like shrieks emanating from down the corridor. They initially merged with my dream which rapidly transformed into a scene from *Deliverance*. I dopily rose to my feet and languidly made my way into the unknown and potentially dangerous wilderness. I was functioning on auto-pilot until the potential implications of the screams hit me. Clad in only my boxers, I half-sprinted, half-stumbled down the public corridor to Eirene's room which I identified as being the source of the cries of terror. I banged on the flimsy door, increasing the frequency and strength of my strikes as I heard the lock being turned, subconsciously correlating my actions with the speed at which the door was being opened. The lock clicked and I burst in on Eirene ready to strike the assailant. Eirene, Emily and Abigail were all staring at a small hole in one of the polystyrene ceiling tiles. "Hamster!" Eirene stuttered in fear and signalled to the vacant hole. As pure unadulterated relief flooded through me, Eirene regaled an elongated story that could best be summarised as she woke up and saw a hamster looking at her through that hole. She's no rodent buff and I'm curious as to how her sleepy eyes in a darkened room could ascertain that it was a hamster and not something less domestically domicile but, due to her traumatised state, I let her believe it was a hamster rather than a rat.

It was 700 km to Almaty, the former capital, which sources predicted could take anything from five hours to five days. Thankfully it turned out to be much closer to the former. We had good reports about the place and the bloke from *Lonely Planet* appeared to have spent his entire Kazakhstan budget there and Wikipedia-ed the rest of the country, judging by the amount of words he devoted to it. We took heed of *their* top accommodation recommendation and attempted to head for Hotel Khazol but soon became lost. The kids were irritable and, naturally in turn, so was I as I lambasted *Lonely Planet* for using maps with phonetically written English road names to direct us down Russian cyrillic written roads. Unfortunately, their guide to dialling codes in Kazakhstan was nothing short of a work of fiction, so we couldn't even call the place. With my limited Russian and the limited road signs that I saw, I attempted to translate between the two before going down the taxi route. I knew I was close but the £20 quote to go a few blocks was obscene so I elected to decline his offer and spend the £20 on fuel looking for the place, which I duly did. Eventually we found it and were quoted £150 per night and £90 per night by its lesser neighbour, a good tactic which helps soften the blow of the £90 place which we took.

After a long day, we finally flopped into our functionally compact room and ate in a very acceptable, cockroach-infested restaurant where dinner was served in the form of a home cooked stew from an animal that wasn't in our *Point It* book. Exhausted, the kids and Eirene fell asleep too easily, leaving me to read Ranulph Fiennes's autobiography and cringe at the true meaning of the word "adventure!"

Next morning, we set off with a hotel-provided Russian map in search of an internet café/coffee shop and a book shop in order to buy an even better map of Kazakhstan. After about an hour I discovered that the hotel map had south at the top and north at the bottom and we'd gone completely the wrong way for almost two miles. I pointed out to the family that if the city was folded in half along a 45° axis then we would be in the right spot, but they wouldn't have it. When we finally arrived at the book shop, a Kazakhstani soldier with excellent English helped the local shopkeeper rip us off for a fold up map of Almaty and the surrounding area. I checked that the map had north at the top but, despite that, the soldier turned it upside down when he was helping with directions.

We found the email café and coffee shop that *Lonely Planet* recommended with free internet which was a little slice of America in Kazakhstan. It was good to hear from everyone back home and fire off loads of emails. I ordered cakes by way of penance and Hannah, who seemed to be showing an increasing tolerance to milk, was permitted by Eirene to have a big square of chocolate which she deservedly tucked into. It was a big jump and we monitored her closely, half expecting her to metamorphose into some sort of alien creature at any moment. Having a milk allergy meant we carried antihistamine medicine everywhere and restaurant visits and menu analysis always came down to the milk question, with birthday parties being an exercise in rigid self-control for her. The specialists we'd seen had given some hope that she might grow out of it but concurred that if it was still with her at five, it would probably be with her for life. Having had it from birth it was just something that we and she both accepted and were resigned to. Now she was chomping away on milk chocolate looking as happy as anytime I had seen her and it felt really emotional. I held back the tears until she said, "I can go for curries with you now, Dad, if you want." She knew how to press the buttons.

We meandered back to the hotel with almost unanimous aspirations to go up in the city's cable car to the highest point in Almaty, Kok-Tobe mountain. I say almost unanimous because Eirene had clandestinely whispered to me, "I'm not going up in the fucking cable car, ok?" Instead, we pottered at the base of the mountain while I groomed Eirene with the idea of staying at a former Soviet observatory and satellite monitoring station base deep in the mountains, about 20 miles towards the Kyrgyzstan border.

At breakfast, I received a text from my mum telling me that my brother Douglas's five-year-old daughter Lydia, who had been born prematurely and suffered a catalogue of health problems, had a collapsed lung again, developed pneumonia and was back in hospital. My tears at Hannah being able to eat chocolate were given some perspective.

Back at the hotel, Hannah and Abigail settled down and Emily dozed off in her now familiar spot - lying on the sideboard with her legs on the bed while I continued to read about Fiennes' fingers falling off and lips sticking together.

With four maps in hand and no booking, we set off for the space station. As we drove up the valley higher into mountains, we were stunned by the immense beauty of it all. If someone had told us that Kazakhstan had places that put Switzerland to shame, we wouldn't have believed them. And quite rightly because they don't but they're not too far off. The roads were really rough with grass covered slopes leading to snow peaked mountains and mesmerising waterfalls. The terrain was such that we concluded that a four-wheel drive was essential, just before we were overtaken by a Lada. The views were so spectacular that it even led Hannah to turn off her iPod. It was a shock and one that we had never expected - the iPod turning off that is. Eirene drove admirably through the rough terrain while I map-read and took videos and photos.

A friend had recommended we stay in a traditional yurt, highlighting it as being the best time of her trip for the remoteness and beauty of it. Eirene was adamant we wouldn't be doing that and was back-tracking on the space centre accommodation after we had passed a good few expensive hotels on the way up.

The observatory was only about 30 km from Almaty on a steep, well-maintained road high up in the Tien Shan Mountains at the boundary between the fir trees and alpine meadows. We stopped to admire the Big Almaty Lake, an alpine reservoir at over 2500m above sea level, which provides the city below with all its water.

It felt pretty surreal turning off a dirt track into a compound containing six massive observatories and a whopping satellite dish with a circumference of about 60m. A Czech family were coming out as we departed and, as always, their English was about a thousand words better than our "Dobre den" Czech. They directed us inside a tired looking barracks-style pink building where we came across an elderly, white-haired Kazakhstani woman with a thousand wrinkles. She neither knew any English nor had her reading glasses on to read our Russian but via a mixture of my dismal pronunciation and better charades we managed to secure a couple of rooms, lunch, dinner and breakfast. I engaged with Philippe, the hairy-eared French owner of a very captivating expedition Land Cruiser, who had a wealth of useful information to part with about the astronomical instruments, the night sky and even the bird life that was soaring above us (Alpine choughs seemingly).

Philippe also told us that our intended port of entry into China, the high altitude Torugart Pass, was closed to all Western traffic for the three months around the Olympics. Furthermore, we learned that we should have registered within 14 days of arrival in Kazakhstan, so it might be more an issue of not being permitted to leave Kazakhstan than being allowed into China. Such rumours were rife within the travelling fraternity and it was hard to know what to believe at times.

I noticed a mountain track heading west and, after lunch, I suggested that the family embark on a good romp up the steep track. Progress was painfully slow with all complaining about having to walk and Abigail had to be put into her baby carrier on my back before we had even passed the entrance gate. Maybe it was the chat with the Frenchman that put it in my head but I ruthlessly frogmarched them, Beau Geste style, up the path. Thirty minutes later, I was reminded why sudden exercise with no acclimatisation at over 3000m isn't a good idea. The walk was cut short and we slowly trudged back down with only me reporting any symptoms.

We made an early start the next day along the much hyped "superhighway" to Bishkek in Kyrgyzstan, which was basically a tarmac road. We had the Tian Shan Mountains on our left with mountain high glacial blue lakes and desert on our right and as we followed the old Silk Road towards the border, we felt like we were heading out on a real expedition surrounded by some stunning and rugged natural beauty.

Unfortunately, we failed to take heed of the hazard warning lights as we overtook the thoughtful motorist in front of us who had slowed to an unnatural 40 km an hour. We, of course, hadn't realised it was a speed trap and were stopped by the roadside sheriff adjacent his shiny patrol car. Even our out of date guidebook warned us of this speed trap. One thing about the former Soviet Union is that people hate the police as much as they fear them. As a result, you will always receive a flash from oncoming drivers warning you of police up ahead. We were initially a little fearful to involve ourselves in this perverting of the course of justice shenanigans, but within a couple of days I was flashing my roof lights and belting out my air horn to all and sundry miles after passing through one. This policeman had us on video doing 66 km an hour on an empty desert road but we countered by wheeling out the smiling, cute kids and showed him our charity drive script. We were let on our way without a fine but during the exhibition, the hazard warning car drove past solemnly and, Eirene reported, the female passenger gave us a resigned shake of the head and simultaneous told you so sigh.

We liked Kazakhstan though didn't fall in love with it. It had its funny ways which was perhaps a throwback to Soviet times. When we tried to purchase two bottles of Sprite for the kids for instance, they would refuse to give them over without putting them in a glass. I tried to explain that bottles were harder to break and more difficult for my children to spill but, although they fully appreciated my argument, they wouldn't budge.

Typically, the kids failed to prove my point and immaculately drank from their glasses without incident.

There was little regard for queuing and no one acknowledged me when I held a door open, let them cross the road or let a car out. It was like being in Croydon. The driving was frightening and frequently witnessed by policemen who did nothing but hold up their white pointy batons to check the papers of the next random driver. We found the traffic rules comical too with road signs to major cities that disappeared at T-junctions and drivers given a green filter light at the same time as pedestrians are given theirs, with the assumption that the driver must look out for pedestrians before they make their turn; something that we rarely saw put into practice.

When we ate out we were frequently asked what we wanted to eat without being given a menu. When we were given a menu, the waiter refused to leave us until we'd read, memorised and decided instantaneously what we were having. Without being sexist, this was an impossible task for my family, believe you me. We were charged for everything individually, so it wasn't uncommon to have a room charge plus a person charge and then a charge for Wi-Fi and for use of the safe and parking. It was almost a case of "Does Sir require lights and a locking door?"

At check-out they delayed giving us our receipt so they could check the room, a practice that is understandable but rarely performed in the UK. On one occasion, after checking our room, they told Eirene that we had to pay for the cleaning of a towel that she had draped over the dirty surface of a washing machine resulting in a black mark appearing on it. She refused and was incandescent with rage. There was no damage to the apartment and it was only a bit of dust on the towel which, if they had cleaned the apartment properly, wouldn't have happened. It was well after lunch before her post-incident rant ran its course that day. However, it was the realisation that only towels with dirty marks on them were ever washed that disturbed us the most.

The Kazakhstan/Kyrgyzstan border town was one very long, dusty, straight road lined with moustached evil looking men chewing and staring as the sun beat down on their dark, leathery skin. At the border, a chaotic melee was in progress with much activity on both sides. People on foot bustled around in all directions, some with boxes and others with suitcases the size of a small London apartment. There were women carrying children in their arms, on their backs and trailing at their sides. Angry people remonstrated at cars that had a blatant disregard for queues and traders peddled their goods while policemen stood under umbrellas eating lollies, wearily watching the anarchy unfold. I tried to pick up the World Service on the long wave radio in an attempt to establish if civil war had erupted somewhere. Having established there was no civil war and after initially being indignant at the queue jumping, we quickly turned and followed the masses, barging into the queue ahead of us. We felt our barging had some decorum, however, with polite waves and nods of acknowledgment as the little battered cars thankfully surrendered to the path of our big monster.

After about 45 minutes of this drama we entered phase two whereby I was ushered off to sort out the immigration documents for the vehicle. A Russian speaking man told me to fill in a Russian written form but eventually capitulated and filled it in himself. After about 25 minutes of scribbling he came out and pulled me to one side. Knowing what was coming I began to reach for the $10 bill I had ready in my pocket but was surprised when he broke out in smiles and asked for my phone number for his sister who was moving to London later in the year. I misread him again as I spat out excuses as to why taking a Russian bride whilst married was against our customs He didn't seem offended at the suggestion and made clear that he merely wanted her to contact me if she needed help. I tried to explain in my broken Russian that I didn't live in London and certainly wouldn't be in London later in the year but eventually gave up and told him I was looking forward to it.

We sailed through the rest of the border without so much as a passing frisk and popped out the other side only to be stopped by the police about 200yds into Kyrgyzstan. This was our third stop of the day and I prayed Eirene didn't perform the routine that I had witnessed earlier that morning. "Kazakhstan is the best. We love Kazakhstan," banded with a big cheesy smile and a double thumbs-up. Admittedly it did work but left me concerned that they might develop their own equivalent of a Borat-style English tourist character. I was sent up the steps of a border post and showed all the same documents to a different policeman. He waved me on his way but not before I raised the issue of car insurance. He laughed heartily and for the first and last time spoke his only English to me. "Kyrgyzstan? No, no," as he waved me on my way.

Philippe the Frenchman had made us aware of some brilliant mapping software that was available for all of Asia. We had some third-party stuff which had a few dots with names next to it but no roads. A town with 10 people would be the same size with the same font as a city with a million people and it served as little more than an expensive compass. He, with the help of three different bits of software, numerous CDs, a PDA [2] and a GPS antenna, had sourced some old Russian army software that contained the most intimate details of all this once great superpower's neighbours and former territories. I was keen to have what he had but it all became too complicated with too many dependencies, so I didn't bother. Arriving in Bishkek I briefly rued it before spending 10 pence or something on a taxi to take us to where we wanted to go. With the unreal prices of accommodation in neighbouring Kazakhstan at the back of my mind, I had erred on the side of caution and made prior contact with a property agent in the hope of sourcing an apartment for a few days. The office was conveniently located next to a DHL depot that we needed to collect poles sent from Prague that

---

[2] Kids – this is a Personal Digital Assistant. Think after books but before smartphones.

would allow us to access our number one spare wheel at the rear.

Predictably, the wrong part had been sent and even more predictably I couldn't find the agent's business in our block. I called them again at very expensive international roaming rates to tell them I was outside and could not see them. She said that she was on the second floor, so I trundled in and discovered the second floor was completely cemented up. I enquired on the third and first floors with no success and frustratingly returned outside to further increase the profits of my mobile phone company. I looked at my car in anguish, exacerbated at my decision not to install the comedy megaphone that would let me shout out "Would the English-speaking lady allegedly on the second floor please get off her arse and come out of the building before I piss my week's budget away on phone calls." I phoned again and was asked to come around to the side but she finally agreed to come out when I refused to continue with this hide and seek lark. Out she belatedly popped armed with a bunch of keys, jumped in the front and directed us off on a route downtown.

We had emailed the company with the very basic requirements of secure parking in a good area which unfortunately she had read as no parking in the worst area in town. We pulled round the back of a block of flats that made The Bill's Jasmine Allen estate look salubrious. It was one of the most despondent and run-down bits of town I think I'd ever seen - and my wife's from Croydon. The locals didn't look too chuffed either and were literally sobbing in each other's arms although we later learned this was down to an ongoing wake. The agent took me to the security entrance and made a show of pressing some numbers on a disconnected numeric keyboard before pulling open the already ajar door. It was the tiniest and noisiest lift I've ever been in and I felt I knew the agent much better after we exited than before we entered. At £25 per night the apartment was great value, although when you incorporate the inevitable loss of car and trip cancellation that would undoubtedly ensue, it was over our budget. I gave her a polite no and reiterated my email request. She then took us to a slightly less bad area of town; a place with no parking to meet a delightful lady who invited us all in for tea and water. I told her it wasn't suitable on the basis that our car would have to be left about a mile away but we did, on her insistence, pop in for the token polite glance around. Behind the high fence was a garden that Mr Miyagi from the *Karate Kid* films would have been proud of (after he'd taken on the underage boy and forced him to undertake lots of menial tasks). It was pristine; wood and stones were ornately arranged around meticulously cared for plants and miniature trees, and not even a pebble or blade of grass was out of place. She showed us our room with four beds where we could all stay together, and impressed me with such an elegant, kindly and professional manner that I would have bought a timeshare from her if she'd asked. No secure parking was a show-stopper though, even when she offered to dismantle part of her garage door and roof. We declined with gratitude and started to head off. But before we did, she came up with the idea of using her neighbour's drive. He agreed, and we agreed, and it turned out to be a great decision as she provided the most appetising and varied local food and just couldn't seem to do enough.

Having dropped off our overnight sacks, we took a trip to downtown Bishkek where we watched the fountains in Ala-Too square and visited the granite Victory monument which was built to commemorate the 40th anniversary of WWII. Its red rib-like structures symbolise a yurt and within them, the sculpture of a woman stands over an eternal flame waiting for her husband to return from the war. With 20 million deaths incurred during the conflict it was unlikely he ever did.

Bishkek is a city that needed to be experienced rather than ticked off on a list and with little to entertain the kids, the marshrutkas (overcrowded minibuses in vary states of disrepair) provided a welcome distraction and talking point although we did find a popular park with swings and slides for the kids in a tree-lined boulevard. We'd heard that Bishkek was named after the paddle used to make its national drink, Kumis, but unfortunately or perhaps fortunately, we didn't have the opportunity to sample the fermented mare's milk on that occasion. However, we did experience the wonderful Osh bazaar, selling colourful dried foods and a whole aisle dedicated to dried cheese balls, which are seemingly a very popular snack.

Later in the afternoon, I nipped off in search of ramp or inspection pit in which to service the car for the first time. I had noticed an inspection pit when I'd taken the car for the equivalent of a £3 car wash and I'd offered them another £3 to use it in the afternoon, but not before spending nearly £90 on 12 litres of semi synthetic Castrol GTX.

That afternoon, I commenced my car tinkerings, sweating away in my new boiler suit, with the usual crowd of onlookers. I felt like a porn star on his first shoot, eager to perform with smiles hiding my nervousness. I held the cliched wrench with trembling hands as I opened up the lubrication. Inevitably a brave local stepped forward from the crowd and became involved. Fortunately he knew what he was doing and over the next hour or so we tinkered away changing air, oil and fuel filters coupled with a fair bit of nipple greasing. I knew he was expecting a few quid and wondered what the hit would be. I offered him 500 som (£1 = 70 som) and he wouldn't take it. Maybe he was insulted, I pondered briefly. I felt bad for my cynicism as he explained that he actually owned the tyre place across the road. Seeing this as an opportunity to give him some recompense, I explained that I wanted the tyres swapped around to ensure equal wear. I popped over and he and his boys changed them over and changed them over good. No machines, no uneven tightening, no careless jacking. On completion I asked him for a figure and he refused and wrestled off the 1000 som I attempted to put into his hand. I drove away with the realisation that if this had been England then I would have probably been hundreds of pounds down. With everything about the people and the area screaming out poverty I was truly humbled. Even throughout it all people came and gave me water, fascinated with the car and to hear what I was doing, each enthusiastically telling others as they in turn arrived.

So it was with a spring in my step and newly found love for mankind and this country in my heart that I returned to our accommodation to be greeted by an ongoing hostage situation.

Eirene barely acknowledged my entrance into the communal sitting room and wasn't speaking at all before I realised that we were running with a Code Red situation. An elderly guest Hettie, a Dutch lady and Swiss resident who had lived in New York, was regaling her life story to new ears in intimate detail.

"I'm a sponsor for the Babushka Society," she droned monotonously. "We provide support for the elderly in Kyrgyzstan where they have no other family support." I wasn't overwhelmingly surprised to learn that there was absolutely no form of government support in terms of housing, pensions or anything for the elderly. The Babushka Society, (Babushka being Russian for old lady as opposed to padushka which is a pillow. I'll never again muddle them up) provides some relief by obtaining overseas funding, predominantly from Switzerland, Denmark and the Netherlands. At €150 a year you can sponsor a specific lady, which although not providing the benefit a big shared pot might, does give the sponsor recognition of exactly where their money is going. Furthermore, I would assume that this makes the sponsor less prone to pulling out when there is an actual person that they've communicated with who would be deprived. Hettie had been asked if she wanted to go out, at her own expense, to visit her lady and see how she was getting on. There had been some communication between them over the years, often belatedly, when Hettie had sent money for hearing aids and waited a year for a reply. Quite recently she had doubled her money to her babushka and was keen to meet her to see the conditions she was in. I imagine when this offer of pay-for-yourself-visits is made to donors, the society never in their wildest dreams expect them to respond positively and book their flights!

Before meeting her own lady, Hettie met a number of others, many in desperate circumstances and flat-bound in high rise buildings with no lifts. All of them expressed enormous gratitude to her for her assistance despite the fact Hettie wasn't directly sponsoring them. It was therefore with considerable astonishment when Hettie went to visit her babushka's residence as it wasn't a flat; it had colour telly, spare rooms and a delightful garden. She wasn't wearing the hearing aid when Hettie arrived but popped it out of its box at the top of the cupboard where she carefully stored it so it didn't get broken. She showed Hettie her new coat and boots that she had bought with her Christmas money and made mention of a leaking roof. The following day the lady gave Hettie a quote for $2,000 for a new roof. Unfortunately for this babushka, her golden hen stopped laying for her the following day when she changed her sponsorship over to someone needier.

Leaving Eirene in the conversational trap she was in, I decided I liked Hettie after all, loved the guesthouse and I loved talking to people. Not as an opportunity to reel out our "look at us" story but to hear theirs. Whether it was the kids or us or the nature of our accommodation to date, I had missed this.

The day was capped by the arrival of a Dutch bloke with blonde hair in a ponytail travelling alone. He lived in Bangkok and I inadvertently nearly asked "How long have you been a drugs mule?" instead of "What line of work are you in?" He was a very affable guy, eager to talk but in a very slow and careful manner, and I felt I recognised him from somewhere.

The following morning, after a sumptuous breakfast, we took a day trip to the Ala Archa National Park, south west of Bishkek. The park, although physically similar to the one in Kazakhstan with its rushing rivers and high snow-capped Tian Shan mountains, contrasted starkly with its Kazakhstan counterpart in that it was devoid of masses of people and litter. The park gets its name from the colourful Himalayan juniper tree, but we didn't see any, nor did we see any of the famed snow leopards or, for that matter, the more common wild goats. We did, however, take an invigorating gorge walk which came complete with fast flowing rapids fed from one of the many glaciers further up the mountains. Our picnic on a ford by the lake was overlooked by imposing mountains whose peaks disappeared into the cloud. I couldn't imagine a restaurant anywhere else in the world that would be so empty with such an amazing view. We watched the kids paddle and munch simultaneously before they directed their attention on a wishing tree, a gnarly, old spruce whose sweeping branches had good luck rags tied to them.

Later that day, Eirene finished off the Ranulph Fiennes autobiography. We had been dual reading it which doesn't work too well especially when she has the habit of reading the end at the beginning and then telling me what happens. She does this with films as well with the element of surprise seeming almost a cumbersome chore for her. Having finished this book first, I thought I would wreak revenge and told her that he had sold most of the cattle at his Exmoor farm. Maybe I was lowering myself to her level, but she needed to be told. Her response was a nonchalant one but inside I knew she'd be seething.

Two American girls arrived in the evening. One was a banker in a nearby "stan" country that I'd never heard of and the other was a teacher at a South Bronx high school. They had gathered here to meet as Almaty city, famed for its international cafes and restaurants, offered both pizza and red wine. Eirene's five years teaching in the ghettos of Datchet near Royal Windsor in Berkshire failed to cut any ice with the teacher so, arguably as an act of revenge for the disrespect, she sent in our kids in to talk to them incessantly.

We tried to secure accommodation on Lake Issyk-Kul, the jewel in Kyrgyzstan's crown, after the owner's sister, who was in the travel business, had failed to deliver. She said she was having great difficulty trying to contact an agent on a Friday evening / Saturday morning but would call us on the way. I followed the owner round the corner to Dostock Expeditions to pay for the traditional yurt that I'd persuaded Eirene to stay in before we entered China. It came to nearly £70 for one night, which I thought was incredibly expensive, so I asked the owner if she had ever stayed in a yurt; she replied that many of her relatives lived in the mountains and she had spent most summers, often reluctantly, staying in a yurt and helping with the animals. "And now tourists are paying nearly £70 a night for the privilege!" I submitted. She let the briefest of smiles escape before adopting her professional persona again.

spent a good three quarters of an hour with our new Dutch friend going through my maps of Thailand, Cambodia and Laos. Not only did he live in Bangkok, but he had lived in Cambodia and spent many months travelling round all three countries by motorbike. I marked my map enthusiastically with his smuggling routes, using a series of clever symbols that I had no doubt would be meaningless in six weeks. We left to a fanfare of waves and managed to navigate our way out of town and onto the road towards the lake in a one-r, passing through a series of canyons, surrounded by muddy brown mountains and patches of snow that they called the Shoestring Gorge. The roads were good but the £8 eco-tax charge just to enter the lake area wasn't so pleasing.

We started looking for accommodation and over the course of the next four or five hours, tried resort after resort, the format with the hotels never changing and the price forever increasing from the initial one stated, despite stipulating from the outset that I needed accommodation for my family of five which comprised of two adults and three children. It was intensely infuriating so Eirene decided to have a shot. She walked in and skipped out shortly after, telling me that it was £60 for us all including breakfast. Her innocence melted my heart and I told her to go in with the exact money and she came back out a short while later, confessing it was now £150. In almost every hotel in Kazakhstan or Kyrgyzstan if a hotel is, say, £50 for two people, there will be a show of not charging for the baby whilst they charge you £100 to share the whole room. During the whole rigmarole we received a text from the owner's sister saying she couldn't contact an agent to make the booking but gave us the name of another place. It was a three-star resort and it ticked all the boxes. They wanted £100 per night for one room on the top floor with no lift but it included all meals. It was very expensive for a three-star hotel in Kyrgyzstan but it had been a long journey, we hadn't had much success elsewhere and it was peak holiday period. I made a mental note to use as much electricity as I could. Little victories.

After the obligatory 30 minutes checking in at the desk, a smooth headed guy wearing a black vest top to show off his muscles appeared alongside with a large man wearing a sailor's hat. The "Right Said Fred" lookalike was hammered. In Pidgin English he introduced himself as Andre and insisted on trying to help us with the check-in process, of which we were now nearing the climax (the handing over of the key). Fearing I might have to start again, I told him about our drive to Australia and he tried to drag me off to meet his mother who lived in Australia.

"Where?" I asked. "Brisbane, Melbourne, Perth, Sydney?"

"Yes, there," he replied.

Our accommodation was delightfully close to the beach of Lake Issyk-Kul, the second largest mountain lake in the world with its own micro-climate, which despite being 1600m above sea level, never freezes. It was so vast that it almost felt like we were looking out to sea, but the water was so still that the fir trees and 4,500m snow-capped mountains opposite reflected in it like an unbroken mirror. The combination of the heat and snow was peculiarly intoxicating and relaxing and just what we needed after our intensely long accommodation search.

Within minutes a lady with a heavily bandaged arm hobbled over.

"Oh my God, you are from Australia!" she declared animatedly. The woman, a cross between Zsa Zsa Gabor and Borat, chain smoked numerous menthols whilst talking enthusiastically about our crazy trip and her life. It was no bombshell to discover that she was Andre's mum from Kazakhstan.

She insisted on us meeting up with her son again and led us to an open-air bar by a large pond. I was treated like the arriving messiah and swiftly despatched to a separate table for a vodka session with Andre and his friends. They were all celebrating the last night of their three day stay at Lake Issyk-Kul before returning to Almaty and they planned to make the most of it. There was considerable vagueness both from Andre and his mother as to the line of work Andre was in and Eirene and I both chose separately and wisely not to dwell on it. Andre was there with his chubby, chocolate munching daughter and his tattooed 20-year-old girlfriend, 17 years his junior. His wife was at home. Within five minutes we were vodka toasting brothers and within ten we were toasting meeting up in London and me going to Almaty. Very obliging but very intense. I once knew a couple of guys who had worked next to each other for 17 years and described each other as "work colleagues." In Kyrgyzstan you were "my friend" in minutes.

We escaped for dinner and headed back to our room but at about 10pm, as I was riding on the back of a pygmy-ridden motorbike in Tim Butcher's *Blood River,* there was a battering on the door. Eirene darted for the bathroom half naked and I opened the door to a glazed eyed Andre inviting me for drinks. He was as drunk as he was insistent, so I consented and we nipped downstairs where he purchased a £1.50 bottle of vodka and we headed off to the disco for more vodka and a bit of *Boney M* and their Ra Ra Rasputin (Russia's greatest love machine). The children in their party fell asleep on their chairs as Andre bribed the DJ to play a traditional Russian song for his karaoke number. He took to the mike and dedicated it generously to his brother who I didn't initially realise was me. Half way through his rendition, one of his friends started barking like a dog at Andre. Others joined in as did I, thinking it was a traditional mark of respect. Andre's face and reciprocal barking

114

of Russian back at them changed the mood and made it clear that it wasn't taken as respectful. One by one the kids were carried off leaving me, Andre, his girlfriend and another girl who had grabbed me for a slow dance. There was talk of swimming at the beach and my plea about my trunks, goggles and towel being in my room fell on deaf ears. Finally, though, I was allowed to make my excuses and crawl back to my room. Their friendliness was of such a scale that my inbred cynicism was permanently wary of a potential scam, but it never came.

Our food at Lake Issyk-Kul was very good although breakfast tended to be a rice/porridge mix with bread, cheese and meat. Lunch and dinner were very similar and came in the form of a meaty/potato soup with bread and salad followed by a main meal of meat and rice or pasta. It felt exceedingly healthy and the kids for the most part loved it. It even led to Eirene saying things like, "When I get back home I will change the way I cook. I can save so much money doing what they do with soup and stew," and then, "I cannot bear another bowl of bloody soup, let's go for a pizza."

One afternoon Emily and I were walking back hand in hand from a great afternoon running around on the beach and splashing in the cool, blue lake with the mountain panorama. I asked her if she was enjoying her holiday and she replied, "Yes I am. I like travelling round the world and going to different places, but I really like being with the family all the time. Anytime I want you, you are there." I was taken aback at her insight and felt the hairs going up on the back of my neck.

"When I'm at school," she continued, "I get bored and wish I wasn't there. I guess it's the same with you at work but a lot worse." I was stunned by what I had just heard from a five-year-old and turned away so she didn't see me well up.

Kyrgyzstan took some time to warm to. On the surface it was dirty, rude, insular, money grabbing and fulfilled the stereotype of a former Russian satellite state. Litter was abundant outside the national park and the roads, health service, schools and general infrastructure, where it existed, often felt like it was third world. Alcohol was so readily available they even served Hannah and Emily a beer that I had asked them to buy on my behalf. The most basic common courtesies were not only ignored but actively discouraged. Waiting for people, no matter how many, to pass through a door before you gets nothing. On the roads no quarter was given nor expected. Kids as young as three stood in the middle of a busy road, crossed in front of us and elicited hoots of derision from other drivers. Spitting was compulsory even, as I discovered, in a lift by the hotel receptionist taking you to view a room you may potentially be renting. Yet it seemed safe and there was no threatening undercurrent of violence. There was something that stopped it and we were not sure what it was, perhaps the old Russian pre-democracy values. From our kids' perspectives, any place that brought out the puddings before the main course had their vote.

It was a country that ranked as one of the friendliest we came across. Total strangers talked to us, helped us and welcomed us to their land. I couldn't help thinking what the Swiss would make of it and I'm ashamed that I managed to live next door to a bloke in the UK for six years and still didn't know his name (if you miss it during the intro it's too late to ask after!). Here we couldn't sit next to someone for six minutes without exchanging life stories. The closed shop that is the mother and baby circuit in Britain could not exist here. I could not imagine me or my wife approaching a foreigner back home in the park, shops, beach or restaurant and start engaging them with enquiries about what they thought of the country and what we could do to help them. It was probably the most unthreatening place I had ever been to. At our resort we felt like minor local celebrities as everyone seemed to know us and were keen to interact with us. I pondered that this must be how Timmy Mallett briefly felt. Russians tended to look down at Kazakhstan and Kazakhstan tended to look down at its lesser minerally endowed neighbour Kyrgyzstan. This made Kyrgyzstan that amiable lad in the road without the ego and easy-to-get-on-with attitude.

Aesthetically it was also one of the most gorgeous countries in the world.

31st July was our wedding anniversary and we had an early wake up with two fully dressed kids singing "Happy Anniversary" to two very different tunes before beginning a massage on the both of us. Emily declared her intention to work in a massage parlour when she was older and we provided some gentle discouragement.

That day we visited Cholpon-Ata, a small resort town on the northern shore of Lake Issyk-Kul. We'd heard about the open air museum and its series of stone circles, tombs and sacrificial burial grounds dating back 3,500 years and its petroglyphs of carved animals and hunters. On arrival though we came across a field with rather haphazard looking boulders and discovered this was their museum. Some of the rocks were carved with art depicting life several millennia ago, showing hunting of animals now on the endangered list. They were dated between 2000 BC and 400 AD and some, despite their constant exposure to external weathering and touching, still showed amazingly good detail. But had there not been a few signs indicating that these 42 acres of boulder-strewn land were a museum, we'd never have known.

We always provided the kids with background and history to where we were, and, on this occasion, I told them the story of the ancient Suka priests who lived in a now submerged village but conducted sacrifices to their gods. Hannah and Emily then mocked those critics that suggested this trip was wasted on them by asking a series of questions and subsequent analysis of where the priests went for poos and wees.

Having spent a week at Lake Issyk-Kul, we headed to Naryn with us all eager to be back on the road. A curious dinner at the resort restaurant had prevented us, for gastric reasons, from leaving the previous day, so we asked reception if we could stay another night. They seemed flattered and I didn't expand on the reasoning behind the decision. I spent most of the day re-jigging all the boxes and equipment in the car in order to make room for the seat in the boot for our Chinese guide. It was a feat of logistical excellence and I succeeded but it was tight with leg room a dwarf would struggle with. It was definitely better suited to one of the kids than a guide who would be giving us directions and constantly jumping in and out of the car. I had put up four 1,000 pound [3] strappings around the adjacent luggage so nothing could move around. It was a cosy box-like set up and the kids were keen to sit there but Eirene was adamant they wouldn't be.

We finally left our expensive holiday resort and observed some gutted fish hanging on a wooden frame to dry at the side of the lake. We turned left into Bishkyl and began an enchanting drive through canyons, dried lakes and riverbeds up into the mountains which stood nearly 4,000m above us. We could see the road ahead of us for miles, with only a few shimmering vehicles coming towards us and glacial blue lakes at the side with an occasional and sporadic white hut in the grassy dunes. We saw some wild goats too as they slowly walked from the centre of the road to the verges on either side of us. We had one night at the Celestial Guest House ("Naryn's Most Luxurious Accommodation") as a treat to Eirene for agreeing to spend the following night in a yurt. There was no running water, but it was comfortable and, at once, familiar.

Some gregarious guides helped us with directions to Tash Rabat, home of our yurt, and they reliably informed us that passing through the Torugart Pass into China should take no more than 20 minutes. Oliver, the German arm of the driving through China company, had also bolstered our confidence a few days earlier, telling us that they had just put some over-landers through the previous week with no problems. For some reason Eirene and I were worried despite their reassurances, perhaps the earlier recanting of rumours by Philippe at the space base sticking with us longer than they should've.

---

[3] This is pounds as in weight. With the haemorrhaging of money that we were indulging in, I just wanted to clarify.

Additionally, though, the pass is a trading one between Kyrgyzstan and China and officially no Westerners are permitted to cross it in their own vehicles. Unofficially it does and clearly has happened but this, together with words of warning from fellow travellers and the fact that obtaining visas involved two embassy visits, some fake plane tickets and a long interview, made me jittery. Until recently all foreign vehicles were banned in China and only a handful of vehicles have subsequently made the trip but my public face provided a more confident front that my thoughts did.

A filling breakfast preceded the picturesque views across southern Kyrgyzstan as we made our way to Yuri's yurt at Tash Rabat. It was a delightful approach meandering along the valley, adjacent to the translucent fast flowing stream, seeing smoke from campfires outside yurts and we arrived at ours at about 1pm. Yuri, Victor, Zowa (Victor's partner) and their teenage son enthusiastically greeted us as we disembarked our Land Cruiser. Zowa in particular looked happier and happier as each of our girls emerged one by one from the car.

All three of ours were very much taken by their kitten and thankfully not the tetchy dog with tiny legs who had apparently never been the same since he was hit by a stick last season.

Had I been looking at a display of postcards, this is the scene I would have chosen. Seven yurts were grouped together in a sweeping green meadow protected by steep low peaks and a picturesque stream. We heard the clanking of containers as a young boy on his donkey passed by, the water splashing inside them. In the distance, a young man was singing. And as we turned round, a herd of wild horses galloped off into the distance having refreshed themselves in the stream.

A chimney rose from the roof of each yurt, but only one was emitting white smoke from a well-established fire, I presumed. As we entered ours, I was amazed at the complexity of the wooden frame work and effectiveness of the insulation. Lattice work formed the bottom third of the yurt, above it wooden ribs created the dome shape of the tent and heavy woollen

119

insulation was placed on top before a breathable waterproof canvas covered the whole yurt. Inside were our beds with traditional animal skin and woollen blankets. A rusty old barrel served as a fire with a chimney pipe rising up and out the roof.

We took a trip to nearby Tash Rabat itself, arguably Kyrgyzstan's most interesting monument. Situated at the junction of several valleys, 3530m above sea level, the crushed stone and clay mortar building with 31 dome shaped rooms was a shelter for merchants and travellers on the wilder part of the Silk Road. Only half of it is visible from the road, the rest is tucked into the hillside and hidden from view.

There were few other people around and refreshingly no barriers, gates or restrictions of any sort that prevented us going in to its tunnelled entrance. We explored its passages and underground tunnels, the presence of graffiti to some extent betraying the wisdom of the decision to grant this freedom. It contrasted considerably with how a building of similar standing would be handled in the UK. But apart from the penis pictures, it looked little different to how it would have done 500 years ago. Surrounded by mountains and rivers and virtually nothing else, it would have been a welcome refuge for travellers on the ancient trade route.

We returned to the yurt and spent the afternoon criss-crossing the plank bridge on the river, walking up mountain paths and playing with the kitten. The kids were in their element and tucked heartily into their dinner. Yuri offered us his Russian sauna, a tent full of bowls of boiling hot water together with a wooden human-sized flat rack and a whip made from leaves. His instructions were specific, and no mercy was to be given. I complied but the kids weren't too keen and Eirene was less enthusiastic about receiving a beating. On our return, Yuri advised us that the best result followed if mum and dad had a "lie down." Eirene eyed me suspiciously and despite his insistence that they would look after the kids Eirene seemed more worried about any further kids and we politely declined. I assured her no money had passed hands and that he was just being hospitable.

As the night drew in, Yuri lit the stove in our yurt and it felt like a sauna itself. The sky was cloudless and there was no light pollution, the sky filled with more stars than I'd ever seen. The children, exhausted from their active day coupled with the heat from the stove, went out like lights. Despite Eirene's protestations I quietly woke Hannah, knowing the other two would be dead to the world, and carried her warm pyjama adorned body outside and lay her down on a fleece in the crisp air. She shivered and looked at me with confused eyes and started to speak. "What are we..." but I interrupted her with my finger on her lips and pointed up to the sky. Her head tilted, her eyes widened, her mouth dropped open and she literally flinched at the sight of the Milky Way and beyond. It absolutely blew her away and she was silent until she saw the first shooting star of her life. "Did you see that?" she exclaimed excitedly without averting her gaze. We lay back, holding hands, both in awe of the naturally beauty of the universe. We stayed there for 20 amazing, profound and touching minutes before we finally succumbed to the cold and returned to our cosy temporary home and fell asleep again while listening to the wool of the yurts gently flapping in the wind.

We had earlier contacted Wang Lun, our guide who was meeting us at the Chinese border, and he had said he would be there at 12 noon which suited us fine as Eirene was threatening us with a 7am wakeup. As I put down the phone, I recalled that all of China works on the same time, Beijing time, despite the fact that it crosses three time zones. This was three hours ahead of us which must be the biggest jump for any border crossing in the world. Several texts and an unintelligible phone call later, it was vaguely established that it was 12 noon Chinese time and 9am Kyrgyzstan time so Eirene's 7am wish was granted.

CHAPTER 6.

CHINA

Tuesday 5 August 2008

Day 97 - Torugart Pass, China - 9,801 miles

The following morning, we were up with the rock petronias (Kyrgyzstan sparrows) keen to give ourselves enough time at the Chinese border. Our enthusiasm for an early departure did nothing to prevent Yuri from bringing out the traditional costumes for the standard tourist dance to the sun gods. Embarrassingly we all loved it, if for no other reason than to see the non-speaking chain smoking Victor reluctantly undertake the Haka whilst dressed like a goat. I think I managed to work out the Russian for "Why do I have to do the stupid bloody tourist dance all the time?"

As we left, we had quite a rousing drive through yurt scattered planes, edged by the most incredible mountains and a sense of true over-landing. The side of the road coming from China was heavily worn in comparison to our carriageway, bearing testament to the heavily one-sided nature of exports and imports between the two countries. Full lorries in, empty lorries out was the story of the road.

However, what had started out as an emotional and friendly farewell to Yuri and his yurts turned into diplomatic negotiations on an international scale as we headed towards the Chinese border. Had it not been for the persistence, perseverance and dial-a-translation service of Wang Lun, then my story might have had to end here. Little did we suspect what was in store.

After about an hour we came upon a building complete with a watch-tower, barrier and machine gun toting, khaki clad teenage boy. He told us this was the Kyrgyzstan border and took our passports inside. He returned with an officer who came for an ogle at the car and then nodded us on our way. China border next. Or so we thought. We drove for about 20 miles with electric fencing running adjacent to us the whole way. The border loomed ahead. We drove past a stationary line of trucks and were waved through the barrier. We were directed to an area outside a number of inspection pits where numerous armed border guards stared at us. Their uniforms looked like the Kyrgyzstanis, as did they, and they curiously asked in Russian if we could speak Russian so I gave them the very best "Zdra Stvuy te" I could muster. They didn't ask me anything in Russian again. A sniffer dog checked out the car and Eirene was escorted with the kids to passport control. I had to fill in a number of car and customs forms and declare my money, books and other stuff which they expressed no interest in seeing. We were sent on our way and as Eirene jumped into the car I declared, "That was easy."

"Yes," she said, "but that was the Kyrgyzstan border."

"So China next," I said and we drove another 30 miles through increasingly more spectacular and wild scenery, the sharp, rugged peaks of the Tian Shan mountain range still dominating the skyline as we continued along this high mountain pass of the old Silk route. I commented to Eirene that I had run out of superlatives and wouldn't know how to describe it in my diary. Her suggestion was that I write that I have run out of superlatives. I agreed but it would have left me in a very dangerous place of nowhere to go if something was then better than this. I needn't have worried.

A climb through the mountains finally led us to what we naively assumed again must be the border, with a queue of stationary and dilapidated lorries snaking their way towards some buildings. We drove to the front of the queue in the traditional fashion, cars always taking precedence over lorries at these places, and on arrival we were greeted by immaculately clad, white-gloved border guards and a number of photographers. I was shocked that the Metro article had reached these climes, but my jovial good humour was soon quashed when we were ushered to the side and watched as there was much rushing around and panicking before a car arrived and a General popped out with his entourage. The left side of his jacket was like a patchwork quilt of colours. The world's most decorated soldier shook a couple of hands, saluted a few times and departed. This time it was clear that there were Chinese here and Kyrgyzstan soldiers back there. It was hard to tell as the typically contrasting physical appearances you would normally associate with a Russian and a Chinese person had been merging for the last 500 miles or so. Our passports were checked and we were waved through into China at last, or so we naively thought (again). We drove down a well-made gravel and sand dirt track road - we were connoisseurs of road surfaces now - with distant watchtowers overlooking our progress. We squeezed past another line of lorries and were greeted with a look of confusion by a group of soldiers.

We established that we were in no man's land, a neutral zone between two countries at the highest and most isolated pass in the world. There were rundown buildings on either side, rubbish flying around in the wind and all that's missing is a bit of tumbleweed and a saloon in this high-altitude desert town. A profusion of differently uniformed men stared at us from all sides and we were waved down by one who couldn't have been any more than ten years old. We tried to tell him that we were meeting a guide here and produced the token Chinese documentation we had together with our passports. He disappeared with them. We were now parked in the middle of a street in a ghost town and all our documents had been taken by a uniformed passer-by for whom I had no distinguishing description of. There were no booths, barriers or painted parking spots that we had learnt to associate with a border crossing. Things didn't feel right. Thankfully, he returned a short while later, but the relief was short lived when he said quite clearly in excellent English, "Border closed," and told us to turn around. Communication was impossible and it became an exercise in stock-phrase repetition. We turned and drove a short distance back in the direction we had come and then stopped and tried to gather our thoughts. We were understandably attracting attention with our Western faces, children, unusual car and the fact that this was a locals-with-lorries-only border crossing, not one that foreign travellers used very often, and I was beginning to see why.

A very small (even by Chinese standards) two pipped officer with an uncanny resemblance to Ronnie Corbett approached us and started to speak in very broken, virtually incomprehensible, Pidgin English. In fairness, a bit like something out of a *Two Ronnies* sketch. We slowly explained our position to him and he told us that the border was completely closed to foreign traffic for ten days and we could not enter. He informed us of another border crossing at Irkeshtamn in Kyrgyzstan that we would have no problems getting through. It was the only other border crossing between Kyrgyzstan and China on the map, looked like it was a 1,000 mile drive all the way back to Bishkek and back down even though it was only about 150 miles as the crow flies. He sensed our desperation and agreed to speak to our guide, Wang Lun, and marched off to get a phone before returning. They had a long conversation before he passed the phone to me. Wang Lun told me that the guide was on the way to the crossing and to just wait and be patient. We then spent an hour talking (in the loosest sense of the word) to Lieutenant Corbett who presumably had been posted there as some sort of punishment. Through some speech and the medium of mime, he told us about his three-year-old daughter and we told him about ours before he decided to trot off.

It had been two hours since the first of our four borders and we started to think about food. One of the dilapidated buildings offered limited supplies but the shopkeeper couldn't have been more helpful. She helped us to buy noodles and then cooked them up for us before taking them outside for the kids. She subsequently returned with coffees for us all at no cost. Eirene was edgy as our car was now symbolically pointing in the wrong direction. German Oliver's and Wang Lun's confidence had rubbed off on me and I was content that all would end well. Eventually a more junior officer came along who disappointingly was neither rotund nor wearing square glasses. He had about 15 armed soldiers with him, one of whom spoke passable English. One pip, a 2nd Lieutenant in British Army terms, shook my hand and his translator, a teenage private, said, "Welcome to China, the host country for the 2008 Olympics. We hope you enjoy your time here." I embraced his hand as the interpreter continued, "The border is closed to foreign traffic, go," and pointed in the direction of Kyrgyzstan. It was a bit of a mixed message to say the least and I begged for him to speak to Wang Lun which he eventually acceded to do. He spoke quickly for two minutes, smiled, hung up and then said, "Excuse me," and pointed in the direction we didn't want him to. The soldiers seemed panicky and wanted us to move quickly and I could see it all starting to go to shit. I looked around for our comedic Lieutenant in the hope he could throw his rank around and buy us some time. A passing guide with very good English graciously involved himself and told us that the border was completely closed to foreign traffic. Had we travelled last night we would have made it through with no problems but today, and for ten days at least, we will definitely not be allowed in. He indicated that the order had come from God's boss and it will not be revoked. Most crushingly, he told us he had spoken to our guide some way down the road and she told him that the border was closed, and we would not be allowed in.

Everyone around was starting to become jumpy but not as jumpy as me and I felt physically nauseous and could sense the imminent re-emergence of the noodles. I continued to stall, seemingly prompting a soldier to climb onto the roof of a nearby building and cock his rifle whilst staring at us. A nearby barracks emptied out on the street and I was starting to think all this might be a little over the top just to move a family. The translator, who was becoming exceedingly nervous as his officer became increasingly impatient with his attempts at moving us, jumped into the driver's seat of our car and tried to start it. I took control and told him I would do it. Frustrated, I quickly drove 20 yards down to the entrance at the front of the lorry queue, coffee and noodles flying everywhere. There were soldiers forming a guard of honour on either side of the road and we realised that the rainbow-uniformed general must be out and about again, or they were honouring our departure. I played my final stalling card and went and took Hannah to the toilet behind some buildings. However, on our return more soldiers were at the car with Lt. Corbett now on plot and crushingly also insisting we go. I complained that we did not have a double entry visa for Kyrgyzstan and we wouldn't be able to return there but they told us it would be OK. We reluctantly left and drove halfway up the winding road and stopped next to the lorries, out of sight of where we had just come from but not of the distant guard towers and the flashing glint of binoculars from within their dark recesses. I felt that we were in our strongest position and that if we headed back into Kyrgyzstan it would be the end of the story. Our paperwork specifically covered us for this border, this was where our guide would be and every single date from then until our departure had specific locations and hotels where we would be, all starting from the other side of this border. The Chinese visa had taken ages, the single-entry Kyrgyzstan visa had a stamp on it and there would be little choice but the thousands of miles back West. The kids seemed oblivious in the back, tummies full and iPods on charge. Eirene was quiet, but we sensed each other's despair. I phoned Wang Lun on the satellite phone as none of the other phones worked. It kept cutting in and out, but I could make him out telling us to wait by the Torugart border and he would sort it out.

"Do not go back to Kyrgyzstan whatever you do. You must get to Kashgar tonight," he warned before the passing satellite disappeared over the horizon and dropped the call. Kashgar was the nearest city to this crossing and was meant to be that night's destination. Wang Lun had sounded confident, but he didn't, to my knowledge, have a QBZ-95 assault rifle pointing at him as we had.

We decided that we had been terribly British about the whole thing and not been insistent enough. With nothing better to do, lorry drivers began to gather around for a spot of pointing and staring. A tall one emerged and asked in perfect English if he could help us. He was from Pakistan and suggested if all else failed we should call our embassy. I wasn't sure whether "These people won't let us into their country" fell within either the remit or jurisdiction of the British embassy in China but at that stage we were willing to try anything and I was grateful for his help. If nothing else, hearing English advice was positive in itself. We waited half an hour before driving back to the border and hiding behind a lorry at the side. There was no sign of a guide, so we spoke to Wang Lun again who said to wait but it might be a couple of hours. I phoned the number for the female guide that we had been given by Oliver in Germany, but she was not our guide and could not help. I was confused and nervous and tried not to show it to Eirene. She had continuously talked about the "What if we don't get into China?" scenario and I had refused to entertain the suggestion, being of the 'cross each bridge as we come to it' school of thought. Maybe not wise but I always think consideration of alternatives diverts your attention and starts to make the alternative more attractive. Reluctantly though I realised and accepted that we would have to start overtly considering a Plan B. Eirene suggested going back to Kyrgyzstan and freighting the car by lorry whilst we found another means of travel but it would be costly, time consuming and difficult to organise even if it was theoretically feasible. Currently we were within a very short distance of the furthest place in the world from the sea and even further from a port that we could use, so that precluded a sailing option. We looked at the maps and overland was not an option. Into northern Pakistan, probably one of the most dangerous regions in the world at that time, from nearby Tajikistan, via Afghanistan, didn't seem realistic and Eirene was very much against it. I couldn't accuse her of being over-cautious with that one. Burma wasn't an option either as they wouldn't let foreign vehicles in officially or unofficially and its doors were even more tightly closed following the deaths of approximately 130,000 people in Cyclone Nargis. China was blocking the way. A 4,000 mile drive through Siberia on the Road of Bones to Vladivostok was a possibility but not one we envisaged when we said we wanted to see the world.

We had now been at this border point for four hours (six hours from the apparent first one) and were playing the waiting game, "hidden" within the queue of lorries whilst realistically expecting to get exposed by the soldiers, tipped off by the Watchtower radios, imminently. The guide, who had been helpful as a translator when we initially arrived in our temporary sanctuary, returned from his Kyrgyzstan drop in an empty bus. I caught eye contact with him and he spoke to me in hushed tones, looking around suspiciously as he did so. It was almost laughable, like an *Indiana Jones* film where the spy surreptitiously whispers the escape options to Indiana, except it wasn't a film and it was getting scarier.

"There has been a big problem," he virtually mouthed, "I could not speak before in front of the soldiers. Yesterday in Kashgar 16 policemen were killed in a terrorist attack with loads injured. Security has gone through the roof and they've closed the borders. Do not tell anyone you know." He nervously looked around him, shoulders hunched and head down.

I felt sick. All this desperate hanging around, pleading and calling was just that – acts of desperation. It was game over. Just as the United States shut its borders to all but Air Force One, the USAF and the Bin Laden family in the immediate aftermath of 9/11, so too have the Chinese, in this province at least. Given the circumstances, the approach of the Chinese authorities was wholly understandable and made their patient manner and friendliness towards us all the more surprising. I returned to the car and discreetly told a shell-shocked and growingly weary Eirene.

We both realised that it was not red tape, wrongly filled in documentation, Wing Lun incompetence or even fraud that we were fighting against; it was a security blitz in which we were understandably less than insignificant at that moment in time. Narrow-mindedly, we contemplated only our own fates before the passing hours moved my mind on to the fate of the dead and injured and their families. The scale and indiscriminate nature of it was massive. If one policeman is murdered in England it is front page news and rightly so. Sixteen is beyond comprehension. We still hadn't moved though, letting hope overpower reasons as we steadfastly refused to accept our fate. Eventually our sombre thoughts were interrupted by the inevitable knock on the driver's window. We turned and saw the 2nd Lieutenant who had efficiently despatched us, standing there on his own.

"Let's take the fucker," I lamely joke with Eirene, who briefly looks horrified. He offers his only English we've witnessed to date - "Excuse me" and points towards Kyrgyzstan. I ask if he will speak to Wang Lun. He shakes his head and repeats his phrase with the corresponding arm movement that jerks towards the nearby border post. I refused with absolutely nothing to back it up. He continued to repeat his stock phrase, always smiling. I try Wang Lun and reluctantly, in the absence of two pip and his working cellphone, use the satellite phone which I had been keen on the Chinese not seeing purely on the basis that they're illegal to own. Given the circumstances I feel I have no choice. Critically and typically it fails with the signal strength repeatedly jumping from five bars to zero and back again. Serves me right for buying a refurbished one. One pip's demeanour changed and for the first time his right hand rests on the hilt of his pistol. It's deliberate and he notices that I notice. I'm expecting him to spit out some chewing tobacco as I begin pleading for five minutes. In the spirit of the

Olympics, he grants me it and walks off. I dial Wang Lun in a panic and, with no army officer present, I naturally connect straight away. Wang Lun repeats his maxim on the crackly line and tells us to stay there and not go back to Kyrgyzstan. Not great for a £10 call. He said he will call us back and the order to let us enter would be coming through soon.

With Wang Lun still on the line, I head off looking for one pip with the sat-phone unavoidably in my grasp, forbidden aerial proudly extended aloft. I can't find him and reluctantly hang up, nausea again returning at the prospect of the bill. Naturally, just as I do this, our smiley 2nd Lieutenant returns but this time with his armed entourage and Mr Corbett. Clearly acting together, this did not bode well. Ronnie explains that he had done all he could to help us, but he was in the army and one pip was in charge of the border post. I now elect to absorb the stark contrast in their two uniforms that I had previously failed to notice. 2nd Lieutenant Smiler starts on his "Excuse me" pointing routine and I reduce myself to pleading, "Please speak with Wang Lun. I promise if you do we will go quietly" complete with improvised sign language. I hold the sat-phone high to the heavens, praying for a signal. I redial Wang Lun and am overly elated when it connects. I carefully hand over the electronic brick to one pip and he speaks rapidly. I'm happy for them to run up the £1.80 a minute + VAT tariff as talk is hope but it's a short and seemingly one sided conversation, abruptly, it appears, curtailed by one pip. He looks me dead in the eye, Mr Nice Guy well and truly gone, and says, "You have 20 minutes," his vocabulary way more expansive than I first thought, and dismissively hands over the Mobell sat-phone.

In every pricey conversation I have had with Wing Lun he assured me that he will call me back. He never did. 19 minutes pass and I call Wang Lun back and pay top money to listen to his stock message that we needed to wait and not go back to Kyrgyzstan. It was undoubtedly good advice, but he wasn't surrounded by a large number of gun-toting border guards who had had their patience pushed to the limit by a foreign tourist less than 24 hours after 16 of their colleagues were murdered. Nor did he have his wife and three children with him in such circumstances. This time, one pip had remained during the awkward and tense countdown. As it hits 20 minutes he points to his watch giving, what he no doubt hoped, would be his final "Excuse me" and points back up the mountain road. I nod solemnly and slowly ascend into the car and systematically go through the car starting drill in the vain hope that either the satellite phone would ring or a Toyota wouldn't start. Neither outcome occurs. With the familiar and normally comforting hum of the 4.2 litre engine idling, I look out the window at the guards and with a big smiling look of expectation, questioningly point left, back in the direction of China. They all laugh except for one pip, his patience now completely evaporated. I check all three mirrors, signal and move off, virtually in slow motion, up the hill towards Border Three utterly gutted. It's unspoken but the children suddenly appreciate the magnitude of the situation.

"Are we going back, Dad?" Hannah says looking up from her console.

"You've got to be kidding!" I say with little playful enthusiasm, "there's no way we're going to Baghdad."

We drive about a kilometre, round a bend and pull over out of sight of Border Four behind a large ridge but still in sight of a couple of watchtowers. It's 5pm and we've been going for ten hours, seven of which had been stuck at this border. The fancy dress yurt gig, a time of fanciful hope, seems like a lifetime away. I'm absolutely pushing my luck but know that Wing Lun is right in one respect – going back to Kyrgyzstan is game over. So, in desperation, I flick the switch and lift the bonnet up on the world renowned reliable Toyota and remove an ignition lead in preparation for the "We've broken down" routine that is inevitably to follow. I idly call Herr Oli in Germany who I know can't help in Hamburg but the act of doing something makes me feel better and, I naively feel, reassures Eirene. Hannah, Emily

132

and Abigail are starting to get impetuous, impatience at the time they've been in the car even by their standards.

"Are we there yet, dad?" Hannah enquires, not for the first time on the journey. Emily follows suit as Abigail watches in anticipation that something is happening. I connect again first time, what with there being no army or border officers around, and Oli tells me Wang Lun had called him an hour ago saying there was a problem but that I must wait. Oli says there has been some sort of bomb and machine gun attack and it's all over the news. He promises to chase Wang Lun and as I attempt to give him the satellite phone number to give to Wang Lun as he doesn't appear to have it, the line drops.

I'm outside the car now, moving around as if subconsciously to help progress matters. I look over and the family are looking at me expectantly, now starting to cling onto any news that's there. We're at over 12,000 feet and the afternoon starts to draw in, the midday 18° starting to give way to a more temperate 12°. I shiver involuntarily and call Shameen to find out exactly what had happened in Kashgar; for the British Embassy number; if she could call Oliver and pass him my sat-phone number to pass to Wang Lun; and to make me feel like I'm doing something useful. Or at least let my family think I am. It goes to voicemail.

We drink the last of our water and share the last slice of bread. Eirene has been superb. Sometimes, like me, she gets stressed at minor things but when the shit hits the fan, and there are armed men preventing us reaching our recently bombed terrorist target destination, and the kids are hot, tired, hungry and screaming, and it looks like her husband has really fucked up, and we still have a long drive back to England and it's holiday over – then she comes in to her own, becoming stoical and clear minded. In the trenches she is great and I see her true colours and take strength from them. Despite this, as we hid in no-man's land awaiting the inevitable armed Chinese patrol to arrive and see through the farcical raised bonnet posturing for all that it was, she calmly told me that if I say, "This is what it's all about," once more, she will punch me. I believe her.

I began to put the jumbled events of the day in some semblance of order. What was clear was that whilst we were out of contact in our yurt, one of the biggest terrorist attacks [4] in China in living memory took place. Wang Lun's successful methods of negotiation to allow overlanders across had failed as one of the most unpredictable [5] border crossings in Asia was now closed to foreigners. No amount of influence can open a border in such circumstances. Plainly Wang Lun and co couldn't say they were giving up on us as we had paid £5,500 for this and we had to be the ones to back out, thus avoiding any recourse for claiming our money back. To ease this transition, they consistently told us to wait and that they were doing everything they could but were also consistent in failing to call us at any point at all. Our only form of communication was the satellite phone without which we would have been in total darkness. Our waiting was a pointless exercise in protecting their £5,500. After all these hours of waiting we decided that we needed a cut-off point. We had a two hour drive back to the yurt, assuming that we were allowed back into Kyrgyzstan and assuming that we weren't held up too enthusiastically at the various border posts in the process. Driving at night, especially in such remote areas, was to be avoided at all costs and I needed to limit the amount of night driving we were now going to have to do. I tendered that I would call Wang Lun at 5.30pm, listen to his wait, wait, wait and go at 6pm. We both recognised that, given all that's happened, no Chinese holiday company was going to be able to get us in. As Wang Lun had said, it's Kashgar or bust - and the bust had won. I tried Shameen again and she answered but the phone immediately died. I later discovered that she was in a meeting in the basement of our old

[4] http://en.wikipedia.org/wiki/2008_Kashgar_attack
[5] http://www.dangerousroads.org/asia/kyrgyzstan/961-torugart-pass-kyrgyzstan.html

work building, to be used as a bomb shelter in times of emergency and therefore not ideal for mobile phone reception. Eirene comforted Emily and stroked Abigail who had been asleep too long. A subdued atmosphere reigned and the now chargeless iPods and Nintendos stayed silent. I looked at the watchtowers, the barbed wire and out east towards the Chinese mountains. Well, at least I had seen them, I mused.

My eyes filled up as I knew that I had failed and our naysayers, of which there were a few, would have their day. Plan B, the 5,000 mile Russian drive to Vladivostok, was unpalatable and that was probably the real reason why I refused to think about it. We wanted the Olympics and a route through South East Asia and into Australia. I felt sorry for myself as I realised we would be back in England in three weeks and Eirene would be with her mum, happy, clean, content and safe. The kids would be with their friends and spending their birthday money and I would soon be on the 7.49 to Victoria with only the Metro and memories as company. We would talk about doing something else or doing this again another time, but we wouldn't. It wasn't the ban on foreign vehicles or the ban on students, which the three kids were categorised as, or the fake plane tickets we'd got as part of the Chinese entry process, or that we weren't going through the approved government agency, or the strange handling of my visa application in London, or that we couldn't be in a set place on a set date 10,000 miles away that stopped us. It was the fact that I looked at my wall map back home and looked at my calendar and plucked Monday 4th August 2008 out of the air as the date we would enter China. Then I thought again and, with the border closed at weekends, elected for the 5th as it might be busy with the build-up over the weekend. That educated re-think fucked up the trip. Or arguably it was the senseless murder of 16 young men that inconvenienced the midlife crisis plans of a selfish, self-centred tourist and his family.

Shock of all shocks, I received no word from Wang Lun who had given me his word he would call back, so I phoned him at 5.34pm. Initial greetings were exchanged and his tone was regrettably and predictably no different from before. Except his words were, "It's OK. You can come through." And that was that. I returned to the car and told Eirene who couldn't believe it nor, for that matter, did I. We decided to play along with the charade, clipped ourselves in and turned around for our drive back down to the border and inevitable gesticulation from one pip with the subtext of, "For the last time, fuck off before I shoot you." We rounded the bend to see a long line of lorries struggling up the hill towards us. All those in the queue to go into China had been let through and they were now letting the other side in. Basically, the Kyrgyzstan into China side was now closed. We moved to the side to let them past and saw a soldier in the passenger seat of the lead lorry. He indicated for his lorry driver to stop and, as the crawling convoy drew to a halt, he began shouting and signalling for us to stop. Jumping down from the high passenger seat, he came rushing towards us, shouting down his radio, and we realised that it was one pip's interpreter, the one who had nervously ushered us from the border area. I made a grab for the map and was interrupted in my last ditch pathetic attempt of asking him for directions to Kyrgyzstan, by him excitedly uttering, "It's OK, it's OK! You can come through."

I wanted to make glorious love to him right there right now. We embraced, we hugged, we patted, we went too far before awkwardly returning to our formal roles of tourist and border guard. I had always been curious how you got the job being the person who tells someone that they have just won the pools or the premium bonds. It must be brilliant to have that moment to change peoples' lives for the better like that; to be the bearer of good news, to always be deeply and fondly remembered in someone's head at one of the most significant and life-changing instances of their existence to date. It would be the antithesis of how people reacted when I, a uniformed policeman, knocked on their door. I might be being melodramatic in my comparisons, but one pip's translator had a little glimpse into that job at that moment. He jumped into the car with us and, as he guided us back down towards the border we thought we would never see again, he hurriedly told us that a high ranking army officer had made a phone call that afternoon paving the way for our entry. All tiredness evaporated as we tried to weave our way past the oncoming lorries before being compelled to drive down a steep embankment and off-road it to the border. This was something that would normally fill Eirene with dread and some compulsive brake leg pressing but she seemed overjoyed. We were directed into the border guard compound and elatedly parked our car, if such a thing is possible.

Two pip and one pip were nowhere to be seen. We saw familiar guards who were now all smiles and genuinely happy for us. The kids greeted them admirably in Mandarin and we popped our passports out again for what we thought would be the final time.

"Empty car," said one of the smiling assassins. I looked forlornly at the packed 3D jigsaw puzzle that was our boot and rapidly estimated that, at best, this was going to take us at least two hours. And so we began.

One by one bags, boxes, first aid kits, shoes and everything else came out with a gaggle of guards haphazardly hunting through them more in curiosity than anticipation of a big drugs or arms haul. Surprisingly they searched many boxes twice, some boxes no times and didn't check the safe, glove box, central console, most of the car or us. Two hours later on the button I tightened the last ratchet on the re-packed boxes and we set off down the road with the warning not to take any "hotoraphs." We followed a ravine of a pass next to a wide, dried up riverbed with the stuff of climbers' dreams on either side of us. We drove and we drove and we worried. Still no final border post or customs.

"We've left our guide back there." Eirene nervously suggested, and I outwardly assured her we hadn't.

We were driving in China with no Chinese documentation or licence plate which would be a first for anyone. We had assumed that at the first border post our guide would be there to run around sorting things out, speaking rapidly in Mandarin. We didn't anticipate that four border posts and 60 miles in we would still be on our own. Finally, we came to border post five, a shanty town with a makeshift barrier across the road and the now familiar continuous line of 6ft barbed wire fence. We drove slowly, hoping our guide would emerge at any point, arms aloft in exaltation at the end of their long wait. I might be being uncharitable to the local population but a number of what I assumed to be prostitutes did pay us some attention but our guide wasn't one of them. We stopped and waited downwind of the harlots, outside a large and immaculate police station being eye-balled by two machine gun carrying policemen inside its high gates.

I took a stroll to the local shop and struggled to find the word for water or a way to describe it by sound or sight. Eventually the owner finally pointed to 40-odd crates of water stacked up to the ceiling behind me. On return there was still no sign of the guide, so I gave Wang Lun a call this time on my normal mobile that had finally elected to show some signs of life. I told him I was outside the police station and there was no guide but he seemed confused. I crossed the road and tried to hand the phone to one of the policemen so that they could explain to Wang Lun where I was. I don't know if it was for security reasons or because it was a pink phone, but his reaction was akin to me handing over a pin-less hand grenade. He shouted at me in Chinese and took a few steps back before one of the others disappeared into a hut. Eventually an officer arrived, took the offending phone and obligingly spoke before handing the phone back to me, whereupon Wang Lun declared that he knew where we were and that we had 70 km still to go before customs. There must be a good number of countries that all could fit into this whopping border crossing. It was massive and if I ever get the time I wouldn't mind coming back here for a couple of weeks and seeing it all.

As dusk descended and headlights were turned on (unfortunately only ours – the Chinese, in an apparent show of virility, refused to pop them on until at least three hours after sunset), we moved on not convinced that our nightmare day was going to be over soon. We drove on in the darkness before a line of stationary lorries finally loomed ahead and we slowly moved ahead of them in the now familiar border tradition, praying that we had finally arrived. Those hopes were dashed when we discovered it was just a police check and we were all ordered out of the car, including young sleeping occupants, to approach a nearby desk. We were allowed on our way and told to keep on driving. Eventually, after 16 hours in the car, floodlights lit up the sky ahead. We approached more barriers, something squirted something on to our car and we were told to stop. Not customs but quarantine. A face masked officer approached so I wound down the window to be told to wind it up again. I had to queue up and pay for the service, while being soaked by the toxic chemicals. When I returned to the car there was an assemblage of police, quarantine officers, army, border guards and customs guys loitering with clear intent that they should be doing something although not quite united on exactly what. On request, I handed over my passports to one of them and was told to drive to a big building up ahead where an immaculately presented border soldier with good English asked for my passports. His name, I later learned, was Zuoshuming. I told him that I had given them to one of the guards back at the place where I was sprayed.

"Why did you give them to quarantine officer?" he enquired. I explained that a man with a gun wearing a uniform at a barrier in a new country we had just arrived in had asked for our passports and that, as a traveller, it was customary in such circumstances to hand them over. This appeased him.

We were led into a darkened customs hall, exhausted children and all, given some landing cards to fill in and then told to empty our car. Lights came on in the hall and from the far end we saw the most welcome spectacle that I have ever seen, well, certainly since the translating soldier showed up with his words of assent. There was our English speaking guide, complete with a rucksack full of paperwork and a whopping suitcase which, without losing a kid, we would have no room for. Our Hamburg agents had assured us that she would only have a small day sack. Nancy introduced herself and in typical British fashion, I apologised for keeping her waiting. She was straight into action brandishing laminated forms and shouting at people who were ordering us to empty our car. They settled on searching just a few bags before deciding to inspect under the bonnet. They asked for the location of our engine number, the second occasion this had happened, and I told them I couldn't find it, so they settled on taking it from my log book and reconciling it with Nancy's documentation. This was of course copied from the logbook, so I was quietly confident it would tally up. Zuoshuming asked if I had any literature on China, such as *Lonely Planet* or *Let's Go*. I saw little point in denying I had a copy of *Lonely Planet,* especially considering one of his colleagues had moved my copy by the handbrake whilst looking to open the bonnet two minutes before. It had slipped my mind, but Eirene had remarked that during the smiling assassin search one of them had opened the *Lonely Planet* book and bent over the corner of a specific page, and then closed it. I handed the book over and he told me that there were inaccuracies within the book, a present from my mum and dad. I assumed it was Tibet related but he said it was regarding Taiwan.

"Ah, the completely Chinese owned state that isn't, in any way at all, an autonomous republic?" I proffered.

"Yes, that one," he acknowledged without a hint of a smile.

He insisted on permanently confiscating the copy and I asked if he could he not just take the relevant pages.

"I don't want to damage your book," he said, shaking his head by way of explanation. Words failed me.

"You should write to the authors and publishing company and complain about the inaccuracies in it," he suggested.

"I can't," I said. "I don't know who the publishers are now you've taken it."

The charade drew to a close with me enquiring what the inaccuracies were as I hadn't read the book and he agreed to email them to me. So I gave him my email address and although I never did receive the list of inaccuracies, we still write to each other to this day . [6].

I later learnt that books are revered in China and encountered a similar approach when we travelled to North Korea a few years later. The written word is sacrosanct to the people primarily as publishing is owned, or at least overseen, by the government. Having something deemed to be inaccurate in published form is exceptionally dangerous as it will be taken as gospel. In fact, North Korea specifically ban the Bible itself as it presents a challenge to the government and may be taken as Gospel. It reminds me of the narration of the lead character, Eugene Jerome, in the 1988 film *Biloxi Blues* after his secret diary his exposed to his fellow recruits. "People believe whatever they read. Something magical happens once it's put down on paper. They figure no one would have gone to the trouble of writing if down if it wasn't the truth."

Of course, in the West, most written words are taken by many with a large pinch of salt, to the extent that there's often some consternation if it emerges later that they're true. However, physically damaging a book, no matter how inaccurate, still goes against the grain.

Zuoshuming commenced his reluctant physical censorship of the guidebook as Nancy returned with another officer, asking me if I had a satellite phone. Considering I'd spent the best part of £80 allowing Chinese border guards to use it earlier in the day I thought it best not to fib. I produced it

---

[6] He now organises tours around China – email him on aimuzi73@126.com

and it was immediately confiscated. I asked "Why?" and they said that it was because it was Olympic year and it was for security reasons. So that cleared that up. Concerned that they might decide to later use it at great expense to me, I battled for the SIM card and won. Encouraged with my success I put in a further bid for the fragile aerial on it but that was put on hold. At one juncture my future pen-pal pulled us to one side to ask what we knew about yesterday's events. Not wishing to dob anyone in I told him I knew nothing. My account of the following conversation was recorded as soon as practicably possible but whilst still fresh in my mind.

Zuoshuming – "There was an attack on some policemen yesterday."

Me (innocently) – "What? They were punched? Kicked?"

Zuoshuming – "No."

Long silence.

Me – "Are they OK?"

Zuoshuming – "No, many died. We must not talk about it"

Me – "Oh shit, I'm sorry. How many died?"

Zuoshuming – "I cannot say. For security you understand. You must be careful what you say. You must not ask about it. You don't need to know."

Me – "OK, I understand. I guess that's why we had the border problems."

Zuoshuming – "You are talking about it. 16 people died. You must not talk about it."

Me – "OK. Sorry. 16! That's really bad."

Zuoshuming – "How did you know 16 people died?"

We carried on waiting, talking to a local worker with excellent English who was elated to be able to show off his expertise at this foreign tongue. Hannah fell asleep in my arms and Emily fell asleep on a raised plastic table. We had formed the mistaken impression that China would have had a public face of friendly openness in this year of all years. I mused to Eirene that we were only a book and a satellite phone down so things could be worse. As she nodded, Nancy tentatively approached us and told us that due to a mix-up, they were confiscating the car. Unlike the others, the car bit was pretty important. She said it was OK as they were sending a taxi from Kashgar for us. She conceded that she thought she had made a mistake and forgotten a certain piece of paperwork and it was her fault and she was sorry. She would be in a position to sort it out the next day when the car would be returned to us. We were so tired and devoid of any emotion that we would have complied with anything she suggested.

I drove my car with her to a nearby compound accompanied by customs officers and watched as they tried to jam the 2.5m high car into a 2m high garage. Eventually I was directed into an enormous empty warehouse and, in typical Chinese fashion, directed to a specific empty space right at the back. We returned to the customs hall and waited for the taxi that turned out to be a 30 seater bus solely for us. We dragged ourselves in, laid the children down in the beltless seats and set off to Kashgar through large, boulder-filled canyons. We were in China, stripped of some of our possessions, all of our car and devoid of any ability to think clearly. But, 22 hours after we set off, we were in China and we were all safe and happy. All that was left for us to do was accidentally leave our passports on the bus, check into the hotel and go to sleep.

CHAPTER 7.

EXPLORING CHINA

Wednesday 6 August 2008

Day 98 - Kashgar, China - 9,925 miles

We woke in the Seman Kashkar Hotel and met Nancy for breakfast. Daylight revealed a dark cloud sitting about 200 feet above the entire town, totally blocking out any view of the sky - but it was sand from the desert and not pollution we were informed. Breakfast was a selection of noodles and eggs - too many eggs for Hannah we were to realise later.

Kashgar is a long standing city that has continually acted as a major communications hub and trading town since its inception thousands of years ago. It is the most westerly city in China and served as an important link on the Silk Route between China, the Middle East and Europe. Its crowdedness and makeshift stalls at the side of the road, selling a myriad of merchandise from melons to machinery, made it feel more like India than China. Had we been travelling through Kashgar in 1273, we may well have come across Marco Polo during his 24 year trip of Asia, documenting his experience of the city. But today, this vibrant town with narrow backstreets of two-storey terraced buildings and open-fronted, colourful shops with goods flowing out to the welcoming streets beautifully yet brutally awakened our senses after the tranquillity of our sleep.

But there's little time to embrace it. Nancy said that we had to go and collect our car but first we had to go to hospital for a medical that was required for our driving licences. Eirene has a thing about hospitals being a place of death and disease and wasn't keen on taking the kids there. Perhaps there was some merit to this but there was no babysitting option, so we took them along with strict instructions to hover above the ground and not touch anything. We crammed into the belt-less taxi, a tautology if there ever was one, and drove through Kashgar's chaotic corridors to the hospital.

China recognises no driving licences or permits outside of their own and when we saw their driving standards we appreciated that we needed to be pretty special to earn one. I guessed my asthmatic concerns in obtaining a licence were unfounded when I saw a one-legged, one-eyed man riding a moped in streets where single person mopeds carried more passengers than a bus. Donkeys and carts dodged taxis, lorries and cars and I guessed that the minimum age limit for driving a moped had to be about seven or eight. The wearing of helmets was apparently strictly forbidden and there appeared to be no rules of the road, but everyone seemed to know them. The driving was just mad.

We made it to the hospital unscathed, although this major city centre hospital seemed more akin to a war-time field hospital with patients lying on homemade stretchers while relatives wafted them with makeshift fans. A steady stream of homemade wheelchairs and similar devices flooded in from the dusty streets. It looked like it was working at over 100% capacity as the infirm and dying lay around on floors and benches and many people wore face masks in the intimately tight queues that snaked through the reception area.

Nancy embarrassingly and efficiently queue jumped us from place to place, tolerating the cringeworthy flirting of the doctors and sorting out the form filling. The eye test was nothing short of comedy genius as Eirene, who has constantly refused glasses and optician visits, stood behind the oche line first, watched on by a packed crowd. Keeping her feet religiously on the line her neck began to crook as the nurse took her lower down the reading chart. Like a tortoise it emerged from out of the recesses of her body until it was almost parallel to the ground. By the bottom line of the script her whole body appeared to be at a gravity defying 45°. She later confessed that the nurse was giving her hand signals near the end to help her.

Afterwards we all waited outside whilst Nancy did some running around. We were shocked to see a crowd watching a young lady lying on the road writhing in agony right at the entrance to the hospital. She had come off her moped, which was lying at her side, and the other party was nowhere to be seen. Unfortunate and inevitable considering the driving but she must have been over the moon at the convenience of the accident, literally smack bang outside casualty. Despite this, for 15 minutes, she lay there holding her hip in obvious pain as no one, not even the watching hospital entrance guards, helped her. Someone took some snaps and three ambulances, sirens wailing, drove out the hospital and carefully navigated around her. It was macabre. It looked, as much as I could diagnose from a distance, that she had fractured a hip or her pelvis and, judging by her screams, was breathing fine. I thought long and hard about it but as she was Muslim and I was a Western male, I thought better than to start prodding around her abdominal region. And she was making a considerable noise which medically is always a good sign.

Eirene's nervousness at being in a hospital where the kids could come to some harm dissipated as we sped away in the taxi, kids on our laps, from the set of *Mash*. We had lunch at a restaurant in the grounds of the hotel and I sat patiently and in wonderment as the adjacent table took it in turns to have their picture taken with a bemused melon eating Abigail. Nancy and I left at about 2.30pm to collect the car from the Torugart border. With a good 24 hours of Chinese experience in my pocket, I cynically and conservatively estimated to Eirene that I might be back that evening. We arrived and took our places on our respective stools in a nearby shop and were entertained by the owner's crocheting. Following a four hour wait, which consisted of a power cut, two-hour staff lunch break, a prolonged meeting regarding the recent terrorist attack and a great deal of Chinese officialdom and bureaucracy, we were ready to go. It was just in the nick of time as I had managed to run through my entire ensemble of daddy jokes, comedy handshakes, shadow puppetry and popping noises with the local kids. As the crowd size increased and my repertoire drew to a close, I felt the increasing pressure that only the greats, like Jimmy Tarbuck and Stan Boardman, would have understood. Although border towns should never be used to judge a country, it was interesting to note the number of nappy-less children on show, with nothing but a large and convenient hole in the seat of their pants. I made a mental note to stop trying to view things through Western eyes; however, I'm not sure if I would ever be comfortable with the propensity for and ease of which physical violence was dispatched upon them by their parents. There's something beyond heart breaking seeing a three-year-old struck with full force from an open hand that merely results in them scurrying away with a tear. I glanced at Nancy for some mutual assurance or even acknowledgement but she seemed oblivious to it or, at least, at ease with the ordinariness of it all.

The car was released and we headed back to Kashgar, stopping for diesel on the way. Or attempting to. At the first garage we came upon, the owners had employed a couple of people to hold up, across the entrance, the surely symbolic barrier of a piece of string with bunting on it. They requested our vehicle documents and passports before allowing us in. Nancy declared this to be a new security measure in light of the attack and was to become a common feature throughout the province. On some occasions Eirene and Nancy had to stand outside the petrol station while I entered on my own, for "security reasons." I only wish they employed this system in England because whenever I fill up at the BP/M&S Garage and Eirene goes in to pay the bill, £20 is magically added to it.

I arrived back at the hotel in Kashgar at about 10pm and grabbed a sandwich from John's café, a famed Kashgar meeting place where, for thousands of years and to this day, travellers attempted to out bullshit each other with stories of their exploits so far.

Our fears about the Chinese drivers were confirmed the following day on our longest drive yet. It was a 750 km trip to Kuqa and as we left Kashgar on a really great dual carriageway, Eirene overtook a car only to pull back swiftly into her lane as she was greeted by an army vehicle coming around the bend towards us at about 70mph on the wrong side of the road. There were no sirens or lights and the other carriageway was open. Nancy didn't seem the least bit phased by this, but our arses didn't stop dilating for about four hours and we never again regained our trust in Chinese dual carriageways and their pretence of one way traffic. En route, we had to make a quick stop at a nearby town to collect our driving licences. Even in my cynical world, I estimated it a couple of hours max. We waited outside a post office-type building for about an hour and a half as Nancy did what she had to do and then we headed off to a vehicle testing centre for another wait. Nancy helped work our way to the front of the queue and our car was driven in by a laughing tester who had never witnessed anything as funny as a right hand drive car. Wait till he saw my shadow puppetry. Headlights and breaks were comprehensively tested with complex machines and then the feared cry went up for my engine number. With all the trouble there'd been in finding it before I was hopeful these guys would know exactly where it was. Another hour and a half later following car manual checking, many oily hands and genuine concerns from me that the number had been scraped off and the engine was nicked, it was found. We were permitted to return to the post office for another hour and a half while Nancy worked her magic. It was a troublingly late 2.30pm and 4.5 hours in total before we set off on our 750 km journey.

With hindsight we should have put our foot down and not put our foot down, so to speak, and stayed where we were for the night. But there was something persuasive about a near stranger with an itinerary that seemed set in stone. With their confidence we bestow imaginary knowledge and experience, often wrongly. We were assured it was all concrete highways and that bit was true. What we didn't account for was 15 separate police checks and stops. On some occasions we were told to empty everything from our car before our angelic Nancy interfered, shouting and waving angrily, until their position inevitably changed. So a top tip for terrorists – take a young, feisty 4'8" Mandarin speaking young lady with you if planning any attacks on mainland China. On top of the police stops, at one stage we drew up behind a number of buses and open-backed army lorries, driving almost at funeral procession speed along the highway with curious soldiers peering out the back. Eirene began to overtake, to Nancy and the soldiers' horror, and we were quickly ushered back to the rear of what turned out to be a convoy. You aren't allowed to overtake convoys for "security reasons" that we stopped trying to work out. Even a parallel and adjacent road was forbidden. We were saluted through police checks and toll roads as immaculately turned out soldiers, guards and police stood to attention. After one and a half hours of crawling at 30 miles an hour the convoy stopped at a toll booth for the large number of occupants to use the hole in the ground facility. An excellent opportunity for us all to pass through but the now large group of cars behind the convoy were told to wait for half an hour in position before the convoy started again. It was starting to resemble the film *Convoy*, with miles of traffic tailing along behind the procession. The talk was that there was an important general in the convoy together with the injured officers from the recent Kashgar terrorist attack. It said something about the patient and unquestioning nature of Chinese people that no-one seemed even remotely irate at any of this.

One of the core rules of travelling is not to travel at night. This charter goes back to the dawn of time and is as relevant today as it was then. Bad things happen in the dark – everyone knows that. As dusk fell, with 150 miles still to go, we finally and unsympathetically rid ourselves of the convoy of bereavement.

Feeling a bit jittery, an offbeat game followed where every other vehicle refused to put their headlights on until 45 minutes after it turned pitch black. The fun didn't end there as numerous unlit donkey carts zigzagged across the road, interspersed with obscured cyclists wearing dark clothes and, of course, no lights.

"Maybe you can't see their lights, Dad, as those legs are blocking them," Hannah submitted, indicating the young children sitting on the handlebars of some of the bikes. It felt like level 10 of some computer game but with only one life left.

When vehicle lights were finally deigned to be turned on, it was to be full beams only. After much scorning we elected to join the anarchy and flicked our beams on when we saw theirs on. They would then turn theirs off, leading us to withdraw ours which, in turn, was taken as a sign of weakness leading to them victoriously putting theirs back on. And on it went.

I later questioned Wang Lun about this and he laughed so much he could only utter "It's true but I have no explanation." By way of clarification, his driver explained that "it's always been like that." We were warned by everyone about the driving, but nothing could adequately have prepared us. No indicators, dangerous overtakes and a complete disregard for other road users. On single carriageway roads adopting a position over the central line was common, preventing overtakes and engaging oncoming traffic in a game of Duel and Darkness.

"It's amazing that no one gets killed," Eirene said exasperatedly. It transpired they do – 68,000 in 2007 and, to put it into context, there are 36 deaths a year per 100,000 vehicles in China. The figure for the UK is 7.

We made it safely to a buzzing Kuqa City at 11pm, put the kids straight to bed and sagged into our own immediately after. The nerve-racking night driving had taken its toll.

We left early the following morning and a little remorseful at not having more time in the bustling town which our travel book had described as "dead." I had particularly wanted to visit the Kizil Thousand Buddha Caves, over 200 grottoes built into the cliff face with cave art from the 3rd to 8th centuries but it was not to be. A fleeting glimpse of the city was all that was afforded to us, something that was to become the hallmark of such an ambitious and rigidly planned tour of this 10 million square kilometre country.

We continued across the seemingly never-ending desert and straight roads in the direction of Turpan. Sporadic forests of poplar lined the road and occasionally they were fronted by a long row of tiny shops with oversized, colourful signs above their doors. In fact, the signs were so large, they frequently not only ran the length of the shop but protruded above the top of the building too. Parked outside were rusty old trucks and buses. Groups of men stood around chatting with not a woman in sight. The roads were wide and the line between road and the very generous unmade flattened parking/walking area was frequently obscured by all the desert sand. Unlike the narrow streets of the UK, land was not a precious commodity, so the distance from one side of the road to the other was something you'd contemplate driving if you needed to do the journey.

In the more remote parts it was like an unfinished backdrop to a play, with undulating empty brown land and a pale blue upper half. There were no sheep, goats or any kind of livestock, no plants or trees nor virtually even any colour - just barren land with an incredibly well maintained road running through it. The only colour in our insipid journey was the bright blue crash barrier which ran along the side of the road. The fact that there was such a good road was incredible as we were driving through one of the highest passes of China and the ever present great mountain system of central Asia, the Tian Shan Mountains.

Numerous police checks slowed our journey and although we were always treated with a healthy mix of fascination and friendliness, we wanted to reach Turpan to see the opening of the Olympic Games on TV. We drove through the mountains as the afternoon heat increased. The higher temperature and work rate of the car led the air-conditioning to fail and the engine temperature soared, a "feature" of the engine management system of our model, Google later informed me. I was convinced that Nancy took our insistence on putting the car heater on at full blast as some sort of strange Western custom or initiation ceremony, unaware that it was an effective way at reducing the engine temperature.

We stopped halfway through the mountains for one of Emily's regular toilet breaks and came across a saloon car stuck axle deep in the gravel. I quickly attached the winch, hoiked him out and we were unexpectedly rewarded with gifts of apples and grapes. I could only guess how long they would have been there had we not come along but their reactions and gifts indicated it would have been some time. After that, the atmosphere in the car for the last 40 km to Turpan was quite buoyant. Eirene was happy at having helped someone, the kids were munching on grapes and I was excited that I was able to use my winch in a real situation.

Turpan is in a large basin, the Turpan Depression, 150m below sea level and famously recorded China's highest ever temperature of 55°. However, much like the oldest pub in Britain, there are many claimants to this title and even more questioning the claims. What wasn't beyond dispute was that it was bloody hot. As we approached the city the thermometer indicated a relatively cool 44°. There is a famous road in Scotland known as the Electric Brae, where it appears that you are driving uphill when in fact you are going downhill. It gets its name from when electricity was first invented and was seen as a strange power, but the effect is actually a very realistic optical illusion. On the road to Turpan we found there was a similar optical illusion. For about 10 miles we drove what appeared, from the lie of the land, to be clearly downhill but which both the car and the altimeter in the GPS indicated was to the contrary.

As we approached the outskirts of Turpan, I mentioned to Nancy about the arrangements for us in Beijing. During the debacle that was our entry into China, she had asked us at the border what star hotels we wanted to stay in and how many rooms would we want. Confusion reigned as I showed her our itinerary which spelled out exactly which hotels we were staying at. Her itinerary was considerably different from ours and, to her knowledge, no hotels had been booked. Additionally, she had been told that our trip fees did not include Beijing accommodation. At the time, we had exhausted kids, no car and our assets were slowly being stripped from us, so we paid little attention. But today, as we approached Turpan, out of the blue she said that her boss, Mr Wang, was coming over to meet us that evening. Alarms bells immediately rang, even louder when we learnt that he was making a specific 400 km round trip from Urumqui, a city we had passed, just to see us. My money was on either a cock-up with the Beijing accommodation or that the train tickets to Beijing (which Nancy had known nothing about) had failed to materialise.

I prepared myself for the worst as I came down to the lobby to meet him after we checked in. He first ran through the itinerary we had, the same as the one I originally had, and showed us an alternative one as there had been problems the week before with entering the outer environs of Tibet. All seemed fine so far but I was cautiously nodding, awaiting the big bang. He told us that there had been another earthquake in the Sichuan province, 6.2 on the Richter scale, but that wasn't a problem. Mr Wang assured us they happened every day and there was only something to worry about if it registered over seven. In England an earthquake with a level of two on the Richter scale is front page news with images of a knocked over plant pots and horizontal wheelie bins. He answered all our queries, even telling us that he had secured accommodation in Beijing, right in town and much closer than we had thought we were going to be. We waited and waited but no big bang came and it turned out that he had come all this way just to meet us.

With my cautious cynicism kicked well and truly into touch, we dined in a private room in a local restaurant and ate a colossal meal whilst he ensured that my beer glass was never empty. He related that on the day of us entering the Torugart Pass, he had gone to the most important government department and obtained a handwritten note attached to our documentation stating, "They must enter China today." He then spent the rest of the day in meetings with numerous other officials and for that reason could not return my calls throughout the day. The attacks had made this his biggest challenge, but he had brought us through and we expressed our sincere gratitude at his efforts as I guiltily recalled my traitorous thoughts on the day in question. The kids were brilliantly behaved and their rapturous greeting of the melon at the end brought great mirth to the table. Having insisted on paying the bill, Mr Wang left us as we headed back to our hotel to watch the opening ceremony of the Olympics.

For the first time in a while, I had the chance to relax and check our website and catch up on some emails. Something prompted me to do a few checks of which IP addresses had been visiting our website and there was an unusually large number from China. I was a bit paranoid and intoxicated, a cracking combination, so penned an email to a few friends and family along the lines of "Bumped into my old Etonian mate, Eric Blair, the other day and he said he'd been watching out for me on my website." Yep, no doubt the world's most resourced code breakers would be baffled as my mates knowingly nodded.

A search for mobile SIM cards, laundry facilities, clothes for Abigail, local road tax and the elusive Toyota part that would allow access to our spare wheel occupied the following morning. Eirene acceded to the kids' yearning for hamburgers and asked Nancy to take us to a local burger place. Hannah had, strikingly for her, eaten little over the last two days but put paid to any concerns by polishing off two full-size burgers and a load of chips. We were quite fastidious about our children's diet but were keen for Hannah to eat and realised that they had a month of Chinese food to come anyway.

Nancy was starting to bond with the kids, who made up a song about her. "Nancy is great, she is our mate. She lives in China, where life is finer," were the core constituents of the mysterious lyrics. In advance of arriving in China, we had had numerous discussions about where she would sit in the car. Eirene wasn't keen on having this extra person imposed on our family unit and wanted to put her in the boot. Not actually the boot, but the third row of seats with all the luggage beside her. I asked Nancy what she thought and she said she would sit anywhere, the most important thing was to ensure the children were happy. Very laudable and although we sometimes struggled with communication, she was extremely helpful and selfless with a quiet strength that she needed with the many police stops we were experiencing. She offered little in the way of conversation or questions but was always happy to give answers, albeit brief ones, to anything non contentious that we asked. In the end, Abigail took the spot.

Not only is Turpan very dry and hot, in fact the hottest place in China, but it also has very fertile farmland due to the ingenious irrigation system which has allowed Turpan to also become famous for its grapes.

Some time to explore the city had been factored into our itinerary and we decided to visit a karez, a well system that was constructed over 2,000 years ago to capture and transport water from the mountains to Turpan. It was considered (wrongly in my opinion) on a par with the Great Wall in terms of building magnitude. The incredibly efficient but simple karez wells were part of a canal system of over 1,100 wells and tunnels which were all constructed by hand. They covered a distance of over 5,500 km and many are still in use today. We were keen to see this engineering feat, and with the temperature heading to 44° again, it was a chance to keep cool in the underground tunnels.

In the museum, a model showed a small boy being winched down a 100m vertical well in complete darkness, to remove mud and gravel from the bottom. The water then emptied into a small reservoir before being drawn into the water channels for irrigation. The temperature in this stone cave was delightfully cool and the girls enjoyed exploring the underground channels that weren't in use. We held them back from venturing too close to those with fast flowing water running through them for fear of them being swept away and embarking on an adventurous irrigation channel ride.

We soon discovered that anything remotely touristy in China came with the associated merchandise, in this instance a labyrinth of shops and their assistants that needed to be fended off before you could leave. To this extend they had fully embraced Western culture. As soon as they saw you looking at something, even if you hadn't picked it up, they pounced, telling you how good it was and what it could be used for. The sales pressure was intense and poor Emily, pocket money in hand, struggled to grasp the concept of haggling.

Emily: "How much?"
Owner: "20 yuan."
Emily: "OK."
Daddy: "No Emily, you must haggle!"
Emily: "19?"
Owner: "Yes."

I took an excited Emily and Hannah to the indoor swimming pool near our hotel. The unlit and filthy changing rooms were home to a rusting bicycle and many small, moving things. Poolside smoking was the norm, alcohol was served freely and I guessed that even petting and running would have been permitted. The roof was open thus facilitating the entrance of numerous shitting birds. Furthermore, of all the staring we had undergone in our travels so far, this was the most intense. It was so unrelenting that I repeatedly checked that I had remembered to put my trunks on. The odour of the open poolside toilets pervaded through the almost transparent curtains and, unbelievably in the midst of this decay and squalor, Hannah and Emily were asked to leave the pool as they didn't have swimming caps on. It took 15 minutes to purchase them, wholly due to the pool assistant steadfastly refusing to either write down how much they cost or take the money from my hand despite my gesticulating. At one point she turned to writing the amount in air, which had she been holding a sparkler might have given me some semblance of an idea. We spent an hour and a half in there, which although serving as an oasis from the outside heat, was not relaxing under the never faltering eyes of every single occupant of the all-male pool. I occasionally embarked upon the stare back game but would rapidly relent as it meant not watching the kids and I didn't want a big poolside kung fu fight.

The next day we headed for Hami, setting off early to collect our laundry from the launderette where Eirene had deposited it the day before. All the family laundry came to nearly £20 and Eirene was as incandescent at Laundrygate as she was at Towelgate, the infamous request for payment for a dirty towel in Astana, Kazakhstan. Although I didn't think it was that cheap for a country famous for its laundries, I thought it could have been worse with some hotels charging upwards of £5 for a shirt. It certainly gave some perspective to her scathing tirade against Madame Jo Jo's £10 fee in Hungary. She tried to move on, but it blew up again when, after a long wait for the actual laundry itself, it turned up wet and un-ironed. She then devoted a considerable stretch of the 500 km trip to Hami analysing the transaction.

We learnt by text that an American tourist, apparently a relative of one of the Olympic volleyball team, had been murdered in Beijing with the perpetrator then jumping to his death. Further, Nancy's phone had been buzzing with text after text coming in from her friends concerned for her welfare and urging us to move out of this troubled region quickly as a terrorist attack [7] had killed many people in Kuqa the previous day, the buzzing town where I had been keen to prolong our stay. This she elected to relay to us before assuring that we would be fine. Hami was our last night in the region before we left the Uyghur people.

Hami, also known as Kumul, is another important outpost on the Silk Route and due to its strategic location, has been fought over many times between the imperial Chinese, the

---

[7] https://www.theguardian.com/world/2008/aug/10/china.olympics20081

Mongols and the Uyghur people. It has a more temperate climate although the city is divided by the Tian Shan Mountains. These give it a kind of dual climate with a river valley and grasslands in the north which are cool in the summer, while in the south, the more arid region has great temperature variations between day and night.

We arrived in Hami and immediately drew a crowd when we parked outside the front of the hotel; the number of starers increasing until there were about 70 locals gawping at us unblinkingly. I felt like I should have been delivering a food parcel or some news of something, at least. Instead, I opted for, "There's nothing to see, make your way home, it's all over here" through a rolled up newspaper but it fell on deaf ears. "We are from Surrey. We come in peace and we mean you no harm" cut no ice either. Nancy suggested that not many Westerners came through this area, especially ones with children.

The hotel porter undertook a token superficial search of our bags, having learnt his search skills from the same school as the Chinese public car park attendants who would ask us to open the boot and then stare silently at the multitude of boxes before closing it. Nancy guided us to a restaurant where the kids delighted in a local delicacy of sweet Hami melon and I delighted in the price of £9 for the whole meal, including drinks, although Hannah was aghast that they neither had nor had heard of chow mein.

"This isn't proper China," she declared authoritatively.

It was over 500 km to our next destination, Dunhuang, over the border in Gansu province. The desert road, a contrast to the never changing plains of Kazakhstan, appeared to alter its complexion more frequently. Barren, yellow gravelly earth gave way to a covering of spiky desert grass as we drove on wide roads across miles of flat plains that disappeared over our horizon and merged into the Gobi Desert. We felt free and like pioneers, the factually incorrectness of this doing little to stifle our elation. We were then presented with hilly terrain and ravenous, craggy landscapes with poplar and willow trees that became more frequent as we approached Dunhuang. There the desert gave way to glacier fed streams and fertile land with agricultural development starting to dominate the landscape. It was astounding and China continued to surprise us.

The town itself was tree-lined and tidy and had a charming appeal to it. Like a group of mini celebrities, we stepped out from our dusty vehicle to a crowd of curious onlookers and checked into our hotel. Nancy, still carrying the guilt from the Torugart Pass vehicle document/confiscation palaver, took us all out for Chinese hamburgers. The market she took us to had the feel of a Hollywood action film. Corridors of hessian sacks overflowed with colourful spices, seeds and nuts. Carcasses of animals hung from poles with dozens of live chickens in tiny cages. Fish stalls displayed their wares in rectangular steel baths next to mini mountains of fresh vegetables, and a myriad of colourful cakes and sweets ran the length of one aisle. We should have been getting chased by suited men through these passageways, knocking over all and sundry whilst being angrily gesticulated at by the owners. Instead, with our senses under attack, we manoeuvred towards a café and took our seats where the cook publicly diced the meat in front of us before filling pita-type bread with it. We thought they were delicious but Hannah and Emily were not so enthusiastic. Nancy appeared with five transparent cartons of a local apricot juice, a drink that seemed popular in the café when I looked around. We snaked our way through the busy cobbled streets absorbing the atmosphere and daily life behind the stalls and tourist market. The girls cautiously spent their Yuan on trinkets and rings and Nancy bought us some sweetcorn which the kids enthusiastically demolished. I hoped this hadn't come from her meagre income, but I suspect it had.

After breakfast, we made our way to the Mogao Caves, home of the greatest collection of Buddhist art in the world. It would have been even bigger but the English, along with other European "pioneers" ransacked the joint in 1900, leaving a peppercorn £240 as payment. It's about 25 km out of town, past the airport and the newly built (but not quite finished) super-duper train station and into proper film set desert of semi-corrugated sand dunes with smooth cliff tops devoid of rubble, gravel or growth. Unusually, I was driving and it took all my will power to avoid a side road and spin out towards them. At the outer barrier of the caves we were told that we needed to remove our two jerry cans from the roof. I explained through Nancy that it was diesel and not readily flammable, but he would have none of it. I enquired about the remainder (50 litres) of the diesel in the tank and I'm told that it was ok. I asked if we could empty the jerry cans into the tank and he gave us a resounding shake of the head. Those cans had clearly been earmarked as suspect. We finally parked up and Nancy informed us that, for a whole multitude of reasons, she could not use her guide pass to come round with us and neither could she be seen to buy the tickets herself. There is a surcharge for foreigners, understandably perhaps as we plundered the place 100 years previously and they've probably still got the hump. It worked out at £14 each and Eirene and I independently compared the price to peak-time Legoland admission, although quite why, neither of us knew. All those long drives on the bumpy roads ensured that none of our children had hit 1.4 metres in height yet so they were free. We were told to wait a couple of hours for an English guide but Nancy managed to scrounge one from the university and we shared her with two Germans who were also driving a Land Cruiser round Europe and Asia.

The caves are cut into a long stretch of cliff and have been tastefully rendered with a 1960s council house stone chip finish. Each cave, of which there are thousands, is under lock and key and, for our £14, only a handful were open to the public as the humidity of visitors can affect the contents. Every cave is covered with paintings, each one depicting scenes from the trade route, cultural exchanges and warriors, with life size Buddhist figurines on a plinth at the end of each cave. Far from wholly being a talisman of Chinese culture, there is much Persian and Indian influence in many of the drawings as well as

Christian, Greek and even Russian. Russian convicts were imprisoned in the caves in 1921 and gouged out the eyes and pulled off the hands of many Buddhas in a fruitless search for gems. The guide's knowledge seemed limitless but unfortunately the kids' patience wasn't. The penultimate cave proved to be a cave too far for them and they were involved in a vicious scrabble over the torch before their quest to touch everything began. The final cave, at the entrance to a seven level pagoda built into the rock, silenced us all. We walked through the gigantic feet of a 45m Buddha, the third largest in the world and the biggest indoor one. It was colossal and completely intact. We craned our necks in awe at the logistical accomplishment that its erection undoubtedly was.

We left the caves and joined up with Nancy, which proved to be the lull before the storm. It started with a flicker of a smile from a passer-by as we took a photo of the kids outside the pagoda. Then there was a kind request to pose with them and within minutes, crowds of tourists were hauling our kids away for picture after picture. My vicarious 15 minutes of fame were quite overwhelming; mothers with children the same age and as beautiful as Abigail (impossible as that sounds!) cast them to one side as they pushed forwards to take pictures with our novel blonde and red haired models. Eventually we dragged them away and were then greeted by children at the tourist shop on the way out, giving over gifts to our three as if they were the Orient Kings. Emily, on the surface at least, claimed to hate it and declared that she never wanted to have another picture taken of herself again. Hannah loved it and saw it as ideal practice for her later career as a pop star. Abigail initially fought it but quickly developed a standard smile and pose for each picture.

Dunhuang felt the most tourist friendly of all the places we'd been to in China so far. A number of road signs and shop frontages were in English and we even met some English girls in an Internet cafe, only the second group of English people we had come across on our travels. We ordered apple pie in a café and it wasn't quite what we expected but the children remarkably masked their distress at the pita bread covered in apple sauce and cucumber that emerged. We talked to a group of Americans who were starting an Internet café in the town, the first foreigners to live in the city, and we realised that this place didn't have long in its current state.

Unfortunately, we were on the move again the next day. We had over a month in China but it is such a huge country that I was beginning to concede that we were trying to do too much in too little time, a feeling that could apply equally well to the whole trip.

Despite all the long car journeys, I relished the time with my family, even missing the kids in the few hours between their bedtime and ours. Despite their moods and tiffs, the time spent with them way exceeded all my hopes and expectations. Emily was becoming increasingly clumsier and more forgetful and, as maddening as it was, it was so endearing and reminded me so much of myself. She was cute, beautiful and intelligent and would do anything for anyone. Her innocuous nature and complete innocence made me love and worry about her in equal measure. Hannah was still guarded of any time I spent outside of her but was improving. She played better with Emily but still had a strong jealous streak that she struggled hard to quell. She was astute and funny and had long waves of role playing greatness where we became her patient, daughter or son and she devotedly cared for us, but I had to stop myself from doing more for her than the undemanding and happy-go-lucky Emily. Abigail was still her mother's girl and this journey was doing little to change that so far. She was becoming more playful and the way she almost buried herself inside us when strangers approached was priceless. The knowledge that it was only temporary made it more precious. Unlike the other two, her language did not seem to have developed much since we left. Perhaps it was laziness on our part as we understood what her novel noises and mispronounced words meant although we always tried to remember to repeat them in clear English back to her. The nature of the drives and days we had meant that Eirene's daily teaching schedule had pretty much been timetabled out of our life although Hannah and Emily frequently requested books to read and maths to do. Any concerns I may have had about their educational development had now been completely eradicated and I knew that they had the intelligence to catch up on their return if there was indeed any catching up to be done.

Eirene and I were great together. We had our niggles but what was important was that they were unusual and we were united in what we wanted to do and how we did it in almost everything. She seemed to be enjoying things more and the longer time progressed without anything bad happening, the more relaxed she became. She loved China and there were many things not to love about it but fundamentally the people were affectionate, proud and hospitable, the food was great and there were no complaints about the accommodation. The children were happy so Eirene was happy and that combination always made me happy.

I was glad things were going well as we had several even longer days of driving ahead of us, the next one being nearly 800 km to Xian. Nancy offered us the superhighway route or the normal toll route and advised us to take the latter. Unlike her boss, whose English wasn't very clear but who understood loads, Nancy's clear diction sometimes belied her lack of vocabulary and understanding. Despite repeated questions, she could not tell us the difference in time or distance between the two options. Knowing we needed diesel and didn't have much cash we asked Nancy if the petrol stations took credit cards like Visa.

"Yes," she replied, "they all take Visa."

We stopped at the first one and I offered my Visa card and both her and the pump attendant shook their heads. Nancy kindly explained, "None of the petrol stations take credit cards. Cash only." Baffled, I headed back to one of my secret stashes in the car.

Nancy was a tremendous asset throughout the trip though and had a certain controlled distance from the children that resulted in them wanting more of her; they battled for her hand and to sit with her at dinner. Having someone tell you where to go, communicate in the local language and sort out directions, hotels, meals and everything else had been like a holiday within a holiday, not to mention the extra pair of eyes and hands she brought to the table. Laos was going to be a bit of a shock when we had to take these tasks back on ourselves.

We had an overnight stop in Lanzhou and as we pulled out of the biggest city we had seen in China so far, over the Yellow River Bridge and up into the mountains, the tide of smog above the city almost blocked it out completely. The population of about three million, all crammed into a valley on the Yellow River, made this city, until about 1998, the most polluted city in the world. It probably still had the same level of pollution; it was just that other cities had become worse.

Our next stop over on the way to Xian was Zhangye, a seemingly very social town despite the fact that we had to drive through a pedestrianised shopping precinct in order to park the car. Its lack of tourism resulted in hand car washes for a £1 and a meal for five including drinks and beer coming in at £3.60. The car park attendant produced two puppies, a cliché I know, and the kids flocked to him. Abigail was very reluctant to put her puppy down and we reflected on yet another compromise of not letting them have direct contact with animals. This was second only to "They must always wear a seatbelt" which failed in the taxi on the first day in China. Fortunately, there was no licking or biting from the outwardly healthy looking pups and I failed to get my money's worth on the costly and painful rabies injections we all had in the UK.

The town was buzzing and vibrant and we were metres from the famous bell tower that marked out the town. We thought we had spotted a children's play park but as we entered, it was in fact an exercise park. We learned later that the Chinese don't do children's parks, just exercise parks, where they learn

164

the skills that will ensure future Olympic success. Nancy, knowing I had an interest in martial arts, asked a group of children wearing kung fu suits whether they would show me some. This was taken as a licence for the big boy in the group to beat the living shit out of the others and I didn't know whether I should clap them, stop them, pay them or put my thumbs up or down at the end of each bout. Our children drew the usual crowd of admirers who were intent on touching, prodding and staring. The friendliness was unparalleled although sometimes I felt uncomfortable and I remembered reading about some pretentious film star complaining about people taking pictures of her without permission. "It's so rude" she complained diva-like but I was beginning to know how she felt when I was playing on a swing with Hannah and a woman stuck her mobile phone about a foot from Hannah's face, grabbed her chin to position her, took her picture and walked off. Hannah said to me that she now knew what it must be like to be in a zoo. I wondered if British people were exclusive in their approach at outwardly not being offended so as not to offend other people's offensive customs.

China itself continued to impress us with arid deserts giving way to green pastures and terraced mountains with contoured lines of vegetation, reminding me of the images of China from my old childhood world atlas. And just as the deserts gave way to greener climes, the Uyghur people gave way to the Han Chinese.

We later received word of another terrorist attack in Kashgar, this time with four dead. Later, I read of allegations and speculation that questioned the veracity of these reports and certainly when we passed the scene of the Kashgar attack a couple of days after, there was no physical indication at all of an attack but this could easily be explained. The only time I really had cause to question the legitimacy of any media reports was when we saw Great Britain near the summit of the Olympic medal table. On leaving Xianjing province though, we went from 20 police stops a day to zero, literally overnight, although we came across one toll booth that was barely visible due to a swarm of bees that a policeman was bravely tackling with a 25ml insect spray. Notably it was also apparent that outside of that troubled province, the Chinese one child policy wasn't as rigidly enforced. We learnt that the policy itself is imposed regionally and not nationally which led to discrepancies in punishments and in the ethnic Xianjing and Tibet provinces, these punishments were much harsher than anywhere else.

The driving continued to astound us when we discovered that green lights at junctions, either for pedestrians or traffic, were not to be taken seriously and in no way could we assume any form of prioritisation or right of way. Together with carts, donkeys, cycles and pedestrians on the motorway, a common sight is a lone woman standing in the fast lane, trimming the bushes in the central reservation with no lane closure around her or even high visibility clothing. The irony, of course, was that China are the biggest exporters of high visibility clothing (along with pretty much everything else). Many of the highways had signs every 2 or 3 km indicating which lane was for overtaking, which was the breaking down lane and which was the normal driving lane. Nevertheless, 90% of the traffic sat in the fast lane and refused to move. Horns sounded throughout the cities despite signs to the contrary, yet there was no sign of the associated aggression you would expect. Motorbike helmets did not exist and we even saw a moped being ridden with four people, a baby and a massive abnormal shaped box on it. The rider, who was holding the baby across her chest, had a mobile phone that she was texting on in the same hand. These people were openly mocking the years of training that members of the Royal Signals Motorcycle Display Team have to undergo.

We could see that China was embracing mass development and technological improvements although much of the population struggled to catch up. Business centres and Internet cafes refused to allow us to plug our laptop in or transfer my emails that I'd written by any other means. They did, however, offer me the opportunity, with smiling faces, to manually retype the emails onto their computer. It was there that I opened an email from Zuoshuming, page tearing border officer, asking to be my friend and pen pal. What a strange and wonderful country.

We finally reached Xian, a 3,000-year-old former capital of China and a big lumbering city with a burgeoning population in excess of eight million. Our hotel sat adjacent to the old city wall, which was easily accessible and would have been a great way to see the city if the pollution hadn't been so dense. Entering by the South Gate, the one used by armies returning from victorious battles, we walked a few kilometres along the 13.7 km wall, passing a fortification tower every 120m. The distance, it seems, of a shooting arrow. At each of the four gates is a bicycle station, a single row of identical coloured bicycles and tandems which can be hired and would probably have been the safest place for us to ride a bicycle in China, but time was against us.

Instead, we arranged for a relaxing foot massage after our long walk which proved to be a rare experience for the masseurs who had never worked on children, with Abigail attracting the most attention although her dainty feet were the same price as my size 11s. There are moments in life when you think "This is it", and as the five of us sat happily together in that room while the ladies worked away on us all simultaneously, this was certainly one of them. We swung a deal with a local restaurant who provided food every evening at a really good price in return for some fawning and snaps with the children, and we all learnt the Mandarin for sweet and sour chicken and egg fried rice off by heart as the kids had little inclination to change their dietary yearnings.

China continued to surprise, not least on our visit to the mind-blowing 2,000-year-old Terracotta Army site when swarms of visitors queued to take pictures of our kids, seemingly the highlight of their visit to this world wonder. The site had undertaken some reconstructions of the life-sized soldiers as they would have been, fully painted. Since they all had individually made heads, which they think represented the actual soldiers, they looked almost real. The warriors stood on guard at the entrance to the tomb of the First Emperor of China, Qin Shi Huang, who had a fanatical fear of death. History has tragically shown that it is egotistical work like this, not great social or economic progress, that create legacies. Seeing the Terracotta Army made it clear why many of today's dictators insist on pouring money into grand buildings and ornate palaces whilst their countries starve.

As we emerged from the grounds of the museum, Eirene made the mistake of purchasing some cute silk dresses for the girls from one of the stalls. We hadn't realised how many other street traders had watched the transaction and subsequently we became a magnet for every trader within half a kilometre who rushed up to us holding out their goods, which ranged from Chairman Mao stamps and coins to hot noodles and fruit; each one greeting us with a well-rehearsed "Hello."

The following day, we left the car in Xian and travelled by sleeper train the 1,000 km to Beijing for the Olympic Games. Nancy couldn't travel with us due to the lack of accommodation in Beijing, so she saw us off at the station and the kids, particularly Emily, emotionally bade her farewell for the three days they would be away from her. The train pulling out was like a scene from *Brief Encounter,* but the girls rapidly forgot the trauma as they absorbed themselves with the bunk beds (individual tellies on each one), the buttons, the panels, the foldable seats and the disposable slippers. This was no Southern Rail. Through the windows, the scenery changed constantly from rural farmland and rice fields with distant mountains to industrial factories and sprawling cities. Eirene had been adamant when we were in the UK that we should fly to Beijing as the train might crash. I tried logic, reason and rationality but she refused to budge so I relented and booked the train anyway. The journey was cheap; a novel way for us to travel and it verged on luxurious. We arrived in the capital at what appeared to us to be the world's biggest station and, after some searching, were greeted by our guide who escorted us to the taxi rank where, due to having children, we were kindly ushered to the front of the queue and into the (naturally belt-less) taxi.

Our smart hotel turned out to be half way between Tiananmen Square and the Olympic Stadium. We left our bags and headed straight towards the stadium area by tube, departing the subway to be greeted by a multitude of local touts, each with no more than a few tickets, all working away under the noses of the police. A girl with outwardly no agenda helped us in our quest and assured us that Abigail would not need a ticket. Although there were a multitude of tickets available, four together seemed pretty rare. English, American and Canadian touts interspersed with the local touts and although some of their physiques appeared to belie the fact, many of the Western sellers claimed to be part of the teams themselves. Fat Danny from Dagenham didn't make that claim when he offered us four tickets for handball that had started about an hour or so beforehand. We gave him 200 RMB (£1 = 13.5 RMB, also known as Yuan) and took a long, convoluted and misdirected route to a stadium that was about 400yds away as the crow flies. Requests for pictures, bored volunteers wanting to chat and the slow tearing of each ticket's counterfoil individually added to our exasperation as the clock ticked away on the validity of our tickets. We finally made it, sat down in excellent seats and watched a competitive match between Spain and Brazil, which despite our ignorance of the rules, game and combatants, was a thrilling game and just the right length of time for the kids. We emerged buoyantly onto a lakeside area that acted as a concourse for the water polo stadium as well. We spent a couple of hours playing in the fountains, sitting in the shade, eating from the limited selection of kiosk food available, absorbing the smells and atmosphere and taking shifts monitoring the constant stream of child photographers [8] that had gathered.

From the moment we left our hotel there was a mass of uniformed volunteers with maps and smiles that were rarely complemented with any English. Some of them carried suntan cream which you could ask to use and all seemed really happy in a delightful *Stepford Wives*-type way. I engaged with an English couple, travelling for two years, who were very much enamoured by the games but reflected that the food choice was limited and, moreover, there was no central social gathering place with big screens. In English terms, a place where you can get hammered and have a fight. They had a point though and from a spectator's perspective it was a little sterile; the food was limited but nothing short of exotic when contrasted against the inevitable hamburger and chips that were likely to greet visitors to London 2012. [9]

For a change we guiltily ate at Pizza Hut in the evening. By Chinese standards it was very expensive and in typical Chinese fashion when we asked for a drink refill and pointed to our glass, four or five waitresses arrived asking if they could help. We nostalgically reflected on the long search for a waitress with titanic indifference which was so commonplace in the UK. The restaurant proudly posted a large billboard-type poster that was tall as my shoulder, declaring that the restaurant had been certified as having a "B" rating in hygiene. The salad area had signs that made it universally clear that only one visit was allowed with the standard issue bowl. For a country well known for its uniformity amongst people, this rule did spark thrilling creativity in the punters. On entering we had noticed a Jenga-style bowl of melon that we thought about ordering before we realised that this half metre tower had been

---

[8] Photographers that photograph children as opposed to photographers who are minors

[9] We subsequently attended the London 2012 Olympics and I would like to formerly apologise for this assumption. The Olympic Park had in fact such a plethora of worldly food that I actually struggled to find chips.

painstakingly built by an enthusiastic customer. Another lady worked with the industry of a starving artist, as she spent the entire time of our visit defying the laws of gravity with her masterpiece of salad. We had become used to people staring at us in China, but the shocked looks Eirene received as she left the salad area with merely a few potatoes and an inefficient stacking of lettuce on top surpassed everything to date.

Despite promises from Danny in Dagenham, four tickets for the Birds' Nest stadium in the morning did not materialise and we spent a considerable amount of time mingling with the touts trying to find something better. A Canadian offered us two diving tickets with a face value of 300 RMB for 3,000 RMB and assured us he paid 4,000 RMB for them and he was just trying to get rid of them. He claimed he was part of the Canadian diving team and pointed to the thinning outline of the word "Diving" written across his chest on his otherwise motif less paper-thin T-shirt as irrefutable proof. We declined his selfless offer and I decided that I should focus on two lots of two tickets separately. The morning events ran from 9am to 12.15pm and it was now 10am. Earlier enquiries with people selling tickets for that day's events had been greeted with derisory sneers but as they realised their tickets were losing value with each minute that passed, they began to gather around us. It was a battle of wills and both buyer and seller were as desperate inwardly as they were nonchalant outwardly. Eirene, stuck in the heat with the kids was becoming increasingly irritable, understandably so. For my part I could not leave Beijing without going to the Bird's Nest. There was a multitude of single tickets available for almost all evening events, but I curbed my mercenary leanings. Finally, I settled on a price of 1500 RMB (£111) for two tickets for athletics from one of the initial sneerers. I set off seeking a second pair before Eirene stopped me and said she wanted to head off home with Emily and Abigail instead.

Had I known quite how painful the 1 km journey to the stadium would be, I probably would have joined her. But I didn't. Hannah and I set off to the second nearest tube station; the nearest tube station, called the Olympic Stadium Tube Station, was closed for the duration of the games for "security reasons." The entire network seemed brand new with new trains, stations and uniforms, and on board, the air-conditioning wafted down our necks while we watched the flashing lights indicate which station we were approaching. We emerged from the brand new, second nearest tube station and were directed by a cordon of volunteers in a big loop, past closed off roads and available concrete standings suitable for buses, to a bus station about 500 metres away. There we stood in a long queue of people next to a longer queue of manned buses as no one moved. Ten minutes later, the doors at the front of the first bus opened and everyone crammed onto the one bus. The bus then took a painful route towards the stadium, passing closed dual carriageways (security reasons) and stopped frequently at traffic lights. We were given eight seconds of green lights for every two minutes 18 seconds of red lights. Yes, I timed it. The fact that the bus was so crammed that the driver could not open the doors, did not deter him from stopping and trying to pick up other passengers. We finally arrived at a packed pavement with a number of other buses at which point the army of volunteers disappeared.

The stadium, an absolutely awe-inspiring sight, was within touching distance but we had to walk away from it before we could go through the first security entrance some way from where the buses stopped. The security entrance, number 25 for the record, perhaps summed up China's efficient inefficiency more than anything else. In expectation of the masses coming through this gate, there was a considerable distance of snake like barriers that ran parallel with each other. When we arrived, there were only four or five of us coming through at our entrance, due to our lateness. However, we were still compelled to walk the full circuit of this snaky path with no shortcuts permitted, during which volunteers directed us to carry on walking as if there was some choice in our pre-determined path. Finally though, and within touching distance of the prize, I dragged Hannah across a massive concrete standing to the stadium where we discovered our entrance was on the opposite side. We made our way round and queued to buy a drink as the heat and effort was taking its toll. After much un-British queue barging by all and sundry, we were finally placed one before the front, behind a colossal lady with bulbous arms. We watched incredulously as she took the opportunity to put those chunky arms on her hips and scan the large neon menu signs visible from miles away. After she departed with her tray of food large enough to feed her stand, I ordered the drinks, some popcorn and a sausage. The drinks arrived but I sighed wearily when I was given two vouchers for the separate popcorn and sausage queues at the far end.

We finally found our £100+ seats just as the last runners of the day left the stadium, leaving us with some women throwing a sharp stick around and jumping into a big sandpit. Nevertheless, Hannah, who lacked great expectations, seemed in awe and it was great to be there. The seats were comfortable and offered a great view of, on the whole, inactivity. The stadium was a masterpiece, a work of art by Chinese artist and architect, Ai Weiwei who came up with the idea of a bird's nest during an intensive brain storming process with the Swiss architecture firm, Herzog & de Meuron. He did not, however, attend the opening ceremony of the Olympics, choosing instead to boycott it because "an Olympics held without freedom and against the will of the people will be nonsense, because no totalitarian regime can play at being a democracy" he was quoted as saying. He was very critical of the Chinese government for their stance on democracy and human rights and especially for exiling his father, the poet Ai Qing, to a desert labour camp during the Cultural Revolution, for being the wrong kind of intellectual. He spent most of his life in America and only returned to Beijing in 1993 to see his dying father. His political views are never published in China and his anti-Olympics views were ignored by the Chinese media. Still, he did a cracking stadium.

My attempts at finding a schedule of events proved fruitless (even the China Daily News, the only English paper in China, didn't offer a schedule for the following day) and the smiling volunteers couldn't understand a word I said.

We eventually decided to leave and failed to find our bus now that the army of volunteers had disappeared, so we walked in the smoggy, tiring heat. Even Hannah, who loved all the attention and the photographs, held her hand up at one point when being approached for yet another a picture, and in the style of a seasoned diva declared "Not today thanks."

We met up with the rest of our clan and Lesley Ashmall from Radio Five Live who took us for our most expensive Chinese yet where we relayed our journey so far to her. She had interviewed us before we left and was now doing a follow-up piece. She told us of her experiences of China both now and when she travelled through it when she was younger.

"I was absolutely gobsmacked when I saw Beijing again," she told us in her lilting Scottish brogue. The kids performed great when they were being interviewed but displayed the perfect yin and yang by running around the restaurant hitting each other with fans when it was our turn.

Time was against us in Beijing but there was a section of the Great Wall about 40 km away that we thought we'd have time to visit, Nancyless as we were. It proved to be a long and convoluted journey and the taxi driver lost his way twice.

I never quite understood the strategic benefit of building big walls to stop marauding armies and people as history had shown that they don't. Nevertheless, it was only when I set eyes upon it as we hit the summit of our climb at Badaling, witnessing its climbs and dips over the mountain ridges as far as I could see, that I truly appreciated its status as one of the Seven Great Wonders of the World. Our visit felt almost fraudulent as we sprinted from the car onto the cable car up to the top, took a few snaps and then straight back down and into the taxi. A place I had always wanted to visit and one that adorned the inside cover of my treasured *Purnell's Illustrated Atlas* that I had as a kid and when I finally stood at the wall, there was little time to savour it. Not for the first time I questioned the point of our itinerary.

With that box ticked we dashed back to Tiananmen Square for another one. Although not quite akin to the experience undergone by the heroically audacious student standing in front of a column of Type 59 tanks in 1989, we did feel vulnerable as we were attacked from all angles with umbrellas, fans and guidebooks, all being cunningly and insistently employed to separate us from our children for their photo calls. In addition, we had more "hello" people, who approached us with their well-rehearsed English greeting before thrusting their wares in front of us in the hope that we'd purchase some Tiananmen Square pictures or Chairman Mao stamps. Stopping to look at anything was consumer suicide as it immediately attracted all the other traders, in addition to beggars and those after more photographs with our kids.

A crowd gathered for the daily lowering of the national flag in the square, but we elected to spend an hour stationary in a taxi heading back to the hotel. By all accounts, Beijing authorities had severely restricted private vehicle usage during the time of the games, but it was still busier than London at Christmas so I could only imagine what it was like when there was no ban.

The final day of our sprint tour of one of the most remarkable and historical cities on the planet led to us meeting up with a friend, Andy Hooper, who was there in his capacity as the Daily Mail's chief sports photographer. He suppressed my normal, natural enthusiasm and jealousy of his work with tales of 18 hour days with no rest, making me feel even more ashamed that he had given up his first morning off to treat us to lunch. We were looking forward to seeing him but afterwards we were both taken aback by just how exuberant we both felt at seeing someone we knew from back home.

He left us as we set foot in the Forbidden City, a city within a city that had previously been inaccessible to outsiders for 500 years. Generations of people had been born, lived and died there without ever leaving the city walls. Again, parallels with Croydon. The place was quite stirring with courtyards leading into courtyards and pagodas adorning the mounts with their respective throne rooms.

"This throne room was the room where the emperor went to think before going to the next throne room," a nearby guide explained confusingly.

The guidebook recommended at least half a day and that is what we roughly spent having the kids' pictures taken; we stopped walking at our peril and eye contact was avoided at all times. At one stage, during some unscheduled shoelace tying, they took us by surprise when the old "sweet handed over to the kid" chestnut acted as the catalyst for a marauding crowd of men, women and children to overrun our position. Eirene was the first casualty, jostled out the way by a lady declaring angrily "My turn, you wait."

The novelty had worn off and we didn't want it anymore so we split up in an attempt to reduce the sore thumb nature of our three child family, but it was a nugatory gesture. Like packs of wolves they hunted us down one by one, dividing and conquering. At one point Emily was on the verge of wetting herself yet still they wanted more. Like the recruits half an hour into *Saving Private Ryan,* we quickly became battle hardened and wised up our tactics. Despite all the activity, we managed to see most of The Forbidden City, albeit very rapidly.

There were certain places we had to see but they were invariably an anticlimax by virtue of the fact that we had seen them from afar so many times before. They offered no surprises and big crowds. There was much to be said for going and seeing and knowing nothing beforehand. I always imagined the undiluted pleasure of seeing the Victoria Falls through Livingstone's eyes and not after I'd heard countless accounts, read pages upon pages of narrative and flicked through a wealth of filtered and photoshopped photographs. The Forbidden City fell squarely into that category. Truly remarkable but, having been built up so much, it ultimately fell short of the hype. My children, however, were Livingstone and hadn't read, listened and looked in advance so I was fortunate that I could take the pleasures from their uninformed faces. Wider reading and the internet had not yet taken their toll on them.

We only had three days in Beijing, a city alive with the Olympic spirit like I would never have imagined. The facilities were absolutely second to none – a superb underground system, when they use it, and brand new stadiums at every turn. Accusations flew of "a smiling face for the Olympics" but from what we saw of the rest of China that didn't hold true and it was a country that was always smiling. Admittedly it put on its best Sunday clothes with thousands of cars banned from the roads, building sites covered with mesh, industrial production halted, spitting actively discouraged and litter-free streets patrolled at night by workers on electric mopeds, feeding off scraps. For a city where smoking seemed to be compulsory, even cigarette butts couldn't be seen. Flower beds sat alongside recycling bins and spectator guides gave instructions on queuing, manners and how to conduct oneself at the various sporting events. For this I could offer no criticism. Like washing a car before you sell it, or preparing lesson plans before an Ofsted inspection, it's natural and should be condoned not condemned. Ai Weiwei has it down as "a pretend harmony and happiness" but the pride was genuine.

We took the overnight train back to Xian and arrived at 8.30am with Eirene having slept much better than on the way out. Morale was high, the family was buoyant and everyone was pleased to see Nancy again and the feeling seemed to be reciprocal. She had gifts of chocolate for the girls who had comedy-sized fans for her in return. Emily in particular had been sobbing uncontrollably when we left for Beijing without her and we worried about what she would be like when he had to say goodbye for good.

Back in our own car, we made our way along a winding road that weaved its way through the base of a gorge of the

Chingling Mountains, the natural divider between north and south China. This was panda country and we all wanted to see a panda. Even the kids lifted their heads from their consoles to go on panda watch. We were briefly teased with a blast of English music, albeit not English tunes, from Xian FM Radio or whatever it was called, before the peaks rendered the signal into silence.

A tissue had caught itself on the front bull bars and it was a waiting game between Eirene and me before one of us broke (Eirene) and asked to stop the car because we both knew, unspoken as it was, that they who called it would have to remove it. We headed for Guanyuan in the Sichuan province, which was the scene of devastating earthquakes that had struck a few days after we left the UK. They were the strongest to hit China in almost 60 years, measuring eight on the Richter Scale; they killed an incomprehensible 70,000 people, injured 375,000 and were felt thousands of kilometres away. I asked Nancy why the parks, roads, pavements, car parks and almost every square inch of the town of Guanyuan was covered in blue tents. "That's where people live now," she said, and I cringed at my naivety. It was 100 days to the day since the earthquakes hit the province many miles away from this city yet the devastation it caused was still in our faces. Occasionally, interspersed between the blue tents, would be the latest bulbous Vango tent, left by the now departed UN who were briefly permitted to visit. The faces of the people showed little attestation as to what had happened and they greeted us in the same way the rest of China had – fascinated and with open arms. Tragic events like these put life into perspective and rightly belittled our minor first world troubles. What was evident was that the best aspects of humanity were there in abundance, working together, sharing what little they had to help rebuild each other's lives.

To date Nancy had always secured us accommodation on or near the ground floor for ease, we assumed, of carrying all the bags.

"I get you very nice view," she declared with great pride, as she handed over the keys to an eighth floor room when, for once, we all would have preferred being under a staircase in the cellar in this volatile area. I had even had nightmares about the earthquake on the overnight train from Beijing, coinciding with the rocking of the carriage.

I couldn't sleep but this wasn't due to any seismic dreaming. It was excitement at a call from the Daily Mail who wanted to do a spread on us the following Saturday after hearing us on the radio. I spent most of the evening sending off high resolution pictures of our trip to the reporter at the paper, excited at the thought of being in this national paper. The Daily Mail's formulaic content repulsed me in the way it grabbed, twisted, distorted and fuelled middle England's paranoia, fears and stereotypes whilst pandering to, nay creating, right wing prejudices [10]. It stood for everything I stood against but hell, my parents loved it and I was happy to compromise all my principles for my 10 minutes of fame. Plucking a few gems from the past, my folks, via the Daily Mail, had reliably informed me that "English has been banned in schools" to which I replied, "No it hasn't, Dad."

"It has," he continued, "they're talking about banning it."

"No, Dad, there is one school, in one borough, where they are offering bilingual lessons to a population whose first language isn't English."

My dad would authoritatively inform me, "You can't get admitted into A&E unless you pay cash up front."

"What happens if you are unconscious then?" I queried.

"It doesn't matter" he states, shaking his head.

And all of this is continuously overlaid with house prices crashing and immigrants on benefits living in £1million houses interspersed with something about Diana. The reverence with which this publication is held above absolutely anything else,

---

[10] Naturally notwithstanding the excellent sports section and award-winning photography

against even first-hand experiences or expert testimony, would lead to probably the proudest moment of my parents' lives. The level of esteem that the publication of our story would raise them to in the Spanish ex-pat community was beyond comprehension. The racist bile combined with my nauseous hypocrisy as I kept my fingers crossed that it would be printed despite my fears of a "British family escapes from immigrants and falling property prices" headline. I quickly emailed Shameen and asked her to sort out the appropriate laminating and framing of the publication.

Sleepless as I am, I belatedly read up about Guanyuan just as we are due to leave. At breakfast I elect not to share *Lonely Planet's* words about the place to Eirene who seemed jubilant about not waking up in a mountain of rubble - "...the site of China's largest nuclear weapons-grade plutonium production facility, so nobody really lingers here..." It just made sense what with her hostility over my proposed Chernobyl visit.

We found our pandas at the Chengdu Research Base of Giant Panda Breeding where among them were two red pandas and a giant panda nursery. There were also enclosures for giant panda cubs, adult giant pandas and sub-adult giant pandas as well as a panda hospital, a panda kitchen and, of course, the obligatory panda gift shop selling cute (toy) pandas in every conceivable panda mould. I think I got off quite lightly having to pay out for only three hand-sized giant pandas. The centre itself is well renowned as it has an international reputation for its work on breeding. Nevertheless, Eirene and I left with a bad taste our mouths at the enclosed conditions the pandas were kept in. In fairness, only slightly more than marginally worse than UK zoos, but sad all the same. They do make attempts at releasing them back into the wild but with a survival rate of about 32%, the light at the end of the tunnel for most of them is a metaphorical train coming towards them.

We were now fully ensconced in Buddha country and spent the day visiting the Jiajiang Thousand Buddha Cliff, which we approached through a small quiet village. We stood at the top of the crooked stone steps and looked down at the Qingy River on our left below us and a wall of carvings on our right. As we descended, it was like looking through windows of a multi-storey building; each of the 200 shallow caves held Buddhas in various scenes and postures. There were over 2,400 incredibly detailed and intricate carved Buddhas dating back to the Tang Dynasty with some still showing details of lapis blue paint. Water leeched from the water table and ran down the red sandstone walls, nourishing a bloom of colourful green mosses which framed each of the Buddha niches.

We then took a river boat cruise to see the largest stone Buddha in the world, whose construction began in 713AD. The Leshan Giant Buddha stands at the confluence of the Minjiang, Qingy, and the Dadu rivers. The Chinese monk, Haitong, believed that the Buddha would calm the waters between the two Dadu and Minjiang rivers to make it safer for shipping. This was indeed what happened but whether you want to believe it was the powers of the Buddha, or the deposition of giant stones in the river while the Buddha was under construction, is entirely up to you.

We had been in China for nearly three of our four weeks and, as we'd established early on, it was a huge country to cover in such a short time. As such, our days tended to follow a similar routine. Within a couple of minutes of waking, the blood would start to return to our numb limbs after a night on the rock hard beds. The little buggers are deceiving as they look like normal beds with legs, sprung mattress, sheets and all the gubbins but they give little more than a degree of elevation above the floor. Eirene had even slept on the floor on occasions just for some posturepedic padding from the carpet.

While Chinese dinners offered a wide and varied selection of food, breakfasts offered the converse, which was typically a buffet of spicy and vinegary vegetables and some meat dishes. Nancy, who only appeared to eat once a day despite our insistent attempts at buying her lunch and dinner, would tuck into all with great zest and understandable repeat visits. On a good day we would have watermelon, a boiled egg and even corn on the cob. On a bad day we would just put some stuff on our plates almost out of politeness. Back in the room, I would be pressed to find some tissues in the car or go looking for some toilet paper from one of the maids. Without exception there was never a spare roll of toilet paper in a Chinese hotel room. More often than not, there was only half a roll or less to begin with, and public or restaurant toilets were always without any relevant material at all. My position was that it was a silent cultural protest by the Chinese, who have virtually invented everything there is except paper. Eirene's position was that they don't wipe their arses properly.

As we prepared to leave the hotel each morning, we moved our belongings down to the car for what became known as Operation Square Peg into Round Hole. We cleared out the previous day's rubbish and old food and Eirene began her jigsaw puzzle of packing the bags and six people back into the car. Nancy had added spice to this by bringing her comedy-sized suitcase, not much smaller than herself. I got the impression that she looked at our limited selection of apparel in puzzlement and I wondered if she had picked up that we looked at her fresh daily change of clothes and varied wardrobe with just a little resentment. When we finally set off, we typically stopped at a supermarket, "just for some bread" Eirene would say. Half an hour later Eirene would return, breadless, with Nancy and three weeks' worth of shopping, which she crammed into my passenger footwell. Towards mid-morning I would start to feel like I was having a stroke, with no movement or feeling down the shopping bag side of my body.

At every junction as we left a town, we'd have to prompt Nancy for directions. Throughout the journey, at any busy junction or motorway exit, she would almost imperceptibly whisper "Wait a moment." Sometimes she would have us sit stationary at busy junctions for a good few minutes before she whispered "left." Eirene would turn left and then her whisper will rise to a loud "No, no!" before we realised that she meant the other left. "Right is the hand you write with," Eirene would remind her again. I'd look at Nancy and realised she didn't understand a word Eirene was saying.

Emily would often, almost subconsciously, ask for the toilet within the first half hour but we had learnt it was a token gesture and merely notice of an 11am requirement. Nancy had no qualms about stopping and asking people for directions, which we did on a regular basis. Only one of the cities we had been to, Turpan, had Nancy visited previously. If the direction request involved Nancy leaving the car, the kids would remind her to put her seatbelt on when she hopped back in. She didn't like wearing a seatbelt and I think she thought we were asking her for her protection. But for the same reason that we tightly secured 20kg boxes with strappings capable of holding three times that weight, we really didn't want her flying around if we had an accident.

As we drove out of town, cars would drive towards us on our side of the road and there would be a few emergency stops as people pulled out from side roads without even a pause, thus allowing Eirene the pleasure of using our air-horn. Signalling for any purpose was taboo and having indicators constantly on for no purpose was actively encouraged. Green lights were treated with caution as tuc tucs (rickshaws with an engine) and rickshaws (tuc tucs without an engine) zigzagged across our path, interspersed with mopeds, as they all vied for space between the multitude of mirrorless lorries. Children as young as one and two ran around the road on their own in their crotchless trousers and grown, suit-wearing men elected to squat down next to each other when in conversation just as one would over the hole-in-the-floor toilets that monopolise the entire crapping market in China.

On the toilet front we were frequently forced to use petrol station toilets which were literally holes in the floor with places to place your feet and no indication of whether you faced the wall or your audience. There were no doors between cubicles and only three foot high walls separating them. Sometimes there was just a shared trench where we could see the previous occupants' digested remnants of breakfast, lunch and dinner. I have no words to describe the stench. Some of them even had a cheeky token charge to use the dirt-ridden dungeons. Eirene would always tactfully let Nancy go first so that neither party had the embarrassment of witnessing or, God forbid, hearing the other doing their business. Nancy would always come out and report that the toilets were fine, which was always at odds with Eirene's subsequent account. On one toilet excursion, though, Nancy quickly returned to the car and vehemently shook her head and, despite some considerable pressing, would only utter the word "No."

Beyond the Olympic capital city, poverty was not hidden. Shops by the roadside with the entire shop front open to the street sold absolutely everything from tyres to sandwiches. The roads varied between tarmac and gravel. Tuc tucs laden with fruit, vegetables and abnormal-sized loads dominated the city roads and we even saw one with a fire on the go in the back. Where there were two lanes the law dictated you drive in the right lane, although protocol dictated that you either drive on the left or straddle both lanes. For a country with some ghastly road surfaces the attitude of the lorries was extraordinary. They suddenly changed lanes for the most minute bump in the road, which would necessitate them dropping their speed down to marginally quicker than stationary. When moving, they would dominate the wrong side of the road for lengthy periods if the surface looked remotely better than their own side. All vehicles would, when we attempted to overtake, stray towards us in some sort of odd token blocking ceremony. And it was wet! We were there in the rainy season and the wipers were constantly on. In agricultural terms, all land was utilised neatly and effectively with mountainsides terraced to waste nothing and the rain presumably suited the countless paddy and tobacco fields that we passed. Patches of mist dotted the mountainsides and, as we drove higher, it became thick fog over the bumpiest roads. We were amused when they turned into tarmac just before the randomly placed toll booths, which varied between three RMB (23p) and 130 RMB (£10). We inevitably came across a slow moving truck and, despite a polite beep from us and an indication that we were overtaking, they still moved out to avoid a rock the size of raisin. We soon realised that leaves strewn together on the road, or a couple of rocks, acted as the Chinese equivalent of a warning triangle.

Pedestrians too played the blocking game, walking four or five abreast, often in the centre of the road and men rolled up their shirts to just below their nipples in some sort of strange attempt at a bikini come crop-top. Pleasingly for our stereotypes, the lantern-type Chinese hats we knew from pictures adorned many in these parts of China. They looked at us in wonderment and embraced us with open arms and a good deal of staring, but there wasn't even a hint of acrimony or fear of attack that might be experienced in similar circumstances in the UK. Their lives looked so primitive and yet they seemed so happy. Putting the driving to one side, we felt safe.

Eirene would drive for the first few hours before we swapped over and she doled out food to the chirping birds in the back. Previously this was something I had done but it became a role she took on since we arrived in China and I was grateful for it, but the format was a little risky. Eirene would unsheathe the sharpest blade of my sponsored Leatherman tool and employ it to jam some sweet bread as I drove over crater-sized potholes, avoiding braking lorries and swerving dramatically to avoid other unexpected obstructions. It was a bit like *It's a Knock-out* with no Health and Safety Executive, but the kids were fed, the car messed up and Eirene somehow managed to avoid disembowelment by hari-kari every time she undertook the routine.

To pass the time, Eirene and I pointed out things of interest and asked each other questions like "What is the biggest mistake you've ever made?" and "Who, if you had to choose, would you arrange to have eliminated?" (These two, we found, were often linked). I learnt that Eirene would have liked a better marriage proposal from me; that she was most scared when we hired a car and drove through winding roads in Cyprus; that she has, in her opinion, made no really big mistakes; and that she can't even name one big breasted weatherwoman (her suggestion of Angela Rippon clearly not counting on either point).

Between three and 14 hours after we started, we would arrive at our destination. Often, we had to ask for directions and sometimes Nancy would hop in a taxi, which she always paid for herself, and we would follow her. Every time she used a taxi, she did a thing that I found really endearing. As the taxi pulled off, she would pop her head out the window and wave enthusiastically at us to follow her. We always did but it left me wondering that there must have been a time as a guide when she clambered into the taxi in front of her tourist group, drove off and then realised, on arrival at the hotel, that they hadn't followed, having not been given an official wave. Nancy was great at sorting out the keys and paperwork with the hotel while we unloaded the car and waited for her return. She would always help us take the bags to our room and make sure we had enough duvets and pillows and that everything was fine. She would then ask us "What time we meet for dinner?" We'd usually settle down and I played with the kids as they often had unused energy from sitting in the car all day. Hannah frequently had a load more energy and our enthusiastic karate fights often turned messy. I begrudged her un-kung-fu like scratching but recalled something similar in the Hall of Mirrors across Bruce Lee's chest in *Enter the Dragon,* so maybe I was being harsh.

We would then meet up with Nancy and were normally not late as the children's empty stomachs mandated a good degree of promptness. Nancy always asked, "Chinese or Western?" and Hannah would always reply "Sweet and sour chicken and egg fried rice please." On the odd occasion we enquired, "Do they have Western restaurants here?" and Nancy would reply, without any hint of a smile, "No." We would amble off to a local restaurant and every time would be greeted like long lost family. A boiling hot bowl of tea was immediately brought to the table and put in front of us all, including the curious, just turned two-year-old Abigail. Restaurants nearly always sold beer although it normally wasn't cold; sometimes they sold Sprite but rarely sold water. Half an hour after the food arrived it looked like we'd emptied everything on the table. Nancy refused to eat saying that she was not hungry. We tried everything, but I guess she felt it would be impolite, improper or against her employer's directions.

Customers frequently came over, smiling and bringing their kids for pictures. The men too would smile, produce prolonged guttural attempts at extracting as much phlegm from the bowels of their gullet as possible, before depositing it on the floor alongside us. Smoke filled most restaurants and the lit cigarettes were discarded on the floor and no one, bar us, batted an eyelid. We normally paid about £8 for all of us but sometimes it was as cheap as £2 or £3 for an evening meal. Western food, on the very rare occasions we would encounter it in major cities, was much more expensive.

Sunday 24th August 2008 though was different to our normal routine. The formula and approach were the same as above, but the first hint of trouble came as we robotically packed the car and Nancy chose at that point to say, "We have a long day today, eight hours at least." It was 10.30am and if we had known it was going to be so long we would at least have gone through the charade with the kids of trying to leave early but our itinerary had it as 350 km and our map said it was motorway. We pointed this out to Nancy, who had been suggesting a wiggly though more direct yellow road, but she agreed and we drove back in the opposite direction along the motorway before turning at a junction and coming back south again. Something happened and subsequent debriefs did not quite establish exactly what, but the thinking was that the motorway on our map that was shown as built and not under construction, hadn't actually been started. Maybe it was a wrong turn or bad directions or misquoted mileage figures but at 3.30pm, after five hours of driving, a man at a toll booth told us we had 400 km to go. Naturally, like any person in the world who was quoting distance, we had to fight to get the actual distance out of him and initially he said it was nine hours. No matter where you are, if you ask anyone local how far X is, they will frustratingly give you the answer in time.

"How far is it from the airport?"

"Oh, about an hour."

"Really? I drive at 5mph – is that still the case or could the speed I drive at in any way be a factor? Actually, I know the speed I drive at and I know my average speed on a motorway in non-rush hour conditions and this, believe it or not, may well be radically different from your own. So, bearing that excruciatingly obvious fact in mind, can we jump straight to the distance part? You know, the part I asked at the beginning?"

This last bit is obviously an anguished internal monologue that rattles on in the background when my mouth is actually uttering "So how many kilometres would you say?"

And off we tentatively set. On our right hand side, a mud-filled shallow bubbling river bordered regimental rice fields and manicured terraces were blighted by the occasional enormous boulder from previous landslides. On our left, lush green mountains rose up from the road, scarred only by ruts of historical and recent landslides. Sensational backdrops lay ahead of us with waterfalls, canyons, winding track ways and even more fields. From time to time, the mountain peaks revealed themselves from their clouded veils. The rain moved seamlessly from a drizzle to torrential and visibility dropped to a car's length in places. Of course, no one put their lights on. It was like a segment from *Top Gear* - the road narrow, barely enough room for two vehicles to pass. On our left were trees and cliffs but on our right, the barrier-free road dropped to... well, I never did find out, thankfully, but it looked a long way down. We approached a long queue of lorries and, as is traditional in China, being a car, we overtook them. We thought it was a toll road, but it turned out to be an accident at a sharp bend where a car going down the hill had driven straight into the side of a lorry cutting the corner coming up the hill, sending the latter nose diving into a maize field. Diesel spilled from the lorry and petrol flowed from the car, the liquid intersection of which was becoming the unofficial gathering point for the smoking spectators. I approached with my shiny western first aid kit, but it quickly became apparent that there were no injuries of note. As the queue built up, with the help of Nancy translating, I offered to move one or both vehicles out of the way to the side of the road with our winch. Both parties consistently refused saying they needed to wait for the police to turn up and examine the scene. In 2007, over 81,000 [11] people died in road accidents in China, equating to one every six and a half minutes, 24 hours a day, every day of the year. For a country and police force so completely unconcerned with road safety that no-one wore helmets, seatbelts, obeyed any directions, flow of traffic or rode a moped with less than two people on it, I assumed they were taking the mickey. But no, it was genuine. We waited an hour for two policemen to turn up, take some snaps and measurements, have a smoke themselves in the petrol pool before eventually instructing the locals to push the vehicles out of the way. They then took this as an opportunity to stand with their hands on their hips and look bemused as cars, buses and lorries from both directions battled to pass through the now single carriageway, over a road full of broken glass and slippery diesel. Unsurprisingly, chaos ensued and more cars were hit. We escaped the shambles after two hours but quickly came to a halt a few yards down the road where buses and lorries blocked both carriageways coming back up as impatience had clearly got the better of those waiting in the queue.

It was now approaching 7pm and we were running really late. We had about 200 miles to go, one packet of Pringles and half a tank of petrol. Moreover, the light was fading and we were going to be driving at night. Not just any night but a monsoony

---

[11] http://english.peopledaily.com.cn/90001/90776/90882/6378731.html

night, on rubbish mud tracks masquerading as roads, with hair pin bends and massive drops at the side. As we pushed forward, the rain seemed to be bringing down half the mountainside with landslides every 300 metres, some almost blocking the road entirely. At one point we stopped as boulders the size of our car reigned down from the high cliffs to our left and passed over our road to other unfortunate roads below. Hannah came out of the car and watched in amazement at the sight in front of her as she simultaneously weed on the ground (pre-planned and not out of fear). Darkness descended and I could sense Eirene's unease but I was driving as fast as conditions would allow. We stopped counting the number of accidents when we hit double figures. One recipient, whose mangled car was blocking most of the carriageway, refused my offer of help to move it out the way. Nancy translated that he could not move the car until the insurance company made it there. It was 7.30pm on a Sunday, 300 miles from the nearest big town so I was mightily impressed with the service the insurance companies provide. No-one complained.

This was Eirene's Cypriot winding roads but worse and it never seemed to end. By 9.30pm we had been driving for 11 hours with only a couple of stops in some petrol station toilets. It was dark. Dark like a city dweller never experiences, no street lights, no neon signs and there wasn't even a twinkle from the electricity-free mountain villages. Thick cloud obscured any hope of moonlight. The frequent flashes of lightning only briefly exposed the heavy rain where it had weathered its own channels as it ran off the mountains to our left, down the road and over the unnerving vertical and barrierless drop a matter of feet from the side of the road. Such was the shuddering I could feel through the car that I started to think there was a problem with the engine mountings before realising it was earth tremors. The headlights struggled to illuminate a stream of moving hillside in front of us and there was only blackness behind.

"How long do you think Nancy?" Eirene quivered.

"Soon," Nancy repeated.

The situation was like nothing we'd ever experienced and I felt out of control, like we were some minor characters playing a part in a choreographed action film, waiting to be written out of the script by some horrific natural disaster. The car was severely tested as we ploughed through mud, up ravines and waded through deep water on the hairpin bends. On another day this would have been an exciting challenge, an adventure to be relived and regaled again and again in the pub. But this time, with the precious load I was carrying, I was scared but tried to show a calm and optimistic exterior.

I didn't think it was possible but conditions deteriorated even further. My mind wandered back to Nancy's boss telling me that earthquakes are a daily occurrence in this region and the crazy paving tarmac bore testament to this. I didn't share it but dwelt on what would happen if one of the minor tremors turned into a bigger one as we perched on the high, narrow roads. Leslie Ashmall, the Radio Five reporter who I had spoken to over the phone before we met up in Beijing, enquired about any hairy moments we had encountered; at that time I couldn't think of one.

Before we left the UK, I had reluctantly agreed to always go on the main roads despite the cost in missed sights and experiences it might have brought. I saw the cost of our equipment and thoroughness of our vehicle preparation as an insurance policy and not something that I thought we would need. We had come across great off-roading routes with river crossings and sludge-filled ravines that I mournfully avoided but this was the deal with Eirene and it was the right one (I suppose!). Risks could wait until the kids had left home. Only a couple of days before we had opted for Plan B of our itinerary as Plan A, towards the grasslands of Tibet, was badly affected by mudslides, making many roads impassable. Having seen the conditions on our Plan B road, I could not imagine how they could have become any worse. If we managed to avoid being knocked off the road by a landslide, the chances of us not coming across one that completely blocked the road seemed remote. I had spades and a winch and other helpful stuff but they wouldn't have moved us past a road blocking landslide, which would mean another six hours driving back the way we came, if that was indeed possible. A sleep in the car, on these vulnerable mountain passes, looked suicidal.

I decided that we would have to stop at the next village, no matter how unlit it was. With this thought in mind, I rounded a bend and through the rain saw a large lorry coming straight towards me. The road was narrow, we couldn't both pass, and he was coming downhill with no sign of slowing. He was bigger than me and that was the clincher. He closed in, 100 metres, 80, 50 and still showed no sign of slowing. His loud airhorn offered no solution and I pulled as far to the right as I could, away from the edge, and into the darkness in an effort to slink against the steep rock.

The right side of the car immediately sunk and we came to a sludgy halt as he drove past without any hint of deviation. It was only about a foot drop from the road side and I changed to low ratio and full diff-lock to try to pull us out as I turned the wheel sharply left. The offside wheels skidded along the side of the concrete verge but showed no sign of mounting it. There was a gap of no more than two feet between the road and the wall of rock which prevented me from turning the car and hitting the verge straight on. I looked around in vain, searching for the lorry driving culprit, in the hope that he had stopped to check on us and pull us out but he was long gone. The car sank deeper as my attempts became more desperate. I tried reversing but to no avail. I reluctantly stepped out of the car, into the rain, and realised that I would have to use the sand-ladders that I had so tightly and securely attached to the roof rack. They were very light and allegedly very strong and replaced my thick and heavy waffle boards that I'd had in my Land Rover days. The rain showed no signs of abating as I set about unpacking everything from the roof rack in the dark. I set them up as a bridge between the drop and the road and climbed back into the driver's seat. As I mounted them, they contorted like liquorice under the weight of the Land Cruiser and I realised that their name might give a clue as to their suitability in this environment and for this purpose. Various combinations of placing them differently didn't help, albeit they were by now virtually warped balls of steel. Eirene and Nancy had joined me in a show of solidarity in the pounding rain under Nancy's small sun umbrella and I gave it one final, tyre ripping attempt to pull us out but it was hopeless.

So there we were, everyone's eyes expectantly on me, with the threat of a landslide avalanching upon us all at any time. I clawed at my brain and scanned the surroundings for a plan C and spotted a roadside pillar 30 yards away, barely a couple of feet high. I elected to forego the fluorescent jacket, warning triangle and safety gloves, and pull the winch kit out from the roof box. I grabbed the winch remote, connected it up and reeled out 35 yards of steel winch cable. I threw a strop round the lone, apparently pointless, pillar and secured it with a shackle which I attached to my winch hook. I didn't check the rigidity of the pillar as I knew that no matter what I discovered, I would still give it a go. I hopped back into the car, turned the wheel hard left into the verge, and pressed the retract button on the winch remote control that clung to my shaking wet hand. I revved the engine in an effort to give it more power. At first, it took up the slack before jolting to a virtual stop as it hit the tension of my wheel and 2.5 tonne car against the verge. My CSE physics told me that at this point, as I optimistically continued to press on the retract button, the weakest link in my chain would go. As I contemplated whether this would be the strop, the shackle, or, more likely, the pillar, the car slowly moved. I kept the button pressed on the remote and the car continued to obey my will and eased gently forward until the front right wheel bumbled over the edge of the verge onto the road. Still shaking and dripping wet, I excitedly continued to gently accelerate and pull us out until finally the car became pleasurably level again. The relief was palpable. We had to quickly attach everything back onto the car and three drowned rats squelched back into their seats. We benevolently allowed the waiting lorry that had just come up behind us to pass in front, something we later regretted, and set off on our way again. The rain was still relentless and the windscreen wipers gave up the ghost.

"OK, we might have to wait here a bit," I announced, far more confidently than I felt, as I pulled over, knowing, from the growing array of rocks on the road, that we would be hit by something from above if we did. It was just the size of the hitting object that was up for debate.

I made the token effort of heading out into the monsoon again to check the wipers, knowing that there would be little I could do to fix a motor here. An equal mix of annoyance and elation hit me as I discovered that the buckle from one of the sand ladder straps that I regrettably omitted to re-attach in my rush, had jammed itself between the bonnet and the wiper. I removed it and the wipers sprung into life.

Nancy had been keen for us to make our allotted town but had, after a united protest from us, conceded that it might be best to find a place at the next big town we came to. After a number of false dawns where what we thought was the outskirts of small town but were just tiny isolated settlements, we finally arrived at the next big place. Nancy fled our car and jumped into a taxi to ask for directions to the hotel, which turned out to be right beside us. Nine hours after asking the man in the hut the distance (yes, he was right, but that's not the point!) and 14 hours after departing, we were all exhausted and burnt out from the hardest driving we had endured to date. We felt like competitors in the Paris Dakar race, albeit with the burden of carrying heavy bags and crying kids up to the room at the end of the most difficult leg. Nancy, as always, literally carried more than her weight and proved to be a top girl under pressure. An hour later, with the kids asleep and Eirene and I sharing a bottle of beer and tucking into a big pot noodle she had made in the room, we kissed and smiled. Again, when push came to shove and we were in the trenches, she had come up trumps without a word of complaint although she did calmly declare at that point that she never wanted to have another day like that again.

When Emily was born, we sought medical advice on numerous occasions as she would repeatedly go blue and stop breathing in her sleep. It was a very worrying time, but it was diagnosed as reflux, quite a common though nevertheless dangerous condition. We thought it had all been sorted but on one final "best be safe" visit to the hospital, following lots of waiting and numerous checks, the doctor walked in as we were holding hands and happily making plans for the rest of the evening, buoyed by the optimistic and reassuring words of the nurses. The doctor looked up from the clipboard she was gripping with both hands, paused and told us they would have to keep her in overnight for some more checks as she wasn't happy. That moment, when we both welled up simultaneously and tears started their journey down our cheeks as we stared open-mouthed at the now shocked doctor, felt like the closest I had ever been to my wife. That was until the evening of Sunday 24th August 2008 when we held hands again. Tragic but true that it is the bad times that unite people and not the good.

Sobering news a few days later reported that an earthquake measuring 6.1 on the Richter scale had hit Panzhihua, the last town we were in. That was minor by Wang Lun's standards but there were 40 dead and 10,000 homes destroyed. Although China had felt like a very safe place to travel with the family, we had actually been playing dodge ball with earthquakes, landslides and terrorist attacks for the last month.

After such a perilous and exhausting journey, we decided to spend a few days at Lijiang. Our plan had been to spend only a day there and then drive north to the multi-named Zhongdian, which was renamed to Shangri-La in 2001 to encourage tourists and is also known by its Tibetan name, Gyaitang. I had heard it was an appealing town by all accounts. but Eirene suggested that we all have a break and spend five nights in Lijiang to charge our batteries, to which I agreed.

The old town of Lijiang is on the Ancient Tea Horse Road, a network of ancient trade routes which is sometimes referred to as the Southern Silk Road. It has a unique style of architecture, history and culture compared to other Chinese cities and it was easy to become lost in the maze of cobbled streets.

Lijiang looked like it hadn't changed a great deal from the one Peter Goulllart penned about in his book *Forgotten Kingdom,* in which he described his experiences of living with the Naxi people, or Nakhi as he called them, of the region during the 1930s and 40s. He considered Lijiang a paradise where the people were genuinely happy and welcoming of strangers.

"In courting friendship with a Nakhi a good deal of sincerity, sympathy and genuine affection was necessary, and also patience. They were a very sensitive people. The Nakhi possessed no inferiority complex but neither did they suffer a show of superiority in anybody. They were not obsequious and did not cringe even in the presence of high-ranking officials or wealthy merchants. Unlike the Chinese in certain parts of China, they were not discomforted or disturbed by strangers of other races."

We spent the four days absorbing the friendliness of these people. The shop staff wore tourist pleasing traditional costumes, although nearly every shop appeared to sell an identical array of trinkets and tat for over-inflated prices and, aesthetically pleasing as it all was, it felt somewhat contrived. Occasionally, however, we caught a glimpse of some originality among the tat when we discovered the odd individual shop selling unique pieces of artwork and handicrafts down a less touristy alley. A silversmith sat outside his shop on a small wooden stool, his anvil screwed into an upturned log which acted as his miniature workbench; an artist painted a street scene in oils, each leg of his stool perched precariously on a couple of bricks to raise him to the height of his easel; and we ate corn on the cob, freshly made at the side of the road.

The labyrinth of a market went on for miles. Plain hessian sacks filled with colourful plant derivatives lined the narrow passages and the air was filled with the rich aromas of spices. We looked pitifully at baby rabbits, cats, dogs, birds and other animals crammed into cages and as my family spent their money on trinkets and clothes, I indulged myself in a 23mm socket. They hid what we wanted to see and exposed what they thought we wanted to see.

To the people of Lijiang, the rivers play a very important role. While building the town, the Naxi people gave priority to the three rivers that flow from the Black Dragon Pool at the foot of Elephant Mountain. Rather than interfering with the flow of the river, as so often occurs in the construction industry in the UK, the rivers were allowed to flow through some of the houses and even their kitchens.

We thought we might pay the famous Jade Dragon Snow Mountains a visit. They are a small mountain range of 13 peaks up to a height of 16,500 feet, each one so high that it is covered in snow all year round. We woke up really early to purchase three oxygen canisters to combat the likelihood of altitude sickness but unfortunately, on top of our £5.50 each tourist tax for the area, they wanted £30 just to drive to the base of the mountain and another £60 to take the cable car up. We compared it to the cost of an annual pass at Legoland and decided that the legend of Jade Dragon and his brother Haba Snow Mountain who fought off an evil fiend would need to remain an unvisited fairy tale. It came as a surprise to us because China had been so cheap and, apart from an isolated £5 pot of tea, there had been a distinct lack of people trying to rip us off.

We did, however, afford ourselves a visit to the Jade Water Village at the base of the Jade Dragon Snow Mountain. Although someone appeared to have had the village away, we did see a large number of streams, hypnotic waterfalls, millwheels and golden statues all surrounded by verdant vegetation and wild alpine flowers. The girls knelt on cushions for photos in front of the impressive towering Dongba human god statue, which stood in a shallow lake. The statue, a female head and body, with hands almost clasped in front of her heart as if in yogic prayer, had a snake's body for legs and cobras flowing down from each of the pleats in her skirt; it is said she depicts the harmony between man and nature in Naxi culture.

We spent two hours allowing other tourists to take our pictures. Abigail caught on to the idea very quickly and posed, like an experienced catwalk model, with her hand behind her head. The girls once again seemed to be more popular than the attraction itself and as Abigail and Emily's profile in holiday albums around China increased, Hannah's popularity visibly waned.

"I'm over the hill," the seven-year-old forlornly told me, as we watched the groups of tourists snapping away at her younger siblings. It is a cruel industry.

A week before we were due to leave China, Nancy dropped the bombshell that it had been decided that no satellite phones would be released back to anyone until the end of the Paralympic games on the 17th September. We had initially been told that it would be returned to us when we left the country. The phone was quite expensive and we were paying an ongoing monthly fee, plus it was meant to be another safeguard for us in South East Asia and Australia. Our mood rapidly changed but we were grateful that she had told us now and not left it until the following Friday when we were due to leave and allegedly pick it up at the border on exit. The problem with the phone appeared to originate from "Big Brother" concerns that it was a very difficult thing for them to monitor. Whatever our feelings on the ethics of that, we could follow the logic to a degree that they needed to retain it while we were in China. Why, though, they felt the need or thought they had the right to hold onto it when we were in Laos and further afield was beyond us.

We were nervous about going into remote northern Laos during monsoon season with three kids and no communication.

Unfortunately, our *Rough Guide to South East Asia*, which was three years out of date, carried with it warnings of bandit attacks and bombs in the north which contradicted the current FCO guidelines. Nevertheless, it was the *Rough Guide's* warnings that stayed with Eirene and she immediately suggested we contact our embassy. She did not want to leave China without the phone when we most needed it. We considered our options and pondered the idea of refusing to leave until it was sorted out. Our visa lasted for 60 days although the documents for the car were only valid for another 10 days. We thought it could be a dangerous game, so we decided to contact the embassy and, adopting the principle of six degrees of separation, emailed every single person we knew to see if they had any contacts or ideas. Some of the initial responses verged on the bleeding obvious but there were some obvious ones that we hadn't thought of, such as contacting our MP and the Mayor of London. Boris Johnson, who had just been elected the day we left on our travels, was not too popular here for some reason to do with breaching protocol by not having his jacket buttoned up. The actual protocol, of course, was having it rolled up to your nipples. We also tried a few newspapers and TV stations as the Chinese were particularly media-sensitive during the Olympics. We did, however, accept that "Family loses mobile phone in China" wasn't really front page news and, juxtaposed with the recent natural and man-made losses of life, fell squarely in the First World problems camp.

Our longer stay in Lijiang marked what we also hoped was a watershed for Hannah. She had been taking too frequent a pleasure in showering misery upon Emily and, on the brief occasions when Emily was absent with a parent, Abigail. She also regularly adopted a stroppy attitude and only seemed to do something if she could see some personal benefit from it. On her own or when she was considerate, she was great; we came to the conclusion that it was probably a combination of jealousy, boredom, genetics and a deep-seated evil borne from the bowels of Lucifer himself. We had tried everything from carrot to stick but stopped short of beating her with the carrot. At dinner, towards the end of our time in Lijiang, we issued our hollow and empty sounding threat that we would send her back home, telling her that she didn't seem happy and she wasn't making us happy much of the time. It fell on deaf ears, so I walked her back to the hotel on my own and told her about all the arrangements we had made, where she would be staying and all the logistic detail that she demanded to know in order for her to grant validity on the threat. By the time we were back at the hotel she was sobbing her eyes out and repeatedly saying "It's not right, you can't do this," between sniffs and sobs.

"You're going to scrub my name and face from the family card," she said, in reference to the hundreds of business cards that we had made containing our contact details and a picture of the family. We said that it was in her hands and she could control her behaviour.

"I know I'm mean and horrible but I can't stop it – I do try. I do it for the reaction. I am happy honest. Please don't send me back." She had a list of child-like and not so child-like things that pulled the strings of my heart.

"I haven't chosen a desk in the juniors."

"What about Ducky?"

"What happens when Nana and Granddad go out at night. Who will look after me?"

"Nana doesn't have Star Wars on DVD."

And, "How can I speak to you whenever I want?" Maybe it was too far. Eirene and I cried silently with her and if she had any doubts about our earnestness, our tears completely eradicated them. She went to bed with the agreement that we would review it in a couple of days but not before she requested a little bag of her favourite Scooby snacks to see her fine for the journey. We went to bed with guilt heavy in our hearts but optimism that we had achieved the impact we desired.

The following day when I entered their room, Hannah was wide awake, hands behind her head, looking at the ceiling.

"Maybe I've been a bit hasty. It might be a good plan after all," she announced. She then proceeded to regale her thoughts about her going back, playing with her friends, staying with Nana and Granddad and having them all to herself. And then there was the food. My God, the food! She had a list of food that she was going to have when she arrived back that she clearly had put considerable thought into. And, of course, Emily now wanted to go. I broke the news to Eirene that our bluff had been called and she'd outdone us again. As Hannah began the early stages of packing her bag we moved to Plan B or C or Z or whatever we were on and desperately tried the boarding school route.

"Nana and Granddad can't have you, so we will have to put you in boarding school." I had concerns that she might start doing cartwheels and excitedly telling us of planned midnight feasts in dorms that she had read of in her *Katy* series of books, or learning magic at Hogwarts, but it did the trick. Good old Hannah returned, and we were all treated to a day or two of sickly sycophantism the like of which had never been seen.

"I've bought this ring for you Emily with my own money."

"Can I help you with that bag please, Mummy? My hands are empty and yours are full."

And, "I love you, Dad. I'm so lucky having the best daddy in the world." Sickly as it may have been it was nonetheless a great relief.

Our next stop was a place called Dali where I scored a cheap victory by briefly persuading Eirene that Dali was a place where traditionally people from all of China would come to rest and muck about. These activities would be undertaken in conjunction with a nearby town called Dilly, hence the phrase. She later exacted revenge by wobbling my chair from behind while I was reading on the BBC news website about the most recent earthquake, and then watched me subsequently try and convince everyone that there had been an aftershock. Nancy too claimed to have felt it, but it turned out that she was in on the wheeze as well.

Dali was a pretty and fascinating town, more buzzing and less contrived than Lijiang. The traditional Chinese buildings, including our hotel, had pagoda-style roof tops, which was a pleasant change from the concrete Western-style structures we'd been used to. Dali has a history dating back to 738. It became a Kingdom in 937 and by the year 1000 was the 13th largest city in the world. It was conquered by the Mongols in the 12th century and became a major transit point for the introduction of Buddhism throughout the rest of China. The old walled town that remains today was built in 1400 by the Ming Dynasty but it has witnessed many attacks over the centuries. The females were considered the most unattractive in all of the East, hence the term "minging." Unfortunately, she didn't buy that one.

The old town is dominated to the west by the Cang mountain range from which the town slopes down towards the enormous alpine lake Erhai. The mountains are said to have beautiful wild flowers, including some of the rarest camellias in China, as well as a rich array of bird life, and are accessible by a chairlift. We'd experienced our fair share of chairlifts on this trip and instead elected to visit Foreigner Street for a Western-style dinner. I chose a curry and rice, which although contestably not Western was nothing short of heart-breaking. I had missed curries more than anything, so it was a tragedy when a bowl of boiled bones in hot water, topped off with some Uncle Ben's, turned up. The kids, however, loved their hamburgers. At one stage, during our Western meal, Eirene and Hannah returned from the toilet for Eirene to discreetly tell me that when Hannah was crouching down on the hole in the floor she let out a loud "No shit." Eirene was gobsmacked and on the verge of issuing the requisite admonishment before Hannah continued "Or you pay 70 RMB fine." She had been reading the sign posted in front of her. In our hotel in Dali, the book in the room demanded "No dirty whoring" (clean whoring ok?) and "You must not become prostitute once in our hotel." The hotel did have a distinct lack of facilities, so I could see the temptation.

Due to the negative impact my earlier curry experience had on me, I had the most disturbing and vivid nightmare. I dreamt that I went for a curry on my return to England with my mate Roger, ordered my favourite dish from our Indian in Caterham and it was boiled bones again.

"It's all changed now," he declared. "That's how they've done it since the Olympics."

For some reason, which I decided was just because I could, I visited a barber after lunch and asked for my head to be shaved bald. My hair had become very unkempt and I'd not had it cut for five months. Unfortunately, my quest for a "Buddha" was hampered by the ladies (Eirene, kids and Nancy) who instructed the barber to give me a number two all over. I ended up with something a UK barber would have given me, and I was cheesed off. So we returned to the hotel and I spent an hour and three Mach Three razors finishing the job. If I'd done this back home, there would be the inevitable verbal sparring to contend with. It would've been frowned upon at work and socially only permitted if you are going bald, are a bouncer or are having chemotherapy, in which case it's perfectly acceptable. Also, I have always wanted to know what my head looked like. Some people seem to suit bald heads and I wanted to put my head up against them. Would I have an unusual one, lacking in symmetry or verging on a pyramid? Or would it be blotchy and like a political globe of the world? I had a number of scars on my head and a particular nasty one from a childhood bump that I was keen to cast my eyes on. I would be defying nature and deciding when I wanted to look at my bald head and not when it did. Anyway, I was pleasantly surprised - I think I have a great shaped head. Right enough there was a big scar and it felt a little unreal to the touch. Rubbing material on it felt weird as did the wind but it kept me occupied. Unfortunately, none of these positive aspects was shared by the family. Hannah cried, Emily was terrified and Eirene threw a quiet one. Abigail didn't bat an eyelid, but it took a good few hours for the furore to die down and I was forbidden from taking my hat off outside.

We received a call from a bloke called Callum at ITN, working for *London Tonight* in the barrel scraping department, who wanted to run our big "Family lose phone" story that night. They wanted a load of video, quotes and us interviewing each other. I then spent most of the night going through and transferring video and pictures before it fell through with the usual assurances that it was going to be run the following night. Thankfully we didn't hold our breath, but they did put in a call to the Chinese embassy in the UK which is the sort of thing we were after.

The highlight on our trip to Jinghong along a series of crap roads that rather incredibly managed to become worse, was Eirene's beaming smile on emerging from a petrol station toilet declaring "They had doors." When we arrived, the kids were ecstatic at seeing a couple of swimming pools and slides in the hotel grounds. From my time in the police, you could bet your bottom dollar that if there was a CCTV camera overlooking a serious crime scene then it wouldn't be working. The same logic ran true for sightings of swimming pools in hotels in China. All credit to this hotel though, as one of the pools did contain a liquid of sorts but it looked like it could have been fed directly from the waters of the Black Sea resort we stayed at in Ukraine.

At dinner, we confronted the elephant in the room and pinned Nancy down on the whole "Chinese eat dogs" myth and almost immediately wished we hadn't. Not only did she confirm it, but she offered us it there and then and provided a pretty exhaustive list of just about every animal in the world that is eaten in China, including snake, rat and tiger. The interesting aspect about eating dog is that it's more expensive than pork, lamb and chicken so they would never covertly serve it to you as a replacement.

I thought I'd get my own back on Nancy after the prank they played on me with the wobbly chair and the earthquake, so I told her all about *The Panda's Paws* restaurant in London, elaborating in great detail about the incredibly intricate dishes they served. The panda is, of course, China's national animal, revered beyond all others and certainly never consumed – well, at least knowingly. It worked, and she was visibly stunned.

"You've got to try it, Nancy. Yes, they're beautiful and rare animals but they're also very delicious." I finally conceded to her that there isn't a restaurant that serves panda in London. And if there was, they would pretend it's chicken.

In the evening, I donned my fashionably oily overalls and headed out to investigate the banging under the car. Previously when I had performed this mechanical ritual in a hotel car park, every man in the town from toddler to octogenarian was with me in seconds, under the car trying to help or head submerged under the bonnet having a good poke around. Although a lovely and consistent trait of China, it can also be a royal pain in the arse. This event was no exception and I gave a couple of lads the standard tour which consisted of a look round the car, a hand gestured explanation of our route on the map sticker on the side of the car and finished off with the handing over of the family business card. After this they insisted on calling a friend to come over and help. The banging seemed to be emanating from the exhaust and they were absolutely insistent I put my tools away. Nancy popped down during this and explained that they were doing it for free. An oily man then arrived, looked at my rear end and told us to follow him to his garage which we did. His garage was a salubrious 12-ramp establishment on the other side of town where the problem was sorted quickly. He refused any payment, but we were invited for tea at the original man's shop. There we were introduced to a large crowd of men and women sitting round tables that looked like the base of a tree with polished tree stumps as stools. It was a tea shop like I'd never experienced. Tea-related carvings and ornaments adorned the walls and shelves. A special tea was meticulously prepared and served to us on a ceremonial tray and poured into a glass for us. Every sip was topped up and the glasses seemed bottomless. Eventually, after many final glass raisings, we made our way back but not without numerous gifts of freshly wrapped tea for us both. The man's name translated as Mr Left, possibly as a result of a childhood accident, but he epitomised the friendliness and hospitality that we found throughout most of China.

After a bad night's sleep, induced by excessive caffeine or worry about the journey ahead, we had a 7.15am breakfast in preparation for what was supposed to be the worst drive of our time in China so far. Memories of our recent treacherous mountain drive in the rain and dark were still fresh in our minds and I was fearful of a repeat. Nancy, and others she had engaged with, predicted a 12-hour drive to Jinghong at best, with substandard dirt tracks in the offing. The roads proved to be bad, but we had seen worse. The scenery, though, had not been bettered, with paddy fields and tobacco plantations giving way to the most remarkable mountains, waterfalls, valleys and ridges. Phone signals quickly disappeared and we felt stirringly remote. Predictably, just before Eirene handed the driving over to me, we hit tarmac which grew into a dual carriageway and a full blown, not on our map, motorway. I was envious she had the mud driving and her feeling was reciprocal over my road driving. However, we were all relived that the journey only took eight hours.

We booked into the town's flagship hotel, a place that was so run down that it looked like the flagship was White Star's Titanic. We were provided with a rancid room, mould clinging to the flaky walls and a stench of old, wet socks hanging in the air. The floor looked like a murder scene and the skirting boards had almost completely disintegrated. We made the mistake of looking under the bed for something we thought we had lost. Sweet Jesus! Six or so used condoms greeted us and some other objects that I will never unsee. During the night, I was woken by some shuffling and a heavy slam of the door.

"I found a cockroach in the bathroom and I was showing him to the door," Eirene explained nonchalantly, conveying its size better than if she had taken a picture. There was an army of cleaners on show, who paraded at 7am in the lobby but subsequently tended to always be in transit and not actually doing anything. It was a dump, the worst in China and probably the worst of the trip, so it was a shame that it marked our penultimate destination in China. But, all things considered, we had been very lucky so far.

Our accommodation in Mengla, our final destination by the Laos border, was consistent with our previous night's hotel. The town was devoid of anything of merit and by virtue of it being a border town that is the sole stepping stone into Laos, it took its clientele for granted. It was frequented by truckers and prostitutes and the room phone rang almost constantly from mid to late evening enquiring if I was after any services. I had developed the habit of asking Hannah to answer those in case my English of "No, no, not interested" was translated as "Get up here now, I want some extras." In other circumstances, employing your seven-year-old daughter to fend off ladies of the night could charitably be described as unusual, bordering on neglect and abuse. As far as I could see it, Hannah liked answering the phone, didn't understand what they were saying, and the girls didn't waste any time. Everyone was a winner.

China was a country I had been really looking forward to visiting and a place that did not fall short. It has chaotic roads, misspent cash, curious rules, unquestioning people, no democracy of note and frequently little in the way of hygiene standards. Poverty barked out from almost every corner, interrupted only by the low guttural retching of phlegm up the throat before it was deposited on the floor. Nevertheless, it seemed to have the happiest and friendliest people in the world. Patient, accepting and absolutely in love with children, which seems a cruel attribute given their one child policy. It was cheap, welcoming and made us both feel safer than we had ever felt in our lives. It has deserts, mountains, tropical forests, delicious food and a history that puts our own to shame. And we loved almost every second of it.

CHAPTER 8.

SOUTH EAST ASIA

Friday 5 September 2008

Day 128 - Muang Ngoy, Laos - 14,501 miles

We left early for the border with Nancy for the final time. She cut effortlessly through encyclopaedia-sized paperwork and we exchanged Dollars and Yuan with an increasingly delighted local lady. She afforded us a perplexingly good rate but always tried to rip us off at the end of each exchange of monies by giving us lower denomination notes than we should have had. This happened three times and in some ways I admired her perseverance and recognised it to be little different from me repeating the same joke until eventually I get a laugh. We were allowed through the first border after tearful goodbyes to Nancy, although that was not a condition of exit. Eirene and the girls were upset to see Nancy go as was I, knowing that the lazy days of directions and accommodation being arranged by someone else were now gone. She had been great for us and my worries about having a stranger in our midst for such a prolonged period of time turned out to be unfounded. We gave Nancy a homemade thank you card with $120 in it that she said she would open later. We exchanged contact details with promises to keep in touch and never heard from her again.

Somehow, we became a little lost when trying to find the Laos border which should have been only a few kilometres after the Chinese border. Due to the rain, a fast flowing stream needed vaulting in order for us to reach the customs building, where I was passed from window to window, handing over money and watching people type my details into various computers. During this bureaucratic endurance test, loads of Chinese arrived and pushed to the front of the queue. I thought to myself, I'll have a bit of that, and so began a constant push-pull surge of people that climaxed when a good dozen of them pushed against me and I gave it the comedy shimmy and they lost balance and flew past me.

I tried to explain that I wasn't coming over the border on foot, that I had a car and family with me but judging by the lack of understanding from the officer, you would have thought I was the first person ever to drive a non-Laos or non-Chinese car over the border. Finally, a guard told me to drive down the road a short distance while my family walked to the same spot and it would be sorted. It wasn't. The guards there didn't want to know and the bloke in the bureau de change also expressed understandable disinterest. So I elected to drive off, just like in Kyrgyzstan, with no insurance or vehicle import certificate, wondering about the wisdom of our impatience.

At each border crossing we always looked out for differences from the country we had just left, a natural border that matched the political one. Even the children put down their iPods for a couple of minutes as we all looked in anticipation at our new country and, invariably, there was never any immediate difference, save perhaps the writing on the road signs. China into Laos was not one of these however. It was coming to the end of their wet season and the tropical heavy rain had turned everything in the countryside lush and green We quickly realised that, unlike China, where every square inch of a mountainside was farmed in some capacity, Laos was just wild, with a fraction of the available land in agricultural use. That, and the roads which were little more than trenches, made us feel that we had arrived in a new world. As we didn't know what the timing would be of our border crossing, and the speed we could drive in Laos, we headed for Muang Ngoy with a number of alternative overnight stops up our sleeve should progress be limited. Our travel plan through Laos was wholly based on the chat I had with the friendly Dutch drugs runner, back in Bishkek, Kyrgyzstan. I had mixed feelings about the fact that most of his suggested markings on our maps weren't mentioned in our travel books, but took comfort in the fact that he had lived in Cambodia and Laos for a couple of years and spent many months zipping around the region on his motorbike. The thought remained though that it could all have been a cunning long-term trap for us to be chopped up and murdered by one of his Laos counterparts. As it happened, Laos felt very relaxed with mighty landscapes of near-vertical jungle-covered limestone cliffs. Our progress was good and no-one was murdered.

Muang Ngoy was one of the most visually stunning places we had been to. Buildings constructed from bamboo and cane topped with wriggly iron roofs lined narrow and dusty streets. Wide drainage pits at both sides of the road required makeshift bridges to pass from road to pavement or entrance. The backdrop was dominated by precipitous pinnacles, dragon-shaped mountains that emerged from the Mekong River, their steep slopes densely covered with gravity defying trees and the occasional flash of limestone that scarred their emerald green faces. At their summits, puffs of stationary stratus clouds hung around their necks. Buildings beside the river stood on stilts to allow for changes in water level and others not as close to the river were raised to protect themselves from monsoon rains and mudslides. Clearly rain was a frequent visitor to Laos. It had a nostalgic familiarity to it as if I'd seen it on some 1970s Saturday morning TV show from my youth. "The Lost Islands" meets "Monkey" perhaps.

Having spent the last four months travelling through non-touristy areas of foreign countries, we were excited to see a white European, not realising that we were going to see thousands of European tourists in Laos. He turned out to be a Swiss computer science student and a great storyteller who recommended the Sunset Guesthouse, if we had the money. The money turned out to be £10 for two bamboo rooms overlooking the river and a guarantee of no mosquitoes. The versatility of bamboo amazed me; from the roof to the balcony, the furniture and the flooring were all fashioned from bamboo in one form or another. Some of the gaps between the floorboards, however, were almost the same size as the floorboards themselves which allowed one or two uninvited insect visitors to come flying around but I felt Eirene's hump was unjustified.

She had been mounting a steady campaign which involved rushing through Laos to reach Thailand as soon as possible. I countered with "Laos is the best country to travel through according to loads of travel websites." But she was keen to reach mainland Thailand which I countered was effectively the same as mainland Laos, but not as untouched or as cheap. Other lame, illogical, irrational and unreasonable points were put forward until she eventually played her trump card. "Malaria is far more widespread in Laos." Admittedly we were having problems administering the tablets to Abigail who insisted on spitting them out, no matter how cunning our approach. Cunning was rapidly replaced with brute force as we were drawn to pinning her down and forcibly thrusting the tablet, in whatever disguise, down her panicking gullet. We recognised that there might be some long term impact on her attitude to medicine and made a mental note to arrange an appointment with a psychotherapist on our return.

We ate well at a riverside restaurant that night, all of us ordering Western food for the first time in months, except for Hannah who ordered her favourite sweet and sour chicken and egg fried rice. We met a couple of English girls, solicitors Juliet and Tamsin, on the bridge and somehow managed to bump into them a further six times in Laos.

The following day as we drove south towards Luang Phabang, Eirene seemed increasingly unhappy. The bamboo hut on the banks of the Mekong with all its uninvited livestock was not her cup of tea so I promised her a posh hotel in Luang Phabang with no gaps in the floorboards. We paid £60 for a palatial room in the Apsara and Eirene was appeased. Over the next few days we were massaged, fed and amazed by all this old town had to offer. There were numerous trainee Buddhist monks wandering around in their orange sashes, which firmly sat in the *Monkey* part of my memory. Our hotel directory warned against handing over our email address or contact details to these fellows as there was a likelihood of subsequently being bombarded by requests for Nike trainers. As many were barefooted or wearing simple sandals I could understand their position.

An old colleague from the police, Justin, had put us in touch with a girl called Jane who ran a bear sanctuary near Luang Phabang. In southern China and Laos, we had seen signs outside shops offering bear bile which we assumed wasn't literally bear bile and, if it was, wouldn't be a big seller for obvious reasons (it being bear bile). Unfortunately, we were wrong on both accounts. To find that bears are hunted in Laos and taken to bile farms where it is extracted through the most inhumane means imaginable was astonishing to us. We were even more surprised to learn that often their paws are used in China for bear paw soup and it is not unusual for the paws to be removed in the restaurant in front of the diner whilst the bear is still alive. Jane, together with her partner Jude, had given up life in the UK to come and help develop the sanctuary in Laos. At the time of our visit, she had about 20 bears of varying ages, none of whom were born in captivity. Some were gifted to donors as cubs; it was seen as a sign of wealth, and then the owners couldn't cope with them when they became full-sized bears so handed them over. Others were rescued from hunters when the Laos government chose to occasionally enforce against the activity. We were given a VIP tour into the bear compound and the kids watched and asked questions as the baby bears fought, climbed and ate in as natural an environment as they were ever likely to see. It was not the first time on this trip that we failed to answer the children's whys.

We took Jane's suggestion and walked up Kuang Si Falls, a 60 metre three-tier waterfall with swimmable rock pools at each level. A forest walk at the lower part of the falls gave us a spectacular view where we watched as the water thundered onto the stage, ripping its way between the layered verdant curtains of primitive foliage. Like a solid sheet of ice, it flowed over the edge, down to the next level, gliding over moss covered boulders before taking its next flamboyant bow.

The water level was high and, much to Eirene's disdain, I encouraged all the kids into the pool and ran with the traditional "snake has me by the throat" routine before finishing off with a comedy drowning. I know one day this will come back and bite me, possibly literally, but until that day I will live my life by that act. We bumped into Juliet and Tamsin again on their rented bikes and gave them a lift back to Luang Phabang. My former police colleagues would never speak to me again if they knew of the assistance I offered those evil lawyers from the dark side. In fairness, I think they were destined for probate or conveyancing as opposed to defence lawyers.

The next stop on our itinerary was Phonsavan, the site of the Plain of Jars, so called because of the giant stone jars of unknown origin that rest on hills around Phonsavan.

The road to Phonsavan was a long and windy one along Route Seven and Eirene voiced her contempt for it. This particular road was described in the *Rough Guide* and on the US Embassy website as "bandit strewn and flying advisable." The official advice from the chap at the Foreign and Commonwealth Office that I spoke to said it was "Nonsense! Maybe if you are American" and that it "could be a bit cheeky but fine for a while now." Reassured by his most English of words and despite seeing a number of motorcyclists with rifles and Kalashnikovs flung over their shoulders, the journey was thankfully uneventful. Although some of the smaller jars had disappeared over the years, about 2,500 still remained for our arrival which was quite surprising considering it was the most heavily bombed area in the world during the American war in Vietnam.

Much of Eastern Laos served as a supply route and staging post for the North Vietnamese during the Vietnam War and it was to this end that the US staged a secret war against it. Between 1964 and 1973, Laos was hit by an average of one B-52 bomb-load every eight minutes, 24 hours a day. The US dropped more bombs on Laos than were dropped during the whole of World War II. Of the 260 million bombs that were dropped, 80 million failed to explode [12], and it is this that serves as America's legacy to their most recent South East Asian trip. The Americans have bombed 30-odd countries since the end of WW2 but dropped the most by some distance here.

Our tour of site three of the Plain of Jars was un-commercialised and isolated. It wasn't very well signposted and we lost our way a few times, but that was to be expected according to our guide book. We parked by a hut and crossed a precarious wobbly bamboo bridge spanning a 10 metre-wide river. The bridge looked like it washed away frequently in bad weather as the only support it had was two enormous bamboo uprights in the middle of the river, their bases plunged into the soft silt of the river bed and secured with natural twine to either side of the bridge. The bridge itself was nothing more than five or six bamboo lengths, stretched across the river and tied together with that incredibly versatile bamboo twine. The bamboo lengths, however, were round and didn't quite stretch across the river, so others had to be attached to them which created gaps and a nightmarish situation for Eirene. The left hand side of the bridge was completely open while the other side had a hand rail of one bamboo cane. I strode across the wobbly bridge first with Emily and Abigail, before photographing a terrified Eirene edging her way across slowly, reaching out for the support of anything she could grab while Hannah followed confidently behind, oblivious to the torment her mother was enduring.

The rest of the path was a little muddy through scenic paddy fields marked out by a number of white flagstones, which denoted that the area had been cleared of bombs and mines.

---

[12] The Guardian - Wednesday 3 December 2008

We eventually reached a Plain (yes I have spelt it accurately, if not correctly) of Jars to find that we were the only ones there. I was immediately struck by the size of these vessels. Each sandstone or granite jar was between one and three metres in diameter and height with the base having a larger diameter than the top. There were about 150 jars at this site, some complete and others broken or on their side and randomly sited on a grassy plane. Over the years, some trees had flourished among them but surprisingly, to this day, the origin of the jars remains a mystery. Local legend says they were created by a nation of giants for a king who needed somewhere to store his rice wine, but more weight has been given to archaeologists' reports that they date from between 500 BC and 200 AD, the Southeast Asian Iron Age, and were more likely to have been used as funerary urns, since human remains and burial goods have been discovered around some.

One of the reasons so little study has been carried out on the jars is that the Plain of Jars is one of the most dangerous archaeological sites in the world due to unexploded ordnance. *The Mines Advisory Group* [13] are still removing as much unexploded ordnance as they can four decades later but, with the sheer volume involved, it's almost a never-ending task. Shell casing and shrapnel was strewn everywhere with many of the larger casings being used in place of wooden stilts to support housing. The farmers have no choice but to farm despite the risks. *SOS Children* [14] had set up a village for those children who were still being orphaned by the bombs continually going off during agricultural activity and unfortunately, their numbers show little signs of dwindling. The country is stricken with poverty, one of the poorest countries in the world, but it belies their friendliness and lack of hostility, particularly to westerners. Shoes on children were a luxury item, any clothes at all on children under five was a rare sight and showers were

---

[13] http://www.maginternational.org/
[14] http://www.soschildrensvillages.org.uk/children-charity.htm

taken at roadside streams. With children everywhere, it contrasted starkly with China which at times seemed like *Vulgaria*, home of the Child Catcher in Chitty Chitty Bang Bang. In Laos, every village, no matter what its size, had a 100 odd children running around with few adults to be seen. Laos strongly discourages the showing of affection in public, and signs to this effect at border crossings and in hotels were prominently displayed, so we hazarded an educated guess at where the adults were and what they were likely to be doing. Most, if not every large town had one gloriously new shiny building with intricate gates and well kempt gardens. These were local government buildings. The cornerstone of every poor country seems to be the misspending of whatever limited resources they have.

Whilst the *Rough Guide* had gone a little astray with their bandit analysis earlier they had also done the same with their Phonsavan hotels. I had promised Eirene the Auberge de Plaine de Jarres but no one had heard of it so I gave her the next best thing, the ironically named Hotel Chitichitibangbang or something like that. Whatever its name, it had too many lizards, mosquitoes and cockroaches in our rooms for Eirene's liking and an emergency summit meeting was called when a tearful Eirene announced, "I want out of this hotel and this country." I asked her for an alternative and offered flights for her and the kids, but it became clear that she was simply just fed up, a reasonably common ailment for many travellers, especially a mum loving home bird like Eirene. The kids hadn't helped, with Hannah back to playing up after the "boarding school threat" and even Emily started to increasingly mimic her bad behaviour when she cut me to the quick by taunting me that Granddad's barbeques were better than mine! That wound may never heal. I admired Eirene even more for agreeing to this journey and a £30 call to her mum that cheered her up considerably was a small price to pay. After killing a cockroach the size of my shoe, with my shoe, we settled down to bed and, for the first time on this trip, I had trouble sleeping. I sensed storm clouds gathering.

We stopped at the famous Vang Vieng, touristy though it was. It gained its notoriety through renting out tractor tyre inner tubes to float down the Nam Song river, stopping every few hundred yards or so at a poolside bar to drink cheap 45% Lao Lao Whisky and get hammered. Over the years this had resulted in a number of deaths from drowning, but it hadn't stopped tourists visiting from all over the world. Despite the slow flowing and very shallow river, presence of life jackets and promise of no alcohol, Eirene banned me from taking Hannah down on a trip. But all was not lost as we managed to find an almost mythical blue lagoon with a cave, reputed to be home to golden crabs. We settled there for the day while the kids and I played in the natural pool and rope swings that dangled from overhanging trees.

Hannah's confidence in the water quickly returned as did her ability to confront fear which is perhaps one of her most endearing characteristics. On three occasions she climbed up a steep ladder to the top of a tree to jump about four metres into the river. Eirene wasn't keen on coming in, but Abigail loved the return of the *Daddy Taxi* of Croatia, and happily clung to my back while I swam around. Emily periodically requested to be taken from one side of the river to the other to be placed upon a suitable mermaid type rock. While we didn't have the pool to ourselves, which wasn't surprising in such a popular location, the kids endeared themselves to the dozen or so travellers who popped in. Amongst them was a group of travellers from Tel Aviv. Stereotypical as it is, Israeli travellers tend, from my experience, to have a reputation as not particularly pleasant tourists. They seem to have an overt brashness and arrogance coupled with a distinct lack of humility that does not endear them to those around them. They tend to contrast starkly with the humble and appreciative visitors from other countries and this group were little different. I'm not sure if it is an inherent trait, a group mentality or just my anecdotal experiences but the growing resentment from others around them is almost palpable. Individually, one to one, I find them no different from everyone else. Maybe it's the group thing.

At one point Emily said to me that she wanted to swim on her own. Knowing that she would sink I asked her for a secret sign if she found herself in trouble. Emily said she would raise her hands in the air and scream.

"That's your secret sign for drowning, Emily?" an astonished Hannah declared, waving her own arms mockingly in the air. "That is drowning, you twerp!"

The travel book marked a non-functional algae-covered fountain as being worthy of a visit in Vientiane, Laos' capital, and that probably summed it up for us. We watched Buddhist monks from golden temples meander along the waterfront which was meant to be beguiling at sunset, but the former French trading post was too inert for a lively family of five, so we moved onto Thakhek, a small border town on our way to Thailand.

With the Beijing Olympics still fresh in our minds, Eirene organised a mini-Olympics for the kids after dinner in the hotel car park. We were concerned that due to the amount of driving we had been doing they weren't exercising enough and although the hotel car park wasn't quite as impressive as the Bird Cage stadium in Beijing, our venue in tropical Laos was certainly far from our local park. We all entered the 100m and 50m sprints and ran nowhere near world records or even PBs. The staff thought we were mad and as it became increasingly competitive, I started to concur with them. But we had successfully worn out the kids, and ourselves, and bed beckoned. It wasn't until 3.30am, as the last moped revved away from outside our hotel that we realised why we were the only guests.

Our entry into Thailand was a late decision. We had been heading south towards the border of Cambodia, when I stumbled on the visa chapter in the Rough Guide which explained that visas on arrival were not permitted at this border. We stopped for lunch at Savannakhet and I popped into the

218

ferry station to enquire about a ferry across to Thailand. The enquiry booth was operated by an unconscious woman lying prostrate on the floor, so I alerted a couple of nearby customs officers of her plight and through their body language and facial expressions they clearly communicated the word "apathy". They didn't speak any English, nor did they score my silent presentation of "I want to drive my car across the river" very highly and I left, no wiser as to how to traverse this river.

We popped across the road to a restaurant where I asked the manager, "Can we across river drive drive in boat to Thailand?" I tentatively submitted complete with arm movements. "Yes, you can drive drive but people find it a lot easier to take the bridge just up the road." His fluent use of English shamed me as he continued to inform us that the bridge our guidebook had said was possibly in the offing, had been offed.

We now considered ourselves experts on border crossings having negotiated our way through every conceivable diplomatic situation possible and we were astounded to find this one verged on pleasurable. The whole crossing took 30 minutes, the majority of which was spent exchanging information, football news, off-roading stories, photos and much shaking of hands with the police officers. I had been expecting something altogether more intimidating and akin to one of the many Thai horror stories we had heard. I determined that border guards and customs officers throughout the world were recruited for their bad attitudes, inability to communicate outside of grunts and megalomaniacal yearnings. The good ones went to Savannakhet.

We crossed the bridge driving on the right hand side of the road and entered Thailand to find we now drove on the left hand side. The road signs were in English, they had lovely smooth roads and instantly recognisable shop and fast food signs. It was as much a culture shock seeing all that as leaving them had been. We stayed at a hotel at Ubon Ratchathani and found menus in English and 7-11 stores selling whatever we wanted. Our air conditioned hotel room, including breakfast for us all, was incredibly cheap. I even bought a mobile phone SIM card from a transvestite shop assistant with painless ease. China was the last place we'd bought one and that had involved a two hour interview and much exchanging of documents and drinking of tea.

The people of Ubon Ratchathani were as genuine and helpful as we had heard and hoped as I discovered when I came upon a picture kiosk in a restaurant and decided to print off some photos from my memory card. I popped my card in the reader and watched it disappear while I waited for instructions to appear on the screen. To cut a long story, approximately one hour 15 minutes short, nine people from various sources and with a variety of tools emerged to extract the card from the depths of the machine's innards, a machine that none of them owned or knew anything about but they were all willing to try to help. We liked Thailand and not just because it had street lights, ambulances and schools made of bricks and mortar. We liked it for its people who had so little to give but gave readily what they could.

We headed in the direction of the Khao Yai National Park, which took much longer than we'd planned. The road surface was good with multiple lanes, but it was a busy road with heavy traffic and frequent hold ups. The road had only just reopened after heavy flooding and sandbags up to one metre high and two metres deep still lay at the side of the road. For a while we drove behind a vehicle that was carrying even more stuff than we were. It was a small van with no rear doors carrying huge bags of produce that sat precariously in the back. The spare wheel dangled from the roof which was even more full than the insides with bags, boxes and what looked like a wardrobe all strapped to the roof, making the vehicle twice its normal height. We stayed well back and overtook it as soon as we could. Health and safety on the vehicles seemed as casual as China, confirmed when we saw a fully-packed school bus with five additional students hanging on outside at the very back. They were perched on the little steps and had to stretch up high to hold onto the rim of the roof.

The following day, we set off for the National Park and enforced an iPod ban as we'd been told that there were all kinds of animals to see, including elephants and tigers, and I wanted all eyes on the lookout. The larger mammals clearly hadn't been told about the iPod ban and weren't coming out in the rain, deciding instead to stay indoors on their jungle Nintendo equivalents. We were excited to see various primates including gibbons and macaques and some deer but not so excited to see the leeches which we hadn't encountered since I flicked one from my arm towards Eirene within 20 minutes of driving in Laos with my window open.

On arrival at the park centre we spotted a rope bridge that marked the start of a 1 km circular walk. We purchased some leech socks for all of us which looked like white gaiters and caused much hilarity among the family. Had we purchased the rest of the outfit, we'd have looked like a family of forensic scientists, but our uniform stopped just below the knees. We sprayed ourselves with insect repellent that was guaranteed to ward off any moving invertebrate within 100 metres and set off on our marathon trek. Although we started out enthusiastically, with Abigail in the Bush Baby on my back, the terrain became a bit rough and my fare dodging passenger began to complain bitterly. Witnesses claimed that I repeatedly bashed her head as I bent low under fallen branches and trees but I, at most, brushed them. The jungle floor was awash with leeches which rapidly attached themselves to our feet and onto the white of the leech socks. Eirene developed what we affectionately called the heebie jeebies and became panicky as more climbed on as quickly as she removed them. I decided not to mention to her that there were over 50 species of snake within the National Park but luckily we didn't see any although we did come across a giant millipede on our path. The trail became more difficult, increasingly indistinct and much longer than 1 km. Perhaps I should've have pressed them for a distance-only measurement.

A couple of shaky bridges over stagnant water proved to be the incentive for one of Eirene's greatest wobblers. Being the pro that I am, I managed to catch it on video which surprisingly didn't seem to placate her. As she searched her legs for leeches, I filmed the surrounding jungle. Then I heard her squeal and as I panned round to her, there was a look on her face that I'd only ever seen in horror movies just before a dagger comes down. Without any pause for breath, she launched into "Get me out of here quickly, OK? Get me out of here, I really don't want to be here, get me out of here!"

When we returned to the car we did a leech strip and search and stripped the kids off before starting on each other. One had climbed through a breathing hole in Hannah's trousers, but we never did find it despite what we told her. I later discovered that another three of the minxes had climbed over the top of my knee high socks onto my bare legs. It was the blood running down my leg that alerted me to them. The little buggers not only have an anaesthetic in their initial bite but they release an anticoagulant into your bloodstream, so I didn't feel them biting and I was bleeding a hell of a lot. I formed the impression from the family's reaction that they were not too enthusiastic about another trek in either the foreseeable or unforeseeable future, which I thought was a bit harsh - until I saw a big fat tourist stripping down in the nearby cafeteria, looking like he had emerged from the set of some S & M movie.

The long and frequent journeys were taking their toll on the children and basically we needed a holiday. The kids needed exercise, lessons, which were difficult though not impossible to conduct in the car, and structure. If we were not careful, Abigail was in danger of turning into Augustus Gloop, Roald Dahl's gluttonous character in *Charlie and the Chocolate Factory*. She continued to amuse and delight us with her little ways. On one occasion whilst firmly clutching a bag of crisps, munching away on their contents, she said "Emily, would you like a crisp."

"Yes please, Abigail," Emily said gratefully, before letting out a shriek as Abigail tried to force a sludgy crisp from her own mouth into her sister's.

So we stopped driving and spent five days in Bangkok. We liked Bangkok. It was crowded and claustrophobic but we enjoyed the cosmopolitan atmosphere, the accommodation, the food and the people. All of the people, except the bloody taxi drivers. The taxis themselves were in very good condition. They had air-conditioning and were readily available and very cheap but unfortunately every single taxi driver was a dirty stinking thief who couldn't find his own house if he tried. They never carried a map, frequently "forgot" to put the meter on or just refused to, drove the wrong way completely and didn't know where anything was. An 8 km journey to a very famous landmark, which should have taken 25 minutes, took one hour 40 minutes and somehow required us to drive 40 km. They earn crap money so the need to rip people off is always there and for that I empathise. It's a bit of a Catch-22 as they won't improve until they earn more money and no one wants to agree to them having any more money until they improve. Of the 10 trips we took in a taxi, and I'm wary how gullible that makes us sound, not once did they take us straight to where we wanted to go.

For some, Bangkok was a living nightmare. On the 4th November 2003, a 19-year-old lad from Bury boarded a flight from Manchester to Bangkok. On arrival at 3am at Don Muang airport he was stopped, a bottle of face cream was opened and a load of ecstasy tablets were found wrapped at the bottom. At that moment the teenager's life ended. He escaped the death sentence and was given 99 years at Bangkwang Prison also known as the "Bangkok Hilton". I decided to visit him.

They call us "banana visitors". People in Bangkok for a few days who think they will pop into the prison, throw a few bananas through the bars in return for a future anecdote and leave, feeling happy about themselves, with a ready-made tale for some other day. Having read a few books about Bangkwang and Plom Pen prisons in Bangkok, I don't deny that they held a morbid fascination for me. Not just the conditions but the fact that a single mistake can have such massive repercussions. I do not condone the trafficking of Class A drugs, although I'm not sure that ecstasy can remotely be considered to be on a par with heroine. You can argue that they know the risks or whatever but you're often dealing with vulnerable and malleable individuals with a desperate need for funds. This makes for a dangerous combination. Someone asked me why I should show any sympathy for these individuals. They make a conscious decision to do something illegal and must pay the price. I agreed but it was the price they were asked to pay that I had an issue with and I think too often the punishment didn't fit the crime.

When I was a kid, we lived near Peterhead Prison in Scotland, famously stormed by the SAS in 1987 during a short-lived siege. It was home to the real hard cases, Category A prisoners. We used to drive past it and I always had this fear that I would end up there wrongly, through some twist of circumstance and it terrified me, leading to many sleepless nights. A few *Hammer House of Horror* films and *The Count of Monte Cristo* (where the count was wrongly imprisoned in Château d'If) enhanced this fear and it's still with me today.

With this in mind and after the peak of all crappy taxi drives across Bangkok, I arrived at Bangkwang and waded through foul smelling water from the adjacent overflowing river, to a desk in a building across the road from the prison. I had been willing to visit anyone and was assured that I could just turn up. I had steeled myself to be sitting across from a sex offender, somewhat different from a drug trafficker, but not strangely in the mind of most prison inmates, who viewed them no differently from any other prisoner. I was initially told that no foreigners could visit today and was sent away. I made a quick call to the very helpful Kate Dufall at the embassy who gave me the name of the now 24-year-old Michael Connell from Bury. I paddled back to the desk, armed with a specific name and was given a pass. I was sent to an adjacent desk and given another bit of paper before being sent across the road through a side gate to the main entrance. I had brought chocolate, toothpaste, toothbrush, soap, playing cards and cigarettes for the person I was visiting but all, bar the chocolate and toothbrush, were taken from me. The convention appeared to be that if it could be purchased at inflated prices in the prison visitors shop and you had chosen not to, then you could not bring it in. The chocolate was English so that was fine and they were out of toothbrushes. I believe similar logic is still being employed at British Airports. The cards, though, were confiscated on the basis that gambling is illegal in Thailand in the same way that drug dealing is illegal in Amsterdam and knifing someone is illegal on the streets of London. After depositing my bag and all money I passed through a metal detector and into a long yard, lovingly furnished with a rich variety of flowers. I handed in my slip and passport photocopy before sitting outside a long line of booths with telephones. Visitors were separated from prisoners by about 10 foot of distance and 10 inches of Perspex. An Australian couple in their 50s, who had come to visit their 32-year-old son, helped me find a booth and we chatted briefly. Michael arrived, and after five attempts at finding a working phone, we settled on the crackly sixth. We exchanged greetings and I started into my defensive "I'm not a banana visitor" speech to this gaunt but otherwise healthy looking 24- year-old.

He reassured me that it wasn't a problem. There were 12 British prisoners in Bangkwang, nearly all from London, and all but one in for drugs. Prisoners Abroad [15] provided a helpful guide on visits in which they encouraged visitors not to enter into discussion of the inevitable rights or wrongs of the prisoners' cases or debate on how badly the system had treated them. Michael had an unexpected outlook and a very philosophical one at that. He had none of the resentment of someone who was unfairly convicted or being treated badly either by the courts or the prison. He freely put his hands up to his offence and offered no excuses outside of highlighting the

---

[15] www.PrisonersAbroad.org.uk

mass difference in the price of ecstasy tablets in the UK and in Thailand as his fiscal motive. He had visited Thailand a short time before and had walked straight through customs without even realising. With this in mind and Britain offering little to him, he returned back home before setting off again on his own with his cache of ecstasy. Wisely he hadn't shared his plans with anyone and no one knew he was catching a flight. Nevertheless, Bangkok customs had a description of him on arrival and went straight for the face cream bottles where he had secreted his tabs. The only explanation that he could offer was that the authorities at Manchester had noticed them in the X-ray as he left and thought it more prudent to leave it to Thai authorities to take the rest of his life away, thus preventing a burden on a British prison for the next 18 months to two years (if that). He showed no bitterness over this nor of his treatment in the prison. Many of the Brits are whingers, he explained, but he had learnt Thai fluently and now had a very good job in the pharmacy. Idle hands appeared to be the greatest enemy with Michael saying that Sunday was the worst day as there was nothing to do at all. He would stay up as late as he could on the Saturday in order to stretch out his lie in on the Sunday. Literally everything had to be bought out of the prisoner's personal funds. I had expected Michael, like many of his counterparts, to be battling to have his sentence served at home. It varies from country to country but the agreement with the UK is that you can apply to have half your sentence served in a UK prison. This could mean that someone caught in possession of a small quantity of drugs could be serving 40 years as a Category A prisoner in the UK whilst watching murderers, rapists and even murdering rapists alongside them, go free. That, combined with the almost constant cell incarceration experienced in the UK, led Michael to probably the wise conclusion that life was better here. This was incidentally a position pretty much echoed by Sandra Gregory in her book *Forget You Had a Daughter,* who painted a bleak picture of Thai prison life. As a British reader I felt on the high ground until she was transferred to a UK prison,

226

a decision she ultimately regretted, where conditions were in many ways worse.

Michael said that he found it difficult to relate to many of the grotesque passages in *The Damage Done,* Warren Fellow's book about time spent in the same prison in the late 70s and 80s, and that conditions had substantially improved. We talked about football and Bangkok and girls and prison life. His dad had been out to see him three times and his brother once. His mum hadn't visited, and he understood why. He would have preferred it if there were no family visits or, if they did visit, only if they were over in Thailand visiting anyway and it wasn't their sole purpose. I wholly empathised with this and could imagine the guilt and pain that such visits could bring. He seemed old beyond his years and not just physically. His honesty and outlook amazed me. As he shuffled off back to the hospital, I departed truly humbled at my daily complaints and grievances. "I'm one of the lucky ones," he told me. "I'm young enough to maybe still have something when I get out. Most die here."

I left some money for Michael and subsequently sent him a parcel through. I had left no address for him to respond to me but knew that a reply would be unlikely even if I had. "I only reply to the birds these days and only those ones with a picture. I've had my fingers burnt once too often," he joked, half in earnest.

I thought about Michael frequently over the course of the remainder of our trip and still do to this day. I also ponder if he hadn't been caught with the tablets and walked through a deserted airport terminal as he had before, whether that would have been it or whether he would have done it again. I think I know the answer, but I still don't think his greed matches his fate.

Despite Michael's enthusiastic recommendations about the ping pong/razor blade act and the fire darts into the balloon routine, I had no opportunity to visit Pat Pong, frequently the only area of Thailand that many visitors do see. I did, however, childlessly visit the Lumpinee Stadium, the world's most famous Thai boxing venue, to witness some bloodthirsty antics.

On arrival outside I could make out a low resonating buzz, almost like a distant rumbling of thunder. It turned out to be the guttural urgings of the 1,000 strong male crowd, whose passion as a group of spectators was unparalleled to anything I had ever witnessed in football, boxing, or any sport for that matter. With a ringside seat in the gladiatorial arena, the low ceiling, smoky shadows and increasingly intense drumbeats raised the atmosphere to fever pitch even before the warriors entered the ring. Each fighter was in peak condition and none seemed to be overtly affected by the exchange of brutal kicks, punches, knees and elbows, with no knock downs or knock-outs to be seen. Having been a boxing and martial arts aficionado since before my teens, I have long struggled with the paradox of my enthusiasm and enjoyment of pugilism against the immorality of it all. My tolerance was stretched during the last fight when two 12-year-olds fought through five rounds of battering each other with no head or foot guards. At the karate club I ended up running in the UK, children weren't even allowed to wear "kid gloves" as sparring was pretty much a no no, as too was the hitting of any bag or pad, no matter how soft. The nervousness and wariness around both litigation and parental concern about bone development and injuries did undermine the benefits of training quite considerably but for good reason. So the two 12-year-olds set into each other as the illegal betters placed their unlawful bets. Despite some of the elbow shots, the most damaging blow in any martial art in my opinion, and some of the duress that the shins were subjected to, neither of them revealed even a split second's fear or pain on their faces. I left having experienced something as enthralling as it was shocking, my moral boundaries stretched yet again and only compensated by the fact I won 1,000 baht on the pubescent last fight!

Although I hadn't seen any ping pong balls, my somewhat self-centred weekend continued with the family on a visit to the Bridge over the River Kwai, about 70 miles outside of Bangkok, near the Burmese border. Through 250 miles of virtually impenetrable jungle, over 100,000 prisoners and Asian labourers from numerous countries died building the railway line that helped enforce Japan's supply line to Burma during World War II. The bridge, having been modified a number of times since it was bombed by the Allies at the end of the war ("in case they come back"), was quite small but nonetheless majestic. The health and safety guidelines adopted by the Lumpinee Stadium were in force here as visitors were allowed to walk between the two rail lines, with girders and big open gaps either side, across the river to the other side. That, coupled with the fact that it was a working line, and everyone had to move to whatever space they could find on the bridge when a train came along, made it quite an intriguing experience. We sat down at what turned out to be the most expensive restaurant in the area. We had studied the menu of a less expensive establishment which looked promising until it listed 'Carp Cowboy Style' and 'Sun Dried Serpent Head' with a Spicy Sauce or Mango Salad as an everyday kind of meal. I drank cold beer and looked at the bridge, pondering what the prisoners on it would have made of the scene now. Like the kids playing and laughing at the Thietvid Memorial, I settled on the opinion that maybe they too would be happy with this vision of freedom and prosperity.

Bangkok had some beguiling parks, in particular Lumpini Park, which stood out for its cleanliness and mass outdoor aerobic sessions enjoyed by anyone who turned up to either participate or just watch. The community feeling was both tangible and for us, atypical, as it is normally reserved in the UK for times of major crisis or when it snows a bit.

Lumpini Park was also well known for the presence of large water monitor lizards, some almost two metres in length. We were treated to the sight of one hauling its massive body from the water before confidently and fearlessly plodding over the grass in cumbersome fashion as if it owned the place. I had read that they do not prey on humans, preferring to eat much smaller animals. However, the literature did go on to say that if it is grabbed or feels threatened by a human, then it may use its teeth, claws and tail to defend itself, which could inflict serious and potentially fatal injuries. We watched him from the safety of the other bank.

A very diverse group of people played basketball together in the court adjacent to the play park whilst a man in his late 50s, possibly 60s, held a ball and looked immaculate in his pressed basketball gear on the sidelines. He stood there patiently, playing the game with his eyes and a nodding head and occasionally bounced his ball and caught it again as he shuffled his feet. He was on his own and somewhere in the recesses of my memory I was him but five years old, watching my brother or some other group of kids, not my age, wanting so much to join in but not having the courage to do so on my own volition. I watched him through watery eyes. I didn't know his story, but I didn't want him to go home on his own with his ball under his arm and put his clean gear back into the wash. I wanted to go and ask those playing if he could join in, but I knew, disregarding the language barrier, the gesture would be self-defeating. I couldn't draw myself away from the scene, but something finally gave in some quarter and he was nodded on to the court. I watched as he joined in and they passed the ball cautiously to him initially and then with increasing regularity. He was slow, he shuffled, he couldn't shoot but his positioning was excellent and he didn't give the ball away easily. He was so enthusiastic and immensely happy. I was enthralled and inspired at witnessing humanity at work.

We'd met a couple called Kate and Guna, again friends of Justin, in Bangkok, who were wonderfully helpful at the time and great animal lovers. We discussed our travel plans with them and they recommended the *Siam Beach Resort* on Koh Chang Island. Eirene and I are not big animal buffs and we were a little nervous that any resort they suggested might be like the set of *Dr Dolittle*. It was a long drive on dual carriageways littered with traffic lights, junctions and towns which meant progress was slow. On the hour long ferry crossing from Laem Ngop we watched the radiant sunset over Thailand's second largest island, Koh Chang. This meant that on arrival, our 45-minute drive to the other side of the island had to be done in complete darkness with unfamiliar sounding nocturnal creatures lurking in the jungle beside us. The kids were verging on extreme tiredness and hunger as we arrived at the innocuous looking *Siam Beach Resort* on Lonely Beach where we were greeted by the staff who carried our bags and led us along a beach lined with palm trees and littered with fallen coconuts. Our beach villa, with all amenities, was only £30 per night for all of us and the straw-roofed restaurant overlooking the sea provided a delicious and cheap dinner. We had found our paradise and not a talking animal in sight.

On opening our blinds in the morning, we were all silenced by our first glimpse of the island in daylight. Dazzling white sands fringed with palm trees flowed into a sea of turquoise where three forested islands punctuated our horizon about a mile away to our right. Not for the first time I drifted back to childhood memories of The Lost Islands.

We had planned to spend two days there and then head to Cambodia for Pnom Penh and Angkor Watt, a couple of do not misses that other travellers had consistently reinforced to us. But the temptation to stay was too strong. The kids had been in the car for too long and temples and Pnom Penh torture schools offered no attraction to them. They loved the place more than Croatia and it was hard to tear them away from the hotel at all. I was frustrated but realised I might have to swallow my ambitions.

The staff doted on the kids and they in turn increased their adorableness and Hannah even managed to charm two freshly made omelettes from the chef at breakfast. Although the skies were moderately cloudy, the temperature was about 30°, so the kids were wrapped up like condoms complete with rubber swim hats for the hours they spent in the pools or by the sea. While Abigail amused herself in the baby pool, we sat in the jacuzzi with beer in our hands, watching them all play as we looked out through palm trees at the Gulf of Thailand.

Hannah and Emily quickly learnt how to order a fruit shake and sign for it on their own and Eirene was happy, happier than I had seen her all trip. We had wireless, which meant she could have video chats with her mum from the poolside. I honestly didn't think Eirene could be any happier, but she peaked when, with our malaria tablets running low anyway, I agreed to give Cambodia a miss.

Koh Chang was a beautiful island and although not frequented by many tourists when we visited, it had the feel of 1960s Costa del Sol. The forests were home to thousands of macaques who occasionally showed up in the town to raid the bins. The kids were keen to go on an elephant ride but our penchant for zoos in the UK had long since dried up and much as they would have loved it, we could not justify paying any money for them to sit astride these chained up great beasts with faces cloaked in misery and hopelessness. And the elephants' faces were even worse.

We did, however, manage to lever the kids away from the pool for a boat trip to visit four islands that promised great snorkelling, deserted beaches and a hot lunch, coupled with the swiftness and comfort of a luxury speedboat. We were taxied to the speedboat along with two Russian couples by a local boy who looked no more than 16. Eirene wasn't too keen on a speedboat, but I assured her it meant less time on the sea and thus less chance of seasickness. She looked resplendent in her favourite swimming costume modestly veiled by a long sarong with an ornate buckle and a thin cotton top. Unfortunately, the sarong ripped as she climbed into the boat and within two minutes of leaving the harbour as we jetted out to sea, the sunglasses did little to hide the tears that were welling up. She was scared and she hated it and the Thai Adrian Mole driving the boat skilfully hit the waves at just the right angle to ensure as much of a spine shattering drop onto the water as possible.

Our first stop was an empty beach where Hannah joined me for some shallow snorkelling in a translucent sea, no longer needing to hold my hand for assurance. Signs in English detailed the decline in turtles and the harmful impact that interfering humans were having on them. Just behind the signs were three large pools containing a multitude of turtles of different ages and sizes all plucked from the oceans by human hands. It turned out that it was a turtle sanctuary with the intention of releasing them back into the ocean when they were ready but quite why they all needed rescuing in the first place remained a mystery.

Back on the speedboat, we headed to the very flat island of Ko Kradad for a deer spotting tractor ride through an incredible jungle with low lying primitive yuccas and ferns, their leaves glowing brightly from slithers of bright sunlight light, which broke through the overhead canopy. The tractor took us to a deserted beach lined with palm trees, a few benches and, disappointingly, a considerable amount of flotsam along the shore, primarily consisting of plastic bottles and old bamboo sticks. As we headed back to the harbour the heavens opened. The destructive breakdown of Eirene's outfit continued as something flew up from the tractor's engine and burned a perfect hole in her costume right in the middle of her back. We sheltered in the cover of a lady's house who brought out tea and cakes as her two-year-old child shared her swing with our children. Eirene wasn't too chirpy and had started to turn her anger, at her almost freely given consent to a speedboat ride, on me.

We were back on the boat again for a trip to our third island where we bought some overpriced drinks from a one-eyed barman on the beach. An Englishman in his 50s came and sat at the bar and struck up a long conversation in English with one of the wholly non-English speaking Russians. He was either unaware or undeterred. A Thai lady, clutching a walkie-talkie, mysteriously watched him from nearby and in what seemed to be a separate and completely unrelated incident, three Thai men emerged from the trees with one holding his chest, clearly in some agony, as he pushed off the helping hands of his two "friends". I felt I was at some sort of Murder Mystery Party and was glad to leave without ever finding out who did what to whom.

Our fourth stop was a tiny, uninhabited island where we had a great experience snorkelling. Despite the limited visibility, the colourful coral and diversity of the fish was quite amazing. Hannah and Emily joined me, but it was apparent Emily was just there for some bobbing around with her life jacket that she had become quite attached to. Hannah and I spotted some yellow and white stripy butterfly fish, brightly coloured parrotfish and a fancy tailed surgeonfish. We didn't spot any elusive seahorses that we'd been told to look out for, but we did see a grouper (a big fish!) hiding in the coral.

We were all reluctant to return to the boat, most of us for what we were leaving, Eirene for what was to come. We sped along for an hour as conditions worsened. The waves became choppier, increasing the impact on our backs as the craft became airborne momentarily before slamming back down on the water. A storm began to take hold and the rain changed from torrential to the next level above, with visibility reduced to about 20 feet. The small tarpaulin above us provided little in the way of shelter and I'd never seen Eirene this angry and scared before. I would guess her infamous drive in Crete was no longer top of her "worst experiences" list. One of the Russian girls had developed sea sickness and the other one had taken to wearing goggles and a snorkel to provide some respite from the monsoon rain and waves hitting her face. They too had started out the trip with some degree of now long gone glamour. We thought we were heading back to the port although the young pilot looked distressingly confused at times as his head revolved like an owl. It was 3.30pm and he put on the boat's lights, his radio-less instrument panel becoming the focus of everyone's attention as he looked nervously at his number two and spoke rapidly to him in Thai. A good degree of pointing ensued before the boat eventually slowed to a halt at a small jetty. There was a mutiny when we discovered that this was the penultimate stop for a tour of a monkey park before we returned to the harbour.

Our young pilot had by now given up the driving seat to the even younger first mate who was clutching a large wound to his abdomen and appeared to have had his appendix removed in the last few hours. He was surprised that we wanted to forego monkey park experience but a mixture of English and Russian shouting assured him we were serious. Remarkably, the journey back to the harbour where we started felt even worse, which took some doing. We finally roped up and clambered ashore, looking like we'd spent three weeks on a fishing trawler in the North Atlantic. Eirene, who set off looking like Posh Spice and returned looking like something out of *Tenko* shouted at me "Never, ever again!" which I'd taken as read three islands back.

We found, in most of the places we visited, that strangers were incredibly kind and caring and lacking in any sort of animosity. Ko Chang island was no exception and we started to think that this behaviour was the norm and the insular inhabitants of the UK weren't. However, some of our less than attractive English men took advantage of this kindness and it wasn't uncommon to see these physically repulsive Western males accompanied by very young and pretty Thai girls. The men fell squarely into two categories – the old and skinny ones with bandy legs and the huge Jabba the Hutt-type specimens with blankets of loose skin and enormous bellies that ran from below their groin up to the lower quartile of their many chins. Since the men were almost always English, the eavesdropped conversations between the unlikely pairings that we picked up was, to say the least, limited. We had mixed feelings on this, but the locals seemed to show no derision to the Thai women. On one side they were blatantly compromising any principles they had and most probably shagging these men just for the money. On the other side of the fence it was the only escape many of them had and we were perhaps kidding ourselves that the

Western basis of marriage, that of the initial rush of love and lust, is any better a foundation for a lifetime's relationship.

"Why would such attractive women want to stay with such repulsive overweight specimens? I asked Eirene later that evening. Her silence seemed painfully indefinite.

A few days later, after Eirene had recovered from Monsoon-speedboatgate, I suggested we take a drive round the island with the intention of visiting one of the many waterfalls it allegedly had. Hannah was not best pleased with this potential interruption to the day's swimming activities and started a campaign to not go, roping in as many allies as she could. However, much to her chagrin, she was overruled by the rest of the family. A few days previously we had inadvertently picked up an Aussie hitchhiker called Bruce (yep, that's for real) and dropped him at his hotel. It was inadvertent in so far as we stopped outside a shop where the bloke was cunningly standing with his thumb out. When Eirene was in the shop, I made some remark about driving round the island and he assured me that it was possible and that the "road under construction" bit over the dotted line at the top of my map was a well-worn dirt track that permitted us access to the full circumference of the island. With this in mind we set off on our waterfall search towards the start of the dotted line a few kilometres away. An overturned lorry completely blocked the road in front of us which meant we had to drive almost all the way round the island and come at the route from the other side, by which time we hoped the lorry would be moved. The dotted line started off well as a single track, recently resurfaced road, but gradually began to break up, cracks becoming crevasses and a few weeds becoming trees. A skirting of grass alongside the road with a few low hanging branches all too quickly became a narrowing tunnel of foliage that we began collecting on the roof of the car. We continued, safe in the knowledge passed on by an Aussie hitch-hiker we had known for less than 12 minutes, that the road was passable. I also had the logic that has blighted expeditions as far back as time immemorial. That of the bloke with his hands on his hips

236

looking ahead and declaring "Well, if we've come this far we'll be as well carrying on." I won't take on a hazard that I know I won't be able to come back through if I have to - but that's about as far as my caution extends.

After about 10 miles, we decided to stop. Decided is maybe too strong a word. The road stopped with a six foot drop into a river but carried on the other side. There was a track to the side that marked a ford crossing. A Thai family who were sitting watching in amazement unequivocally assured me, without a word of English, that I could not take the car across. I waded over and thought I could but they indicated, again without a word of English, that there was another crossing further down so we drove on to find that one.

On reaching the next ford, I urged Eirene out of the car with the video camera to film me drive down a steep bank edge into the river and cross it. Forgetting my statement of 10 or so lines before, I realised that the steep bank I had descended might be a tad more than tricky to ascend if we had to come back this way. Normally, I would have attached the winch higher up the car with the controls plugged in, strops ready and a suitable tree or two checked out, just in case I became stuck, but I was too excited. Filming done, she hopped back in the car and we carried on through thick foliage.

"Where are we going?" asked Emily.

"Through the jungle!" I said excitedly.

"How interesting," announced Hannah. "We already went through the jungle. We already saw monkeys. We already saw snakes. We…" At this point she was interrupted by a traffic report from Abigail tunelessly singing "Muddy car, muddy car, muddy car." It was accurate as we indeed were bumping our way through muddy puddles on a muddy track lined with dense but lush green vegetation and coconut trees.

A few wrong turns later and we were being shaken from side to side as one wheel then the next dipped into and out of brown puddle-filled ditches. Recent mud slides crossed our path and landslips took some of it away on the other side. The girls squealed in the back and announced that they were holding hands. Eirene pretended she was having fun on a fairground ride and tried to reassure them. She was being unexpectedly calm and comforting, this normally being her position either when she is genuinely not worried or when she is at rock bottom and trying to be strong. The detective in me suspected the latter.

Suddenly the track opened up, the jungle gradually became less dense and we dodged coconuts that lay in our path like driver training cones. We came upon a wooden hut on stilts which overlooked an untouched beach. It felt like we were the original founders on this beach like the backpackers in Alex Garland's book *The Beach,* although the backpackers didn't have three ravenous grumbling kids with them on their quest to get away from it all.

So we left our deserted beach and continued on another track to re-join the "main road" but this started to narrow until a landside and road collapse made it about eight inches wide. At this point we realised we had to turn around. Eirene looked at me and I tried to hide my excitement at the return journey through the jungle. Eirene was seething at Bruce and wanted to find him to give him a piece of her mind. If Bruce is reading this then I'd like to apologise for completely fabricating that you gave any such advice about being able to drive all around the island - I just wanted to have some fun. There's definitely something more assuring and authoritative when a stranger spouts something as opposed to a close family member.

CHAPTER 9.

THE BREAKDOWN

Thursday 2 October 2008

Day 155 - Cha-am, Thailand - 16,954 miles

We reluctantly and eventually left our island paradise and headed back to mainland Thailand. Eirene felt genuinely sad, which manifested itself by her heavily tipping our favourite staff - not an easy choice. One of them, a teenage girl who was expecting her first baby in a few months, looked on the verge of collapse when the kids gave her 1,000 baht, the equivalent of about a week's wages.

Somehow we had lost our return ferry ticket and although I tried to play the previously reliable "our baby has eaten the tickets," routine, the heartless wench would have none of it. Still, our position was better than that of two girls from Nottingham who were arguing in the queue in front of us. In an effort to conserve funds, they had bought a bus and ferry ticket from a man in the street, missed the bus and had to pay for a taxi, only to discover that their ticket didn't cover the ferry either. They were sisters and physically and mentally diametrically opposite. One, a lawyer, was very pragmatic in assessing the situation and considered their options now that catching a bus to the airport once they arrived on the mainland was quite remote. The other, a mathematician it transpired, felt their energies would be put to better use by going back and "stringing the fucker up by the balls." In the fashion of a pendulum I guessed. When they were out of legal options we offered them money, drinks and, as we didn't have room for two of them, a

239

lift for one which they politely declined. One of the unexpected things we discovered about this trip was how some people asked no questions at all and accepted your quest with as much indifference as if you have just announced you were off to buy a paper. Many would leave you at the end of an hour's conversation, knowing as much about you as when they met you, having volunteered all their salient experiences and finely tuned ditties. These two girls were stimulatingly different and after we had spent an hour exchanging our stories we uniquely left them having learnt as much from them as they had from us.

With great skill and greater luck, we managed to drive over Bangkok without driving through it and eventually found a motel about 100 km south, which came with insect-infested corridors. Interestingly, en route I decided to stop at a garage and check in the footwell under the steering column as there'd been water dripping on my shin. That was not the interesting bit. The interesting bit was that during my rummaging, I discovered a solid black plastic lump taped up inside the electrical wires of the loom. I wasn't quite sure what it was or how it got there but I thought I'd blame the Chinese who had our car overnight on our arrival.

The next day we took what we thought was a short cut down the coast, but it soon turned into an indistinct path before disappearing altogether. We soon found ourselves in thick jungle again, blazing a trail over vines and around trees while chinks of sunlight lasered through the thick canopy and made everything outside our windows seem alive. The car performed admirably but, despite my regular plotting of our position, we became lost and were forced to retrace our route.

While I was sure we were still rapidly heading south, we realised that buying the highly generic Rough Guide to South East Asia was a false economy. I thought it would be three or four books combined but with the same number of pages and same font size as a specific one for the country but realised The Hitchhikers Guide to the Galaxy would have served us better.

We drove past an unappealing bamboo hut for rent on the coast five times whilst seeking alternative accommodation. The only other alternative was a place called the Peace Resort, right on the seafront, where we probably would have stayed but not a soul would speak to us (so pretty peaceful in fairness). The owner of the hut appeared unoffended when we finally pulled in on our sixth attempt. He told us a worryingly cheap price before giving us a tour of his "bungalows". The bungalow lived up to our meagre expectations, but we accepted it anyway and endured an uncomfortable night.

Tsunami warning signs and directions to the nearest high ground, a legacy from the 2004 Boxing Day disaster, were in abundance everywhere. The disaster, triggered by a massive undersea earthquake off the coast of Indonesia, had heavily affected this region and all of the western coast of Thailand. Between 230,000 – 280,000 people had lost their lives across 14 countries by waves up to 30 metres high in one of the deadliest natural disasters ever recorded. In clumsy geological terms, the Indian plate had moved under the Burma plate and pushed it down, creating the earthquake. It caused the entire planet to vibrate by 1cm and triggered other earthquakes as far away as Alaska. US$14 billion were donated in the subsequent humanitarian operation. A friend of mine from my gym experienced it with her boyfriend and went on to raise money at subsequent events in the UK. Some of this money had gone on these helpful signs every 100 yards with the advice "In event of earthquake or tidal wave move to high ground" and a picture of a man running from a large wave. I was surprised we hadn't introduced a similar scheme in the UK with equally obvious images. "In the event of drowning swim to shore" or "If heavy object coming towards you move out of the way".

After breakfast we headed south to what Eirene decided was a "nice looking place on the map." We had only driven about 10 km from our hut, when, as we were rounding a bend, Eirene announced that the power steering had gone. We stopped, and I checked the steering rack and topped up the power steering fluid. We decided to drive back to Ranong, about 70 miles away, where we'd seen a Toyota garage. It was like driving a 55 ton Chieftain Tank but through clenched hands and a sweating brow, I manfully guided us to the garage. Maybe it says something about the reliability of Toyotas or the friendliness of Thai people, but we felt like kings on arrival. Seven mechanics crowded the car and a similar amount of female staff swarmed around the kids. Water and tea were brought out and our girls were guided to a play area as I looked for the "Millionth Customer" sign but couldn't see it. They continued checking our car while they drove us to a restaurant and picked us up an hour later.

We patiently sat in the waiting area as Abigail hit Emily on the head with a large mallet and I stewed whilst watching one of the mechanics potter around in the engine, cleaning out the air filter and topping up things. The car had been with them for four hours and I knew they were building up to monumentally screw the rich foreigners. Finally, Sannan, the boss, emerged to tell me that I needed a power steering pump and they didn't have one.

"How long will it take to get one in?" I enquired.

"Two months," he responded with a straight face.

It turned out the biggest diesel they had in Thailand was the three litre engine, so they had never seen a car like this. Bangkok had none in stock either, so it was left with us to source a part. I prepared myself for the bill, for spending loads of time and achieving nothing at all and then Sannan said, "No charge," on the basis that they hadn't fixed it. I inwardly cringed whilst contemplating the inner scorn that I'd been storing up. We drove off, tail between our legs, as all the garage staff came out to the front to wave us off. We found someplace to stay and took stock of our position and options.

****

We were about 100 km north of Phuket and we saw what aesthetically appeared to be a luxurious hotel, the Royal Bangsak. We pulled in and discovered the inside married up with exterior. It was nothing short of opulent and it was empty, so we pushed for a great rate. Had we arrived three weeks later, the price would have been £160 a night but we bagged a room for £32. The staff felt like old friends and couldn't dote on the kids enough. Our room was superb, the pool heavenly and the beach deserted.

I couldn't relax though until I'd sorted out something with the car. I contacted Alison and her hubby, fellow over-landers, who we were hoping to meet up with in Malaysia. She was in Kuala Lumpur and I asked her if they had the part there and if so, could she have it sent to us. Alison had never met us, yet she happily drove 40 km there and back for the part we needed. She then took it to the FedEx office where she arranged to send it off to the garage in Ranong, paying for it all upfront for us. We decided to choose the Toyota garage in Ranong to do the work, although it was some way back, on the basis of their approach to us. More importantly though, time was ticking on our 30-day Thai visa and Ranong, being right on the border with Burma/Myanmar, was more convenient to do a "visa run" - a quick nip across the border and back, for an additional 30 days. We were over the moon and the hotel set us up with a daily phone call to the garage to establish if the part had arrived. If we had called them ourselves it would have taken 10 minutes at least before we were put through to Sannan. We spent the next week in a jumbled haze of swimming in the pool, eating and visiting the tropical James Bond island, Khao Phing Kan.

Unless you don't have a TV, you couldn't fail to recognise Khao Phing Kan and its associated gravity defying

243

mushroom shaped limestone rock, Ko Tapu, as seen in The Man with the Golden Gun and various exotic perfumes for him and her. Until the island appeared in The Man with the Golden Gun in 1974, tourists rarely visited the place. However, all that had changed. and it proved difficult to take a photo with just our family and the island in the shot. A boat ride took us under overhanging rocks dripping with stalactites and hanging vines. We explored bat-filled caves filled with slippery rocks at low tide and marvelled at the amber coloured ancient rock art. We abandoned our boat in favour of canoes and navigated mangrove forests and low roofed caverns and dined on fish in a restaurant on a floating village called Koh Panyee. It was only at low tide that we could see the village was built on a series of stilts, although the effect was fascinating when all the stilts were hidden at high tide.

It had been a great day, an exhausting one, but I was relishing the time I had with the family. Hannah had been showing a multitude of strops interspersed with flashes of perfection and unmitigated love. She told us that she didn't even know what "Hello" was in English anymore. However, over dinner, on witnessing Emily's contented consumption of after dinner chocolate ice cream that she couldn't have due to her milk allergy, she provided a venomous commentary.

"Watch her big chocolate-smudged balloon face polish that pudding off," she spat out vitriolically. She was the master of over-reaction and seemed to let the littlest things upset her for a long time. Mind you, her screams of "Snake! Snake!" as we walked along a path in the hotel gardens were justified as she had narrowly missed walking on a black snake crossing the path. A member of staff was with us and, just as you watch the air hostess for a worried reaction when there's turbulence on a plane, I studied hers. I was seeking nonchalance and a wise chuckle but was given panic as she swiftly picked up Abigail and ran in the opposite direction and I followed suit, remembering to grab a child myself as soon as I'd taken a snap. I was later to learn from an expert15F16 that it was a posh sounding monocled cobra with venom deadlier than king cobras.

Back at the hotel, Emily dressed up as a fairy and told us that she could actually feel her wings but "every time I try to take off, I fall over." Hannah was a little unfortunate when I was a bit over zealous with her in the hammock, which tipped up and she landed on the ground with a thump. No amount of apologies or promises from me would appease her wounded hand. She merely wanted to stroke her pained hand with her newly found shell, her "only friend". Seconds later the screams erupted again as a crab emerged from her comfort shell and nipped her already painful hand.

The menu at the hotel was limited and communication continued to be a major problem. What arrived in front of us was fairly random and Hannah's request for plain boiled rice caused considerable difficulty. She had five days of rice soup and rice pudding before it finally arrived. I had to admire her perseverance. We worked our way through their menu a number of times in varying combinations and it was starting to become a trifle tedious when word reached us that the part had arrived at the garage. We decided that I would drive up early the following morning in the hope that it would be done that day and I would be back at the hotel by 5pm to collect the laundry. Hannah begged to come with me, but Eirene overruled her, which turned out to be a wise decision as it was to be four days before I saw the family again.

---

16 Vern @ www.ThailandSnakes.com

CHAPTER 10.

THE VISA RUN

Saturday 4 - Monday 13 October 2008

Day 166 - KhaoLak and Ranong, Thailand - 17,129 miles

The journey started out great. There I was, in the car, windows down and music that I like blaring out of my iPod. No longer did I have to endure the kids' favourites, *Fast Food Rockers,* singing "Let's eat to the beat, Kentucky Fried Chicken and a Pizza Hut". And then it happened. As I slowed for a hazard I heard a displeasing rattle coming from the engine. I slowed even more, and this prompted the engine to cut out. I stopped, opened the bonnet and had a dump in a bush. I don't know why, maybe it was nerves. The engine was boiling and the radiator pipes were untouchable. I had barely started to tinker when a man stopped on his moped, told me not to touch anything and returned in a Toyota Hilux. He towed me to a nearby garage who didn't do very much but the car started again. I heavily recompensed the Hilux guy and gave out some of the Chinese tea gifts we had to the other guys. Had I known that this breaking down lark was to be like *Groundhog Day*, I may not have been so generous with my gifts. I broke down a further four times, only managing a couple of kilometres at a time, as I tried to limp to Ranong.

Unexpectedly, every time I broke down, people stopped and crowds gathered to help. Despite this, none of them was of any material use and every time I turned my back they had jointly made up their minds to do something stupid, like taking the radiator pressure cap off and sending 12 litres of boiling hot water and anti-freeze into the air. Although putting negatives to one side, a fat woman fell over while running away, which amused us all.

An HGV turned up with a massive water tank trailer, parked adjacent to my car and poured 2,000 litres of water onto the radiator. I had no idea what was going on and tried desperately to explain that besides cracking the engine, this was unlikely to provide a long term solution. My lack of Thai proved to be a lesson in patience as each person tried the same things others had, including pouring antifreeze into the windscreen wiper fluid tank. It was like some lame slapstick sketch with activity going on as soon as my back was turned. Unlike the Chinese, who have an uncanny ability to fix things by improvisation, the Thai people only seem to have the enthusiasm for it.

Finally, someone offered to tow me to a garage where I was shown a dipstick with oil on it and told there was metal in the oil. There was nothing they could do to help and by now it was gone lunchtime, it was boiling hot and I hadn't eaten. The only positive was that Hannah wasn't there. The guy kindly called Toyota Ranong and asked them to drive the 100 km to come and collect me and the car. They said they would and it would be two hours. Two hours and, I kid you not, three seconds later, he turned up. I was learning to respect estimated travelling time a lot more.

His car looked a bit small for towing, but he had some sort of lift mechanism at the back which managed to raise the front of my car. We settled in for the long journey to Ranong, and I anxiously watched as he clicked his seatbelt into the solitary seatbelt clip. As a result of the driver clearly forgetting on the chicane-like bends that he had four tons of vehicle loosely attached behind him, a terrifying rollercoaster ride ensued, and I was grateful for the little distraction my Rupert Everett autobiography (that I had picked up at a hostel) offered. I imagined the headlines – "Married British man found dead at bottom of cliff with a Rupert Everett book and a greased Thai mechanic."

Surprisingly, we made the garage in one piece and they began to look at the car which they continued to do the following day while I stayed in a local hotel and repeatedly asked myself if I had checked the power steering fluid level properly. Having not heard anything for a whole day, I made my way back to the garage to be told that a number of the engine gears had been damaged as a result of the power steering problem. They said they would be able to make a list of parts for me but again I would have to source them myself. It was Saturday and I was pissed off. I spoke to Eirene and she agreed to come up with the kids on the Monday morning. With nothing else to do, I did what any other married 30-something bloke would do who suddenly found himself without his family for a weekend in a foreign country - I rented a moped from a lovely chap called Supat and zipped around the stunning coastline supposedly looking for a beach resort for us all. Actually, I was seeing if I could go faster than 100 mph which I'd never done. I also read books, pottered round the shops, listened to the house band play *Boney M* numbers, ate and drank lots, slept in, watched the England game on telly and was ripped off in the hotel massage parlour. Refreshingly, I'd remembered to bring my laptop but forgotten the charger so was guiltless in my lack of emails back home. It was a very dark cloud but with a delightful silver lining.

By the time the family arrived on the Monday I had their room sorted out at the Tinidee Hotel, further accommodation arranged in the Buffalo Bay Club, seemingly the best resort on nearby Ko Phayam island, and a visa run to Burma. I'd even arranged a little treat for Eirene – a taxi to the big Tesco store on the edge of town. Despite my three days of singledom I had missed them all terribly and was over the moon when they jumped out of their minibus on Monday lunchtime. Eirene was very happy with the hotel and we were all happy with the food and interesting new menu.

Eirene and the girls had sourced a great deal at the local hairdressers; Abigail had a trim and Hannah and Emily had their long locks chopped off into adorable bobs. As part of the deal they threw in Eirene's haircut for free, which was quite apparent. I was surprised they even knew who Kevin Keegan was.

Strangely, we were all very excited about going to another country for 30 minutes and at nine o'clock in the morning, our visa run driver turned up for the Burma visa run and crammed us into a tiny car like illegal immigrants. He took us to a port bustling with activity where we filled in our departure cards before being shown to our transport. The boats were long, open wooden affairs with a couple of benches and were attached to each other in such a way that we needed to step on a number of other boats to reach ours. A silent American and a pensive Malaysian man joined us, but this might have been an illusion as our kids were being pretty noisy. Transporting three under eights over six wobbly boats with slippery decks was a trial worthy of any TV challenge show. Each of the boats was a different height with differing sized gaps in between them and we lost points if we dropped any of the kids in the water. With maximum points achieved, we set off across a large bay towards a dot on the other side. We slowly passed a rock in the channel manned by some men with guns. Eirene, not a great fan of the high seas as I may have previously reported, was over the moon that this was it. But it wasn't, we had another 45 minutes to go before we arrived and as soon as we did, a virtual banner was hoisted above our heads saying "We're foreigners. Please screw us."

The contrast with Thailand could not have been starker. Everyone tried to scam us from the minute we stepped off the boat. As we neared the end of the walkway the uniformed officer asked us for photocopies of our passports which we had seen no reason to bring and the visa run company had seen no reason to inform us about. They offered to photocopy them and one of our newly self-appointed "helpers" made to grab our passports and run off with them, but I held on and accompanied him. I dutifully paid him the rip off charge for the photocopies and asked him why he had made two of each when the officer had only wanted one. He suddenly couldn't speak English. I returned to find an agitated Eirene with the three kids. I could see she was unsettled and, despite no knowledge of the language, was concerned at crude comments being made about the kids. Judging by their body language, I could see what she was getting at.

Next up was the immigration officers who wanted $10 for each visa stamp. No discounts for kids so we produced our $50 and all were returned as they were "dirty".

"The bank only accepts notes with no marks," the officer said. Two of the notes had small pen marks on them but the other three literally looked like they had been laundered. They would have none of it and we, as they'd hoped, began to hand over more notes for their checking in front of our burgeoning crowd. A token one was accepted but the rest were turned down as they were all given a ringside look at how much money we were carrying.

"You can pay in Baht," the uniformed man kindly offered, "500 baht ($18) each." I queried the preposterous amount but to no avail and paid up as every tourist before me had and every tourist after me will. We headed back to our boat with 30 days more on our visa and a wife who now seemed elated to be clambering aboard a rickety speedboat. Our driver was waiting on our return and after scaling over twice the number of boats as before, I was disappointed to learn from him that our experience was not isolated by any stretch of the imagination.

Armed with our list of parts for the Toyota, Alison was straight on the case and we headed off to Buffalo Bay Club.[17] on nearby Ko Phayam island, run by a Russian named Dmitri, who was very welcoming on the phone. The boat broke down a few times on the way over to the island and Eirene dropped Abigail's bag in the sea when we arrived on an otherwise

---

[17] http://www.buffalobayclub.com/

eventless journey. Dmitri had offered us moped lifts and I briefly imagined what Eirene's face would be like, before politely declining. We opted for the tractor-trailer option and had a relaxing putt-putt through jungle to the resort. Like almost all places, we should have known by now not to believe their websites. The kiddies club was a snakes and ladders game in the corner of a restaurant. The room, at 1,500 Baht (£23), did indeed have air-conditioning but it was another 1,500 Baht per day if we wanted to turn it on. There was satellite TV, but it didn't work due to a storm destroying the satellite two weeks previously and although the menu was truly wonderful, extensive and highly varied, none of it was available. There was scuba diving but the visibility in the water meant that I could barely see the glass in my goggles, and the children's pool was bright green and less clear than the sea. It was though, a splendid resort in an alluring bay and we had caught it at the start of the season. Dmitri was a great host and the menu improved considerably over our time there and was ultimately excellent. There was also free and fast wireless which allowed us to Skype and email to our hearts' content. On the day of our arrival in the late afternoon, the tide receded by over a mile and the sea became like a millpond. Dmitri was nowhere to be found, nor troublingly, were any of the staff and when we finally found him he declared, "Did I not mention, the tide here varies by up to four to five metres often in as little as an hour." I put our bags back in our room, got the kids down from the trees and prepared for a day on the beach.

We had the sun, sea and sand and the days idled by and I, despite the lack of almost any other people in the vicinity, developed a cold. The great thing about being in this region of the world is that, for a man, you can bypass the man-cold and man-flu dramatics and go straight for the malaria theatricals. I genuinely talked myself into having it until Dmitri told me to take some paracetamol and cut down on the beer. His advice proved to be nothing short of medical brilliance and my malaria was cured within the day.

This brought us to Saturday 18th October and a logistical operation unfolded that made Operation Overlord, the invasion of Normandy, look like child's play. Alison had managed to source all but one of our parts from Malaysia but the final part (part number 13525 - 17030 Idler Gear for the record), was not available nor could her dealer source it from Malaysia. I followed the same logic I used as a teenager with the ladies, namely, don't put all your eggs in one basket and quantity was the key. So I contacted every single person I thought could help. Toyota head-offices in Indonesia, Japan and the UK had more important things to deal with and did not reply but a Toyota dealership in Perth, Australia did and told us they could deliver it and it would be with us in 40 days. I made contact with an old police friend whose brother lives in Japan, as well as Eirene's aunt and uncle who have a sister-in-law in Japan. The parts guy in the garage that fitted out my Toyota in the UK proved his consistent self by being spectacularly unhelpful. Finally, I turned to Frog Island 4x4, a company that had quoted me for my work to my Toyota, but I had eventually turned down. With this in mind I contacted them with some trepidation, but they proved themselves worthy people.

This was how the plan was to unfold. At 0800hrs, my 73-year-old dad, who was in the UK for the weekend visiting his sister, was to depart the south coast's crumbly capital, Worthing, in his Nissan Micra hire car, complete with barley sugars and a full and comprehensive operation order, and drive to Kidlington, Oxford, a place he knew well from his time as a civilian police driver. I had sounded my dad out about this via my mum and she had insightfully replied that he would be more than happy to help but insisted that he would want the address of where he had to go. Dad was then to meet a man whom I will only refer to as Steve, as that's the only part of his name I knew. Steve worked for a Toyota garage and told me that the part may or may not be arriving on Saturday from the supplier in Belgium. If it arrived, my dad was to collect it and return to Worthing where he was to hand it over to Anna, the girlfriend of Eirene's

252

cousin, Corin, who lives in the Worthing area. Anna was then to hand it over to Corin's sister, Kirstie, before dropping Kirstie and her mum, Lynn, at Heathrow at approximately 1800hrs the same day.

The latter two agents would then take a flight to Bangkok to visit their dad (vis-à-vis, Uncle Jason), arriving on Sunday afternoon. Instructions had been sent to Uncle Jason, telling him what to do with the package in terms of couriers and addresses. The package would then arrive at the garage in Ranong on Monday or Tuesday, at the same time as Alison's parcel with the other parts, arrived from Malaysia.

Simple! Maybe not my first choice of elite personnel for what had become "Operation Condor" but we were in desperate times and these were desperate measures.

My Dad

The pick-up man and lynch-pin of phase one of the operation has the map-reading skills of Mark Thatcher. He never drives alone and needs someone to tell him his every move. He has not embraced satnav. He's never had an accident in 50 years of driving but has witnessed hundreds in his rear view mirror. However, I have never produced a more comprehensive pack in eight years of planning operations in the police. Explicit directions, when to refuel, aerial photographs, tons of phone numbers and a Plan B and Plan C. He's notoriously early for everything. We once arrived at Heathrow at eight o'clock for an 11 o'clock flight, that being 8am for an 11pm flight so I was concerned that he'd be staked out in the Hertz Micra opposite the garage on the Friday night.

Cousin Kirsty and Aunty Lynn

They are my mules. Their task, on paper, is the simplest of them all. Put their hands out when they are given the package and again when they hand it over in Bangkok to Uncle Jason. They have two major bridges to cross:

Bridge One is when the lovely girl from British Airways asks them "Has anyone asked you to bring anything on this flight for you?" In Operations HQ we know this to be a critical point. Both are inescapably honest and wholly incapable of telling even the simplest of fibs. A verbose and jumbled account of being handed a package by the father of a cousin's partner outside a pub in Worthing to take to Bangkok and post was inevitable.

Bridge Two is when they arrive at Bangkok airport with the green channel on one side and the red channel on the other. There is about £20 of import tax and VAT to pay on the item so they have a Matrixesque choice which is always dangerous. Green or red. Green means a walk of dread looking more suspicious than a first time drugs courier. Red means danger, admitting something to the uniformed men of the world's highest sentencing country. The choice is theirs.

Uncle Jason

Codename UJ is handling the Bangkok side of the operation. His task again seems a simple one. Receive package, call the FedEx number we have given him and stay in the same place until they come to collect it. What in fact will happen is that he won't do anything on the Sunday after he receives it as nothing happens on a Sunday (apart from FedEx who said they can collect it) and it won't make any difference if he leaves it until Monday. So on Monday he will go to work and discover that there is a FedEx place not far from his home and he will arrange to drop it off there that day. He's late, the place shuts at 5pm so he leaves it till the following day. The following day he goes there at 4.45pm and he has forgotten the bit of paper with the address on where it is to be delivered. Wednesday comes and he has both the piece of paper and the package. He fills in the delivery address incorrectly and opts to save us a couple of quid by going for their five day super saver delivery package as the overnight one is too expensive. Five days later an empty box arrives at Toyota in Ranong. Maybe I'm selling him unjustifiably short but I'm nervous.

The brains of the operation is Anna so all my dealings are going through her.

Tuesday 21st October arrives and we have a Code Green situation. Everything seems to go perfectly to plan. The part was collected and delivered to the Phase Two operatives who take it to Bangkok and pass it to Uniform Juliet without a sniff of trouble. The only slight delay was UJ asking us if we wanted to pay £150 for a man to drive it down to us the next day or if he should use Express Mail Service at £1.20 which guaranteed next day delivery. With hindsight, my paranoia and level of concern had proved very harsh on these devoted family members who were all going out their way to be very helpful. The only slight problem we had was that Sannan, the lovely English speaking bloke at the garage, had gone into hospital in Phuket for an operation. We had told the garage twice, in calls in Thai and in emails that there would be two deliveries and that one of the parts they wanted had already been included in a delivery they had received earlier. They evidently did not understand this bit as on contacting them after they had received the initial delivery, they told us two parts were missing. My Keystone Cops had turned into the SAS and I was confident the operation had been a success.

We had plans to leave Dimitri and Ko Phayam and move back to the mainland the following day, in preparation for our car being ready and fully operational by the close of play. The kids had taken a shining to Vin Diesel's "The Pacifier" which Dmitri lent us. It's like Kindergarten Cop but the acting is worse. It's a pile of tosh, banal and predictable at every clichéd level but the kids loved it. There were no books to read so I thought I might enter Mastermind when I returned home with the chosen specialist subject of *Rough Guide: South East Asia 4th Edition, Published 2005.*

Since the water was slightly less cloudy, the snorkelling conditions had improved and Dmitri took Hannah and I out for a free scuba diving lesson. But after spending about an hour and a half preparing the tanks and strapping himself up like a gimp, Hannah declared in the first five minutes that she didn't like the air, so that was the end of that. Dmitri then offered us some bikes but the one offered to Hannah had stabilisers with no wheels, just the metal fork bit, and my saddle was lower than my knees. Foolishly I elected to give it Joe Large and Charlie Big Potatoes before coming off spectacularly in the deep sand (who would've thought) in front of the hotel manager and my eldest daughter. The cut on my knee barely elicited a tear.

Dmitri had been great and although constantly in a state of activity in preparation for the forthcoming season with equipment for his kiddies club building up almost daily, he always took time out to do stuff for us. He even took Hannah and I out to his fishing nets to see what the night's catch had brought - not very much it turned out. About half a kilometre of fishing nets had fetched up a stingray about the size of mobile phone and another slightly larger but skinnier fish. There were three or four other ones in there that had been freshly decapitated by other fish and crabs as well as two big pink jellyfish which thankfully weren't on the menu.

At dinner, Eirene and I sat looking out at the beach as it came alive with a variety of crabs all scurrying around, digging, fighting and, from our wine-fuelled observations, wrestling. That night though, there were one or two less as Dmitri, bored with the daily Mexican pizza and tacos combo he prepared for me nightly, had suggested that I try something different. Crab! He sensed my unease, witnessed by the fixed glazed smile on my face and said that if I didn't like it then he wouldn't charge me. So there was my "something different", a plate of legs and arms and big shells and 100 crabs eyeballing me from the beach. A set of tools, evocative of a 17th century dentist's kit, was laid next to me. I selected the tools I felt would be most appropriate at extracting meat from the crabs and tucked in. The rest of my family were so keen that the man of the house should have the big meal that none one of those little minxes took even a morsel from me. I ploughed through the limbs and housing for what seemed like hours (Eirene said it was two hours) before finally putting the pliers down to one side with my fatigued arms. Dmitri bounced over, keen for feedback. "I'll certainly make a contribution," I offered. That night, the branch tapping on our window merged into a cast of crabs banging on our door as sleep subsumed me.

Notably, a lovely French couple had arrived with their two boys and young girl that day. They were based in Thailand and they, as well as their eldest boy of seven, spoke very good English. Dmitri had informed us of their impending arrival about five days previously and Hannah and Emily had been running around, holding hands, and arranging all the toys they thought they might be interested in, in anticipation of them coming. "The boys are coming!" they squealed, when the time began to draw close. They were the first people outside of Dmitri and his staff that we had all met for a while. The children duly turned up and ignored their efforts of neatly laid out toys. I watched as Hannah desperately tried to engage them, delighted and excited with the newcomers. They barely granted her a glance. She was nervous but confronted her fears and tried again and again but to no avail. She backed off. It was just a little thing, but I was chuffed with her and wanted to just grab and hug her as I watched her squirm in discomfort, trying to hide her embarrassment and disheartenment. I felt sad for her but proud of her ability to stick her head above the parapet, face her demons and be able to engage anyone.

"These are some of the most powerful characteristic that anyone can possess," I told her.

She harrumphed, "I'm not bothered," as another of chip of childhood innocence fell away rapidly replaced by the safety of cynicism.

We woke the following day to another cloudless sky with a deserted beach and the charismatic Dmitri, who told us not to bother going to see about the car until they said it was ready. Fellow over-landers that we'd met earlier on in the trip, Dwight

Wood and his lovely wife Tessie and two kids, Loong (18) and Lewis (5), arrived in Ranong and called us up at 1.26pm. They were in an internet café about three miles from the port they needed to be at if they were going to catch the last boat out to us at 2pm. We were messaging on Skype and I was telling them to "Go Go Go!" Unbelievably they made it and even made it to our resort when they didn't even know where we were. They were inspiring and were driving in a £300 Citroen ZX from the UK. Dwight is the sort of bloke that could try his hand at anything and improvisation was his middle name. His wife was from Singapore and seemed wholly un-phased by his mad antics. She was great fun but if you fed her drink after 8pm she changed. Her recounting of an occasion with the Chinese guide ("Get in the fucking car" repeated five times) scared us all. Loong is probably the most balanced and sociable 18 year old I had ever engaged with and I include myself in that. Lewis was five, turning six, and very handsome. Hannah loved him, and Emily confessed she would like to kiss him on the lips. They were great company and a great respite for us. Interestingly and predictably, now that Hannah and Emily were playing with Loong and Lewis, the French kids decided they were missing out and started the engagement process. Hannah somewhat cautiously welcomed them in to the inner circle.

Throughout all this, a feeling of foreboding started to form in my head. It was confirmed that the garage was right and a part that Alison's Malaysia man said was included in an original part he sent, wasn't. The clan could have easily brought it over from England when they came but we didn't think we needed it. I set all the hares running again and ordered it from the UK as well as back through Alison's Malaysia man whilst making enquiries with Dubai, where there was a rich stream of Land Cruisers and their parts. The UK guy had to order the part from Belgium, so Dwight put me onto a Belgian traveller they had met, Hendrick, who made enquiries for us and was in a position to send it out. The Dubai people said "Yes," and added that we should email them. Everyone was offering us the part and I kept the hares running. The following day Alison confirmed to us that her Malaysian man had received the part and it was on its way. She would collect it as per the usual custom and arrange for it to be couriered for us and it should be with us early the following week.

On the Friday, we left by a less posh tractor trailer than the one in which we arrived. This was often the case seemingly. The Woods came with us as they smugly announced that they intended to drive down in their fangled working car towards Malaysia. The day started badly with a call from Alison who announced that the part had turned up, but it was the wrong part. In fact, it was the original part that they had already sent through to us. Uncharacteristically I'd made the mistake of cancelling my hares. I was back on to the UK bloke at 8.30am UK time and he was not in. I called him at 9am on the dot and he immediately told me not to worry and that he had cancelled the order. How painfully efficient, I thought. I then had to ask him to cancel the cancellation, which he did, and he emailed back to say that it should still arrive on Saturday.

We waited at Oscar's, a bar by the port, for the 2pm ferry. It was an ex-pats bar recommended in most of the travel books but as I have recently discovered, this entry in the guide books has now been removed, which probably happened shortly after we visited. The guy that ran it was a painter and decorator from the Midlands. Ironically, the place hadn't been painted or decorated in years, furniture laid toppled over, the floor last saw a broom when the walls last saw paint and it reminded me of when I was in the police and attended a burglary. Together with the home-owner, I'd surveyed the devastation and wanton damage that they'd wreaked on the main bedroom. "Thank God they didn't touch this room," she said, a split second before I was about to put my foot in my mouth.

Oscar's menu was limited to beer and/or bacon sandwiches. The toilets were on a par with the Hellraiser toilets from Ukraine - Ukraine just winning by a sheet of loo roll - and the clientele looked like they were from Mos Eisley Cantina, otherwise known as that weird alien bar in *Star Wars*.

We headed for the Tinidee Hotel, our logic in leaving our paradise island being closer proximity to the garage would make things happen quicker. It wasn't something I wholly concurred with, but I could understand that it felt like progress to Eirene. Dmitri again warned us against this foolish move, but we knew best.

The Woods found a hotel that was almost exactly 10% of the price of our stay at the Tinidee. I vented my frustration at the nature of some of our trip and suggested that "there were better ways that we could have done it!" Every different, memorable and enjoyable bit of accommodation: the space centre in Kazakhstan, the overnight train journey in Beijing, the huts on the side of the Mekong in Northern Laos, the Yurt in Kyrgyzstan; Eirene had been vehemently against them all beforehand but praiseworthy after. One might therefore surmise that my next quest for something a little out of the ordinary would have been more receptively received, but no. If there were "Travelodges" all the way along we'd have stayed in them. She had consistently been an advocate of the expensive, the posh, the bland and the branded hotels, and the Woods and their carefree attitude brought it home to me. The kids love camping and not once had Eirene agreed to us using the tents or cooking on our own. I moped and whinged and complained and sulked, concerned we were missing out on as much as we were spending.

For once we did not have dinner in the hotel and Dwight and his family dragged us out to a restaurant in town. Despite losing our way at times while I was navigating, we came across a restaurant with no menus and no chefs that was simply wonderful. The food was freshly cooked which I definitively knew as we had to cook it ourselves. A charcoal-stained terracotta bowl of flaming coals was positioned in the centre of our table, supported in a rusty metal framework. That kept it just off the table. A circular metal cooking plate, about the size of a very large dinner plate with handles, was placed on top. It took the form of a gently sloping mound in the centre with slits to allow the heat to cook the bite sized pieces of meat we placed on top. Around the mound was a moat filled with a couple of centimetres of warm liquid, which cooked and steamed our vegetables. It was fascinating and so different to anything we'd tried before and we all loved it. I slumped into bed monumentally frustrated.

When I woke the next morning, I realised that I had been a bit of a twit or maybe I've spelt that wrong. When we were students we had nothing, and it seemed even less when I became a policeman and Eirene a teacher. The occasional holiday was sourced for £100 and camping wasn't unusual. As we grew older and my salary increased, holidays were top class villas in Portugal or a cruise and weekends away were often £1,000 or more in luxury hotels. The kids arrived and Eirene had a new car, money, time, no job and it stayed like that. And then this travelling thing came up and I refused to let go. Eirene agreed to it, possibly not quite appreciating the implications of her suggestion, we told everyone, our bed was made and then we were off. Things weren't great at times and she missed her mum and with me suggesting shit-holes we could stay in, it just wasn't her anymore. The budget was massively blown by this time, but I realised it was a reasonable price to pay. Eirene's caveat before we left was that she was to drive and that we don't do anything stupid. If she'd thought about it she could have asked for decent accommodation and I would have agreed. I would have agreed to anything and perhaps wouldn't have been so pissed off. I concede that I'm more than a little bit hypocritical, as I'm the first to grab a beer from the mini-bar or order what I want from the menu since South East Asia was half the price of everywhere else we had been to with twice the standards. I felt better and apologised to Eirene who, to her credit, said she would be more open-minded.

Dwight and I decided to nip up to the garage so he could check it out. He seemed content when he was shown a series of sheered and almost bald gear cogs. "You need the part," he declared. We'd left Tessie swimming with the kids and, on returning to the hotel, I was dismayed and delighted, but probably more dismayed if I'm honest, to see Emily doing front crawl across the pool. I had spent the last six months with them continuously and was only away for an hour when I missed one of those great memorable moments that tend to happen when you are at work. Tessie, who I discovered couldn't swim a stroke herself, had managed to coax Emily into swimming on her own. I was over the moon. I crossed my fingers that this wouldn't be like the time she managed to ride a bike without stabilisers before never riding again.

It was time to go our separate ways again and we waved all four of them off in their 16-year-old car with improvised Halfords trailer. During the course of the previous night and that morning, both Tessie and Dwight had mentioned about taking Hannah with them and us all meeting up in Singapore. In written form, in the cold light of day, this may seem an unusual, even sinister, offer, but it wasn't. It was actually one of the most generous offers I think I'd ever had but we kindly declined.

It was now Tuesday and our part still hadn't arrived. In fact, it had only just arrived from Belgium to the UK that day. Despite two emails and a phone call to the Oxford parts man requesting an expediency courier, he struck up a deal by opting for the UPS Super Saver which took until the following evening before the part was even picked up from Oxford and delivered to Abingdon. A journey even a Bangkok taxi driver could have bettered.

Eirene suggested we start moving again and I was with her on that. This nice hotel was pissing me off with its lovely smiley staff, crystal clear pool and trendy outside jacuzzi area with four multi-temperate plunger pools. Eirene loved it but remarked to me in the foyer "The one thing I do hate is that awful music they're always playing over the speakers in the background." I hadn't noticed it, well, not until that moment, and then from that point on, it was all I could hear. I suggested venturing out for dinner, a break from foyer music if nothing else, but all were against it. I insisted and then partially regretted it the moment Emily managed to bite her finger eating soup. Coming back, it was a very serene evening. Emily and I sat on the veranda overlooking the pool outside the restaurant after dinner. I had a beer, she had a hot chocolate, the house band was playing Eric Clapton numbers and there was a programme about climbing Everest on the telly. Emily prepared herself for bed and when I checked on them Hannah was on her knees in the prayer position saying, "Dear God, make sure my family is safe on this trip. Make sure the world is safe from this money problem. Make sure the car is safe from them mechanics. Amen." Emily on the other hand did what she normally does and adopted the praying position but instead of saying a prayer she held her breath until her face reddened.

Economically, globally, times were interesting and Hannah had silently picked up on snippets of our conversation where we were remarking on the apparent collapse of countries in our wake as we headed out East. Banks were shutting down and the High Street, including Woolworths, was gathering victims. We'd left with oil at an exorbitant rate per barrel which impacted us heavily, but the instability back home was to result in me putting virtually every penny we had into the safe confines of gold. Hannah hadn't remarked on this at all but little ears listen and I was perturbed that this was something of concern to a seven-year-old.

Fri 31st October 2008

Day 184 - Ranong, Thailand - 17,129 miles

The days seemed to revolve around sleep, the pool and food – basically a cruise without the nausea. We didn't rise until about 8.30am, except for the previous Saturday when Dwight came round at 7.30am and we had to pretend that we'd been up for ages and that was the norm. We'd have a buffet breakfast, which, if the Germans had been in, literally looked like a battleground. We would then make our way back to our room where we camped for the morning, checking emails, Eirene doing lessons for Hannah and Emily, me taking it in turns to alternately wrestle and cuddle one while she educated the other and then us all jointly shouting at each other a lot. On the stroke of midday, Eirene would begin the shuffling of the flock for lunch and we would go downstairs again and participate in the receiving and examining of menu routine even though we all, even Abigail, knew it by rote. On our return upstairs, we would spend a considerable amount of time preparing the swimming costumes. I'm unsure if this was deliberate or if we were subconsciously stringing things out, like a prisoner in solitary confinement when he has a simple task to do. We then splashed around in the pool for a couple of hours before the cry of an approaching dinner. Back to the room, which had now been made up by the maid who had given up on her pre-2pm attempts, and the kids trashed our freshly made beds whilst we showered them and prepared for dinner. As always, we would be first for dinner and we'd play the menu game again while the kids ran around on the karaoke stage until the intermittent arrival of the individual dinners. We would then watch the karaoke people do their Thai songs. We'd gone off the duo next door and their Eric Clapton numbers because Emily had started singing "woots on her wake up" thinking this to be the actual words to *Wonderful Tonight.* And then it would be back to the room to put on some cartoons that Hannah would authoritatively announce were "not appropriate for Abigail".

I'm perhaps being a trifle unfair as there were some memorable events above and beyond the circumstances described. On one occasion, we all took a taxi to Tesco, which although proved to be as painful as I would've predicted, did fill the kids with a greater anticipation than the Great Wall of China and the Terracotta Army combined. Eirene and the girls did, by conservative estimates, in excess of 30 laps of the same two clothing aisles while the locals had a good grabbing of the kids session. Seemingly, you can grab strange kids and literally pull them away in the opposite direction from their parents, but photographing your own kids dancing to music or sitting in the trolley is banned and strongly reinforced, so I discovered. On another occasion, we did a treasure hunt one morning in which Emily performed particularly well and Hannah solved some pretty cryptic clues. We would also walk into town through a market selling pig heads, shark fins and a diverse range of fruits and vegetables that I'd never seen before or since. We were greeted with frantic, shabby streets lined with crumbling colonial-style buildings. Red and gold Chinese lanterns hung outside some shops but were almost obscured by the abundant rows of spaghetti-like power lines strung down both sides of the road. We shared the road with a mixture of mopeds, modern cars and colourful, windowless local buses.

Without our own transport, distances travelled were short. Public transport was painful, a hire car cost a fortune and moped taxis for the five of us looked incredibly dangerous. We were worried about the car. On the surface we were upbeat but underneath we were thinking about what we were going to do when the wrong part was finally delivered, which seemed inevitable. I wanted to go back off to Dimitri's island as hanging around in the hotel seemed rather pointless, but Eirene was concerned about the annihilation the sand flies seemed to wreak on the kids when they played on Ko Phayam's beaches. She was pretty thorough with the repellent, but they still left Emily's feet looking like pepperoni pizza. Hannah hadn't been well either for a few days and she had needed the doctor. Although she seemed to be much better, it was arguably (I argued it was) not a good time to go to a remote island with no medical facilities. However, I was very happy at fooling Hannah with the old pizza gag when I told her that during her illness the Doctor had said all we could give her was pizza and pancakes to eat. "Why's that?" she said, her eyes lighting up. "Because it's the only thing that will fit under the door." Bob Monkhouse RIP.

According to the online parcel tracker, our part had arrived in Bangkok a few days ago and hadn't moved since then. I had formed such a negative mindset that if it was the right part it wasn't going to solve the problem, or if it did, it would only be for about 100 miles. Time was running out and we needed to get to Malaysia and onto Singapore if we were to meet the shipping schedule. I called up UPS and they told me the part was scheduled for delivery on Monday, a mere two days away.

At 3pm Eirene reluctantly, but wisely, finally let me nip off on the moped, leaving her with the three girls, to go and look at a Japanese World War II barracks and POW camp about 20 miles north. I knew that I was taking a risk that on my return Abigail would be doing an Olympic standard gymnastics routine as Hannah and Emily proudly held up their doctorate certificates, but I hit the open road and felt as happy as I had in the 30 minutes driving up from the Royal Bangsak hotel before the car broke down.

However, on this 30 minute mark the back wheel started wobbling and sliding away from under me, but in Sheene-like fashion, I managed to control the skid by braking. The back tyre was as flat as I felt. A bloke pulled up with his wife in a pick-up and I asked him if he would give me and the bike a lift to Ranong for 150 baht. He agreed, and we set off. I was hopeful of a quick turnaround at the bike place and the chance to get back on the road to the camp again, but unfortunately the bloke's driving made my father-in-law look like Lewis Hamilton. Not only did he drive exceedingly slowly but he was texting on two phones at the same time, so it was probably just as well. Two petrol station stops later, he dropped me at the bike rental place and refused all payment. I was keen to make a quick getaway but the once-friendly Supat destroyed the dream. Despite a line of other hire bikes on offer, I had to wait for someone to come and fix this tyre. Also, I had to pay. I had laughably thought that he would have been offering my lift some money on arrival and offering me refunds, but it wasn't to be.

"You sign contract saying you bring bike back in same condition you get it," he said.

"But I haven't done anything wrong – this is wear and tear," I pleaded.

He wouldn't have it. As we sat there, watching the clock tick by, waiting for his mobile tyre repair operation to turn up, I tried working the logic with him.

"So you never need to do anything to these bikes at all. Just wait for a renter to go out and it goes wrong and he pays?" There was no reply.

Eventually his guy turned up and the cost came to 100 baht, about £1.60, so I dropped the L.A. Law routine and swallowed it. It seemed that the air valve had broken off (a wear and tear or bad fitting job) but not before it was too late for me to go on my jolly. I returned to the hotel room a broken man to find approximately 60 lobster-red people in Speedos around the pool. The Germans had arrived – cancel breakfast!

I finished my latest book, *The Lost Executioner* by Nic Dunlop, which is a great account of the Khmer Rouge genocide in Cambodia. It focusses on Comrade Duch, the top man of S21 Tuol Sleng, the former interrogation and extermination centre in Pnomh Penh. The book had its flaws but overall it set Nic aside as a pioneer in his research. Moreover, the book made me want to go there and I reflected on our decision not to visit the country but then I realised that if we had gone there, the car breakdown would have occurred there and not Thailand. The two countries, even today, are strikingly different.

Being in Ranong was a good time for books. There was a massive book shop in town, although only about 30 centimetres of its shelving was devoted to English language books. You'd struggle to describe the choice as diverse with the works falling into two categories: Despondency and despair in South East Asia jails and Learn Thai. Of the former category, I had pretty much gone through them all, which, at £7/£8 a book, was a costly business. I had read of hell in Indonesian prisons [18], hell in Thai prisons [19] and hell in Cambodian prisons [20], the last one being a very powerful tear-jerker. I found Debbie Singh's book, *You'll Never Walk Alone,* particularly inspiring and even wrote to the author in Australia to share my thoughts and mentioned that we'd be heading to Perth later in the month. Eirene also started reading them, naturally, for her, from conclusion to introduction.

We were now 17,000 miles and six months into the trip and I was starting to feel that I should be doing something else with my life on our return to the UK. These books in particular and this trip as a whole were leading me to want to do something of more value than data modelling to third normal form in System Architect. I didn't really know what that was (the data modelling and the something) but I had felt like that at 21 and joined the police. 16 years later, I was feeling it again with the same level of sincerity as I felt then. I wanted the house in the country, no money worries and the worthwhile job but they didn't seem to go hand in hand. I thought I might join the Red Cross as a volunteer and do something worthwhile like swelter in the heat at village fetes and drop injured footballers off stretchers.

I liked Thailand although there seemed a clash between third world poverty and first world technology. On finishing school, it appeared that everyone was presented with a moped and a Liverpool shirt and every street had a *7/11* store in it. We found the Thai people so helpful and warm-hearted, completely

[18] "Hell's Prisoner: The Shocking True Story of an Innocent Man Jailed for Eleven Years in Indonesia's Most Notorious Prisons" by Christopher Parnell. Published by Mainstream Publishing

[19] "The Damage Done" by Warren Fellows - published by Mainstream Publishing Company. "Escape: The True Story of the Only Westerner Ever to Break Out of Thailand's Bangkok Hilton" by David McMillan - published by Mainstream Publishing. "You'll Never Walk Alone: A True Story about the 'Bangkok Hilton'" by Debbie Singh - published by Booksmango

[20] "First They Killed My Father" by Loung Ung - published by Perfection Learning

lacking in any form of menace. In banks it wasn't unusual to see a teller counting and sorting bundles of high denomination notes on the counter with no barrier between them and the public. The touching of heads, however, is considered very offensive except if it was our kids' heads in which case it was considered compulsory. There was littering and smoking but completely incomparable to the levels we experienced in eastern European and central Asian countries. Pictures of the King and Queen adorned almost everything, including road signs, calendars, inside taxis and on posters in every single shop, restaurant and home. In fact, just having the one picture in your shop seemed to be considered disrespectful with two or three being the norm. We had even seen shops that only stocked pictures of them. We assumed that not all of them could be for sale. Even when browsing a Thai website, they would appear as a pop-up just like Viagra or winning an Apple product did on Western websites. Much of the Western culture, like films and football, had been absorbed but so much of it had been ignored, like music. Very few Western bands and artists appeared to have made much impact, although I did see a Richard Clayderman section in a shop in the High Street.

I was thoroughly enjoying all the time I could spend with the kids. Even Abigail was growing closer to me and finally becoming outwardly affectionate. Sometimes I thought Eirene didn't agree with our direction or appreciated what we were doing, but then I would hear her on the phone to her mother reciting verbatim something I had said that she liked, or telling a friend that she felt like she was "stuck in the best July of our life. None of us are ageing." I'm not sure if I was advocating better communication between us or more eavesdropping on my part but it made me feel happy.

On Monday 3rd November, the UPS website said the parcel had been delivered. Too excited for breakfast, I headed up on my 125cc to the garage, straight through the front doors to be greeted by Sannan, the boss. His face gave nothing away but then in all the time I'd know him (almost three weeks now),

269

it never did. But his opening greeting of "It's the wrong part" gave it away. He showed me the old part and the new part that had arrived, complete with the part number attached to it that he gave me. Although both "vane pump gear" they were completely different. Other than "I think it is the wrong part number we ask for," he offered little more. I was so angry; I didn't hang around for an apology that was unlikely to come. I headed back despondently to see Eirene and the girls. Eirene looked almost childlike when I told her the bad news. Time was running out for us to reach Singapore for the ship to Australia, for the family and other commitments. Naively but understandably, we had arranged to meet and travel with Eirene's mum and her aunt in Perth on a set date and this self-induced restriction was forcing our hand. I spent the most part of another day emailing and calling to try and source the right part and I belatedly found a wonderful website that told me the right part number. Of course, the one we had ordered was for a Russian-made Land Cruiser. Toyota, in order to avoid import taxes, had a collection of Toyota badged cars throughout the world with internally manufactured parts, which made them all different country to country. This contrasted starkly with Land Rover, who had one set of identical unreliable parts available throughout the world.

I had started to hate the sterile Tinidee Hotel, now not least for its constant xylophone music playing throughout the hotel 24 hours a day that wouldn't be justified at Guantanamo Bay. It would steal a few bars from a well-known song, drawing you seductively into its hypnotic drone, before spitting you out as it headed off into its own pointless and repetitive melody. Maybe they were worried about copyright, but it certainly didn't bother the rest of Thailand, judging by the diversity of counterfeit products. We eagerly watched the progress, or lack of it, of a new part shipment which had taken 14 hours to travel to Cambridge from Peterborough, clearly not via the direct A14/A1(M) combo.

By the next day, Thursday, it had reached Bangkok. It had only taken 40 hours in the end. Singapore was about 1,000 miles away and we needed to be there by Monday morning. I was hopeful that it would arrive that afternoon, be fitted Friday and then we could be on our way.

We decided to hire a car for a day as we were in desperate need of a change of scenery and it was Eirene's philanthropic response to my despondency at not going back to Dmitri's island. We drove for two hours across the mainland, excited at the change in scenery, when suddenly the phone rang at midday. It was DHL in Bangkok.

"We have the parcel," they told us.

"We know," we told them.

"It's still in Bangkok," they said.

"Why?" we asked.

"You need to pay the £8 import tax."

"Why can't we pay it on delivery like we have with every other delivery from every other courier company? And why are you only telling us now?" I asked abruptly.

I had read in numerous places that it was considered terribly impolite to lose your temper in Thai society. I was terribly impolite. Nevertheless, they won. Obviously they didn't take credit cards but wanted us to pay the money in cash to a branch of Bangkok Bank before they would let it go. So that was the end of the day out. We made it to the bank, queued up, paid in the money coupled with the requisite fee for paying cash into the bank. But the task was not finished as the paying in slips had to be faxed to DHL which couldn't be done at the bank. Finally, with it all done at my end, they told me that it was unlikely the part would arrive tomorrow and would probably be Saturday, leaving us a load of night driving to make Singapore. I may have been terribly impolite again, but they did say we could collect it from Bangkok (a round trip of over 700 miles) but they needed to know in the next 30 minutes as they had to pass it onto the local post. Despite my best attempts, I discovered the world didn't revolve around us, so we elected for the conventional postal method.

Saturday arrived. I shot straight from my bed to my moped and arrived with the sparrows at the post office, which was shut, but the sorting office at the back was open. Bribes, smiles and bows galore granted me access to the man who could have been holding my part. He wasn't, but it was right behind him and he handed it over. I checked it and it was the right part. With my Ark of the Covenant safely secured to the moped, I drove like the clappers to the Toyota garage and greeted Sannan as he arrived for work. He looked at the part and, without a flicker of emotion, nodded his head. He thought it could be done by lunchtime, so I rushed back and was received like a returning Prisoner of War. I was the alpha male, head of my empire and ordered the family to pack. "We're getting out of here!" I declared. They all obediently and enthusiastically started packing and we arrived at the garage by 11am with bundles of luggage in tow. I sought out Sannan who told me that when they put the part in the car and turned it over, the engine "made a noise." I told him not to worry and that, from my experience, all cars make a noise when they start. Nothing was going to affect my elation. We took the kids to a fast food restaurant across the road where we bumped into Dmitri. He greeted me with "What the hell are you doing here?" before moving straight into "I told you. You should wait at island. It is never ready in Thailand until it's ready." It was great to see him, if a little embarrassing. We passed on our great news and he smiled in his inimitable way, his cynicism not wanting to burst our balloon.

On our return to the garage, I saw the mechanics dismantling the whole car. There were screws, bolts, pipes and car bits scattered, in no resemblance of order, amongst another car's bits. I wasn't filled with confidence, but they painstakingly and painfully took each bit apart, examined it, cleaned it, sanded it and put it in the big pile. I, too, was a pain as I hovered over their work while Eirene attempted and succeeded in keeping

272

three children entertained in reception for several hours. At 3.06pm, they told me they thought it was a rubber gasket that had gone and caused the noise but they thought they could have it done by 5pm or 6pm.

Our target of driving over 1600 km to Singapore in approx. 40 hours by Monday was still theoretically doable, so Eirene readied the kids for pretty much the night in the car as we watched the clock. Five o'clock came and went, as did all the staff, bar three mechanics and Sannan. At 6.48pm, everything was done and put back together. I'm a pacing vulture as they carefully put the final pieces of their jigsaw together, cash at the ready to tip the mechanics as the key is turned. It turns over but doesn't start. They try it again and it still doesn't start. A scurry of activity ensues with much pressing and turning of stuff and it nearly starts on the next attempt. More rapid Thai, prodding and looking and they try it again. It refused to burst into life. I start to head back to the darkened reception area to tell Eirene that it wasn't going to happen and we would have to return to the xylophone music. I'm nearly there when the car joyously breaks into life. I turn immediately and sprint back across the workshop, but they don't look happy. My elation shrivels as their eyes now look knowingly at each other and not the engine. A rhythmic banging is emanating from the engine. It sounds like a heavy object hitting a fan which, metaphorically and literally, it virtually is. Sannan looks at me and emotionlessly as always says "The engine bearing has gone. We can fix it, but the engine will have to be completely stripped and rebuilt. Minimum of two weeks and two months for parts." It's like a bereavement. Eirene is now next to me, although I didn't see her come out. Sannan looks at her and says, "I'm sorry." The others are looking at me. I look up and the kids are at the reception window clutching their teddies, looking out at me, ready to go. Eirene starts crying. "It's over isn't it?" she says. I nod and skulk to the back of the car for no other reason than to hide my own tears.

Back at the Tinidee, the hotel staff somehow knew of our bereavement, probably from our faces, and treated us accordingly. We talked over our options which seemed very limited. We could fly to Australia to see Eirene's mum and then fly straight back but we couldn't see the point in that. We could fly round Australia, only seeing the cities but we didn't like that option. Or we could wait in Thailand for two months and then have the car shipped back to England and fixed at a massive cost. Those appeared to be our only options. The only thing that was certain was that Eirene was going to see her mum in Perth in 11 days on the 19th November and it was made clear that that was written in stone. "We're fucked" I thought. I looked up and asked the children for a hug, but they ignored me and carried on watching the telly. "Fair enough" I acknowledged.

I don't think I had ever felt so low in my life as I performed a mental inventory of our situation. For starters, it looked like the trip was over and the car was going to cost a fortune to transport and fix. The parts and transport costs had not been insignificant at the time but now, in the grander scale of things, could be considered peanuts. If we returned home, we had nowhere to go home to. We had no house, no car, a load of money spent, a trip half done and a wife whose list of favourite people didn't have me in the top five. Eirene needed to be in Singapore to travel to Thailand and I needed to sort out the car, either fixing it or having it transported somewhere. The kids unanimously wanted to go with their mother and I felt as lonely as I did a fool. I'm not sure what the opposite of rose-tinted spectacles was, but I'd managed to get myself a great 2 for 1 deal at Specsavers, whatever they were.

The next day things didn't feel any better, so we left for Dmitri's island to re-group and decide what to do. Eirene offered no resistance at all and Dmitri kindly picked us up from the port in his tractor without even a hint of smugness. He gave us a discount on our previous food and accommodation stay and threw in free air-conditioning, which had been one of Eirene's bugbears about coming back here.

I booked Eirene and the kids on a flight from Phuket to Singapore for Wednesday and arranged the taxi to take them the 300 km to the airport. Dwight, who was now in Singapore, agreed to pick them up at the other end and take them to a hotel. I started making arrangements to have the car transported to Malaysia so it could be dealt with by a garage owned by Alison's friend. The guy was recommended and Malaysia had more parts available. Plus it was in Kuala Lumpur which would make subsequent remote shipping considerably easier. Dmitri shook his head and said in his imitable Moscow accent "It will be difficult. It is best you keep car in Thailand and sort it here. Getting it to Malaysia very difficult." As the days passed the bugger proved to be right again and I was beginning to learn my lesson.

The next day I saw Eirene and the girls off to the airport but as we made our way through the jungle on the back of the tractor to the waiting speedboat, a typhoon ominously hit the island and the only shelter we had was under a big sheet of tarpaulin. When we arrived in Ranong, we were pleased that from the selection of pot-bellied, leery, smoking taxi drivers on offer to us, our taxi driver was smart, cheerful, spoke some English and had a very modern air-conditioned car. We collected some belongings from our car at the garage and I said farewell to my family and forlornly watched them drive off. Supat lent me a moped for a few hours and I made my way towards Burma, this time via a five-star casino, to extend my visa for another month as it was due to run out the next day. I made it back just in time to catch to the speedboat, a 30 minute trip that avoided the two hour slow boat which frequently breaks down I was told. After two hours and numerous breakdowns in the speedboat, I was dismayed to see the slow boat overtake us as we bobbed around half way between Ko Phayam and Ranong. I finally made it back to Dmitri's and settled down to a long night in front of the computer while I tried to arrange transport of the car to Malaysia. Living the dream.

The drama of the last few days slowly evaporated and a sense of perspective came in. I decided that we could still carry on with a hire car in Australia. It wasn't what we planned but labour was cheap in Thailand and I had a few good leads on transport. Any worries and woes I had were smoothed by Dmitri who laid on a few complimentary cocktails for me that evening, knowing my family was absent. It was Loy Krathong, a Thai festival of light, which is traditionally spent with a loved one. Dmitri's wife and family were absent as well and, like a couple of straight, married men approaching middle age, together we watched the small candlelit boats slowly drift out to sea as their airborne counterpart lanterns floated skywards toward the full moon.

The following day, I finally began to make some headway with the car with an English guy running an expat motor firm in Bangkok agreeing to act as my middleman to handle the repair and engine replacement of the car at a specialist garage near him. I paid him more than I should have and more than I thought we initially agreed, but my hands were tied and I think he knew it. The Malaysian transport option never had legs and I finally heeded Dmitri's advice. The plan was to ask the Toyota garage in Ranong to sort out the transportation of it to Bangkok and I was chuffed to receive an email from them.

From: Toyota Ranong
Sent: 14 November 2008 08:25
To: info@drive-to-oz.com
Subject: Transportation car for you

Dear. Mr. Graham

Toyota Ranong clearly give know in about [story] of car your transportation go to Omyaichiangkong Co.,Ltd Nakhon Prathom which , our way will use in car your loading , by company truck way has will the calling picks the freight , 20,000 amounts are baht , which , this price has totaled up something the insurance between the transportation is that already , and ? at you fully company way will manage the transportation give you immediately , and the part in about [story] of expenses , your way will must have payying for Toyota Ranong orderlily before the transportation , when , the transportation has been doomed to die Nakhornpathom already has will an officer comes to do taking car your reaches to do repairing next.

If you have the doubt or , inquire the data adds, contact with done to a turn Toyota Ranong Call Center: 077-822822.

Yours truly,

Mr. Jirasak

Toyota Ranong Toyota Dealer's Co., Ltd

So with all that ambiguity cleared up and all the ends tied, there was an emotional hug from Dmitri, after he unsuccessfully tried to charge me less than half of what my room rate should have been. I really loved that place and grieved at having spent so long at that cursed Tinidee in Ranong.

Eirene and I travelled for six weeks in Greece between our second and third years at university. It was a great holiday, an eye opening trip and probably the moment, at aged 20, we both realised that this was it and that we were for each other. But five days of that trip was spent in Ios and it was crap. I was frustrated at not having a job and then even more frustrated when I did, working for 80p an hour washing dishes in the dark, as my girlfriend carried plates to tables and received tips as her lecherous boss tried it on. We also met up with a lovely English bloke and his girlfriend who we watched, five years later, on some documentary, as he gave his account of his armed robbery conviction and subsequent escape and recapture. When we think of our trip to Greece we have a habit of thinking of just those five days. Not the three weeks before nor the three weeks after. The darkness colours the whole. And I was worried that our car problems and prolonged stay in that sanitised anaesthetised hotel would become our los.

My 8.30am moped arrived, driven by a Jimmy Krankie lookalike but smaller. He or she was minute. We made it to the port where, once again, the speedboat broke down a couple of times on the journey across. When we eventually docked, Eirene's old taxi driver was waiting for me and we stopped at Toyota on the way for an incomprehensible conversation with the bloke who wrote the above email. I handed over a mere £100 for them failing to fix the car and taking a long time to do so but it was a fraction of what I would have paid in the UK for a similar failure to fix it. I was carrying nothing more than a small rucksack and it seemed amazingly easy to travel without children. But not something I yearned for.

While sitting in the back of the car, I decided to have a read of my *Lonely Planet Australia* book while the driver did his Ayrton Senna impression. He also had an incessant nose picking problem which reached such a height that I was fearful his head would cave in. When I mentioned it to Eirene later, she told me that she was convinced there couldn't have been anything left at all by the time he dropped her off a few days before.

Regrettably I decided to stay in the centre of Phuket, which was a town like Ranong and every other Thai town but bigger. The only thing that stood out as different was the gun shop and the prices which were steeper now that I was further south. Before I checked into my hotel, I was assured that it had wireless and this was confirmed by the receptionist and her two co-conspirators. However, on arrival, they all denied any existence of wireless but that I could readily connect to a Hewlett Packard printer at the office block opposite and pointed me to the £10 per hour machine sitting in the corner of reception. Well, the joke was on them because I discovered that if I put my laptop straight out, parallel to the ground, on the right hand window of my 12th-floor room, I could muster something between connected and one bar from a router somewhere.

Unfortunately, this was the time that an old work friend called Clare elected to send one of her three megabyte "Why women are better than men and penises are stupid" type emails. I prayed that in years to come this sort of file could be passed seamlessly on a pointless social media site and not by email. The long and short of it was that I had to stand holding my lifeline of a laptop containing all our photos, films and my diary for almost 30 minutes wearing nothing more than my boxer shorts. I felt like I was in Guantanamo Bay/Tinidee Hotel as I stood with my arms outstretched at shoulder height, holding the heavy Sony Vaio as steadily as I could. In fairness though, the penis/stupid men email was worth a smile so I forwarded it on to all my contacts as was the tradition.

The next morning, my pre-booked taxi driver turned up 45 minutes before I'd requested him and, in fairness, he did have the air if not the looks of my dad. He did, though, break all land speed records in driving me to the airport a mighty three and a half hours before I was due to take off. I thoroughly enjoyed my flight with a window seat which was normally only reserved for our kids who would fail to even glance out of it for the duration of the flight. I, however, grabbed the window of opportunity quite literally and spent virtually every single minute of the flight relishing the view as I watched the people, houses and cars diminish in size to dots and rivers and roads to lines. I exchanged some pleasantries with a couple from Leicester who were on a three-week South East Asia/Australia trip for her 60th birthday. As seemed to be the pattern, and perhaps it was my inquisitive nature, we departed with me knowing, amongst many other things, the weight, time and date of their grandchildren's births (apparently unusually heavy for a Gemini) and them knowing that I was sitting next to them going from Phuket to Singapore. It had been a matter of days that I'd been away from my family, but it seemed a lifetime.

Singapore was a posh airport with only four controllers at the passport desk catering for 200 passengers. Two of them did nothing as they were in charge of staff and some special card holders of which there was none; one of them actually managed to manicure all her nails in the 45 minutes we queued so perhaps I was being a bit harsh when I said nothing.

As I only had hand baggage I waltzed straight past "baggage reclaim" and through customs to be greeted by Eirene and the three kids for the first time in any flight I have done. Normally they either don't show up or are late. It was brilliant but unfortunately Eirene was desperate for the toilet so immediately departed for 20 minutes with Hannah. I subsequently established that she had been sharing a compact flat with a friend of Dwight's wife Tessie that was accommodating six adults and seven kids. I felt it was a bit cosy, so I suggested we move out to a hotel or apartment of our own when I arrived there, but Eirene insisted that I had to experience the experience that she had experienced. I didn't know if that was a good or bad thing.

We headed into town and bickered with each other over a direction dispute but that was the norm for us. It had become somewhat of a tradition that in times of prolonged separation we have a good punch-up when we eventually meet up. We headed for Raffles Hotel where I had been keen to have a cocktail in the Long Bar and where Dwight and family were waiting. There are certain things you have to do when you go to certain countries, the must-dos and can't-be-misseds, the places that are distinctly associated with that country and which you will be asked about on your return. The Long Bar at Raffles is one of them, although I'm trying to have it removed from the list. It's one of the world's most famous hotels and where the "Singapore Sling" cocktail was invented, and rather morbidly where 300 Japanese soldiers committed suicide following the liberation of Singapore towards the end of World War II. When I saw the prices they charged I was sorely tempted myself. The place had been completely rebuilt numerous times and was luxurious, although they still encouraged the throwing of your monkey nut shells onto the floors. At least I hoped they did or I was just arriving after some uncouth guests. The place attracted many Brits who would have a Singapore Sling - but only the one after they gave you the bill. Dwight and his family had looked after Eirene and the kids from the moment they arrived, so we took them out for dinner at an outdoor place and had a steamboat, a restaurant where you cook your own dinner at your table, not entirely dissimilar to what we'd had in Ranong with them. It really was a tremendous business concept and I could imagine the bank manager's response to the initial business pitch. "So people come to you and pay over the odds for the food and drink at plastic tables outside on the pavement and you have no kitchen or anything like that and they pay you to cook it themselves?"

I found Singapore to have a strange socialist culture. It is probably one of the most capitalist cities/countries in the world but with a tremendous social influence from the government. Buying and renting is not easy and there is a mass of social housing, in the form of towering tenement blocks, each with its own personalised and large sequential number emblazoned on the side. Ours was Block 830 (between 829 and 831). There are walkways, alleyways and parks in the middle, with little sunlight and the occasional underground supermarket. Everything about it sounds like the Jasmine Allen Estate off *The Bill* or Broadwater Farm, except it's not. It's everything that it was designed to be in the UK but just didn't work. In the UK, these tower blocks alienated people and isolated previously thriving communities. In Singapore it's been the opposite, with the communal park areas used and shared by all for a myriad of differing activities. In the UK, it proved to be a hotbed of un-witnessed crime, the numerous stairwells and overhead walkways acting as escape exits for the growing minority. In Singapore, it's as safe as houses so to speak, with everyone looking out for everyone. There was no litter, no graffiti, no smell of stale urine and even the lifts worked. It felt impersonal and no less claustrophobic but there was no fear and street crime is almost non-existent. We arrived by bus with no louts, no swearing, no spitting and no intimidation. The pavements of the country bore testimony to the prohibition on chewing gum sales and the low level of crime to the severe sentences dished out. In 1994, an 18-year-old American student, Michael Fay, was sentenced to four months in prison, four strokes of the cane and a $3500 SD fine for criminal damage. It would have been six strokes had President Clinton not appealed for clemency. It was a bitter pill to swallow for the otherwise law abiding Fay and I'm aware there's a Clinton joke there somewhere as well. The ground floor of every block in Singapore is an open pillared area and on the night we arrived, a massive open-air wedding was taking place. It was vibrant and compelling.

Our host Carol and her husband, a man whose name I never, ever remembered, no matter how many times anyone repeated it, had four children aging from 11 months to 11 years, completely looked after by two Filipino maids. Carol and hubbie were rarely to be seen, working on a multitude of jobs ranging from crane operating to picture processing. The maids did everything – cooking, cleaning, feeding, disciplining, driving, teaching and everything and anything else. Even when mum or dad were at home, their roles did not waver one iota. If there was a family picture to be taken, then the kids were handed over to Carol. If a baby Carol was holding began crying, the baby the maid was looking after would be moved from its cot/baby seat to accommodate the blubbing new arrival. It was a very strange dynamic and we couldn't help thinking that if they didn't have the maids and maybe sold their brand new Toyota people carrier, then they could have more time with the kids.

Dwight was keen to give us an experience of Singapore that we wouldn't find in a hotel. I think he picked up that I wasn't happy with the Holiday Inn/Tinidee setup in Ranong and had acted accordingly, not least because everything in Singapore, including hotels, cost a fortune. The one thing, though, about living as a guest in someone's home, even if you are paying $50 dollars a night for it, is that you compromise your standards in many ways. If the family in question choose to swear, it's something that you either accept or don't. Hannah and Emily, on meeting me at the airport, thought the place was great as they ate cake for breakfast and watched violent, bloody Japanese cartoons which ran continuously on the TV. Abigail became increasingly frustrated as their second youngest made it her life mission to take and hide every single toy that Abigail picked up. They were, though, a very loving and giving family who treated us like special guests, making us feel as comfortable as possible in their humble abode.

Singapore proved to be quite spellbinding. Coming from Thailand as we just had, their shops, restaurants, roads, infrastructure and architecture seemed to be from another age. Their swimming pools and leisure complexes were vast and spotlessly maintained and staffed, with almost nominal entrance fees. They say that people who haven't been to Singapore for five years struggle to recognise the place. They have an island called Sentosa, accessible by a cable car that bizarrely goes through the centre of some buildings on its journey down, that they've turned into a massive holiday complex with amusements, rides, beaches and a varied choice of sports, foods and activities. It's on the way to rivalling some of its Disney cousins in the US and, at £6 for a pint of beer, I think they'll have the funding to do it.

We indulged our slight hankering and ventured on a night safari at Singapore Zoo, which was a pleasant surprise. We journeyed through jungle in an open-sided electric bus with uncaged animals roaming freely and crocodiles that seemed to be within touching distance. We then drove on to another geographical time zone where the giraffes paid little attention to the new batch of transient travellers who continued their adventure through Equatorial Africa, where the commentary turned to the lions on the right. There were no barriers or glass and perhaps half the excitement was due to the fact that the papers were still covering the story about the Malaysian worker who had, just a few days before, unsuccessfully stormed the lion enclosure with a large mop and a bucket over his head.

We alighted from our bus and headed for an animal show where an Americanised Singapore girl regurgitated a rehearsed spiel and encouraged some trained animals to perform for a peanut. Every single animal refused to perform as requested, no matter how many treats they were given, which at least showed that they weren't beaten into performing. The only animal that did what it was told was a humongous python that emerged from under the seats of the central section of the audience. Volunteers were requested and promised Baskin Robbins vouchers in return. As we were sitting at the front, the kids tried to push me up every time they requested a volunteer. I'm not big on snakes and Hannah wasn't far behind me on that either. When the snake appeared, I clung to my bench, my nails wedged into the crevices of the wood, whilst trying to nudge Eirene forward with my shoulder.

The show reminded me of an account by my friend, Neil, who visited a bird sanctuary off the A3 in Hampshire. They arrived late for the eagle show, the eagle having already departed from the leathered wrist of the demonstrator. They then listened to a 45-minute increasingly desperate fill-in spiel from the eagle man himself, before he finally put his big gauntleted hands up and apologised for losing the bird.

In Thailand and much of South East Asia, there is a respect for foreigners that perhaps parallels the disrespect that too many people in the UK have for our own foreigners. Money, success and achievement of outsiders, so widely castigated in the UK, was admired there. People looked at our expedition fitted out car with genuine admiration and staff in the finest hotels honestly did not appear to hold one ounce of hostility towards us. With this admiration for money and high standards in mind, I detected a slight sense of disenchantment in Carol and her husband (I really wish I knew what his name was, but it was just too late to ask) when we clambered into their car and headed for the "Budget" terminal at Singapore's Changi Airport, one of the world's finest airports. Their family were levered into every available nook and cranny of the car for a rare day out as we headed to the airport, us *Farangs,* as the Thai people called us, occupying the bulk of the main seating area. As always, with 13 people in an eight-seater people carrier, we yet again silently compromised our near elastic standards. I don't know if it is a British thing, or just our own personal weaknesses, that insist on us failing to conform to the most basic of safety standards just so that we don't offend hosts that we will never see again. We had initially made strident attempts at going for the taxi options, which wouldn't have had seat belts in it anyway, but they wouldn't have it.

I checked the bits of paper as we drove and again reiterated that it was the "B" terminal which mystified him a great deal.

"Is there no such terminal?" I enquired.

"There is," he responded, "but it's the budget terminal."

"Do they not fly to Australia from there?" I asked.

"Yes, they do," he replied.

They had actually built a special terminal very quickly, they told me, just for two or three budget airlines that flew from there. Occasionally, you have terminals primarily employed by the budget airlines in the UK but you don't specifically label them as such. I felt I should have a bell and be chanting "Unclean! Unclean!" By the time we arrived at the airport, they had resigned themselves to our destination, but we were all surprised when we saw the brand new, smart building with no queues, loads of shops and a free kids' playground. We said our thank yous and goodbyes and made our way through to the departure lounge area.

Eirene and I were excited. This point marked the end of stage four with our final stage, Australia, upon us. We ascended the plane's steps, as buoyant as we had ever been, good seats sorted and the future ahead of us. Eirene was seeing her mum and I was delaying, for a little bit longer, the inevitable feeling of senselessness that commuting and tapping a computer for the next 30 years would soon bring.

CHAPTER 11.

AUSTRALIA

Wednesday 19 November 2008

Day 203 - Perth, Australia - 17,129 miles

The plane landed 20 minutes late and as we queued for another 30 minutes, waiting for our baggage to come out, a bloke with a radio had his dog sniff every crevice of us and our hand baggage. We assumed he worked for the airport authorities. When the bags finally popped out, the traditional "who gets to sit on the trolley" fight ensued.

Every time I emerge from airside into the passenger terminal, I always scan the raised signs with people's names on them hoping beyond hope that one might have my name on it. For some reason there is something extremely agreeable and comforting about someone coming to meet you at arrivals.

I'd been in touch with my cousin in Australia in the hope of meeting up with him and the rest of the family when I arrived in Perth, and he had responded by saying his dad would pick us up from the airport. We had lived in Maidenhead for many years, a 30 minute drive from Heathrow on a good day, and there weren't many good days. As a result, I'd watched my parents be at the beck and call of every man, his dog and their friend arriving there, wanting to save money on a taxi and inevitably accommodation. For that reason I'd turned down the kind offer, knowing neither where Uncle Richard would have to come from or where, at that stage, we would be going to and so we had arranged a hire car.

However, being unable to break with custom, I scanned all the name signs being held up by relatives and taxi drivers as we emerged into the passenger area. A man started walking forwards as we emerged from arrivals as though he knew me. He introduced himself as Richard Taylor, my Uncle Richard whom I'd never met. Uncle Richard knew we didn't want a lift and he knew that we had a hire car arranged but, despite that, he thought he would come and say hello and give us his number.

After Uncle Richard helped me find our hire car, we said our goodbyes and headed off in the wrong direction to our rented apartment that Eirene's mum, and very entertaining Aunt Maria, had occupied for us that afternoon. Eirene was over the moon to see her mum and the kids responded in the manner that we had hoped they would, especially Abigail who wouldn't let go of her. Excitement overruled tiredness and we stayed up late into the night talking and chatting.

Over the following five days, I managed to squeeze in three curries without anyone noticing, I think. We had our first childless evening when we ate out with Corin and Anna, Eirene's cousins and our "Operation Condor" stalwarts, who were visiting Australia at the same time as us, along with Eirene's Uncle Jason and Aunt Lynn. We all took a trip to Rottnest Island together and they, without complaint, tolerated our children's stop/start antics as we sailed to and then cycled around the island.

Located just off the coast of Fremantle, south of Perth, Rottnest Island was an old Aboriginal penal colony in the 1880s. It's a popular escape bolt for the city dwellers who affectionately know it as Rotto. Almost everyone who visits it hires a bike and cycles the 12 km around the island, stopping off at one of the 63 secluded white sandy beaches. We were no exception. One of the first animals we saw as we left the cycle hire was a quokka, a tiny fluffy kangaroo-like creature that has flourished on Rottnest Island due to the lack of habitat destruction and predators. Although not much bigger than a domestic cat, they are extremely cute and are so used to humans that they happily pose for photos. I say happily because their faces look like they have permanent smiles which has earned them the title of happiest animal in the world. It was so relaxing, and strange though this may sound, we felt like we were on holiday.

Perth is not widely regarded as a domain of the young and I could see why. It was not without its crime though, as the papers were keen to proclaim, and not without its racism, as the taxi drivers consistently showed us. It was clean, upbeat and spacious, with lots of space which they used by installing wide pavements, wide roads and wide houses.

The gift of space spread to its famous park too, Kings Park. One of the largest inner city parks in the world at over four square kilometres with two thirds of that being natural bush land. It was a favourite meeting place for locals and tourists to use the free BBQs overlooking the city and Swan River. However, the weather had been, by Australian standards, poor, but by UK standards, an Indian summer. As a result, there was rain for an hour most afternoons which precluded the obligatory Kings Park BBQ. We enjoyed Kings Park but despite its location on top of Mount Eliza, we felt it did not quite justify its lofty position in the Perth Tourist Attraction charts. It was, however, top of my annoying place names failing to use singular possessive or plural possessive apostrophes.

I contacted my never-seen cousin, David, who was married with two children and we arranged to meet at his sister's house, my never-seen cousin, Michelle. She, her husband and three children, lived in a very rural area on the outskirts of Perth in a barn-type property that they were in the process of developing. As I've said before, I'm not a great animal lover; I wouldn't harm them but I have no desire to live with any and was therefore amazed to discover that all animal loving genes had been given to my cousin Michelle. Her place looked like an animal sanctuary with alpacas, horses, parrots, hermit crabs, rabbits, dogs and fish, and her door was open to any other creature that wanted to pop along.

Uncle Richard and Aunt Heather joined us, and we were made to feel like part of the family. I didn't really know any of these relatives, so expected to feel little. Growing up, my family consisted primarily of my brother and my mum and dad, but this extended family gathering really did give me a strong sense of belonging that I hadn't expected. On the way back home, I repeated like a mantra "That was really, really nice" to the frustration of my fellow passengers who had regularly experienced the feelings of wider relations since birth. But it was really, really nice!

The loveliness didn't stop there as we also had a wonderful lunch the following day at my uncle and aunt's elegantly furnished house, which had all the hallmarks of a prospective battleground when the kids saw their low-level delicate ornaments. My aunt's wise head avoided the scene with a strategically placed outside tea party.

While in Perth, we managed to squeeze in a meeting with the author I contacted while in Thailand, Debbie Singh, at a BBQ in Kings Park, of course, now the weather had relented a little. She was really encouraging and supportive of our trip and proved to be inspirational company. She devoted a large amount of money and time to help her brother, who had been convicted of cheque fraud, to be released from a Bangkok Prison, only for him to refuse all contact with her when she succeeded. A bit of a spoiler, but that was tantamount to what the blurb on the back of the book says anyway. The whole thing changed her life and that of many others as she, with the help of contacts she had made in Thailand, continued with charity work after his release. When we spoke, she was a social worker dealing with juvenile offenders and I couldn't think of a better person to undertake such a role. I went to great lengths with my kids to emphasise that these are the sort of people that should be inspiring them, and not their TV and music icons.

From Perth, we were due to head to Adelaide and there had been a concerted campaign for us not to drive this stretch, especially the infamously tedious Nullarbor Plain. There had even been a suggestion that we put our newly hired Land Cruiser on a train, but the drive was something I was really looking forward to. The nothingness had a strong attraction to me in much the same way as moorland and desolate mountain ranges in the UK did. Eirene and the children decided they would fly so that they could spend a bit more time with her mum who was visiting other relatives in Adelaide. I was going to do it on my own or with any kids that could bear to be parted from their mum and nana; so basically on my own. However, it just so happened that an old workmate, Simon, an unemployed city trader (so there is some justice somewhere), was on a round-the-world trip and agreed to join me. The plan was that we'd pick up some Swedish hitchhikers, have a run in with a token serial killer and play a suitable soundtrack of us driving along straight desert roads. The reality was more *Brokeback Mountain* than *Road Trip*.

We all picked up Simon from the airport and set off to collect our hired Land Cruiser. From the ads I had seen in internet cafes, Land Cruisers and Volkswagen Campers were frequently coming up for sale, so I worried as to whether I had made the right decision in choosing the costly rental option. I reasoned with myself that I would be given a top notch model in great nick and that the hire company would replace or repair it if there were any problems at all. We arrived at Britz Rental and found a run down, scratched and dented basic model with a considerable leak from what appeared to be a defective gasket in the transfer box. There were no mechanics there and they couldn't fix it. They offered us a Nissan Patrol but, we were reliable informed, "It was not to be trusted." The tyres were technically legal, but they told me that I'd be liable for any accidental windscreen or tyre damage. I enquired if I was covered if it was non-accidental, but she firmly told me "No!" That worried me because we had hired a Kia people carrier for nine days in Perth and Eirene had managed to reverse it into a wall.

Britz, like many firms, offered a price match but failed to deliver when I produced an offer with identical conditions for an identical vehicle at an identical pickup location for identical dates from their company for $900 less (£1 = $2.40 at the time). "The agent shouldn't have offered you that price," she directed. When you meet up with people and make arrangements to be in places for certain dates it restricts many things, not to mention your negotiating position, so we bit our tongues and went for it. We felt a bit deflated as we shopped around, seeking cheap imitations of the essential equipment that we already had in our car in Bangkok.

Both Abigail, who over recent months had been rapidly turning me into her best mate, and Emily, howled as I reversed out the driveway. Fortunately, it was because I was leaving and not because I had run them over. I saved my howling till the end of the driveway. Simon and I headed south to Pemberton and Eirene flew with the kids to Adelaide the following day.

We were barely a few hours into our drive and our snake and kangaroo count was rapidly increasing. The kangaroos had the uncanny ability to stay completely stationary until the video camera had performed its prolonged boot up procedure, at which point they hopped off. We made it to Pemberton just before the hotel closed at 6pm. They were not night owls. The restaurant was already closed but we found ourselves in a nearby pub, which looked like the set of the *Accused,* listening to locals becoming increasingly boisterous. We left just prior to the third rendition of "Kill the English" or something similar. Like me, Simon's Scottish, but he has the accent that I've long lost and he looked disappointed to leave the xenophobia.

We followed the coastal route around the south western chunk of Australia as opposed to a direct route to Adelaide. With no frequent toilet breaks, constant shepherding or slow eating that I would normally have associated with family travel, we made excellent progress. Simon was able to go to the toilet when we stopped for petrol and not 10 minutes afterwards. He could rapidly digest a menu and make a prompt choice which he would then stick with. And he could walk from one place to another without distraction, so he was just the ticket for expediency.

We climbed a large, red mountain way off the beaten track. Although it was about 100 times smaller than Ayres Rock, less busy and had no curse, my aspirations to have a quick week on the Pennine Way on my return to the UK before looking for work were dashed in the first 200 metres of the walk as I was struck by another curse – that of the unfit who hadn't exercised for about eight months. I was aware of a deep heaving from within my lungs and raspy exhalations from outside of them and couldn't believe I was doing triathlons 18 months previously. I resolved to address my decaying state with the usual extreme training and dieting binge when we returned home. In many ways, I felt that I had climbed my own Ayers Rock by the time I made it to the top and certainly felt cursed, despite the outstanding views over the tree canopy for hundreds of miles in every direction.

We continued south on our journey to the point where the Indian Ocean meets the Southern Ocean. I don't know what I was expecting but, had it not been for signage, I would never have known that the ocean I was looking at had changed. There was no join and they both looked the same colour. We stopped at the famous tree top walk in Walpole, a series of suspension bridges that climbed and traversed treetops in an ancient forest. The public were invited to walk along, bounce up and down and move rapidly from side to side in an effort to bring them down or maybe this was just us. It was quite a remarkable experience and appeared to come from the same school of thought as the cook your own food steamboat restaurants in Singapore and Thailand. This one was based on the business plan of building a couple of metal bridges up in the trees and charging people $8 to walk around them for 10 minutes. We left satiated and alleviated of our $16 and refused the temptations of the compulsory gift shop that encloses the exit of every single tourist attraction in the world. We made Esperance a few hours after nightfall with scant regard to the 5pm arrival deadline that my travels had so far dictated. Simon secured a tremendous $135 a night deal in the Best Western there (for those of you reading this 10 or more years after 2008, this is an attempt at sarcasm) although it did have internet access and a fish and chip shop round the corner. It was a basic hotel, but the guestbook told another story and appears to have been nicked from The Savoy. "The miniature tray of tea-making condiments was an unexpected delight" – Alison M, Fremantle.

The Nullarbor Plain is flat, arid and frequently featureless so Simon and his personality were well at home. At over 77,000 square miles, it has claimed the lives of many early pioneers and travellers, being described by the explorer Eyre as a "hideous anomaly, a blot on the face of nature, the sort of place one gets into in bad dreams." It is still considered a legendary drive despite the fact that it is now all tarmacked, with petrol stations 200 km apart at the most. With this in mind, we headed off full of enthusiasm, still exchanging stories, events and catching up with missed months. I missed the family but, and I don't want to sound too much like *Blackadder* and "Bob", Simon's company made a very obliging change, despite my initial swipe at the beginning of this paragraph. Above all, though, it was an unmitigated pleasure to break my swearing famine. We hit Norseman (that's the name of place just for reference) 200 km later and were starting to run a little dry. I filled up with diesel and it was apparent that Hobson's choice of either take it or leave it was the primary economic driver behind the rapidly increasing pump prices. We turned right at Norseman and onto the big one, The Eyre Highway. It was 700 km of very straight roads to Eucla, just near the border with South Australia and, at over 150 km, the road has the longest entirely straight bit of road in Australia. I used it to run out a few old chestnuts, periodically enquiring with navigator Simon whether it was straight ahead. He in turn, the first four times at least, dutifully glanced down at his map but if you ask him he'll deny it.

To relieve the boredom, I engaged Simon in a little bet. Simon, being the catalyst for the global recession in my eyes, had bought my 4.26-4.28 spread at 4.10. In layman's terms, at 4.10pm I proclaimed that the next vehicle that we passed, excluding burnt out and abandoned ones by the roadside, would be in the period 4.26pm to 4.28pm, me therefore holding a three minute banding. He thought this was optimistic and believed it would be later. At 4.25pm a small dot was sighted on the horizon and at 4.26:30pm it was clearly identified as an oncoming road train, one of the enormous trucks with multiple trailers that frequented the route. At 4.28pm it was clear it was going to be close and I was jittery. My foot was pretty much touching the radiator as I tried to squeeze every last ounce of power out of the vehicle. It was exciting stuff and we were both absorbed. It hit 4.28:30pm and it was no more than 750 metres away. Simon, with his First-class honours degree in maths from Imperial College and a master's from Cambridge, appeared smug as he toyed with the mental arithmetic. He adopted the aforementioned face indeed when, at 4.29:02pm, we passed the road train. I hoped he was happy at his humiliation of his comprehensive (albeit not comprehensively) educated chum. It seemed he was.

After that surge of adrenalin, the rest of the journey passed uneventfully until we hit the town of Eucla that turned out not to be a town but a motel with a petrol and weather station attached and the freedom to charge what they liked, which, by God, they did. We arrived at 6.45pm and the multi-skilled receptionist/cook/bar lady/cleaner/owner asked us if we wanted to eat as the restaurant had shut and the café was just about to. Two bottles of Miller beer came to $17 so we'd at least made happy hour, but we really needed much more drink to disguise the expensive and dreadful burgers that followed.

The car, despite its dilapidated appearance, just kept going and we can vouch for the effectiveness of the windscreen wipers that were in constant use for two days, wiping the red dust from our view. We continued along the barren Nullarbor with nothing more than dead kangaroos and "Beware of Camels" signs to break the monotony. Occasionally we saw a School Bus stop and realised that at the very least there must be a homestead within a few hundred kilometres. Now and again we saw, what we first thought, was a zebra crossing on a very flat section of the road. Signposts indicated that it wasn't anything as useless, but it was in fact markings for the Flying Doctor Service. Our road had suddenly become a runway and at any moment a Hawker 800 could be careering up our backside. Naturally it never did.

We stopped off at Iron Knob, a dusty old mining town where Billy Connolly was reputedly and repeatedly addressed as a poofter by a barman there on account of his earring. Like many of these small towns there were houses, a few shops, a garage and all the makings of a town but absolutely no one around, not even at the garage, although the census taken two years previously declared a population of 199.

Further on, we hit our first set of traffic lights for about 3000 km, a sudden and welcome realisation that we were approaching civilisation - or at least Adelaide. We arrived victoriously circa 5pm outside Aunty Maria and Uncle Tim's address in Gladstone Street, having not asked for nor been offered directions. I had thought the family would have been waiting to greet us but, as was to be expected, it was the wrong Gladstone Street, the genuine one we found after a few phone calls and some directions. The kids were over the moon to see me; that interpretation I deduced from the fact that they didn't immediately dive on the plastic bag of tat kaleidoscopes I was holding. There was more of Eirene's family visiting and it was great to see them all. There was a place in the bed next to my wife and my mate Simon checked into the motel round the corner where Eirene's brother, also called Simon, was staying.

We spent four days in Adelaide with all the extended family which would be best summarised as follows:

High breakage count of various bottles and bowls and the like. Unfortunately, I am unable to blame any of our kids for that and have to own up to all of them.

Kathy (Eirene's mum) woken up at 3.30am and again at 4.15am the night before her flight back to the UK (in which she was guaranteed no sleep) by my brother Skyping me on my laptop which I had left in her room as it was connected to the internet, downloading films for the kids' iPods. Very embarrassing, which leads me onto ...

Eirene's Uncle Tim leading me through to the aforementioned room and showing me a number of emails from his internet provider indicating that he had massively exceeded his 400mb limit at 15c a megabyte. They even charged him the additional for the cost of data in sending the emails to say he was going to be charged the additional cost of data. Me showing considerable embarrassment at this, followed by consternation that he didn't tell me about his "limited plan" before he let me use his connection.

Me doing mental calculations that brought the bill to about $400 (£50 a film)

Him being angry and blaming my friend Simon, who had used my laptop for a few emails.

Toilet getting blocked on the morning of our departure.

Other than that, it was a great visit and the kids loved the company of their cousin Emma, the garden and last but not least, our embarrassment.

Adelaide is a wonderfully green and clean city with an abundance of fantastic vineyards within easy driving distance of the city. It was originally planned as the capital of Australia with large pedestrianised squares and the whole city surrounded by parks. It is also one of only a few cities in Australia that has no history of convicts. We visited the Rosemount Estate, home of our favourite wine. Wistfully, before we had even made it through the cellar door (for the record none of them were actually doors to cellars), we were ruthlessly informed that our favourite wine was a "C" grade, which isn't good apparently.

Furthermore, Rosemount was owned by Fosters who owned over half of Australia's vineyards, including Penfolds and Lindemans. What's more, Rosemount wine was made up of not only their own grapes, which they flog to hundreds of other wineries, but of hundreds of other wineries' grapes as well. It was like finding out my favourite football team didn't actually have any players at all from the town it represented, but brought in a load from other places thousands of miles away whilst the home-grown players, the ones that I wanted to see, were given away to other clubs. How stupid would that be?

After saying goodbye to the family, it felt good to be back on the road again, despite the fact that we were not in our own car with all our off-road gear and winch, first aid equipment and extended fuel capacity. Eirene was driving, and the kids were in the back and we felt free and content, just the five of us on an adventure for the first time in over two months. This was also the first time Eirene had driven outside of an Australian town and she passed comment on the tedious nature of the drive and the banality of the scenery, which I saw as varied, colourful and so un-Nullarbor. Maybe it was best she flew that bit after all, I thought to myself.

We were heading for Mount Gambier and had been given numerous explicit directions and instructions by well-meaning family and friends. There was only one road, signposted in English, and we had a map, which was more than could be said for the first 17,000 miles of our journey.

It brought to mind a bloke who gave me directions to his house once, to look at a car I was keen to buy. No word of a lie, 15 lines of directions accounted for no more than about 500 yards of one stretch of straight road. Still, they were all being caring and helpful and remiss in recalling that we had driven a fair bit already.

We drove through quaint colonial-type towns and discovered Robe, which despite being "South Australia's favourite seaside town" was quiet, enchanting and right on the sea, where Emily and Abigail played in a well maintained park as Eirene and Hannah sat on a rocky outcrop atop a small island a few yards from the shore. All were happy, and I knew Eirene was thinking "Could we live here?" but by the time she left her little island she had enough reasons to convince herself that the answer was an objective no. There was only one real reason, proximity to her mum, but she unnecessarily justified her position with lesser points.

We arrived at Mount Gambier, famous for its "inexplicably" blue lake that fills most of the hollow within a dormant volcano. I say "inexplicably" but I think that might be tourist bumph in order to throw in a bit of mystique. I'm sure if they put their minds to it someone could work out what chemical process it is that changes it from a startling cobalt blue colour during the warmer months and back to a cold steel grey in the other months and publish the formula on their website and brochures. I really feel my letter, email and comments on their website to this effect were largely a waste of time.

Our accommodation lay next to it and we were happy with our "holiday cottage" (read mobile home) that was $80 less than the recommended "Retreat" (read big mobile home with more tellies). As it was December and we were in the legendary Australian summer, we'd taken heed of all the advice about the heat and stocked up on factor 50 sun creams, summer clothes as well as half-season sleeping bags that were virtually sheets. We didn't bring fleeces or raincoats, thinking it would be warm and dry all the time but it was unseasonably cold so we rushed to turn the heating on in the "cottage". I fired up the barbie, publicly concerned about the hungry kids but privately freezing. As the sun went down I perched there, on the crest of that volcano, while turning freshly captured meat over a roaring fire just as, I envisaged, the Neanderthal Naismiths in Stone Age times had. I pushed it too far, however, when I gave it a grunting "Man get food. Women clean" come dish washing time at the end of dinner and was accused of misogynistic stereotyping. I have a familiar feeling that Captain Caveman Naismith would have been given similar short shrift in his day.

Despite the time of year, the place was very quiet and didn't appear to be fully up and running. There was a large inflatable jumping pillow, about six metres by 20 metres which the kids loved. Post dinner, I joined them and explained the merits of British Bulldog to them. They brashly attempted to attack in one solid group before adopting a pincer movement with Abigail sent up the middle as a distraction. I rapidly turned into Competitive Dad and dropped my substantial weight within feet of them in an attempt to fell them, but with little success against their nimble movements. I stopped short of full-on body slams.

After the kids had gone to bed, I sat down at the computer to do some work and picked up an email from my mum which made me laugh. This was the breaking news from the ex-pat community on the Costa Blanca.

From: Madelene Naismith
To: info@drive-to-oz.com
Sent: Sunday, December 07, 2008 9:16 PM
Subject: Your photos!

Met Vera for a coffee today (she's now walking with just one crutch in the house, so coming along fine) and she was saying that at the Saturday coffee morning, Betty wasn't speaking to Beryl, but WAS speaking to Gladys, who barely managed to speak back to her, but neither Betty nor Gladys are speaking to Thora. Beryl wasn't speaking to anyone. Vera says she might not go again.
Lots of Love
Mum

We stayed at Mount Gambier for a couple of nights exploring limestone caves and searching for waterproofs and fleeces, the latter being incredibly difficult to source out of season. We couldn't believe that after seven months on the road, the first time we had to move our heating switch in the car to the red bit was in Australia in December – their summer.

The pamphlet stand in our holiday park reception was a caver's wet dream with activities ranging from day-long extreme caving to wheelchair-friendly sink holes which had been converted into gardens. We'd have to indulge to some degree so we set off for a day at Naracoorte Caves, a World Heritage site visited by Richard Attenborough, just over an hour's drive from our campsite. We had to swap seats after 20 minutes for Eirene to have a powernap (as passenger for the record). After months of sitting around and then being flown around I worried she had lost her driving legs.

With activities above and below ground, Naracoorte Caves proved to be a great hit with the kids. We took a tour of an underground cavern which contained models of extinct indigenous animals with animatronic tails and speakers in their arses that scared the kids enough but not too much. They delighted in following a path painted in the pattern of the red-bellied snake which led them to the Wet Cave which despite its name was notably quite dry. It was just the right length for them and with robust limestone columns and chunky stalactites hanging from the roof, atmospheric lighting and smaller tunnels to peer in to, it was just adventurous enough too. Back home we spent another cold night around the BBQ planning our route for the next day and drinking our C-class wine.

The following morning, despite our recent euphoria, Eirene was in a bad mood and the kids knew it and eventually experienced it. I did what I could by badgering and poking her constantly for the first few hours of our journey, but it just seemed to make things worse if I'm honest. She had cheesed me in turn by asking me what I was doing as I was busily packing the car, cleaning it out and doing the usual checks. As the delightful scenery encompassed us, the atmosphere lightened and the mutual moods abated as we contemplated how many visitors to Oz witnessed the between city side of the country. We pootled south and onto lunch in Portland, a thriving harbourside town immersed in indigenous history and home to one of the world's earliest sites of human settlement. We saw absolutely no trace of them, so we took the town's word for it before continuing along the coastal road to Warrnambool.

I had been pushing for some camping, but Eirene rightly pointed out the cold weather was not conducive to our playschool-like equipment. We found a holiday park with a cabin and headed straight to the beach which was only a few metres away. We watched a bloke kite surfing, flying through the air at an impressively scary height while holding onto a parachute with a board, slightly larger than a skateboard, strapped to his feet. His activities should have been a warning to us that swimming was not the best course of action here. The sea that looked so inviting soon proved nothing of the sort with strong winds, luckily pushing us back rather than out. Disappointed, we walked off to an enormous adventure playground, so large that just finding our way around it was an adventure in itself.

Over lunch, we discussed the possibility of an early start the next day to see the sunrise over the Twelve Apostles, one of the highlights of the Great Ocean Road on one of the greatest drives in the world (not my words, the words of *Top Gear* magazine). The rocky outcrops that are the Twelve Apostles, although there are only eight now (so a bit like Sevenoaks but not really), held a particular interest for me as they were in that *Purnell's Illustrated Atlas*, the fount of all my geographic knowledge when I was very young. I had always hoped that I'd see them in real life one day, and even the prospect of it was really evocative of my time growing up in Newburgh, Aberdeenshire.

The only flaw in Eirene's sunrise plan was that it would necessitate us mobilising our children by 4.15 in the morning, no mean feat indeed. The old cynical, irritating Graham would have poured scorn on this idea but the newly reformed, suitably inebriated and happily watching *Long Way Down* Graham, was bigger than that and endorsed her objective and offered full support to the campaign. All of this despite the absence of an alarm clock and with knowledge of how cold the mobile cabin outside of blankets would be at that time in the morning.

Our departure proved to be a mere three hours later than anticipated but we were still the only car at the Bay of Islands, the first viewpoint on the road where we stopped, and we huddled up in sleeping bags on the wooden walkway to eat our cereal. As we munched, we watched the effect of the winds blown up from the Antarctic forcing the waves to pound aggressively at a load of little and ever decreasing rock outcrops that were almost disappearing in front of our eyes. Bowls not quite empty, a family of Japanese tourists stumbled on our spot and it felt akin to having set up home in Ikea and then being discovered by the first shoppers of the day. We rapidly and mischievously packed up and went on our way complete with a strong nod of confidence from Hannah to the tourists from Tokyo.

With a camera in one hand and a kid in the other, we trotted off to a good number of often familiar sounding spots along the coastline. We walked over the quite rousing and empty *London Bridge*, minus its adjoining bridge to the mainland, courtesy of a relatively recent collapse that left two tourists stranded on the outer part of the bridge. Wooden decked paths guided us to appropriate viewpoints and led us back to the car park and, although it felt sterile, it was safe and prevented the inevitable decay of adjoining land that unfenced routes would have brought. *The Arch* was exactly that, a large natural limestone rock with a stunningly precarious arch. The road earned its accolades. There was one natural and amazing rock structure after another, dotted along the whole coastline and, unlike the many of Australia's other roads that we'd experienced to date, the landscape constantly changed. Occasionally it even took a turn to sweep inwards towards sprawling pastures and thick forests before swinging back to the rugged coastline.

As we approached the Twelve Apostles, we spotted a place offering helicopter flights over the attraction. Having never been in a helicopter, and following the cancellation of our Matterhorn Cessna light, I voted for a stop and check of the prices which was enthusiastically endorsed by the kids. For a 10-minute flight, they quoted approximately £130 for the five of us, charging Hannah and Emily as one and putting Abigail in for free, so we decided to go for it. Luckily, they failed to charge me any extra when they discovered that I was coming in at 118 kilos on their scales and I asked for a recount, as I began taking off my Crocs and light fleece. The operator insisted it wasn't necessary, but I insisted it was as it was being written down somewhere and I've always been a staunch advocate of accurate record keeping. Formalities and corrections complete, we all excitedly piled into the chopper and adorned our headphones with microphones, which was the highlight of the trip for Abigail. The pilot gave a brief warm up to the rotor blades and we drifted off into the air on this clearest of mornings. Having studied that blue atlas for so long as a kid, I would never have dreamed that my first real view of the Apostles would be from the same angle that the picture on the cover was taken from. Admittedly, there were fewer of them now than in my atlas pictures and even quite recently one of the apostles had popped its clogs. The fragility of the others was obvious to even the inexperienced and untrained eyes of the other passengers. Eirene hid her vertigo well by nervously taking pictures of everything she could and after everyone, including me, tired of my "Broadsword calling Danny Boy" *Where Eagles Dare* impressions over the helicopter mike, I settled down to concentrate on the wonderful view.

Despite the weighty cargo, we landed safely and, still buzzing, headed off down the standard decked pathways that led us to the viewpoints for further pictures. Nostalgia reigned when the kids were grabbed by a number of Chinese and Japanese tourists, some of whom insisted that I, and not their watching partner, take the pictures and ensured our kids were smiling straight at the camera as they were gripped tightly around the waist. Time was no object for them but was ticking on for us, so we decided on one more stop, at Cape Otway lighthouse. The road down to the lighthouse was more rewarding than the lighthouse itself which demanded $50 for us to climb its spiral staircase. We elected not to pay and play and openly mocked the sign at the door that said "Cape Otway Lightstation. Highlight of the Great Ocean Road."

The route to and from the lighthouse wound through a koala-adorned forest with a cuddly and slovenly koala draped in almost every fork of the roadside eucalyptus trees. Cars stopped and occupants surrounded the bases of the trees for a photo opportunity. The koalas were pretty laid back and we quickly established that it was gauche to involve oneself in another car's koala unless invited. I've read that there's a similar rule in dogging. We discovered our own koala tree and found our children even more nonchalant and slovenly than the koalas themselves as they reluctantly moved from the car, the few yards to the tree. In somewhat of a role reversal, it was Eirene and I acting like excited kids.

Our drive continued on to perhaps the most dramatic part of the Great Ocean Road, a cliffside route that offered award winning views of the Indian Ocean as it curled around the contours of the receding coastline. Once again, the place names weren't as inspirational as the views. Peterborough and Torquay didn't really sell themselves but we settled on the delightful Anglesey, an oxymoron if there ever was one.

At $135, that night's mobile home was the most expensive but also the best yet. The facilities were great with plenty of activities for the kids to do, including another giant jumping pillow, and this time our cabin even had heating, something we still yearned for as we approached the peak of Australian summer. We also met some fellow travellers, complete with kids and relished their company which, due to the isolating motel and hotel accommodation experience, was a relatively unique and refreshing experience for us so far on this continent.

As the sun started to descend, kangaroos approached our cabin, but the kids barely cast a glance before their gaze returned to *Barbie as the Princess and the Pauper*, the 2004 Mark Twain DVD classic. Emily had chosen that film because she knew Hannah would like it, but Hannah was upset that Emily had chosen it and berated her for her choice which confused her ginger sibling. They were both unhappy anyway that the chunky neighbour's kid had demolished their Scooby snacks with one scoop of her shovel-like hand. However, they both still hypnotically watched it and ignored the wildlife, now literally on their doorstep, and our associated calls. I decided that the mountain (our kids, not the kid next door who was nowhere near the size of mountain) would go to Mohammed so I turned it off, dragged them out and forced them to enjoy themselves. They were greeted by a 10 – 15 kangaroos of differing sizes and ages sniffing around curiously, their distinctive shape silhouetted by the setting sun. I looked at the kids who nonchalantly observed them from the door. Nothing. Absolutely nothing.

In the evening, when all around us slept, Eirene and I pampered ourselves by watching *Meet the Fockers* over a bottle of wine with a surreal *Skippy* looking in from outside.

The next day, our destination was Melbourne with the intention of seeing more of Eirene's family and I was beginning to doubt whether there was any left in England. Eirene contacted one of her cousins with a view to meeting up, but we were a bit surprised when he suggested 6.30am. We came to a compromise of 7.30am. Their hours are a bit different there.

Despite the rain, we ventured to Albert Park, a popular inner city escape and home to the Australian Grand Prix. We had planned to use one of the many public BBQs that were positioned around the park but, even though it was raining, all were taken and surrounded by organised defensive walls of lunchtime workers. We finally found one that had no cover, so I got cracking on the sausages whilst treating the burn to Emily's wandering hand.

I learnt several things that afternoon, including the fact that these public gas BBQs will turn off with no warning, that if a beer says draught on it then it has a twist-off cap (I broke the bottle in half attempting to forcibly remove it using an aged old technique I'd learnt but cannot share) and that it is socially acceptable for people to turn up at a clean public BBQ, use it and then leave it filthy.

Eirene's cousin's arrival at 7.30am was manageable and we found him great company for the hour he had with us before heading off to work. We then visited Aunt Geraldine who wasn't as impressed as we were at our family leaving her house and possessions in exactly the same condition as we'd found it.

Abigail had passed her cold onto me and, inevitably and scientifically, being a man, its symptoms quadrupled in strength. I felt miserable but managed, between shouting, to grab an hour's sleep in the car as we headed east-ish. I woke up and settled into *Lonely Planet,* which for once painted a very accurate picture of a place called Lake Entrance and nearby Lake Tyers.

Aboriginal legends state that one day, the sea came in land to rest among the wooded hillside and fell asleep. It never woke and is still there today as Lake Tyers. I don't think all of that is entirely true, but it was a wonderfully tranquil location, surrounded by dense woodland with lots of nesting and feeding birds at the lake itself.

We checked into a near-empty caravan and camping park in the now standard torrential rain, after buying an additional fleece for Abigail. The holiday park wasn't big on marketing with its sole board at the entrance consisting of lists of rules and what the camp does not have (linen, guest parking etc). The park was run by the Uniting Church in Australia that used it as a retreat for youth camps and ministers but, when not otherwise occupied, opened it to the heathenish general public. Apart from being over-charged, we also established that consumption of alcohol at the BBQ areas was strictly forbidden which, for me at least, begged the question as to the point of a BBQ. Our deluxe cabin, however, had captivating views over Ninety Mile beach and the lake which I relished whilst firing up the BBQ.

After the kids bedded down in their sleeping bags, Eirene and I took a trip down memory lane with a look through a load of pictures and video on the laptop, dating back nearly eight years to Hannah's birth. I was astonished how the mannerisms of the children were so similar and how their personalities were there on show at even a very tender age. Four hours flew by and we retired to bed, happy in our refreshed memories. But just before she dozed off, Eirene mentioned feeling clucky and something about a fourth. I slept with one eye open and popped my playboy pyjamas on.[21].

We left the brotherhood and drove by Lake Entrance. In the UK, Lake Entrance would be called something like Lakemouth or Lakeside but in Australia they have a bit more of a "say what you see" Catchphrase approach. For example, Muddy Creek, Watery Creek, Pink Lake, Blue Lake, Ninety Mile Beach etc. You get exactly what it says on the tin, the Bay of Islands being a good case in point. The exception to that rule is static mobile homes which are called everything from luxury cabins to log cabins and holiday villas, but never what they actually are. We searched around for places that offered wireless Internet, but the search proved to be a waste of time and we failed to find anything cheaper than $6 for 15 minutes. I could print and post my emails for less than that and, with the speed of some of their connections, probably quicker as well.

With the Australians' propensity to name things as they see them, we avoided Disaster Bay and instead headed to Twofold Bay in Eden and in particular a cove which was comfortingly named Snug. Eden lived up to its name which the

---

[21] Well known for their anaphrodisiac (as opposed to aphrodisiac) properties.

guidebooks described as "the sapphire coast" and I found it incredulous that the sea could be this colour all year round, being almost bluer than Blue Lake.

The weather started off pretty miserable the next day and I was still nursing a man cold, so we initially entertained the kids indoors. I suggested that we make a promo pop video for *Daddy Naismith and the Dodettes* with our only track, *You're going to get the Finger of Boon*. This was a method by which I extracted laughter and fear from the children by putting my finger between their neck and shoulder, just inside the collar bone and gently pressing, but not in a Vulcan death grip fashion you understand. It had initially been called the Finger of Doom, but Emily changed it. The kids' enthusiasm knew no bounds and they took to it wholeheartedly. The lyrics were sorted out, the stage was made, the equipment sorted, the choreography and costumes finalised and by lunchtime the band had split. The camera hadn't even started to roll before artistic differences between the lead singer (Hannah) and one of the dancers (Emily), who refused to dance, resulted in a big spat. They vowed never to work together again. Officially family pressures were blamed for the split.

When the weather improved, we spent hours on the empty beach in the afternoon and Eirene managed to cunningly conduct a variety of lessons with the sand as her blackboard and I attempted to teach any stragglers some basic karate kata. In a sense, and almost literally when the tide started to come in, they were stuck between a rock and a hard place.

The next lesson we had to teach the children was that of the meaning and use of sarcasm. We discovered that they thought a dump was something beautiful because whenever we saw an incredible sight like the view from Ko Chang Island or the Great Ocean Drive, Eirene and I both exclaimed "What a dump." Lesson learned by both sides and I smiled when Hannah said to me "I really didn't know what sarcasm was."

Eirene had been fighting the camping caper for a while but despite her campaign of "bad weather is on its way" whenever she spotted a distant puff of cloud, I finally managed to persuade her to give it a go after I found us a dream campsite in a place called, and I kid you not, Pretty Beach.

There were a couple of other occupants but there was still lots of space, shade from the trees, the aforementioned pretty beach, a barbie, immaculate toilets and showers and loads of kangaroos hopping around. The kids built their own pretend BBQ adjacent to mine and loved the climb-in roof tent that we had on the car. I was very proud of my quick erection of both tents and BBQ and dinner was great as the weather held out and exposed a glittering sky devoid of almost any light pollution. The place and moment was idyllic and if ever there was a chance to flog the camping lark to Eirene then this was it. As we sipped from our wine glasses by the dying embers of the fire, we took in the stillness of the night and I felt Eirene's head fall onto my lap. I reached down and began to stroke her curiously short, spiky hair but as I came to her long pointy ears I screamed and leapt higher in the air than you've ever seen a 117.5 kg man jump. Panic ensued and I was up in the roof tent before the 4 kg possum, a furry, semi-arboreal marsupial, made its own terrified way back to the bush, Eirene's guffawing echoing in his long hairy ears.

I wasn't particularly looking forward to Sydney, thinking that it was just another city. But I was quite surprised at its cosmopolitan streets, laid back yet busy vibe and spacious botanic gardens with inquisitive ibises, long-legged wading birds with big, down-curved bills. We buoyantly zipped over the iconic Harbour Bridge in our car, our enjoyment only slightly tainted by Eirene's paranoia about not having an electronic tag pass, and then turned around and immediately came back over again as if that would placate the authorities.

We asked a number of people to take pictures of us with the world famous Opera House in the background. Despite our constant request to just stand on a specific spot and press the button for the head and shoulders shot we wanted, the first four groups insisted on walking back and taking the picture they

309

wanted. It's hard when people are being, or trying to be, helpful and giving up their time but it's even harder to curb the impulse to shout "Just do what I fucking told you, for fuck's sake. Stop fucking moving and press the one button on the camera." I sometimes wonder if I'm getting less tolerant as I move into middle age. Finally, the picture we wanted, one of the few family ones we have, courtesy of a delightful couple from Yorkshire who had been travelling for 15 months. "You can always tell a Yorkshireman, but you can't tell him much apart from how to take a simple snap," I think the phrase goes. Or should go.

Our accommodation in Sydney was very mixed, from a noisy, badly managed boutique hotel to a meticulous serviced apartment. The first night we stayed in the Bondi Hotel on Bondi beach which sounded idyllic but would not have looked out of place in 1995 Sarajevo. It was a dirty shithole but seemingly good enough for the police, who turned up in considerable numbers complete with sniffer dogs during the early evening whilst we sat impassively in the bar, racked with unfounded British guilt. There's something about the brass neck of a place like this that asks you to complete a guest feedback questionnaire on departure that I really do admire. "The Sydney drugs squad and associated canines were remarkably systematic and thorough in their search of our apartment" GN – London.

Our second Sydney night was a complete contrast. A luxurious apartment, much cheaper, cleaner and quieter than Bondi, with everything we needed, including linen. We had planned to leave Sydney early but elected instead to take the kids to the *Star Wars* exhibition at Sydney's Science Museum, having missed the one in London that Hannah really wanted to visit. It was very well put together with models and props from the original films clearly labelled and plenty of space to move around. We posed with C-3PO and Chewbacca, studied "elegant weapons from a more civilised age", like Darth Maul's double-bladed lightsaber and played on ground craft rides that they frustratingly allowed children on as if they were toys.

Hannah loved it but Abigail and Emily found most of it a bit over their heads so we also visited Zoe's House. Despite how it sounded, this was a building and construction play area aimed at three to six year olds with foam bricks and wagons they could push to carry their load to the conveyor belt. They loved it.

We popped our car into Britz in Sydney for a list of major and minor things to be done, such as the cabin filling up with smoke when we were driving, black fumes spurting out the back and oil dripping from the drive shaft. Of course, none of that was fixed but they did lend us a motorhome for the day and gave ours a wash when we collected it. I was not happy with the amount of money we had wasted on this, but I laughed outwardly when one of the girls at reception, with the Britz "No Boundaries" logo just behind her head, talked through with another customer the extensive list of boundaries that they imposed in terms of terrain and geographical location.

We reluctantly left Sydney having enjoyed pretty much all of it. We had one last foray across the bridge to the echoes of Band Aid's *Do They Know it's Christmas?* on the radio, before we headed north towards the Gold Coast, stopping frequently at empty beaches and little towns. At one cove lunch stop, we were approached by a two metre-long goanna that was patrolling the picnic area looking for snacks. A keen zoologist may tell you that a goanna is any of several Australian monitor lizards of the genus Varanus and that they are carnivorous reptiles, ranging greatly in size, with predatory and scavenging behaviours. I will tell you that when you first see one of these fuckers, it's like you're in Jurassic Park and they absolutely scare the shit out of you. I was genuinely not interested in having anything to do with her but my attempts to ignore her, like in the world of dating when I was a teenager, just seemed to make me more and more attractive to her. As she waddled towards me flicking out her long tongue, again a memory from my teenage dating years, we were reliably informed by a fellow visitor that they eat anything they can overpower. This one had her bigger mum nearby we were told, so we shortened our lunchbreak and hastily returned to the Landcruiser before the shadow of mum had a chance to hit our car.

The mood in the car was not good as Eirene was feeling grim with a pounding headache which fuelled her reluctance to go camping. It would only have been our second night camping, the kids loved it and it was cheap, although probably too late to have much of an impact on our out-of-control budget. I pushed for it and Eirene conceded, even acquiescing to my request to nip down onto a beach close to the campsite with the car.

This stretch of coastline allowed cars to actually drive on the shore itself and I planned to drive onto it, spin around and come back before hitting the Mungo Brush, our campsite for the night. I knew that I should be letting the tyres down to 15 psi or so before doing this but also recognised that any delay or hesitation would be pounced on by Eirene who would deny me this most brief and simple pleasure. Travelling with kids and a wife massively out of her suburban area of expertise meant the more reckless endeavours were frequently nipped in the bud. I completely understood that but still missed it. So it was with a childish foot on the accelerator and tyres packed with air that we hit the beach before starting to slow down in the soft dry deep sand and coming to a complete halt.

As all four wheels spun in vain, I looked over to Eirene who had slowly bent forward and placed her head in her hands. I looked over her shoulder, towards the incoming tide and, as she became upset, I surveyed about 50 miles of deserted beach. As wobblers go this was the business. In her tired, vulnerable state, about 16,000 km from Surrey, I realised I may have pushed her too far. Between wails, she made it clear that she wouldn't be assisting with my tyre deflation or digging request. Our rental car had no winch which could have effortlessly pulled us out of this mess from a nearby post. As I cursed my big end and dug deeper, I tried to put the adjacent howling to the back of my mind. As fortune would have it, another four-wheel drive emerged on the horizon and slowly, painfully so, made its way towards us. Emily spotted it too and a cry of hope went up as the tide crept, not so painfully slowly, towards us. Our car was axle deep in sand as the Mitsubishi, with two sturdy blokes in the front, drove straight past us, ignoring my gestures and disappeared into the distance. It has to be said that towing a car out of the sand when in the sand yourself is tricky and should be attempted with some caution. Nevertheless, those two blokes were, and always will be, wankers in my book.

Mercifully, left to my own resources, my tyre reduction and digging worked and we slowly managed to drive out of the sand and back onto the highway as Eirene's sobs ebbed away. We made Mungo Brush just before dark for this second night of camping.

The campsite itself provoked a less dramatic response from Eirene, which was surprising considering it had no showers. In fact, it had no water at all and the toilets were the green environmental non-flush type. Literally a hole in the ground with a plastic lid over a pit which must always be kept shut, for when it's left open, it resembles the fly scene from *The Exorcist*. The location beside a lagoon was beautiful with untouched natural wetlands but I feared a sleepless night when copious carloads of teenagers arrived. However, our tiredness quickly took hold and we went to sleep in our ground and roof-tents. I was in the latter with Abigail as Eirene's contempt for camping was only outweighed by her fear of heights and ladders, so the high ground was mine. There were dingoes everywhere so I was sure to run a register on the kids the following morning, just as three girls from the nearby teenage camp approached us to apologise for the previous night's events, the fights, the swearing and the broken glass. I told them sincerely that we had heard nothing but was inwardly slightly miffed at missing an entertaining exchange of "Leave it Bruce, he's not worth it."

As I was packing Eirene's tent away, I optimistically proffered that despite the dingoes, the toilets, the teenagers, the snakes and the stuck in sand debacle, this whole camping lark wasn't too bad. She wasn't listening though, transfixed on something else between us. I followed her line of vision to the scorpion that I had just unknowingly revealed underneath the spot where she had been sleeping and decided to wind my neck in for the time being. "Best get ourselves a roof tonight," I wisely contemplated, so we headed off to a cabin in Eungai Creek, world famous for its buffalo milk, that evening. On first appearance it looked terrific. It was up on stilts, overlooking a river with flawless lawns approaching it and Eirene immediately suggested we stay here a couple of days. However, later on in the evening, after examining the cleanliness of the cutlery and the build quality, she harshly relegated the place to one of her bottom three places she had stayed in. Rather surprisingly the "hamster" place in Kazakhstan earned bottom spot. We were slowly learning that linen, in all these mobile home/cabin places was the exception and not the rule.

While talking with a neighbour in the morning, they recommended nearby Bellingen and Dorigo along Waterfall Way as well worth a visit. So, despite Eirene's impulse to drive on like the clappers and not go out of her way, I subtly and discreetly navigated us up the mountains through English-like countryside, past waterfalls that crossed under the road rather than over it and eventually reached a dirt track for four-wheel drive vehicles only. The "road" was remarkable, taking us through three national parks with world heritage rainforests and sub-tropical forests alive with bird song. So compelling was the journey and the environment that we drove 35 km past the large signpost for the campsite we wanted and had to retrace our steps. The campsite was full, notwithstanding two compact spaces that we were quickly informed were parking spots for the adjacent tents. The place was packed and newly found neighbours with their tents almost caressing each other exchanged pleasantries and talked, without a hint of irony, about how great it was to get away from it all. We elected to depart and scooted down the road where we found a holiday park with a swimming pool, play park, big plots, spaces, laughing staff, super facilities, including Wi-Fi and, best of all and somewhat unusually, camp fires were permitted too. Despite the ants crawling all over us whilst collecting firewood in the snake-filled (if my imagination was to be believed) nearby dark forest, it was a tremendous find that placated us all.

I picked up some emails one of which was from my brother about his youngest daughter Sophie, which highly amused me.

"...I think she may be developing a stammer, so she has been referred for speech and language therapy. We've tried all the standard parental treatments, mocking her, pulling retard faces when she talks, walking off tutting, slapping her to break her out of it and cold water immersion but, to be honest, it just seems to make it worse. We shall see what the modern quacks can do. Tina thinks I should stop forcing her to clean the chimneys but Lydia doesn't fit any more and I'm not paying for it."

His girls have suffered a load of illnesses, in particular Lydia who was very premature (31 weeks) and he's struggled through so much crap with his kids and their health problems. I admired him for his humorous approach to something which would be a mountain to most other parents, including us.

Hannah, after initially receiving the cold-shoulder treatment from two or three boys in the play park, quickly orchestrated the campsite's children, mobilising all the girls and their younger brothers, and held court on a fallen log. The two or three boys decided one by one to join them. Eirene had a cunning plan to empower Emily, who was being bossed around with Abigail and the rest of them. We called her over and gave her a big bag of marshmallows with instructions to give them to who she wanted if their parents said it would be ok. Eirene started filming and we had a quick sweepstake as to how long Emily would have hold of them before Hannah persuaded her that it would be in her best interests if she held them. At that time, all Emily's pocket and reward money resided in Hannah's purse for "safe keeping". However, nothing so subtle occurred.

We'd barely settled on the odds when Emily arrived at the group with a bag of marshmallows in her hand, screaming her delight. Hannah immediately ran up to her and grabbed them out of her hands before rewarding her loyal lieutenants. Sometime later Hannah argued 'til the cows came home that Emily had voluntarily handed them over, a position endorsed by Emily. Even in the dark we could see Hannah's face turn red as we replayed the virtual mugging on the camera.

We spent 10 days in one place over Christmas with Eirene's brother Simon and his family, in a $5m house with a pool, private jetty and a staggering view over the main river towards the skyscrapers of Surfers Paradise. Despite the initial two or three days where I admittedly struggled to come to terms with the missing apostrophe, I soon became at one with my environment, nights in a tent a distant memory. Everyone around there relished in the display of wealth, with endless streams of parties at increasingly bigger houses where we quickly became blasé at the expensive champagne and nonplussed with the tennis courts and boats. I went from the wide-eyed innocence of Dick Whittington to a blasé David Beckham in a matter of days. Their kids appeared to have been conceived as trophies, judging by the time the parents spent with them and all the children above nine had their own little boats, toys and wardrobes like little princes and princesses. It would have taken only one parent to buy a horse and the whole town would have been engulfed by stables and instructors charging a fortune to stand with their hands on their hips, watching little Tarquin ride round in circles.

I think I mentioned that we had met people on this trip with who we engaged for an hour and then left with them knowing no more about us than when they met us. Most of them lived there and I could count on a Norfolk hand how many people said, "Tell me about your trip." Maybe I was being arrogant, thinking that I should have everyone held captive with my every word as I held court with tales of guns, bombs and earthquakes. But it wasn't that. I would have felt the same if I had flown there for a holiday and worked as an accountant. It's the bubble that the people were in, the complete lack of one single inquisitive bone in their bodies, the ability to talk wholly and solely about themselves and their own world for the duration of any conversation, that I found difficult to comprehend.

Perhaps the area was so shallow and self-obsessed because it should be. The global meltdown was on the verge of deeply affecting Australia and these people seemed like they were on the brink. In many ways, it was like the last hurrah as the ambassador hosted one final party in some remote English colony with the revolutionaries battering down the doors as the band played on.

It was, however, an enjoyable and relaxing, if not costly, time and the kids relished being in a stable environment around people they knew for a decent period of time. They loved playing with their cousin Emma and felt like they had found Aladdin's Cave when they saw the toys, dresses and games that were at their disposal. For my part, despite trying as hard as I could, I was consistently humiliated at WWF Wrestling on the Xbox by my nephew Reece. I really appreciated the hospitality that Simon and his family afforded us, but Simon couldn't understand why I didn't want this lifestyle and I couldn't understand why he did.

When I'd visited the Gold Coast three years previously, plans by my niece, Claire, to take me to Byron Bay never came to fruition. We didn't stop on the way up this time as we knew that we'd be spending 10 days with Simon and his family and that we'd probably have a day out there but, somehow, it didn't happen. Everyone we had spoken to recommended the place so we decided to take a detour and see it. Despite it being in the opposite direction of travel, I was desperate to see the most easterly town in Australia, having heard so much about its surfing beaches, sunsets and notorious traffic problems.

I hadn't actually heard about the notorious traffic problems until after we'd attempted to visit. 100 km into our journey and, despite the rain, we joined the end of an eager queue of traffic, 5 km out of town, and waited patiently for 15 minutes as we moved about the equivalent in metres, progress that only Field Marshall Haig would have been happy with.

Byron Bay was cursed. We decided it was not to be, so we turned around and headed off to the less populous recommendations of Natural Bridge, which was part of the Springbrook National Park, where we embarked on an 800 metre walk past a deafening and plunging waterfall over Cave Creek. We wandered through ancient rainforest where the trees were bound with creeping vines and vertical roots and swathed in moss and enormous ferns.

The 800 metre walk turned out to be slightly longer than advertised and on the final straight I had to carry Abigail, while Hannah and Emily competed for who could complain the loudest about the length. I'd say it was a tie, but I acknowledged that the less physical effort they did in their daily routine, the less they wanted to do and, with our constant car-based travel, we were authors of our own destiny in this respect.

We were a stone's throw away from where they filmed *I'm a Celebrity ... Get Me out of Here* and, although Eirene was anxious not to camp, we secured camping adjacent to the Australian Army's Land Warfare Centre at Canungra which was slightly disconcerting. That evening, Eirene and I drank wine around the campfire as the kids slept and we talked late into the night (circa 10.30pm!) before we climbed into our sleeping bags. At about midnight, though, the sounds of the jungle escalated. It started off with clicks and low pitch wails then progressed to gradually unnerving screeches before throaty rattles started reverberating through the forest. The noises played like a repetitive musical cannon, with each round bringing in another new creature with gurgling moans and soft hoots. I tried not to think what insects and animals might be causing this indigestible cacophony and it just seemed unreal, almost fabricated. I recalled the *Not the Nine O' Clock News* sketch where the rhythmic thudding of the train on the train line caused one passenger to pop his head into the carriage next door to see a British Rail conductor playing the drums. The noise was so loud, verging on deafening, and so varied, like nothing I had ever experienced. It was without respite, until the first heavy plops of rain started to fall. From my lofty position in the roof-tent with Emily, I listened as the rain began to chuck itself down, as the British Rail guy now played his drums on my canvas roof. It rained on and off throughout the night, very heavily at times, until a 6am wake up from Eirene caused me to pop my head out from my snug and dry surroundings to see that she and Hannah had very wet pillows and heads. To someone that could barely tolerate idyllic and perfect camping, I knew this spelt trouble. It continued to rain heavily as we tried to pack our wet belongings away as patiently as we could muster and, after a quick shower inside followed by a heavy shower again outside, we left on empty stomachs for the north. Eirene, perhaps not surprisingly, was in a foul mood and I foolishly and harshly said that it would be easier to travel with Paris Hilton than her. Perhaps if my head and pillow had been soaking wet I might not have been so chirpy myself, although the offer of the roof-tent was there for her. We both had a two hour stew before I did my regular and probably justified apology.

We had a long drive on a rather soggy day that took us up through Conondale National Park, noted for its ancient forests, waterfalls and diverse range of plants and animals, in fact very similar to Springbrook National Park down the road. I mention Conondale National Park, not because it was particularly noteworthy, but because I have the map open in front of me as I write this. Navigating through these parks with just a road map of Australia was like driving through London using only a pencil sharpener globe of the world. There were paths, roads and tracks leading off in every direction and eventually and probably inevitably, we took a wrong one and ended up on a Camel Trophy extreme 4x4-type route up and down some mountains that understandably increased Eirene's angst. We kept on and ended up back at the same point, like a scene from *The Blair Witch Project*, but eventually managed to backtrack and made it out without any panic stricken monologues into the camera. It was late by the time we emerged and we were left to endure condescending, although probably justified, sarcasm from one too many Noosa Heads' accommodation owners basking in their 100% occupancy rate. Noosa was a trendy destination with beachfront cafes, bars and restaurants and spectacular beaches and was extremely popular, particularly at this time of year. One of the hoteliers even managed to reply to my polite enquiry about an available cabin with a sneer and a "You've not done much travelling round here then?" At least he deigned to reply; some just laughed and one, like a night cashier at a UK petrol station, didn't even use any sounds at all. I overtly wished them all well and covertly wished the global meltdown provided a slow and painful demise to their smug and comfortable existence.

It was already late as we forlornly headed north for another 40 minutes, moving away from the rich coastal suburbs before we came across a pub in the arty looking town of Kin Kin. Kin is the aboriginal word for a black ant that used to be very common in that area. I can only assume that the first people here initially spotted two of them.

In previous months and other countries, my recce to a prospective hotel would have included a list of 10 memorised questions, a visit to the room/cabin in question and then some hard haggling. I once attended a week-long intensive negotiation course at a country hotel in Oxfordshire. It was one of those courses where the course carried on into the evenings and you never knew when the game play had stopped. On the final night, the excellent instructor said that now and then, when he goes out with his wife, it gives him the simplest pleasure to accept the first price that is thrown at him. He sometimes just couldn't be bothered going through the whole performance that negotiation is. This is where I was and, with the sun long gone, I knew the balance of power lay firmly with the landlord. More importantly, so did he.

As it turned out, the room in the pub proved an inspired choice. My wife was truly elated, verging on ecstasy, that there was a washer and spin dryer for her to use and the menu was excellent. We were even unnecessarily offered earplugs for the house band that had packed up and gone home by 9pm. A fortuitous stop, but within three months the town was to be devastated by flooding when almost a metre of rain fell in six hours, destroying livelihoods, houses and infrastructure, literally overnight. April is some time past the natural wet season, but such is the unpredictable nature of Australia's outback.

Our next stop was Maryborough, a wholesome colonial town noted for two things. It was the only place in Australia where an outbreak of the pneumonic plague occurred in 1905, and it was the birthplace of Pamela Lyndon Travers, author of Mary Poppins. The town had started to embrace the whole Mary Poppins theme with a life-size bronze statue of her, erected outside the old bank premises on Kent Street. The town had olde worlde New England-type housing, a load of old Vauxhalls outside the leisure centre, where the Australian Vauxhall Owners Club held their annual rally and, delightfully, numerous free Wi-Fi signals. I picked up some emails and saw that Tim and Maria had invited us to stay in Adelaide if we were passing back that way. The internet cost alone was too prohibitive, but we were touched by their invite.

The roads were abnormally twisty for Australia and somewhat convoluted as we made our way north to Tin Can Bay. "I Spy" proved to be the popular classic that it had been throughout the last eight or so months and Hannah peaked when it was my turn.

Me: "I spy with my little eye something beginning with 'I'."

Emily: "Hannah."
Mum: "No, an I."
Abigail: "Hannah."
Mum: "No, an I."

It quickly descended into farce before I began handing out clues. The object they were trying to guess was Identity Bracelet or Identity Tag that I had on my wrist with my personal details, emergency contact number, allergies etc. When we started the journey we all had them on, but it became impossibly painful to ensure the kids wore them all the time and when Eirene stopped wearing hers I gave up but continued to wear one myself. So the clues began.

Me: "If you had asked me five months ago I could have seen five but now I can only see one."

Hannah: "Car."

Mum: "No, an I."

Me: "It's inside the car."

Hannah: "Us."

Mum: "No, an I."

Me: "In the front."

Hannah: "You."

I looked at Eirene waiting for her contribution. Nothing came back.

Me: "Where did I work before we went on this trip?"

Hannah: "Passport Office."

Me: "And what else did I work on?"

Hannah: "Identity cards."

Me: "That's it – so …?"

Hannah: "Nothing."

Me: "I'm wearing it."

Hannah: Silence.

Me: "On my wrist."

Hannah (so excitedly): "I've got it – name tag!"

Mum: "No. Identity Tag."

Hannah: "Do I win?"

We secured a cabin in Tin Can Bay, metres from the daily dolphin feeding and started planning our trip to Fraser Island later in the week. It started off great with a short meander down the road to where people were gathering in numbers in anticipation of the dolphin feeding. We stood in the water and watched one swimming a few feet away from us, occasionally brushing the children's legs. Its dorsal fin bore the scars of a recent shark skirmish that had claimed its mother but otherwise it was perfect. We managed to obtain the last morsels of fish to feed them and I filmed the kids as they cautiously reached towards the dolphin, faces open in awe, as it took the food from their hands. And all this at no cost!

We later visited the tiny town of Rainbow Beach in order to obtain permits for camping and vehicle usage on Fraser Island. The beach is famous for its multicoloured craggy rocks, which are made from an array of coloured minerals in the sand making the dunes 80 different colours. However, Aboriginal legend says the dunes became that colour during an attack on a rainbow spirit, which plunged into the cliffs after losing the battle with an evil filled boomerang spirit. I felt those warring spirits were still around when I broached the subject with Eirene of taking the four-wheel drive trail that led through the forest and along Rainbow Beach itself, a drive that was highly recommended in *Lonely Planet.*

Eirene refused to go down that road literally and metaphorically and was adamant that we took the long and sturdy tarmacked road to Rainbow Beach. We had a satellite phone, an emergency beacon, a spade, a tyre compressor (and the knowledge to deflate the tyres), the tide times and other people travelling the route, so I saw it as a very safe risk. Eirene couldn't understand why I wanted to do it and I couldn't understand why she didn't.

"But we're going to be driving on the beach when we get to Fraser Island," she offered, a fact that she had only recently realised to her horror, following her publicly aired anticipation about going there. She even suggested that we should not take our four-wheel drive onto the island, but we should go on a $250 organised trip. Her logic appeared to run along the lines of "We are going to have fun next week, why do we need to have fun now?" Naturally I had the hump in my inimitable way and Eirene suggested that I was very lucky to have a wife who had come and done what she had done. "Most women would jump at the chance," I said assuredly. "Especially with me," I followed less confidently, glancing down at my growing belly. But I bit the bullet and took the concrete road route and, on arrival at our accommodation that night, the lady owner recommended the same four-wheel drive beach route. Eirene, to her credit, finally conceded and we set off to the drive before realising the tide was in. As consolation, though, we were able to drive through 20 km of rainforest and onto Freshwater Beach instead.

There are many things that will stick out on this trip but emerging from jungle, straight onto a wide empty beach stretching for miles and miles with the sea lapping at my tyres as we sped along it, was right up there. Perhaps it was the heat, but I felt like one of those X-Wing fighters, emerging from the claustrophobia of a Death Star tunnel into the wide open space of space itself. The waves were pounding in as we zipped along but the family weren't having it. Emily wanted her iPod, Hannah was trying to torment Abigail and Eirene had a face like a smacked arse. She said that it did absolutely nothing for her and it was, and I quote, "unremarkable." I persevered, never one to let sleeping dogs lie, and queried how anyone could find something like this unremarkable but she maintained her position and said, "It's the same way people don't like green." For once, I prudently decided not to explore this further although did consider that, absurd as it sounded initially, perhaps Glasgow Rangers fans might hold such a position.

Later I recalled Ranulph Fiennes in one of his books describing his thoughts when he looked back on the journal he'd kept while travelling, recounting that he had blown such insignificant things out of all proportion. I felt that maybe this fell squarely into that category. I wasn't sure of my need to enforce my position on the rest of the family. If I found something profound, delightful or compelling, what was it that made me want my partner and children to feel the same? Was it not enough that I did?

I think I have a different attitude to most people and it's absurd to expect the same in others. Climbing the Sydney Harbour Bridge was an exhilarating experience when I did it three years prior to this trip and one I heartily recommended to Eirene. She didn't do it and doesn't know what she missed. I constantly press on the children to experience as much as they can, even if only once, as long as it doesn't do any harm. They can wind me up something rotten when I ask them, for example, if they would like to go and feed some wild dolphins and they say "no" straight off. Feed the dolphins and if it turns out to be rubbish, don't do it again and then you can say your "no" with some authority and experience next time. Eirene's refusal is a tad more justified as she has acrophobia anything more than two rungs up a step ladder.

I was feeling pissed off because we only had six weeks left of the trip and we seemed to be losing the stomach for it. Eirene wanted to be home with her mum, and the kids, believe it or not, were bored with the variety. I was dreading looking for an IT job and was desperately searching for options I could pursue on my return. I didn't like being on this trip with people who didn't want to be on this trip and so readily showed it. Negativity brought me down and it was a vicious spiral. I was being Fiennes melodramatic and I knew it, but I didn't know if I could face the battles to encourage Eirene into a campsite where we could save a fortune and the kids could be in the fresh air and meet other people. It became such a battle that I inevitably relented and paid 10 to 20 times the cost for a crappy mobile home as we strived to reach some middle ground. I yearned for a trip where we camped in the bush and on beaches and took the less trodden, more difficult route. But I knew I was wrapped up in myself. I promised no risks and recalled the "stick to the main road" vows that I made before we departed.

I told the girls we were heading to Fraser Island the next day, arguably the most alluring island in the world. But they and Eirene seemed more excited before we visited Auschwitz and you would have thought they were on the train to there, judging by their faces. Emily and Hannah's behaviour had been intolerable. Emily was now either constantly complaining or asking for things, sometimes combining both, and Hannah was intent on bringing misery to the other two. Maybe their mood rubbed off on us or ours on them. I understood their positions, empathised with their despondency but still struggled to restrain the urge to yell out "Why don't you all fuck off, you ungrateful wankers." I guess really the trip was my escape from my unsatisfactory life. This hadn't come from Eirene or the kids – they were content with their lot back home and yearned for little outside of that. When you take people from that and then present them something that they never said they wanted, it's hard to criticise them when they make clear they don't want it.

I know with hindsight and a competently produced video/picture montage of our trip to some poignant music that all this will be forgotten. And the only, one-sided, record of it will be this. Eirene's brother Simon, when we were out for a drink one night, candidly said that what we had done would be so far outside his own comfort zone he could not comprehend it. He said he would rather lose absolutely every penny he had, this being his worst nightmare, than travel in a car for the distance we had travelled with his family. I should have been grateful that Eirene proved to be as open-minded as she was.

As it transpired, our three nights on Fraser Island was just what I needed and the kids had a great time too, making new friends at each of the three campsites we stayed at.

It is a diverse island that claims to be the largest sand island in the world, with rainforests growing in the sand beside crystal clear freshwater lakes and white sandy beaches that border the sea around the circumference of the island. It plays host to tens of thousands of migratory birds each year and the waters around its shores, although dangerous to swimmers, contain endangered species, such as dugongs and turtles. It had a 58 mile beach, naturally called *Seventy Mile Beach*, a stretch of sandy highway on the east coast of the island where four-wheel drives speed up and down, occasionally interspersed with wide channels and creeks that need to be waded through depending on the tide. It's grippingly gorgeous but I recognised the hypocrisy of our appreciation of it as we left our big carbon footprint all over the place. Travel was dictated by the tides and in the two hours either side of low tide the beaches filled up with thirsty 4x4s like some sort of monster truck convention. The sea itself was empty of humans, bar some fishermen, as the tides, dangerous rip-currents, sharks, stingers, blue bottle jellyfish and a load more lethal creatures ensured that no human should enter it. Although sea swimming was taboo, lake swimming was encouraged and the translucent, almost thermal, freshwater creeks looked void of any animal life. The kids adored it.

Following the brutal death of a nine-year-old boy in 1991 and numerous other attacks by dingoes, campsites were classified as fenced or unfenced, the less expensive option being unfenced. I began our dingo attack training within minutes of arriving at our first campsite at Waddy Point in the north of the island. I emerged from behind buildings, tents and trees and started barking manically at the kids and, after a while, their response became textbook – folding their arms, staring me straight in the eyes and slowly walking back. Even Emily gave me the appropriate response as she slept peacefully next to me at three o'clock in the morning. You need to keep them on their toes.

The island also had a maze of sand tracks crossing it, some in very soft sand, which required a decent bit of skill with the car. Having said that, one of the scenic drives around the island, classified as being "for experienced four-wheel drive users only, highly remote and exceptionally difficult – allow four hours", took us just over an hour and wasn't a patch on some of Eirene's Kazakhstan and China driving or even our *Blair Witch* forest of the other week. I was disappointed that all fires were banned and that I couldn't drink loads of beer whilst turning a few bits of meat on the barbie.

Eirene certainly wasn't enjoying the Fraser Island experience as much as I was and may have reproached herself for suggesting this four-wheel driving and camping Mecca. It was high season and some of the sites were cramped but Eirene tolerated it because the kids were happy and enjoying themselves. Even the presence of a girl from Croydon, Eirene's home town, and the ensuing "do you know ..." chatter, failed to lift her spirits. The wet weather ensured the floor of her tent was soaked each night, although I repeatedly offered her the roof-tent. However, the presence of a large python on the outside table at one of the sites almost clinched an early exit from the island.

The night we arrived at that campsite, the wrinkly and deeply tanned park ranger paid us a visit to tell us about all the evils his campsite held. He was a bit like the sheriff from *First Blood* in his initial encounter with the hobo John Rambo. In fairness, he didn't smash my tail-light with his baton but he did seem to only just tolerate us outsiders, despite us effectively being the source of his income and reason for his role. He took great delight in telling us that seven of Australia's most deadly snakes were to be found in the environs of this campsite. "Wow, seven's not bad. We thought there would be hundreds of snakes," I submitted, but he ignored my repartee and warned us about picking up any objects in the dark. "But that's how I met my wife," I continued determinedly, but it was hard audience, so I took my bows and called the gig to a premature halt before I ended up in his cell-block, being sprayed with freezing cold water. I was of half a mind to highlight that he probably meant venomous when he used the word poisonous, as it's unlikely we would be harmed if we cooked and ate one of the slithery creatures. A little voice in the other half of my mind fortunately told me to keep that thought where it was.

One thing the island did excel at was exploitation of visitors under the pretence of additional costs in transporting goods to the island. All goods, including petrol and diesel, were twice the price of the mainland. I bought the "additional cost" concept to an extent but saw it for what it was - a licence to print money for people with little in the way of choice. I questioned one of the purveyors of highly priced goods as to why the inflation/deflation of tyres, something that was essential for accident prevention, cost $2 at his garage. His reply mystified me. "Exactly," he said, "that's the problem." And quickly moved onto the next customer.

I thoroughly enjoyed Fraser Island and, had the weather been better and pythons hadn't occupied the table next to us, I venture to say that Eirene would have enjoyed it too.

Back on the mainland, we stopped at the first town, Hervey Bay to have a puncture repaired. I was pleased that Australian tyre centres actually fixed punctures and didn't try to replace them with a set of four Fandango wheels and £500 a piece tyres, tracking, balancing and VAT, including tyre disposal. I also posted a small novel of documents to Bangkok, which were required for the transportation of our Land Cruiser back to the UK. Despite Hervey Bay being the number one transit spot for vehicles going to and from Fraser Island, where tyre deflation is essential, no garages supplied compressed air. One of them even offered as some sort of explanation that "we had to get rid of it as everyone coming off of Fraser Island wanted to use it." "That makes sense," I acknowledged and we both nodded sagely at each other, whilst I contemplated how many deaths the nearby roads had claimed over the years as a result of people having to drive in fully laden cars on tarmac with near flat tyres. Here's hoping there weren't any hazards that could suddenly hop out in front of those vehicles causing them to have to brake urgently.

We headed north and took a little detour off the main road to visit Australia's weirdest named town, The Town of 1770, although predictably "The Town of" bit is pretty redundant in most commonplace references to it. It was previously called Round Hill after the nearby creek until 1970 when, 200 years after Captain Cook landed there, they thought it would be a nice touch to rename it. This is celebrated every year in May with a

Captain Cook Festival when everyone rues the fastidious minute taker at the 1970 meeting who was present when the Mayor said, "This shouldn't be the town of Round Hill – it should be the town of '1770'". The town of "The Town of 1770" is little more than a small fishing village, virtually unchanged for nearly 250 years and, being off the main tourist route, is quiet and unspoilt. However, enough tourists visit each year to warrant guided family kayak trips in the creek or amphibious vehicle tours which cruise off the coastline of 1770 and Eurimbula National Park. We paid our respects and continued northwards up the coast, half listening as the young lady on the radio warned of impending cyclones and road closures in the Cairns area.

Morale was high again as we crossed the tropic of Capricorn and settled in Agnes Water for the night. Had we known that we had been snapped on a speed camera that day at a cost of $133, plus a $66 administration charge from Britz, then we might not have been so chirpy. Who was driving is still the subject of some debate. Eirene says it was me and I'm turning the other cheek.

So we moved on to Yeppoon where we stumbled across beautiful accommodation, a house on the beach with unbroken views and the sound of the surf closer than if we'd been camped on the sand. It even had wireless Internet if I embarked on a complex acrobatic routine near the back porch.

We ventured out on a circular trip to visit a crocodile farm and the Capricorn Caves, a "Top Choice" according to *Lonely Planet,* which described it as a "rare acoustic and visual treat." However, Eirene recounted all our cave visits on the trip so far, which I took to mean she was caved out, so we gave it a miss. Our visit to the crocodile farm was equally unsuccessful. As we entered the farm, we saw a couple of the little critters in pools surrounded by chicken wire. A lady greeted us in the car park and said we had missed the tour but that we owed them money as soon as we drove into the park. We didn't pay and drove off back where we came from, but I immediately regretted my failure to make some sort of "snappy" type pun in our brief exchange. Eirene said it wasn't worth driving back to do and I eventually and sullenly accepted it.

We drove inland towards the Eungella National Park after leaving Yeppoon, purely because *Lonely Planet* had spoken harshly of the coastal area of Mackay but praised the land west of it. Despite the continuous rainfall, the park was pretty outstanding; a meeting of tropical and sub-tropical foliage, with flashes of colour from honeyeaters and parakeets and forests that chorused with wildlife songs.

After traversing several rivers and creeks and driving on unsealed roads, we came across some remote accommodation. A note stuck to the gate informed potential guests of a minimum two night stay at a cost of $310 for a damp hut beside a mosquito-ridden river. We elected not to get fleeced but soon discovered that in Australia, the more remote locations were, the more expensive, no matter what the accommodation was like. We stumbled in and out of a few places before returning to Broken River, a campsite that sat adjacent to some water that I guess at a push could be described as broken. The place had a pool in the form of a large concrete bowl full of leaves and branches with some water sprinkled on the top. The food on the menu was extortionate and the cabins had a paint scheme straight out of a 1970s sitcom. Still, it had an open-fire and a platypus viewing platform at the nearby river. We'd never seen a platypus before and in fact most Australians never have either, which probably accounts for why when these strange looking creatures were discovered in the mid 1800s, they provided much amusement to the British biologists who thought they might be fakes.

The area attracts visitors from afar, solely to witness these elusive, flat-nosed, venomous, beaver-looking creatures do their swimming, the best time to see them being the morning and evening when they pop out for a stretch of the old flippers. If you ask me, the place had been marketed by the guys who did Loch Ness - I made four visits, admittedly with three noisy kids, who would have scared any living creature away, and didn't get one sniff of a platypus. Glacially rocking turtles sunbathed on top of each other on nearby rocks (well, that's what I told the kids), and a few fish swam by, but there was no sign of the egg-laying mammals. After my final unsuccessful visit, the following day we set off on an unsurfaced road and navigated one of the most engaging stretches of country that we had seen since arriving in Australia. It gave us both a taste for more outback trips as we travelled along 100 km of empty dusty roads with lakes and mangrove swamps on both sides. It was with some dejection that we eventually hit the concrete and found ourselves a cabin in a miserable, wet holiday park.

The park owner warned us at check-in to "beware the road north of Ingham", sounding like a cross between the pre-incarcerated Rolf Harris and Brian Glover in *An American Werewolf in London*. The flooding from the recent cyclone had left the road closed to all but large 4x4s and lorries. We carried on towards our fate, witnessing the vastness of the submerged fields on either side of us that occasionally made a dash to join up with each other under our tyres. A few kilometres north of Ingham, we came across a queue of stationary traffic and sat obediently for 10 minutes until three large lorries and a group of 4x4s drove past us on the wrong side of the road. We tutted in the traditional English way and then, as more overtook us, I became braver and turned my tutting to tooting and blasted my horn in disgust at their queue jumping antics - that was the work of China, not a civilised left hand drive country like Australia. With that we decided to follow suit, having realised that we were in a queue solely occupied by cars. We came to the front of the queue, drove past a phone-wielding policeman and followed a couple of trucks into a raging river. The river had well and truly burst its banks and a strong current of water, half a metre in depth, surged from our left across the road. Eirene was questioning her sanity yet again and her dismay was compounded both by the number of abandoned, submerged cars off to our right and me looking like Jack Nicholson in *The*

Shining. We made it across with a surge of adrenaline and headed along the near empty roads, overtaking the lorries that so callously overtook us previously. My dad, a man who had little time for vehicles making progress past him and would always brand any overtake on him as either the work of an idiot or, at best, conclude that the person wouldn't get there any quicker, would have been utterly contemptuous of my advance.

After the excitement of our submarine driving, the rest of the trip was a bit of a let-down with its lack of livelihood-destroying floods. We took a detour to Tully Gorge and asked an elderly Tully resident which road it was that we needed for the gorge. He helpfully told us "The Gorge Road," and that it was "out of town." Wasn't after a grid reference but keen on a little more than that. We stumbled upon it and it passed through hundreds of acres of banana plantation and sugarcane before establishing itself alongside a fast travelling creek. It ended in a dead end, so we retraced our route and elected to plonk ourselves at Mission Beach, the seaside town which was made famous, and famous really is the wrong word, by Edmund Kennedy who landed there in 1848 and managed to traverse 42 km of jungle in nine weeks before meeting an unfriendly local who speared him. Little more is known about his fate, other than he was thought to have been speared near the bottom of the gorge by some Aborigines, which does sound like a very painful demise.

Despite widespread protestations to the contrary, I elected to employ the services of Mission Beach tourist information in our search for accommodation. They came up with a beautiful apartment, hence why I'm emphasising the protestations, that was luxurious, affordable and had the obligatory pool as requested by Hannah, Emily and Abigail. It was also only about 100 metres from the beach, which had a backdrop of tropical rainforest.

The following day, we reluctantly left our deluxe Mission Beach resort and headed north towards our goal, our aim, our Mecca – Cairns – thus fulfilling the latter part of our tagline

"From Croydon to Cairns" that we'd put on the website and the little business cards we gave out. We hadn't, in fact, left from Croydon but nearby Warlingham and Cairns wasn't actually going to be our final destination but that's the seductive power of alliteration for you. We hadn't intended to stay in Cairns, only pop in just to say we had been there and take a snap at the town's sign as the place held little for the visiting tourist other than a stepping stone to the Great Barrier Reef. However, Barrier Reef trips from Mission Beach were a lot longer than their Cairns' counterparts and that assuaged Eirene's nervous sea legs, so we elected to stay in the north Queensland city.

The lady running our accommodation in Cairns kindly booked us up on the *Calypso 2* and threw in a bottle of wine as part of the deal so there was commission somewhere, I cynically concluded. Despite repeated requests, no one would tell me what had happened to *Calypso 1*. The whole trip was meant to cost an all-inclusive $420 for the family for the day but on arrival, they dropped the bombshell that Abigail had been omitted from the figure quoted and it didn't include the fuel surplus levy. "But oil is at its lowest price for 18 years," I argued. "Still not cheap though mate," was his considered reply. Nor did it include the eco tax, the rental of stinger suits for the wife and kids, soft drinks, water, GST (VAT) and rental of a seat on which to sit on. I made the last one up, but I wouldn't have been surprised at what was nothing short of piracy. Still, the trip had to be done. The escalating price included a trip out to the main boat from the shore in an inflatable dingy that hadn't been inflated and had a water level inside it that matched the water level outside. Hannah, without a hint of sarcasm and with all the bluntness of a seven year old, said that she wished she had brought her fishing net to catch some of the fish inside.

The main boat was relatively small although 16 of us was about the right number. We were informed that we had to pop into Dunk Island on the way out to the reef to pick up a few more passengers. 44 to be precise. By the time they had clambered aboard it was beginning to feel like the top deck of the Titanic. Perhaps an appropriate analogy as just as we arrived at Dunk Island to collect the surge of other mugs, the boat caught fire. Much rumbling was coming from the Captain's deck and the smell of burning was becoming stronger, but I assumed I still had the burning smell that was a constant in our Britz rental car, up my nose. In terms of PR and attempting not to induce a panic, the opening of a hatch in front of us all was misjudged. Plumes of dark acrid smoke poured forth and word circulated of someone witnessing a lick of flames. More Dunkirk than Dunk, people still queued to board and there was something grotesquely "head in the sand" about the whole thing. The billowing smoke worsened before it improved and the same went for the Captain's mood. He plonked himself down the hatch only to pop up minutes later with a completely blackened face. It was as if it had been applied purely for comedy affect. I attempted to elicit a picture, he refused, and I took it anyway, much to his disdain. He did look mightily pissed off and I'm guessing the last thing he needed was a punter sticking a camera in his face whilst his boat, come to mention it his livelihood, was going up in flames. Mind you, sitting with your wife and three kids on a packed $550 trip whilst oily smoke covered us wasn't what I needed either. I was British and nearing the end of my tether and was of a strong mind to make clear to the Captain that I was indignant as a consumer and TripAdvisor would be getting a strongly worded review in the morning. I bit my tongue and refrained from the feedback for the time being.

Eventually the fire was put under control and reassurances given that there was nothing to worry about, albeit we could all now have an educated stab at what happened to *Calypso 1*. The masses joined our boat and included what looked like a German Village People tribute band and a man with a false leg. Oddly and nonchalantly, his wife, who was loyally aiding him on his every step, carried a shopping bag with a spare leg sticking out.

I had elected to do an introductory scuba diving trip and Eirene had elected not to. I suspected that she was being less than generous and just wasn't keen on the whole underwater thing. I had begun to suspect this on our honeymoon in the Dominican Republic 10 years previously, when she declined scuba lessons in the halcyon waters of the Caribbean, saying that she would prefer to go back home in England in the channel. I smelt a rat, although did accept that she was an active social member of the university scuba diving club in her first year or joined up at least in Freshers' Week.

After a tranquil journey on, for once, a brilliantly sunny day, the boat finally slowed to floating speed on the reef without any more blazes. First, we were all going to do a bit of snorkelling so we began the prolonged process of changing the kids, putting on wet swim suits, changing goggle sizes, fighting over flippers, putting on stinger suits, taking them off and putting them back on again this time with the legs and arms the right way round. More sun cream was applied, water wings inflated and finally we all made it into the water just as most people were leaving after their first hour swimming.

I was now on the cusp of submerging myself for the first time in one of the seven natural wonders of the world. I waddled to the end of the boat, sat down and elegantly rolled off the end of the boat, facemask tight to my head, as I dunked my face down into the Coral Sea ready to take the moment in. No David Attenborough documentary could have sufficiently prepared me for the extraordinary range and variety of different shapes and colours that attacked my vision. It was truly like another world and I felt like the girl with kaleidoscope eyes - nothing could have taken away the wonder of that first moment but in fairness the kids had a bloody good try. Despite their buoyance, their party trick was to latch onto my every limb rendering me virtually immobile. They dragged me down as they simultaneously put their finger in the top of my snorkel and pulled the mask off my face. I was beginning to wish that we'd followed through on our earlier discussion about hiring a babysitter and heading out with just the two of us, but it hadn't happened. For Eirene, less confident in the water, I think it marred her experience somewhat and the whole snorkelling experience became nothing short of a battle for survival. We were soon waved back in and I was taken away to adorn my scuba gear, leaving Eirene to entertain three kids on board the cramped decks of the boat in my absence, feeding them constantly until my return.

The voluptuous Nicole taught me and another couple the basics of diving and I did manage to take on the important elements of what she was saying, namely "Hold my hand when you are down there" and "This is the signal if you get cramp. Show me where it is and I will massage it." It got me thinking that the old groin injury might flare up again. There was also some other mumbo jumbo about what to do in a major emergency and some hand signal thingies but seriously, I asked myself, what's the worst that could happen? Finally, we were allowed into the water and, limbs to myself, I submerged and miraculously continued to breathe. Despite the experience of my recent sortie on the surface with the goggles, two feet under the lopping waves was a different kettle of fish. And what a variety of fish were in that kettle – within seconds of going under, a giant manta ray cast an enormous black shadow on me as it glided effortlessly overhead. I moved deeper and further from the safety of our vessel, following Nicole and the two others on the excursion. Where the reef ended abruptly in places, it was like the edge of a cliff which disappeared into a deep blackness that made me feel cold to the core despite the warm waters. Multicoloured fish swam around purposefully, seemingly ignoring our presence completely. Our leader pointed out rocks that, on the click of a finger, winked at us with hundreds of small dotty eyes; plants with hundreds of spaghetti-like orange strands with white dots on the end almost glued to our hands when we brushed against them. In amongst them were clichéd *Finding Nemo* clown fish, identical in colour to the strands of the plants behind them. They were more curious, coming to look briefly at the visitors before quickly darting away at the merest of movements from us. Rude looking clams, about half a metre in length, shut tightly closed at the merest touch. What we could and couldn't touch was carefully regulated but what we did experience was simply wonderful. One grey plant, on being gently lifted up, had the most vivid and almost luminous purple underside. Rhythmically undulating jelly fish floated by as the line between animal, vegetable and mineral became very blurred. Shoals of multicoloured and even transparent fish weaved around us, while a group of fish near the bottom appeared asleep, completely still, and all pointing in different directions. Some appeared to be eating or cleaning bigger fish and then, just when we thought we couldn't be in any more awe, we saw the biggest of them all.

Probably the biggest worry for anyone swimming in Australian waters is the "S" word. At that time of year, shark attacks and near misses were all over the news, complemented with the obligatory pictures of gigantic bites in surf boards held up by a smiling guy wearing a vest and surf shorts. In reality, there was an average of one death a year in Australia, which made the seas almost infinitely safer than the roads. Still, a shark, like a snake, instils fear in the human mind. It was with some surprise that, as one came close to us, I was wholly absorbed and that this wasn't some HD telly but the real thing. She (I've no idea if I'm honest) was about two metres long and clearly way more scared of us than we were of him as she quickly departed. Still, it was pretty mind blowing and, as we came to the surface at the end of our 30 minutes underwater, all I could I utter was "Fuck me." Which apparently, Nicole revealed, was still top of the pops of phrases to come out of the mouths of reef and scuba virgins after their first soiree. The whole trip gave me a thirst to do it again. To devote a whole holiday to scuba diving and the exploration of the mysteries on our doorstep. What it also did was take the shine off the remainder of the snorkelling we did, like having to go Wembley to watch England play after seeing Barcelona v Real Madrid. As we headed back to port, still with no inkling of fire, I pleaded with

Eirene to go and do one tomorrow and I would look after the kids, but she wouldn't be budged.

We felt Cairns had been given a bad press. People, some books and us had said it was merely a gateway to the Great Barrier Reef and nothing as a town. We found it to be a small, green, tidy municipality with a charming port, interesting markets and wholly unworthy of the disdain and scorn which had been poured upon it. And to top it all, the whole town had been under six feet of water three days before we arrived and there was barely a hint of a sandbag anywhere. "All washed away" Hannah suggested.

It would appear, however, that the *Lonely Planet* writer had a relative in Cairns, as the book was rich with places to see and things to do. For the first time in nine months, we planned the following day the night before and set off with a clear goal in our heads.

We visited a riveting fig tree, thought to be over 500 years old. I know you are wondering how a fig tree could be riveting but far from it being gloomy, dank and swarming with insects as the early explorers to the area described it, we found it to be bright with a well maintained but not obtrusive viewing platform, although I have no doubt the forest was still swarming with insects, judging by the constant clicking and hissing of cicadas. The old fig had a curtain of aerial roots which hung from the top of the tree like long dreadlocked hair and established themselves in the ground. Even the kids stared at it for about 10 minutes, helped by my elaborate spinning of a fairy story into the history of the tree which they bought hook, line and sinker.

Before we left Cairns, we had a big press conference with *The Tableland Advertiser,* now that we had finally achieved our goal. Bafflingly, we could not find any bunting or trace of my friends Paul and Andy who had said nine months ago, whilst drunk, on the eve of our departure, that they would meet us there. Still, it was pouring with rain and we probably wouldn't have opened the car doors if we had found them anyway.

We were up in the Atherton Tablelands, an area of heavy forestation and dormant volcanoes, where erosion had contributed to the colour of the red clay soil, deep river valleys and vertical drops. They in turn have created the famous Millaa Millaa waterfall circuit, a series of stunning waterfalls that cascade over worn basalt columns and plummet into stunning swimming pools. One of them looked just like the one from the old Timotei shampoo advert but I figured that there must be thousands around the world that look like that. I would have liked to go in for a swim, despite a disconcerting pain that was growing in my leg, as I've always loved waterfalls for some indeterminate reason. Perhaps it's the childhood fantasies of treasures and secret passages that lurk behind them waiting to be discovered, or maybe it's just the potential danger coupled with their natural beauty. Eirene had become a bit of a buff on chasing waterfalls and had moved from the apathy of Switzerland to a keenness way exceeding mine. Despite that, we felt like we had reached waterfall saturation by the end of the day, although we particularly liked the volcanic pipe crater and Dinner Falls that we stumbled on towards mid-afternoon. The water at the top of the Hypipamee crater was so still that duck weed covered the surface. The eerie atmosphere was heightened by the tall chamber walls that rose high above us, giving credence to the legends surrounding the crater of two young men who cut down a sacred tree and were swallowed up by the large hole. It is said that when a rock is thrown into the crater from the viewing platform, a loud bang is created when it hits the water which then echoes all the way up the chamber walls. We refrained from testing the theory, fearful off upsetting any resting Aboriginal spirits. We continued on to the three tiers of Dinner Falls, where the upper section had a distinctive triangular shape which was formed of an elongated peak of rock, a bit like a mini mountain, running down the middle of a gently sloping waterfall. The water ran over the top of the mini mountain and down the valleys on either side before gathering in a clear, green pool which contrasted magnificently against the red bedrock.

We had lunch at the tea shop Eirene had mentally logged earlier and it was there, amongst their glossy shelves, that I discovered that the waterfall in question actually was the one from the Timotei shampoo advert.

As we continued heading east, we were tempted to take in the Undara Experience, a series of very wide volcanic tunnels, hundreds of kilometres long that were cut out by lava flows millions of years ago. I like my caves and even Eirene would have made an exception for this except, according to *Lonely Planet's* prices from three years ago, it would have cost us over $100 for the cheapest trip; so we just drove past it, resolute in our new found belief that the best things are free. We stopped at a place called Mount Surprise which sounded like something out of a Carry On film. It was fortunate we stopped as, due to flooding, it was where the road ended. We took a cabin and struck up a conversation with an off-duty policeman who was on holiday with his family in his police car. Or he'd had a mental breakdown, kidnapped a family and was on the run with a tied-up trooper in the boot. Either way, he was well informed and told us a river had burst its banks just past Mount Surprise and that he had been there for three days. It sounded like the start of an episode of *Skippy the Bush Kangaroo*. The water level was 1.7 metres but he was hopeful that we would be able to cross the following day. The town of Mount Surprise is small, with a population of 60, but had somehow managed to produce a massively thick tourist brochure of almost no substance at all. One section that I did find interesting detailed that the local school had just six pupils spanning eight school years and just one teacher. Music was taught via the telephone and I imagine honesty must have played a key role. "Well done Bruce, you're sounding more and more like the actual Beatles every day. And yesterday, it was like Abba were in your living room." "Why thank-you Mrs Simpson, it's just practice, practice, practice."

Some grey nomads [22] who were camping at Mount Surprise told us that the depth of the river had gone down to 0.7 metres during the night but had risen again to 1.7 metres in the morning. They added that it might recede later that afternoon or it might take six weeks, so that was helpful. At about 1 km wide, it was not so much the depth but the speed and power of the flow of the river crossing the road laterally that shocked us. One of them said that the river had been like this every year since he was a boy, 50 years ago. I asked him if there was any talk of them building a bigger bridge and he earnestly said that there had been some. I playfully asked another chap in his golden years "Can I not just take a run at it in the car?" and he playfully replied "Best not. My son did that four years ago in his truck and now he's in a wheelchair." On that sombre bombshell, we made our way to Charters Towers to join up with the main road to Mount Isa. One of the guys had incisively pointed out that this was the main road across Australia and that the army and civilians were working 24 hours a day to rebuild it, the physical structure of the road having been literally swept away, leaving a large chasm. Other than the Nullarbor Plain route, this was the only remaining artery across the Australian sub-continent, so there was indeed some impetus to have it repaired.

It was a long, uneventful drive where only three cars passed us and all three were depressingly the same colour, so I lost that sweepstake. The dusty sun-damaged landscape never varied; dry, red earth with poor quality grass either side of the road, loosely speckled with drought-tolerant, skinny, spindly trees that led to low red, earthy hillocks 50 odd metres away. Occasionally, a primitive road sign indicated we were at a township but, apart from that, there was no other indication of life. The only time the scenery changed was when I was so absorbed in sorting out a game for one of the kids, we drove past an eagerly (by some hours) anticipated petrol station and I missed it. I was genuinely angry with Eirene for not telling me.

---

[22] Or, as they are known in the UK, Caravan Club Crumblies

"Did you want something from there?" she asked, looking somewhat confused, as she thumbed back in the direction of the garage. But, of course, I had no yearning to view the veritable mix of wares that the outlet would stock – the oil, the water, the brake fluid et al. I just wanted to have a look at the only noteworthy thing visible outside the windows of our car in the last five hours! I publicly stewed and privately and tragically made a note of the garage's location, just so I could check it out on Google Earth later. It wasn't the same.

I have to say that I really love the Outback. I've always been attracted to the barren and desolate, both people and locations probably, and Australia had it in abundance. The remoteness of it all makes it so tranquil and, although uneventful, I found it the most satisfying of all our driving. I didn't realise how much I had missed it until we started doing it again, and I really would savour at some point to drive across Australia west to east, through the middle, on its desolate, unsealed tracks.

I also noticed, whilst studying the map in some detail on the drive, that there is a Croydon about 400 km from Cairns, which would now account for some of the disinterest we experienced when we told people that we were driving from Croydon to Cairns.

Everyone seemed to be back in the way of travelling. The pre-Fraser Island tension had completely gone and a different bed every night wasn't just something we had adapted to but something we looked forward to. Emily's intelligence continued to shine through and her ability to laugh at herself and mock others who don't reminded me of myself. If I'm to be believed though, all their positive traits emanate from me! She had learnt, as a result of Hannah's incessant teasing, how to tease Hannah and how not to let it annoy her most of the time. On one occasion, when I was preparing a BBQ, I realised I didn't have enough charcoal. Emily, who had been the target of some degree abuse from Hannah, immediately offered me some of Hannah's Christmas presents (she had received a couple of pieces of coal as well as the normal presents) which had the desired effect on Hannah. Abigail, though, had picked up on everyone's bad habits, imitating and refining them ad nauseam. I constantly told them how much I loved them and how beautiful they were till they were sick of hearing it. Even Abigail told me that she knew that already.

Since my inaugural scuba dive, I'd had a continual pain in the right leg, especially at night. It had been worsening and the hour between waking up in pain and when the painkillers subsequently kicked in, dragged. Things hit their peak as dawn broke in our cabin at Charters Towers when, on a scale of one to ten, I rated my pain and misery at a nine - and by God I've had some colds. So there I was, discreetly and selflessly quietly writhing in agony in bed, desperately changing positions in a futile attempt at some respite, when Eirene took the bull by the horns and started ringing medical numbers for help. At one stage I even suggested an ambulance, but Eirene suggested we go to A & E in town and shrewdly added "Let's take the kids in with us as that will make them see us quicker." The waiting room was like some sort of zombie film, although no one was manifestly displaying injuries that one would immediately think worthy of casualty, unlike me with my sore leg. It was 8am and the very benevolent lady behind the cage told me that it was going to be a long wait. When pressed, she confessed that no doctors would actually turn up until 10.30am which, for any Accident and Emergency, was a bit of shocker, even by NHS standards. She suggested we drove to the local surgery that would see patients without appointments between 8am and 10am. The kids choose this time to be impeccably behaved so Eirene dropped me off at the surgery and I told her I would call her later. I brought a book, *Can't Be Arsed: 101 Things Not To Do Before You Die* by Richard Wilson [23], a great anti-list book that I would strongly recommend, and headed into the surgery.

---

[23] Not the "Victor Meldrew" / "One Foot in the Grave" Richard Wilson although I concede at this point I thought it was.

There were no wire bars defending this receptionist but I resisted the opportunistic urge to attack her. She told me that it would be 30 hours before I could be seen, which put her caged counterpart's paltry figures into perspective. I failed to convince her of the severe nature of my calf twinge, so I limped out and promised myself a cup of tea and a quiet read of the paper before I called up Eirene. Moments like that have to be grabbed whenever one can. I bought the paper and skipped over to the coffee shop before almost being clipped by a tatty looking Britz Land Cruiser. Drat - my lift back to Zombie Island had arrived.

Steeling myself for a long wait, I had a Subway baguette, took some painkillers and settled down to read more startling financial news that boiled down to worldwide property prices were falling and global unemployment was rising. It was a bit like the reporting of Diana's death, massive news as it was, but there wasn't actually enough news to fill the column inches. You know they're getting desperate when they start reporting on what others are reporting and one commentator even reported on that. I had barely tucked into the latest high street retailer to shut down story when the doctor called me in. He was a delightful Scotsman called Dr Kenny Clark. I mention him not as an aide memoire for any future litigious reasons but because he was a doctor who seemed genuinely genuine and talked to me like a human being, telling me his thoughts as he carried out his examination. He thought it might be a clot and recommended I wear some girly tights, maybe to take my mind off it, and gave me a blood thinning injection in my stomach. He told me I needed a scan, but the machine was a 300 km round trip away. He pulled a few strings and facilitated me having one the following day, giving me a needle to inject myself with in the interim. Having seen *Pulp Fiction* over four times, including the disturbing Travolta/Thurman adrenaline injection scene, I felt more than qualified to do this. So, I bid Dr C farewell and we retraced our steps back to the coast to Townsville Hospital, a modern building with lots of flashy equipment for some sort of scanny thing.

As one of only two concrete roads across Australia was still blocked, we thought about flying from Cairns to Darwin and picking up a new rental car there. A carless policeman (surely not?) we encountered told me that the main Barkly Highway, the one they were working on 24 hours a day, would be impassable for two months. He was one of those annoying people who are incapable of saying "I don't know" or "I have no idea", almost seeing it as a weakness. Actually, people that say I have no idea annoy me as well because they do have an idea. They're just being lazy and using the wrong turn of phrase. If the policeman had said he had no idea when the road would be open, I would have known that it wouldn't be open yesterday, as we know it wasn't, and I would have known that it wouldn't be open in five billion years as mankind would have met their demise at about the same time as the sun and wouldn't be able to continue maintaining roads. So he would have had an idea. Quite a wide spanning one but an idea nonetheless. There's a school of thought that may say I'm a pedantic tosser, and admittedly I do irritate even myself sometimes, but it was my own time in the police that produced this idiosyncrasy. I lost count of the number of times a witness would, when asked something like "How tall was he?", respond with "I've no idea." "Well do you have a range at all, madam?" I would probe, and inevitably they would come back with "No, I have no idea at all" which would lead me to turn to my partner and say, "I think this could be Stevie Simms." My partner would nod knowingly. "Who's Stevie Simms?" the lady would enquire. "He's a well-known burglar that frequents this area. He's a midget-come-dwarf, no more than three feet tall." "Oh no! He wasn't a dwarf, definitely not," she would start to say in a panic, worried that she had inadvertently condemned an innocent man to years of cell-bound confinement interspersed with occasional breaks of midget buggery. "But you said you had no idea, madam. We have to take your first account" my colleague would interject. "Are you trying to protect Steven Simms madam? How long have you known him for?" etc etc. So I'm making this up, most of it, but it was tempting and it continues to irritate me to this day. And for the tree hugging anti-police brigade amongst you, Simms had no problems in prison and easily escaped by darting through their legs.

If I couldn't drive because the road was closed, and I couldn't fly because I had a clot, it did make things a bit tricky. These were the thoughts floating between my ears as a young woman began lubricating my leg with KY jelly and rubbing a barcode scanner into my groin. This should have been pleasurable, but my mind was on other things as I sat on the raised bed at Townsville Hospital. Astonishingly, after 20 minutes of prodding and probing, she kicked my bleak outlook into touch and told me that I was all clear. There was the natural caveat that a doctor would have to look at the results to confirm but they were hardly going to disagree with a specialist operative like herself. The doctor, who looked briefly uncomfortable when a packet of Marlborough fell out his top pocket as he bent down to pick up some dropped papers, confirmed the prognosis (I'm going to be fine) and said that he thought there had never been a clot. We could fly and I wasn't going to die. I guiltily reflected on my website posting and Facebook status that read like an obituary and nearly caused my mum to book a ticket straight out. I was elated when I walked out the hospital doors to phone Eirene to pick me up, but that rapidly dissipated when it dawned on me that I still had the excruciating pain in my leg except now with the knowledge that the medical services had no idea what it was.

Unfortunately, I couldn't share my initial elation or new found desperation with Eirene as she was engaged for two hours. Eventually I established through various channels that the engaged tone that Telstra so helpfully put on the end of the line when I dialled the number wasn't an engaged tone but meant that the number did not exist and I was dialling the wrong one. The correct number was on my website but the hospital couldn't give me access to the Internet and it was 4am in the UK so I couldn't really call anyone there. I could, of course, with no qualms call Shameen, but I couldn't remember her number either. The hospital rather helpfully did recommend a shopping centre 5 km away that did have Internet access and there was one taxi at the rank and no queue, but an ungrateful lady with a baby arrived seconds after me so I had to give it up and wait 20 minutes for another one. Things didn't improve at the shopping centre, when I had to wait another half hour for one of the six spotty youths to run out of money Facebooking and Twittering their friends next to them just so I could logon to a website for one minute. Foolishly, having finally obtained the number, I didn't have change for the phone or a pen. So whilst I repeatedly chanted it under my breath, I spotted a card shop and asked if they had a biro I could buy. The lady led me to a display of gold plated pens starting at $150. "I can't see a biro," I said. "We don't have any," she said. "Fuck you," every bone in my body demanded I utter but "Thank you for your help," came out instead. I next tried a newsagent and picked up a biro on the counter and handed over $5, still trying to keep my mind focussed on the 10 digit number that I was repeating like a Buddhist incantation. He handed me five cents change back with the biro.

"$5 dollars for a biro?" I said in shock, "I only bought it as I wanted change to use the phone."

"Ah, we don't do change here, sir," he said.

I eventually found a payphone, waited patiently to use it and even more patiently as I explained to a bewildered wife where I was and how to get there. After 30 minutes of hanging around and no sign of Eirene, the McDonald's cleaner was in on the act when, on being asked where the nearest pay phone was, looked me straight in the eye and directed me to their toilet entrance. There wasn't one there and the manager told me there hadn't been one there for three years.

Eventually the Gods got bored and I met up with Eirene and the kids who gave me a nod when I climbed into the front passenger seat. After much deliberation, we decided to head inland towards Mount Isa as a website had told us that the road in question would be open to light traffic in two days. When we finally found Internet access, I was able to update my Facebook status and reassure my mum that I now had longer than a few days to live and that I wasn't going to lose my leg either. I also picked up an email from Uncle Tim in Adelaide who told me that after the letter I penned to Telstra, they of the stupid engaged-but-not-engaged tone, they had offered him $315 refund which softened the Internet blow considerably. A sleepless pain-filled night followed.

I learnt a few things over the following days on our drive to Tennant Creek in the Northern Territory. First of all, Cloncurry, a little town on the Flinders Highway, was not only the location of the Flying Doctors TV series but also the birthplace of Qantas - **Q**ueensland **a**nd **N**orthern **T**erritory **A**ir **S**ervice, hence the name. The initial chairman apparently was either a not particularly ambitious fellow or, like most people in business, came up with the catchy acronym first and let the meaning develop after. The clocks changed by half an hour when we crossed from Queensland into the Northern Territory, a reason for which I have not yet established. Neither did I fathom why, if a place name had the word "Creek" in it, then this was a licence to charge 50% more for fuel and top rates for bottom accommodation.

We received some advice from a resident in Mount Isa who said "Don't ever consider having a form of holiday or break in Mount Isa and don't have lunch in the beer garden of any pub." The holidaying in Mount Isa bit we could readily understand; it was a dusty mining town with questionable levels of lead in the atmosphere and the main tourist attraction was an old mine named Hard Times Mine, and once a year there was a Mount Isa Rodeo. We'd missed the rodeo so with little to keep us there, we decided to move on after lunch in the beer garden. This part of the warning also came to fruition when we realised that a load of flies had stayed after the last rodeo just in case some tourists popped in.

On a quiz on our trip so far, I asked Emily, "What was the name of the place that we had been to that had rivers as roads?"

"Sounds like here," the five year old said. She had me laughing with admiration at her wit, but the correct answer was of course Venice and she needed to learn that funny is good but right is better. I deducted her a point and she lost the tie-break to Hannah. A harsh lesson indeed, but one that needed to be taught. Fact not fun and that, to me, should be the tagline for all good parents. The big revelation on this part of the trip, though, was the most dreaded words my youngest daughter could have uttered. While offering Abigail help with her shoes, she cut me to the bone with the words, "By myself!" I welled up – the end was nigh.

Tennant Creek demanded and was successful in obtaining $146.50 for a cell, the un-roundedness of the number being a pathetic attempt at inferring there was some sort of scientific analysis involved in the pricing. It was almost dead centre in the middle of Australia and was previously a prolific mining town, but they had all long since stopped digging. There was a sign listing all the attractions on offer, which included the *Social History Museum* with the words "Freedom, Fortitude and Flies" in brackets underneath and a toilet sign that pointed to the bush. However, the town had a surprising number of museums not listed on the sign, celebrating everything from Aboriginal beliefs and culture to the old telegraph station, which, in such an isolated place, was probably in its day the most important building in the town as the critical connection to news from the outside world. We visited a mining museum, which was advertised as having an underground tour. After watching a video, a portly guide who looked like he'd spent all his life in the Outback, handed out hard hats and noise cancelling ear muffs and led the group into a cool cave to give a first hand taste of what it was like for the miners. The noisy, big machine washed the stones while the sorting and selecting process was done by hand. At least, that is what would have happened, but we turned up half an hour after it "opened" and the cleaner told us there was no staff as they weren't expecting any visitors. The local council brochure quoted it as a "very good and active mining museum" but it was all glossy lies.

We carried on north towards Darwin on a well surfaced road with trees on either side heading into the distance and nothing changed for seven hours. I stayed alert for all petrol stations but there was little to report on that front. We stopped at a pub in Daly Waters near where there was a big telegraph pole meeting when they were building a line from north to south, much like when we met the French in the middle of the channel when the tunnel was built. If you ask me, the guys coming from the north were taking the piss, having only done a fifth of the distance the guys from the south did. The pub is exceptional though. It served the local airfield, a centre for the London to Sydney air race of 1926, a refuelling stop for early Qantas flights to Singapore and a World War II Airforce base. Amy Johnson, the first woman to fly solo from England to Australia, famously landed there in 1930 on her epic flight to Australia, also having left from Croydon. The inside is absolutely covered in cards, flags, coins, notes and clothing memorabilia of every kind. It's like one of those theme pubs you see in England where they randomly attach a wagon wheel to the ceiling as if that's the natural way things used to be. It's listed in the *Lonely Planet* as a must see and, with a population of eight, I guessed their business wasn't made up of regulars. In fact, out of the 10 other visitors that were there, we were the only ones eating, with the remainder taking pictures, looking at the walls, filming themselves and sadly attaching their picture or card onto something (mine is to the right of the bar as you come in). Hobson's choice perhaps dictated the attitude of the staff who were as rude, ignorant and narrow minded as they wanted to be, to such an extent that it was like it was an act similar to those gimmicky restaurants where the staff are deliberately contemptuous of their customers. I, in fact, read that at one such establishment in London, complaints had been received that the staff had been "perfectly civil" and that the experience, as a result, had been "ruined."

To their credit, though, they had a couple of petrol pumps outside where you fill up and tell them how much you've put in. I liked this concept of trust, much like the old lady with the jam and honesty box on her table at the foot of her garden on some country lane in England. I filled up the tank for $8.63.

The only other noteworthy aspects of Northern Territory driving are Stonehenge-like termite mounds and an inordinate amount of World War II historical sites. I thought I was going mad but according to both Wikipedia and my own recollection, no World War II land battles were ever fought on the Australian mainland. It seems that every single portacabin site used for a couple of weeks whilst assembling troops had become a shrine and if there was not one of them in sight, then there would definitely be an HMAS Sydney Drive, Road, Avenue, Crescent or Boulevard in remembrance of one of their battleships that was sunk almost 70 years ago.

We arrived in Darwin having spent last night in Katherine, a good few hundred kilometres to the south. Katherine's campsite was very spacious and cuddly kangaroos roamed freely, although the campsite owner irritated us by charging an extra $5 per person for sheets after we had paid and entered the cabin. "Oh, so your children that we've already charged extra for actually want to sleep in the beds?" being the logic that was applied. The town itself was strange and appeared to have a drink problem. We ventured out on a rare evening excursion and it was like stumbling onto the set of "Night of the Living Dead." There were several drunken people from an Aboriginal community stumbling along shouting loudly, repeatedly and unintelligibly and who were joined, to my eternal shame, being from Glasgow myself, by a drunken Scotsman who out-shouted the lot.

We stayed at the same campsite that we'd stayed in on the way up to Darwin, the one where the proprietor had the uncanny ability to know when one of your party was absolutely

352

desperate for the toilet and the air-conditioning wasn't working in the car and anarchy was starting to take over as the family patiently waited outside. Accordingly, she strung out the booking-in procedure to 21 minutes. On two occasions, having completed all the boxes on her little computer screen, I watched as she closed the form with a click of the mouse and then a further click on "No", when asked if she wanted to save it. She then angrily shook her head whilst sighing deeply and lambasted the software before starting again.

Katherine had the almost Orwellian feature of speaker clad lamp posts constantly pumping out positive and upbeat music throughout the town centre and I assumed the intention was to detract from the numerous jobless alcoholics inhabiting the benches. It reminded me of when Eirene was recently held in a telephone queue for five minutes whilst waiting to transfer money from the West Bromwich Building Society, listening to The Beatles "Here comes the Sun" in the background. Despite potentially the greatest financial crisis in history, I think the purpose was to subliminally leave potential withdrawers with a positive and upbeat outlook on life by the time they are finally connected. Maybe it was the Dudley accent on the other end of the line, but it didn't work for her.

It was pissing it down again and the Victoria Highway, the gateway to Western Australia, was closed. To make it worse, Cyclone Dominic, a well-educated sounding tornado, was apparently on its way too. I enquired about extending our Britz rental vehicle as it was due to expire later that week. The car truly was a bag of shit both inside and out and it made our old Land Cruiser look like a Toyota Prius in terms of fuel economy. Despite buying and fitting a new fuel filter (for the hire car) I still hadn't achieved more than six miles to the gallon. I wouldn't have minded if I was making attempts at breaking some land speed records but the top speed was 68 mph (109 kmph) which, for a 4.2 litre turbo engine, was not good. The internal burning smell and external cloud of black smoke emanating from the rear were also still with us. I have a million, ok 23, other complaints of a lesser nature but those were the main ones. On the positive side, though, it was a four-wheel drive with a fridge and a roof-tent, so we did want to extend it as Britz seemed to be one of the few companies that rented this type of model.

We had rented it at $110 a day and with the peak season coming to a close and the distinct absence of tourists in the north of Australia because of the pissing rain, I was hopeful of a better deal. I naively thought that as we had already (naively again) given them $7000 plus $7000 deposit for a long term rental, a further extension would change the price significantly. And it did - $146 per day. I checked their prices online for an identical model from Darwin and dropping it in Perth and they quoted me $109. I was tempted to hand it back and then walk to the vehicle collection queue and rehire it (but now washed). However, we eventually agreed over the phone to put the proposed charade to one side and they relented and gave us the fractionally reduced price.

We were now in Darwin for Australia Day, otherwise known as the day the English settlers turned up and invaded Australia, bringing upon its indigenous populations years of extreme abuse and violations of basic human rights. It is a big family occasion in Australia.

Darwin hadn't exactly gone mad, it had to be said, laying on a fun run and a couple of fetes but, to be fair, you can normally only tell it's St. George's Day in England by the additional bunting around the front of pubs. We had decided to stay in our campsite for another night, despite Eirene immediately going to reception on arrival and cancelling the second night of our stay on the basis of the strong smell of damp that impregnated the cabin. Eirene made herself suspiciously busy the morning of our second day, which meant I had to go on her face saving trip to book in for another night. The smell faded and then disappeared after a while as every single smell will if you spend long enough in it. But on this most sacred of days, Eirene was on an anti-Australia rant. There were many great things about Australia - their litter free streets, their national parks in which pretty much every sight was free (unlike China who will charge you to look at a mountain) and their commendable approach to public safety when it came to driving and skin cancer. Today's venomous rant from Eirene was directed against their Neanderthal approach to the roads system. The Victoria Bridge currently had about three metres of water above it which made the Victoria Highway impassable. The other option was 2,500 km away on the south coast. Basically, every year the rains come and the same roads flood, the country grinds to a halt and everyone waits. The impact on tourism and business in general never seems to be costed. I found it difficult to disagree with Eirene as, in my mind, it was all about expectation and the managing of it. We expected Kazakhstan to have shit roads and we were not disappointed but that wasn't a problem. We expected Australia, as a first world country not to, but it frequently did, especially in the north.

Her Australian negativity was put to rest and mine fuelled when we attended Darwin's major Australia Day event - a 21-gun salute and jet flypast. I was expecting the hairs on the back of my neck to stand up as I witnessed the power and precision of the Australia military at their well-rehearsed best. What happened was four guns fired a few times, each five minutes late, three jets turned up even later and a gaggle of Australian soldiers tried unsuccessfully to march in time in their crumpled fatigues. I'm no jingoistic military fanatic and wasn't expecting the Nuremberg Rally, but I'd lost my military display virginity at the Earl's Court Royal Tournament when I was 15 so was ill-prepared for the shambles.

After the first cannon fired, the synchronised bawling from 40 under three years olds, including Abigail, drowned out much of the remaining discharges. Still it was short and sweet and the kids hadn't seen anything like it before so it pressed the buttons in that respect.

On the good news front, I received an email from my mum that began "Stan and Sylvie" and, for the first time in a long time, didn't end with "the funeral is on Thursday."

We found ourselves low on fuel as we approached Pine Creek. Eirene had a cloud over her head for most of the day and I think she was looking forward to going home in a couple of weeks. This impression was indelibly formed when she said to me "I'm looking forward to going home in a couple of weeks." Having learnt from *Top Gear* that even using the radio in a car can affect fuel consumption, we switched off anything remotely electric, turned the air-con down and I drove at the optimum speed for fuel economy, 90 km per hour, and just made it to the garage. I filled up the car with 135 litres of diesel. Perhaps not too newsworthy in itself other than the fact that the capacity is only 130 litres.

We stayed in Pine Creek by the southern entrance to the famed Kakadu National Park. Like most things that are famed, I hadn't realised it was until the guide book told me so. Australia has literally hundreds of national parks and often the only thing that sets them out as a national park is the sign as you enter. A couple on Fraser Island had strongly recommended Litchfield National Park to us and although I thought we were waterfalled out, Eirene still wanted more and so began our quest to find bigger and better ones. Our first stop was a swimming permitted rockpool named Buley. Birdsong intensified as we approached the oasis and as we exited from the path, we were greeted by two glorious looking swimming holes. A small waterfall showered into the pool on our right and slipped gracefully over the edge at the other, continuing gently down the river.

Abigail couldn't wait to jump in, but the transition from the safety of the chlorinated swimming pools to the dark and wild rock pools of the notoriously dangerous Outback made me slightly more apprehensive. However, with goggles on, the murkiness was no more and a world of little underground caves and freshwater fish opened up for exploration and discovery. The water was energising and just the perfect temperature.

Swimming in a living ecosystem with the scent of the leaves and the sound of the water rhythmically gliding over the rocks just couldn't compare to the chlorinated campsite pools that we encountered to date.

A loaded gun couldn't have coerced Eirene in but bribery, blackmail, child psychology, a bit of cunning and some kidology finished off with a push, saw Emily and Hannah in. Once in, they too came under the spell and I almost needed a loaded gun to get them out. We had the whole place to ourselves and it was a pleasure that was as near to paradise as I had ever experienced. I yearned to submerge myself and kick off from the side of the pool, through the cool waters, and swim to the other side. Every attempt was hampered by two or three kids shouting for the daddy taxi, standing on my back and grabbing every available limb, thus making the process of swimming impossible and drowning a real prospect. And then it hit me. I imagined the very real moment when I would do this sometime not too far away in the future and suddenly realise I was on my own and the kids had long gone their separate ways. I stopped resisting and embraced them and the moment.

Eventually and reluctantly, we morosely headed off, crossing from the Northern Territory to Western Australia. Despite numerous roadside and guidebook-based warnings, Eirene had mistakenly purchased a large amount of fruit and vegetables in Katherine before we left. Due to some fruit fly problem, trafficking of this sort of merchandise over the border was prohibited. After about the 18th sign warning us of this, we decided not to have a mass fruit picnic with the associated stomach problems but sat on our hoard, electing to see how things panned out. Undeniably not the most socially responsible or ethical approach but we had bought all the "gear" in a reputable outlet and it was all currently stuck in a fridge where no life could survive. So we crossed the border and were waved to one side by a very slim man in his late twenties with a full beard, who immediately reminded me of an irritating and backstabbing shitbag I used to work with. I had briefly thought it was actually him and found myself unnaturally elated at his decline. This chap lacked none of the charisma of my erstwhile colleague and promptly and officiously began his examination. Within seconds, Eirene had sung like a canary. It took all my willpower to stop myself shouting "Take her, take her. She bought it. I knew we had an apple but that was it and it was for personal use." To cut a long story short, $70 worth of fruit and veg was deposited into their compost heap whilst we admitted everything, asking for two pieces of broccoli and a cauliflower to be taken into consideration.

Eirene's mother had previously told us the mother of all urban myths when she said that if we run over a snake they can, no matter what your speed, curl around your front axle and slither into your waterproofed foot well before biting you. So, despite our cynicism, when we did accidentally drive over a snake, we spent the next 20 minutes nervously checking the foot well with regular furtive glances over the forthcoming days. Ironically, the only account we heard of a snake bite in our time in Australia was news that Paul O'Grady, aka Lily Savage, had been bitten by an adder in his Kent home.

The rivers had fully absorbed the roads and we now found ourselves trapped in a town with an unpronounceable name with nothing more than the renowned publication *East Kimberley - A Glove Box Guide* for guidance. Even the locals changed how they pronounced Kununurra when I changed to how they had been saying it. The glove box guide was a well put together and ingeniously flannelled compendium to the area that included a tree, a closed crocodile park, a viewpoint and a garden containing many trees planted by the rich and famous, including John Farnham (Australian singer of 1985 "You're the Voice" fame) and Princess Anne (privileged UK Royal of never changing hairstyle fame). To top it all off, I had purchased a 24 hour internet card, only to find that all internet and mobile phones in town had gone down due to one of those all absorbing rivers sweeping away 40 km of fibre optic cable. It was like being sold a cinema ticket only to discover the projector was broken and known to be so at the time of the sale.

We decided not to rush the celebrity tree garden and the big tree in fear that we might have to stretch these things out over the next 10 days. Eirene felt unsettled by our captive state and didn't even break a smile for my Rainbow joke when we saw a real one over the Bungle Bungle mountains (Rainbow. Bungle – get it?).

Despite our current predicament and mutual feeling of claustrophobia, life was good. The kids were happy, Eirene and I had our own little jobs and a healthy rhythm had developed. It had been three days in the same hotel and we almost felt like we had laid down some roots and Abigail's Catherine Tate-style cackle was coming on great.

Our lack of routine had become routine and it struck me how much life had changed. After repeatedly telling kids not to play with matches, every night they would set out the matches and we proceeded to play card games with them. In the UK, a drive to my brother's near Leicester, a journey of just over 200 km, would be the subject of intense debate along the lines of "It's not fair on the kids." And, if we stayed in a hotel, lights would be left on at night so the kids wouldn't panic if they woke up not knowing where they were. Now our plan, as soon as conditions allowed, was to drive over 1,000 km in a day before the waters rose again. We would leave having no idea where we would be staying and when we found a place, the lights would be off.

We called up the recorded road conditions number at 8.30am on the morning of the fourth day only to be told that the road was still impassable, so we paid for another night, indulging in a curiously satisfying mutual Britz slag-off with some fellow Britz haters at reception. I popped into town for a haircut by an 18-year-old who was keen to point out my thinning top, oblivious to the adverse effect it could and would have on her tip. I emerged with an excited Eirene telling me a lorry had come from the west as if it was the fulfilment of some sort of prophecy.

"The road might be open," she suggested so I phoned to listen to the recorded message that I was sure would tell me it was impassable. The recorded voice seemed quite excited as well and, unless it was my imagination, appeared to be rushing the non-descript roadwork problems as she worked east towards us. It was open and passable to high clearance four-wheel drives.

We packed with some vigour and within 30 minutes were enthusiastically driving out of town, a gratefully received refund from the hotel in my wallet and *arrununuK* in my rear-view mirror. We were all jubilant and buzzing, singing through our entire repertoire of songs. Seven hundred kilometres and seven hours later, approaching Fitzroy Crossing, that initial enthusiasm had waned somewhat. So far we had only come across a few puddles but, civilisation in sight, the road turned to a river and we started driving through deep water for about 2 km. Lights I didn't know existed flashed up on the dash and the silence that comes at such stressful moments settled upon us. We finally made it through and started on the songs again until we pulled into Broome, four hours later. I turned to the *Lonely Planet* again as it promised a wide range of cheap accommodation, but our first port of call proved anything but. The inn was full, but the sympathetic receptionist did make a few phone calls for us as she nostalgically recalled her times as a kid sitting in a car waiting for her parents to sort out a bed for the night. She told us Grant at the hotel next door had a room at $120 that could take all of us.

Confidently I tried next door, whereupon Grant quoted us $215 per night for a minimum of three nights. I asked about the $120 he had mentioned to the girl on the phone and silence reigned. Then I realised that he wasn't actually Grant and hadn't been phoned up at all and then he realised that I realised, so I tried the next hotel and found Grant waiting patiently at the reception of a luxurious and exclusive range of apartments with air conditioning, washing machine, dishwasher, big wide telly and a communal pool. Despite our keenness to make up ground, I booked us in for three days. Everyone was delighted when they emerged from the car and saw the place I'd rented, but little did they know the horror that was to follow the next morning.

Pediculus humanus capitis, also known as lice. Eirene had been scratching her head and complaining of unbearable discomfort for a few days. I paid lip service to it not just because I am a callous shit-bag but because in all the years I have known her she has been devoid of any form of mild illness, injury or symptom. Every symptom she's ever had she describes in extreme terms - "agony", "torture", "excruciating" and, of course, her favourite "unbearable." But during a random inspection of Emily's head, Eirene uncovered lice.

"Her head is crawling with them," she shrieked. I just wished she had been exaggerating this time. I know the party line that they are common in kids and it doesn't mean anyone is saying anyone is dirty or anything like that but deep down I knew the truth – we were scum. If word of this leaked out to anyone then we would be forever known as those Nitty Naismiths. Eirene wanted to go and sing like a canary to Grant so all the sheets could be changed. I urged her not to for, if nothing else, the sake of our family name. She ignored me and reported back that Grant had treated her like she had Aids and not in the aware and post- *Philadelphia* 21st century way she'd hoped. The silver lining was that I was the only one who wasn't infected due to the ban that Eirene had imposed, many moons ago, on the kids using my hairbrush and me from using theirs.[24]. I had always objected to this unwarranted stigmatisation, especially when she could use theirs and they could use hers, but the solitary confinement I endured had inadvertently reaped the benefits.

---

[24] Years later, when pressed, she said that it was her belief that my emerging male pattern baldness could be transferred to her and the children by shared use of a plastic brush.

Our time in Broome, other than having the family infected with lice and being called a "baldy old cunt" by an abusive teenager who wasn't pleased that I didn't know the location of the nearest bar, was very enjoyable. Eirene took Emily out for her much awaited birthday meal, Hannah having been taken in Luang Phabang in Laos. They ate delicious food served by an unhelpful waiter who, she later revealed for some reason, was balding. Over the duration of our time in Broome, the kids played brilliantly together. In fact, the only point of conflict I can recall came when Hannah suggested they play Cinderella and Emily refused to "play the blinking cat again."

We arrived in the reasonably sized town of Karratha with, to all outward appearances, a decent range of accommodation on offer but nothing much else of note in the local area. As it was off-season, and we'd previously had no problem sourcing accommodation, I expected to find a bountiful supply of rooms at competitive prices. So it was with something of a swagger that I entered the Best Western in town, carrying the gift of custom for the grateful business owner inside. I left with a quote of $295 for the family room, news that the town's other two hotels were closed and directions to the local campsite that could do us a cabin for $270. Nowhere on our journey have such ridiculous prices been bandied around with such straight faces. In transpired that mining is at the forefront of Karratha industry and with mining comes contractors earning a wad of money. High demand and short supply raised the prices and made it a no-visit tourist area. With light fast ebbing away, we opted for tents at the campsite at $62 per night with charitably no charge for Abigail. Before turning in for the night, we had a worrying chat with the manager, who was concerned we had put our tent up on top of the sprinkler that was going to turn on automatically at 4.30am but left us with a "you should be all right I think."

The sprinkler didn't turn on but it would have been an appreciated relief if it had. Despite having all the tent doors, bar the insect netting, wide open, there was not a whiff of a breeze.

It was a spookily still and muggy night, carrying with it a level of nocturnal heat that I have never ever experienced. At 3.34am I couldn't stand it any longer and headed off for a cold shower. As I emerged from the confines of my canvas home and adjusted my eyes to the night, a young Indian-looking couple, dressed all in white and holding hands, walked past me, not even giving me a glance. I said hello and they didn't react in any way but they seemed to be talking to each other and although only a few metres away, I couldn't hear anything. I popped on my shoes and turned the corner only to see them a considerable distance away, as if they had sprinted and suddenly stopped. More freaked out than scared, but not half as much as when the hot water came out of the cold tap in my eagerly anticipated cold shower.

In the morning, I asked the down-to-earth site manager if there had been any reports of ghostly apparitions or the like in his time there. A frown briefly appeared and just as quickly departed his deeply furrowed face.

"Why do you ask my friend?" he said quickly, as he threw a furtive glance sideways. I explained what I had seen the night before and as my tale came to a close, he leant his head conspiratorially towards me.

"There was a story, the previous owners told me, of a young couple involved in an illicit love affair in the latter part of the 19th century. They used to stroll through the woods here and then one time they were ambushed and set upon by a mob. They died in each other's arms just over there," he whispered, pointing towards the nearby corner adjacent to my tent.

"You're kidding!" I said astonished.

"Yes I am. You must have been pissed," he said, chuckling to himself at his little victory.

We hit the road for another 500 km of intolerable heat, tarmac and bush with only a narrow miss of an emu proving remotely noteworthy. Our air-conditioning system had started to become increasingly intermittent and I was slightly miffed when we stopped at a roadhouse for a break and I saw a prison van pull up at the pump. The prisoners were allowed out to stretch their legs, although there were some rumblings among them when the last rapist out of the back of the van failed to close the door thus upsetting the air-conditioned environment within. I'm not of the "have them break rocks and throw away the key" school of reform, but something about their two toileted, air-conditioned super-van stuck in my throat.

It felt like we had started to develop a touch of cabin fever on these long drives. There is a school of etiquette that dictates you should raise your right index finger skyward from the steering wheel by approximately two to six centimetres when another vehicle passes you in the Outback. Eirene and I decided to break with protocol and invented our own waves, culminating in an elaborate, burlesque, jazz hands routine that puzzled all who witnessed it.

We had completed exactly 21,000 km around Australia. The day's journey was a long but reasonably uneventful one, except for a chance meeting with a solo, heavily laden German cyclist who had also just completed 21,000 km. It gave our trip a bit of perspective and I envied his ability, dedication and free spirit. The cold can of Sprite I handed over didn't really reflect the degree of my admiration, but he seemed grateful and surprisingly chatty for someone who needed every last molecule of oxygen for his endeavours.

The rest of the journey I played *Carcass Count*, a game where I mentally count the number of carcasses at the side of the road and award each animal points based on their likelihood of being hit. We gave ourselves one point for a kangaroo, five for a cow and 10 for a camel because everyone should be able to avoid hitting a camel (and I suppose a cow for that matter). But, in a single 1 km stretch, I created what arguably was an unsurpassable record with an astonishing 66 points.

The rarely acclaimed north western coast of Australia proved to be simply amazing. We took the mostly unsealed coastal route from Exmouth to Coral Bay, going through the Cape Range National Park and Ningaloo Marine Park in the process. I found Exmouth to be a rather unremarkable place with nothing of note to comment upon, except that I helpfully but erroneously left the light on in our outside cabin toilet in case anyone wanted to go during the night. The morning debrief revealed that Eirene's entry into the said toilet at circa 3am was like a scene from *I'm a Celebrity* meets *Indiana Jones,* such was the level of insect infestation that I had created.

The route from Exmouth had been recommended by my cousin's husband who had lived in the area for a while. What he had omitted to tell us and what the park ranger subsequently filled us in on, was that we had to drive across a river to reach Coral Bay. Many vehicles had been claimed at Yardie Creek, partly I guess because the maps, both paper and Google, showed it as a road. By the time we were there we either had to risk it or drive a convoluted 350 km back to the main road.

I checked out the crossing which was essentially where the flowing freshwater from a large gorge poured into the sea. It was about 15 metres wide and I was immediately filled with confidence when I noticed numerous tyre tracks in the sand heading into the river. I started to wade across on foot and can't for the life of me recall if it was the water lapping at my testicles, a stingray lapping at my feet or the smooth, apparently untouched, sand on the other side that brought the hazards of the exercise home to me. It was about 100 metres from the mouth of the river and thought I would move up towards the sea and establish the feasibility of a cross there. It looked a goer. There was a good incline into the water to set us off and some decent rocks underfoot for grip. I returned to the car and regaled an open-mouthed Eirene, who had witnessed me silently dancing up and down near a stingray whilst gripping my clangers, with details of the plan.

The Eirene of old would have staged a sit-in but such was her faith and, let's face it, weariness, that she meekly acquiesced and gave the kids a sandwich. The plan worked to perfection except that I didn't actually know what to do or where to go once I made it onto the trackless other side but hey, we were across. Miles of remote driving, interspersed with marauding emus and petrified kangaroos, followed. It ended with a victorious drive into Coral Bay, a captivating end of the road seaside town. Initially, there didn't seem much to do in Coral Bay with only a few over-priced shops and quad bike hire. But the bay itself was a snorkelling and swimming paradise, with bleached white sand dunes and beaches contrasting starkly with the turquoise water. The sea was so clear that we secured a trip out to a reef in a glass bottomed boat. It had a grand array of fascinating coral and as much freakish fish as the Great Barrier Reef had on the east coast without all the publicity. We had the boat to ourselves and the kids impressed us with a bundle of diverse questions that kept the Captain on his toes, albeit he stumbled on a few of the mermaid ones.

From Coral Bay, we headed up a little spit of land to Denham and Monkey Mia where they feed bottlenose dolphins on a daily basis. We had intended to stay at Monkey Mia but it was a very popular holiday destination and the cost was too prohibitive. We made Denham quite late, however, having heroically rescued two girls and their hired VW camper from the sand along the way. Denham was just as spectacular as Coral Bay and it wasn't far to drive to Monkey Mia for breakfast with the dolphins, but by the time we sorted ourselves, they had been fed and were long gone. Turtles were still hanging around though and we thought we saw some sharks swimming around in Shark Bay from the cliff tops at Eagle Bluff.

We then took a sandy trip to Cape Peron North and on the advice of our campsite owner, didn't deflate our tyres. We subsequently became stuck in the sand and Eirene, now old hat with this, barely raised an eyebrow, before I deflated them in the blistering heat. However, on arrival at the Cape, one of the tyres was now permanently deflated which, naturally of course, was not covered in the $109 daily rental. Words cannot adequately convey the abject wretchedness of jacking a car up on soft sand and changing a wheel in that level of heat, as sand flies compounded the torment by simultaneously vomiting and crapping on my face.

As I undertook this superhuman feat, Eirene's growing ability to treat the abnormal as normal was highlighted when she shared a nearby "toilet" with a foot-long iguana in the same cubicle. Her only remark on the intrusion was that "he looked the other way."

As Perth, our final destination, drew closer, my mind kept turning to what I would do when I returned home. It wasn't a fear of not finding work, which maybe it should have been in the current climate, but a fear of finding it. A return to office life scared me and would, I feared, eventually suck the life out of me. I was no different to millions of others; the only difference was that I now knew the grass was greener. I had tasted the nectar and it was so, so sweet.

On our last evening before Perth, we played outside our beach cabin, Eirene's favourite accommodation to date by far. We cooked outside, played games on the beach and paddled in the sea before settling down for the final time on the penultimate night of our expedition. I couldn't, or didn't, want to sleep, so took a walk along the beach at 1am, with a full moon and the gentle ebbing of the sea as company. Lost in my thoughts, I perched on a rock for almost an hour, my eyes fully adjusted to the night. Eventually I took myself to bed and promptly slipped into a deep slumber. Despite my late night, I woke early as did Eirene, and we were both somewhat muted as we packed up for our final leg.

Our trip was not to end with a whimper though. There was to be one last twist on the trip that nearly broke us.

Eirene had charitably suggested that we drive off-road along the coastal track from the Pinnacles as she knew how much I'd love that. The pinnacles are large limestone pillars of unearthly shapes and varying heights from a few centimetres to over five metres. These golden pillars stretched as far as we could see, over dunes dotted with green gorse bushes. A clearly marked road took itself through the pointy rocks which are part of the Namburg National Park, a very popular tourist attraction along the Turquoise Coast.

The national park lady at the entrance had a face like a blind cobbler's thumb and an attitude to match. She gave us a map of the route we needed to take and warned that "If you get stuck, you'll need a helicopter and it's not cheap." "The kids would love that," I remarked, as we departed her world weary gaze.

We stuck to the path for 40-odd kilometres, the shrubbery diminishing the further we drove, until it led us straight into a steep 10 metre sand dune that dominated the skyline. I reversed, went back the way I came and steered off on an alternative track on the right, following my nose in an attempt to navigate round the obstacle, before we ended up back at exactly the same spot. A closer inspection of the primitive map the grumpy lady had given us led us to the beach path and all looked good until we came across a soldier parked across the path in his camouflaged Toyota, signalling us back the way we'd come. "I'd let you through," he benignly offered, "but there's a high chance you'll get bombed or shot at." I wasn't keen on turning back and having to face Roz from *Monsters Inc.* again, so we headed inland in search of a route parallel to the beach that would take us south to Perth. Tracks we followed betrayed us, rapidly disappearing, and we ended up driving hastily in a series of mountainous dunes, desperately trying to maintain momentum and not let the soft sand clinging to our tyres drag us to a halt.

I began to sense Eirene's frustration at herself for this off-roading gift to me. Every morsel of her body was on edge and the tension was palpable. Worse followed when the iPods started to die and the kids began to take an interest in our predicament as I headed up and down steep dunes, knowing that any loss of movement would result in no further movement for a long time. And then, inevitably, it happened. I slid down a steep sand dune and straight into deep, soft sand, our car quickly coming to a halt as we literally experienced a sinking feeling. This was the trigger for a guttural wail from the deep recesses of my co-pilot and navigator, but I thought better of pointing out her latter role at this juncture. I knew she had been trying to keep it together but her internal unease was incorrigible and its eventual manifestation inevitable.

"Jesus Christ, get me out of here! What are you doing? Get me out now! Now! Now!" she exploded, in a virtually ear-shattering crescendo, her crimson face fuelled with equal measures of rage, panic and fear. Her formerly well-groomed, but now brittle, nails clawed deeply at my sunburnt forearm, which was dropping down the gears in a futile attempt to maintain a degree of traction. The free-flowing tears did little to dilute the pure intensity of her rage. Her fragile psyche, pushed and prodded once too often, had finally cracked, and irrational and futile as she knew her demands were, she was broken, with all sense of logic and reason long since departed.

"Get us fucking out of here!" she very deliberately and precisely ordered, gritted teeth serving as the only shield for her children's ears to the unprecedented obscenity. I flashed a glance at the rear view mirror and absorbed the look of fear in the girls who intimately appreciated, if not understood, the impending anarchy. In unison they pounced on the moment, feeding it with their own hysterical contributions, as their mother began to loudly sob.

"Daaaaaad!" squealed Hannah, her shrill pitch inciting a panicky hand to grab my shoulder, desperately scrabbling the clammy cotton into her tight little fist. "Dad! Dad! Dad!" she chanted, ineffectually trying to dominate proceedings as Abigail picked up the mantle and emitted a demonic screech at a level that belittled any previous submissions during the first two years of her life. Her wide eyes, urgently flicked between all parties, simultaneously seeking clues as to the source of the pandemonium and the corresponding assurance that it was going to be OK.

Emily's hands were on her face, her middle fingers pressing troublingly deep against her eye sockets. Her head began to bob, noiselessly at first and then soft and incessant gasps arrived. There was no fight as she surrendered to the cracks that were appearing in her safe world.

So it was to be an ignominious end; four wailing women and a marooned and virtually invisible car, dusk but a few hours away. I adopted the calm and controlled face that served me so well in the police when I was completely out of my depth and had no idea what to do. I indulged myself with a few seconds, soaking up the scene, hoping it would buy me more time before the next wave of hysteria. We were in exceptionally soft sand in a hollow, surrounded by steep dunes that seemingly offered no exit or opportunity to traverse in any way. Ahead of us there was a 20°– 30° incline that, with a tarmacked surface, was no challenge. Stationary, with sand up to the axles and no propulsion, was a little trickier. The nature of sand driving, and I speak as an expert of some six weeks on this matter, is to make sure your tyre pressure is very low, choose the right gear and don't stop. If you become stuck, then there are a number of options, including winching (that being on the vehicle in Thailand), using sand ladders (they being on top of the vehicle in Thailand) and a load of bracken and stones under the wheels (not too common in this sort of desert). I had one chance to lever the vehicle out by driving. If it failed, it would just result in deeper holes in which to rest our crappy Britz tyres. On my side was the fact that when I realised I was going downwards quicker than I was going forwards, I surrendered and didn't wheelspin myself into a deeper hole. If only I could harness the energy within the car, I insolently pondered to myself.

So, with all the poise and authority I could muster, I popped the car into reverse, slowly eased the clutch up and began rapidly wiggling the steering wheel back and forth in a desperate attempt to grip something. With the crew seconds away from a full-blown mutiny, this was my final act before nihilism truly reigned.

On an administrative level, flights would be missed and there would be an exorbitantly high cost to extract the shitty car from the shitty mess I had dragged us into. And then there was the helicopter to pay for. On a more practical and immediate level, we were in a desert and should stay with the vehicle. But we had a limited amount of food and water and no phone signal. Furthermore, no one was expecting us anywhere for some time so it would be a long time before we'd be reported missing. So we should walk, shouldn't we? All of us together, including the children? It wouldn't be far. Much to dwell on but we would have a night stranded in the desert to consider and contemplate our fate and further actions. Therefore, it was with some acknowledgment to a higher power that the car did actually start to move. It was the briefest of progress but it rapidly began to rein the silence back in, as all eyes focussed on the languid passing of the land outside their windows. I wiggled the wheel more and more, accelerated a little harder and that brilliant Britz car that we'd loved and respected for 13,500 miles pulled it out of the bag. We began to reverse more rapidly and I gave it some throttle and accelerated us jubilantly out of there.

There's something distinctly arrogant and special about a footballer who performs some bit of genius yet manages to retain the composure and blank expression that you might otherwise associate with him successfully lacing up his boots. On the rare occasions I scored a goal, I would turn into a banshee, unable to control the moment of playground greatness. But today I was Cantona with his collars up and the banshees, my family, had been silenced and were now looking on in wonderment at my achievement. Well, that's how I read it, but the moment was mine.

I had little time to dwell on the success of the exit as I reversed some distance before hitting a short plateau that would serve as a springboard to the ascent of the lesser of the inclines. Without further delay, I moved forwards and accelerated hard on what little descent we had, before hitting the 20° – 30° with some speed. We had about 20 metres to do but the car started to slow as the initial surge wore off. I was in second gear, rightly or wrongly, and knew that any gear change at this moment would guarantee an abrupt standstill. Our automatic Amazon wouldn't have had that issue, I briefly contemplated as I kept the accelerator flat against the floor, every ounce of hope and effort attempting to push the pedal through the shell of the car. She, for I'd now personified her, painfully plodded onwards and upwards, managing to maintain the low rev progress as she gratefully grappled herself up the last few metres to the top. We levelled out and I was elated to see no steep drop in front of us. I immediately turned right and took the route of least resistance easterly, avoiding the dips and dales either side of us. Ingrained in my head was the thin black north/south road 5-10 km inland on the nonsensical map the national park lady had given us. The land began to flatten and the sand turned into shrubs which merged into thicker bush that we pressed through, our windscreen taking a battering in the process. Eventually, I predicted vocally, we would hit the highway but instead, on emerging from a particular dense bit of shrubland, we hit a six-lane motorway currently under construction. The workers simultaneously stopped their inactivity and stared at us incredulously as if they'd seen a Japanese soldier emerging from the jungle years after the war had finished. A blond girl in her 20s wearing the obligatory workman's hat and fluorescent jacket, approached and, on seeing the kids, controlled her Anglo Saxon when enquiring who we were and how we had managed to get there. Eirene played the pathetic female English tourist to a tee and we were directed to head 40 km south, down the unfinished motorway, and we would hit Lancelin. We turned right on a compressed gravel surface that was nothing short of heavenly, a heady mix of relief and elation amongst us all. I looked across at Eirene as I slipped into fourth gear and I don't think I had ever seen her happier in the 20 years I've known her. I made a mental note to get ourselves into more hopeless situations just for this.

We made Perth as the sun went down and handed the Britz car back. The receptionist asked if we had had any problems. I told her I had emailed them a month ago with my

20-odd issues but hadn't yet received a reply. She asked me for them again and I said that I would only be repeating what I had put in the email. She insisted so I started to list them and after five her box was filled up and she stopped writing.

It was Valentine's Day 2009 and I had promised Eirene a tin foiled pre-heated meal on a plastic tray, complete with plastic cutlery, and I didn't let her down. Yes, we were flying back and I hadn't seen Hannah that excited since we arrived in China and she discovered she would be having sweet and sour chicken with egg fried rice for the next 35 days. Window seats and aisle order had long since been established but they were asleep shortly after take-off.

After leaving Singapore following a quick stop-over, our BA 747 touched down at Heathrow 10 minutes early and we had our bags off the carousel in pretty quick time. I was filming, and admonished for it by a member of staff, as we came through into the public area of arrivals, the kids living off the last few drops of adrenalin in anticipation of seeing their grandad waiting. The camera was on its last legs in terms of battery life and film length, but I had just enough to capture the moment the kids set eyes on their grandad. We scanned the crowd excitedly but he wasn't there and we headed outside the terminal into the bitter February morning to await his arrival, the kids shivering in shock at the end of 10 months of continuous spring and summer.

Eventually Eirene's dad, Peter, turned up and we hopped into the toasty Ford S-Max we'd lent him whilst we were away. Eirene and I had agreed that in a bid to arrive home swiftly, she would drive and nip her dad's *Driving Miss Daisy* impression in the bag. This was not to be as he insisted on driving to make up for his belated arrival. I don't think I had ever seen the M25 in as much detail as on that trip back, but on arrival at their house, our temporary accommodation for the following few weeks, a mass of bunting was on the outside and at 6am, my brother and his wife were there to greet us, which we were chuffed to bits with. Within minutes, events had taken a surreal turn when an English bloke with a tartan skirt and a knife in his sock turned up, carrying a set of bagpipes. The slow drive had, for once, been a deliberate attempt to allow the family and friends who subsequently arrived, to get there before us. A completely unexpected but very welcome surprise. By all accounts, the country had gone down the plughole in our absence. The kids were beside themselves, running around with their friends and dressing up as princesses. We were home. "How was it?" they asked blearily, and we didn't know where to begin.

Sunday 15th February 2009

Day 291 – Warlingham Surrey - 30,853 miles driven

CHAPTER 12.

EPILOGUE

THREE MONTHS LATER

May 2008

We had changed and we hadn't realised how much. It had happened imperceptibly slowly over the weeks and months, but cumulatively it was quite considerable. The girls have the social skills to talk and play with anyone and the maturity, borne out of necessity, to do the same with themselves. Hannah no longer resents her siblings and with their wealth of experience came an adaptability that we could never have envisaged. I barely recognise the words I've written about their behaviour in the early part of the journey and am ashamed to realise that being good doesn't seem to be noteworthy for this writer. Reading back on my words now, I also realise that Eirene didn't have the hump a lot - I just wrote about it a lot.

Hannah and Emily have merged back into school as if they had never been away and were afforded another hero's welcome by their old chums. They have both slipped back onto the birthday party and after school club circuit and there are no concerns from their teachers. At home we fight the ongoing battle to prevent their diction slipping back to its pre-trip standards. Abigail, being the only child not at school yet, is currently being spoilt by us both.

We're all closer to each other. I love and respect my wife more than I thought possible. I realise that our coincidentally identical family values have probably done more to ensure the success of the trip than anything else, and I now feel upset when the kids go to school and miss sharing a bed with them as we often did.

Far from scratching an itch, in many ways I've made it worse. Eirene, who saw this is a one-off concession to me before we buy the big house, has changed. She wants more and her previous life isn't enough for her now. The only thing worse than the trip being an unmitigated disaster is it being an unmitigated success. We did so much in preparation for our departure but nothing for our return and I discovered that the excitement of going away is directly proportionate to the sense of distress at coming back. Britain is a great country, though, and there are many things we take for granted that other countries don't have. Despite our itchy feet and love of the places we visited, there's nowhere else we would rather have our permanent home.

My pre-trip safety concerns proved to be unfounded although ironically, we were all bed-ridden with various colds and other ailments within weeks of our return. My concerns about the dynamics of us all gelling had little merit and we've gained an insight into each other that maybe we didn't want but I'm glad we did and we're stronger for it.

Would I do anything differently if I was to do it again? Maybe. There's something to be said for just getting up and going and sorting things out on your way. We were over cautious and highly prepared and didn't need most of what we carried, but were greatly comforted by having it nonetheless. Someone once said don't take things that you could do with, only the things you cannot do without. As it happens, almost a third of our trip was spent without most of our stuff, as it languished in a Bangkok garage. Maybe I read up too much on some places, as there's great merit in experiencing something in its pure form for the first time without the prior contamination of other's opinions. And we were rushed. We could have spent at least two years doing our trip and we probably spent too much time in the car and, as regrets go, not having it in Australia was our biggest. The trip was incredibly expensive, especially the way we did it, and was a sizeable chunk of our next house deposit, but what we had in return is priceless. There was a guy that Ewan and Charley bumped into in *Long Way Down*, their motorbike trip from the UK to Cape Town. He was travelling through Africa on his own and the only things he missed were salt and vinegar crisps and toasted cheese and ham sandwiches. That's about what it amounted to for me.

I signed on for the first time in my life and might, they say, receive £60 a week, although it costs £10 and two hours to physically go and sign on. An interview beckons and, if I'm lucky, endless commuting and office politics await. Then there will be stern but familiar-faced fellow passengers around me whom, if I'm fortuitous, I will be on nodding terms with after a few years, in stark contrast to unconditional friendliness of people we met as we travelled further and further east. If I'm offered the job, at best I'll see the kids for 30 minutes, five evenings a week, plus weekends, a fate more synonymous with a divorced dad. When we were travelling I had the habit of checking what the time was in the UK and would be suitably chuffed if it was during office hours. Now I'll be doing the same in reverse.

So I dust off the suit, don the constricting tie and trudge off to the station, a good luck peck from Eirene on my cheek and a blank notebook in hand ready for the interviewer's cross examination. It's standing room only on the 7.52 and I awkwardly rummage around for my iPod earphones, plug them in and press shuffle without managing to sexually assault any of the passengers in the environs of my personal space. *Summer of '69* comes on and I'm immediately transported away to sunny Croatian mountains, the kids bouncing around like Sid Vicious in the back seat, going mad over it, as Eirene shakes her head and smiles at its umpteenth rendition. My eyes well up.

We all want more. After the initial euphoria of our return wore off, we were left with only pictures and memories. Driving to Australia is fairly unusual. Taking three young children is verging on unique. What I didn't realise was that doing a trip of this kind and not wanting more would probably be a first. They say once the bug has you, that's it. I hope it has us.

As I set off this morning, Hannah reminded me of some minor thing that had happened when we were in Kyrgyzstan. She remembered and she was happy that she told me. And then she said, "You look like you're going to cry" and then she said, "You miss it and you miss us, don't you?" and then we both shed a tear.

The Land Cruiser was fixed and returned, Expat Motors pulling it out of the bag, and now it sits forlornly on the drive, humiliated by its daily school run.

Abigail is finally out of her much-loved travel cot and if anyone is going past Lake Balaton in Hungary, despite numerous requests and hollow reassurances, Emily's still waiting and sobbing for Poley and Monkey.

4 Years Later

February 2012

The longer legacy is now apparent. Hannah vividly remembers most of the trip and things that we don't. Emily remembers a great deal, but Abigail remembers nothing. We have a large collage of pictures hanging up in the kitchen as a constant reminder of a time when we were only accountable to ourselves and many of life's external pressures were absent.

Holidays are different. We watched *Raiders of the Lost Ark* one night and decided to take a month off over Easter last year and drive to the lost city of Petra, although not so lost now, in Jordan via Syria. Between planning and departure, the Arab spring commenced, which detracted us from spending more time in Syria. It was a worrying drive through the country with our phone bleeping with texts from the Foreign and Commonwealth Office telling us to get out. We popped in on Svebor in Croatia on the way back and managed not to break anything or anyone.

I drove the sand dunes of Morocco and have my eyes on further North African trips. We climb mountains now and plan to sail ourselves around the Med next year. We did Disney Florida and I think it left us all with an unspoken feeling of not belonging somewhere. Five years ago, we would have possibly revelled in it but not anymore.

We settled in Kent, for the schools, where we knew no one. Eirene and I have worked out that there won't ever be another big trip like that, but the kids haven't.

Hannah is starting to distance herself from us in a natural way that someone entering their teens should do. As the complete openness goes, so her maturing years bring with them greater self-reliance. Communication becomes reliant on the state of her hormones and Emily will soon follow.

I am back doing a decent job now with a mortgage and all is well. After a dalliance with selling the car, we elected to keep it and I use it in the winter to help transport essential workers into hospitals, police control centres and the like. I swear I can still sense its humiliation on the school run though.

Sometimes at night, when the kids are finally settled, something will come on the TV that takes us both back. "That's just like" I will start. "Laos, where we saw that guy with the gun on the bike," Eirene will finish. And the moment passes as we fondly recall or maybe wistfully yearn for the time when we were all together, sharing and experiencing people and places for the first time. When we had time to talk and find out things about each other that we never otherwise would.

We saw our children grow at that time of innocence when they believed every single thing we said, and wore their hearts, hopes and disappointments on their sleeves. When they cried because they were hurt or sad and laughed because they were happy, and nothing was hidden. And we realise it was about the journey, not the destination.

There are many reasons, most of which are justifiable, why you wouldn't embark on something like this. But just do it – things will work out fine. Better than fine. I promise you.

Emily's teddies never arrived from Hungary.

10 YEARS LATER

February 2018

I've finally finished this tome. I had wanted to write it as a legacy for the kids and so I would remember what I otherwise would forget, but it became a burden. Another thing on the never shrinking to-do list. And maybe I had something left to say that I wasn't so sure I wanted to say. So, I've finished it, and this is the end. Reading through this again has been an evocative and touching experience. I'm 47 and people my age are starting to die. Eirene is 48 and we were just past our mid-thirties when we embarked on that voyage. We've done lots more exciting stuff even since the four-year epilogue. A road-trip up the west coast of America from LA to Vancouver. We did do Disney – we hated it and the kids loved it. The Maldives was just like the brochure promised and we've been back to China as a stopover on a trip round North Korea (before it's too late). Next year we're off to Ecuador and Peru for a month.

I learnt to sail and we chartered boats and sailed the Med but, Abigail to one side, the family didn't get the bug. I want to walk to Everest Base Camp – the others, bar Abigail, don't. They have their own hopes, aims and priorities and are embracing their desires. Last summer, Hannah went away to a number of festivals, had a weekend in a cottage with her friends, did the American road trip with us, had a week in Rhodes and finished off the summer with a parachute jump with her cadet friends. In between, she picked up her GCSE results of 10 A*s and one A (maths!). She is a brilliant and popular kid who seems to excel at everything she tries her hand to but, like any teenager, sees only her flaws and thinks everyone else is better than her at everything else.

Emily is chomping at the bit to follow. She is in the first year of GCSEs, has a part-time job, a really good and close group of friends and is excelling at school as we'd expect. Her and Hannah are as close as I think two siblings ever could be. She has a maturity beyond her years and it's been hard to not treat her like an adult since she said to me at age 6, "I know how to make people like you. You ask them about themselves".

Abigail is at big school with them and cannot do enough sport. She's a Leicester fan and an aspiring goalkeeper. The jump to grammar school has been water off a duck's back for her. She still has the simplicity of childhood and is never happier than when playing sport or eating snacks. We cycle together, play lots of tennis, kick a ball round the park and did do kickboxing together. But I sense the shadow of adolescence on her and these innocent times changing, so I embrace as much of her life as she will let me whilst giving her as much space as she asks. All involvement with her activities, and with all the kids, has been with their consent and approval and I think that's important.

The kids rarely, if ever, fight amongst themselves in no small part to Emily who is the glue of the family in many respects.

Workwise, I've managed to orchestrate a freedom in my job that means I don't have to commute and, for the most part, I get to see the kids plod out the house to school and spring back home from it. Concerts, shows, matches and events – I've barely missed any and for that I am so grateful.

All of what we've done since, though, have been holidays, adventurous as some of them have been. We barely wasted a weekend with lots of outdoor pursuit trips and camping galore, but the appetite for those family affairs has waned considerably as they've grown older. The girls are 11,14 and 16 now, and the older they get, the less they want to do with us as they naturally seek their independence and the company of others. We had our moment and we've given them a good foundation.

The car, aka the "Jungle Explorer Happy Madoddi Bus", as the kids so succinctly named it (another example of when democracy produces a result that no one actually wanted in its entirety), is gone. A little Korean-made car went through a red traffic light and found itself embedded under the bull bars at the front. The driver was fine, thank God, and our car was driveable but with a dented bull bar and some headlight and panel damage. The underwriter came out to have a look and wrote it off. "There's parts on this car that we cannot get replaced at our body place," he told me, "I have no choice". I bought an economical, but characterless, Toyota Auris in its place, homage to the Toyota brand if nothing else. I bought the truck back from the insurance company and sold it to an Irish fella who had the appetite and enthusiasm for its rebuild, as well as plans to drive it to South Africa, which I gave my blessing to.

I didn't realise how much I would miss it when it was gone. It was a cumbersome and thirsty beast, ill-suited to the streets of Tunbridge Wells. But, sitting on the drive as it did, it gave me hope that we could, if the desire took hold of us, be on our way anywhere within a day. And it was the hope that I missed the most.

We found out last year Hannah had a tumour at the base of her brain, a benign one, but one that has resulted in several life affecting facets for her and us not least of which was severe depression brought on, we understand, by the medicine they gave her. She had been planning and fundraising for a trip to the Amazon rainforest for a year, but her condition prevented her going, hence our spur of the moment US trip. It's been the worst year of our lives bar none. We didn't know this was around the corner. The tumour has been removed and we seem stable again as she prepares for University and all that it brings. We've done lots, so much, but at times I wish we could go back to the innocent and carefree times of that drive and the simplicity of it all. It all went so quickly, and I thought there would be so much more to come. I've been really lucky, fortunate to have had such a rich family life.

But sometimes I have this dream. It's a warm but pleasant early evening and I'm standing near to the check-in at a busy airport. The smartly dressed British Airways staff are busy tagging bags and typing into terminals as zig-zagged stanchion barriers, with their pull-out belts, guide the position of the queuing masses. I catch sight of them as soon as they come through the automatic doors. They're a curious cross between excited and reluctant as they push a trolley containing two cheap and newly purchased suitcases. The father is ill-dressed for his destination, dark Berghaus t-shirt and those light-coloured trousers with all the pockets and zips on them that travellers' favour. The side pockets are bulging with passports, papers, mobiles, earphones, chargers and no doubt a wallet, with a mix of cards and currencies. He's immediately preoccupied with the screens hanging down opposite the entrance and his partner, a slim and attractive girl with shoulder length brown hair in her mid-30s, is preoccupied herself with her youngest girl, a chubby-cheeked effervescent toddler, clamped to her hip. A dominant girl of about seven or eight, clearly the eldest judging by height, wearing blue leggings and a white cotton top with green arms, comes to a halt next to her mum. Loyally and obediently trailing behind her, desperate to keep up, is a beautiful red-haired smiling girl who looks up at her elder sister in wonderment, hanging on every word or movement she has to offer. All of them have well-worn red and white rucksacks on and a skin colour verging on olive except for the auburn one who is alabaster white. The mother utters something before heading off to the nearby benches, children in tow, and settling down to get something out of her bag. The dad stays put, absorbing the contents of the departure screen whilst rummaging around in his pockets, one hand gripping the trolley handle.

I furtively approach and am almost upon him before he looks up and gives me a friendly and expectant smile, and then narrowing his eyes as if in recognition, but he can't place me. Before he can speak, I lean forward and whisper in his ear,

384

whilst glancing over at his family who are a hive of excitement, wholly oblivious of us, as they chatter, point, poke and play amongst themselves. "Stop," I instruct. "This is it. You're not going to get this again. They're bright, able, articulate and confident kids," I say, as I nod in their direction. "What they're learning," I continue, "they won't get anywhere else. And you won't either. Listen to me. Drive back home. And then drive to South Africa. And then South America. And then carry on after that. You can budget. They've done a great job on the car in Bangkok. It will go for years. You can make this happen." I want to shake him and tell him that over the next 10 years things are going to change radically, but that's against the rules. They've only let me have a few minutes. "What do you think you're doing getting on that flight? Where do you think you're going? What do you think you're going back to? A better life? Really?" I utter frustratingly but with a hint of growing anger. He takes a step back and we look each other squarely in the eye. "You don't know what's around the corner," I finally say, as I put my hand on his shoulder and nod assuredly. He breaks the gaze, turns and walks slowly over to his family, pushing his trolley with him. They look up as he arrives and he crouches down and talks conspiratorially. Open-mouthed, they absorb every word and I watch their faces change as they begin to register what he is saying. The kids then all turn as one towards their mother expectantly, the youngest pulling persuasively at her top. She looks at them all before looking back at her husband lovingly. She breaks into a smile before mouthing something and nodding, a trigger for the kids to start cheering, jumping and hugging each other. The wife and husband embrace before turning around and heading back out through the automatic doors, all holding hands. He doesn't look back.

The End

APPENDIX A: THE INVENTORY

Item	Notes
1st Aid books	
1st Aid kit	
2 x way radios	
Black water containers	
Break bleed bottle	
Calculator	
Camera and charger	
Camping stove	
Car manual	
Clothes	List out all clothes
Coke	For illness
Compass	
Computer translator	
Cutlery, plates and pans	
Door wedge	
Dried food and tins	
Emergency blanket	
Fuel and cost log book	
Games	
Gas cooker with spare cannisters	
Hand cleaning gel	
Haynes Manual	
Head torch	
Ipod Nanos	
Jerry can filter	
Jump cables	
Kelley kettle	
Laptop (international access)	
Lonely Planet Central Asia	
Marriage Certificate	

Item	Notes
Matches	
Micropore water purification tablets	
Money belts	Try Masta travel health
Mountaineering food packets	
Normal phone	Find out which network is best
Patriot roof rack	
Satellite phone	
School work	
Shortwave radio	
Sleeping bags	
Sleeping mats	
Snatch block	
Soft cooler bag	
Spade	
Spare memory cards	
Suntan cream	
Tent	
Thermarest	
Torch	
Tyre gauge	
Universal bath plug	
Video camera	
Washing line	
Washing soap	
Water purifier - consider hand held as well - nature pure and micropore tablets	
Waterproofs	

APPENDIX B: PAPERWORK

Item
Birth certificates
Car insurance
Carnet de Passage
Check all passports valid
Credit cards
Driving licences
Entry visas (Person)
Entry visas (Vehicle)
European breakdown cover
European Health Insurance Card
Exit visas (Person)
Exit visas (Vehicle)
HIV test certificates
International driving licence
Local currency
Lonely Planet/Rough Guide books
Maps
Medical insurance
Numbers of all embassies and names of relevant contacts
Numbers of Toyota dealers
Photocopies of everything
Press releases
Shameen - power on account
Shipping company arrange Singapore
Sponsorship
Travel insurance
VEL copy
Website & donation page

*All scanned and electronic Versions Stored Online

Appendix C:
Pre-departure Tasks

Task	Priority	Done
Budget - work out	Med	√
Medical - what jabs/pills	High	√
Plan Route	High	√
Channel Tunnel/ferry	Med	√
Email others for backup vehicle	Low	√
Speak to school re. self-education	Low	√
Car Ferry to Oz and back	Low	√
First Aid course	High	√
Language course	High	√
Stickers for car	Low	√
Domestic arrangements	Low	√
Toyota garages	Low	√
Prepare folders	Low	√
New laptop battery	Low	√
Folders with clear bits in for paperwork	Low	√
Email people who have done it in Landcruiser/China	High	√
Jason the Pharmacist at Nomad Travel	Med	√
Paul @ Footloose	Med	√
Print our FCO advice pages	Low	√
Speak to the goose	Low	√
AA/RAC (sponsorship when does E expire?)	Low	√
Think of more potential sponsors - insurance sponsors	High	√
Sort out blog for website	Med	√
Btopenworld - can I keep email address?	Low	√

Task	Priority	Done
Return flights from Prague	Med	√
http://www.worldtravel-overland.com/index_files/asia.htm	Low	√
Get a letter from your bank verifying that you are trustworthy and have sufficient monies to fund your trip.	Low	√
If your GP is half decent he will understand the need for a letter that states you are suffering from a condition that requires you to carry your prescription medication.	Low	√
Look through all other trip websites	Low	√
Keep sponsors in loop	Low	√
Do I need valid MOT and tax all the way through?	Low	√
Sponsorship from self-storage companies/speak to Andy Self	Med	√
PDF for sponsorship form	High	√
Speak to Paul re Wipac products	Med	√
Call SIM	High	√
Inform credit cards and bank and phone companies travelling and Power of Attorney	Low	√
Scan and email all docs	Low	√
Look into Garmin 276c (check sponsorship status)	Med	√
Get routes disk from Paul	Low	√
Look at www.globalrally.org.uk and meandmylou	Low	√
World Health Organisation	High	√
Vaccinations check with AXA	High	√
Speak to Shameen re support and do pack for her and sort out Power of Attorney	Low	√

Task	Priority	Done
Speak to insurance bloke (card) re travel and vehicle	Med	√
Speak to satnav bloke re satnav phones	Med	√
Get Vodaphone phone	Low	√
Dog tags including medical alerts for kids	Med	√
Make up ID card with fingerprint etc	Low	√
Shortwave radio	Low	√
Consider video camera	Low	√
Consider dictaphone	Low	√
Speak to roofbox company - 1.4m x 2.5m (minus wheel diameter) re what boxes they can configure - minus 85cm diameter	High	√
Singapore AA (why did Paul mention them)?	Low	√
Get total off-road mag re grills and companies	Med	√
Design better logo and sticker for side of vehicle	Med	√
Ask Paul if I need an exhaust gas thermometer gauge	Med	√
Ask Paul if we need to change cambelt	Med	√
Say to Paul to get keys done	Med	√
Offer Paul money	Low	√
Baby seat pics	High	√
Download new website template and update site with pdf and sponsors name down side and new sponsors	High	√
Get picture of vehicle from side and front	High	√
Put sponsor contact details in sponsor tab	Low	√
Cancel Frog Island	Med	√

Task	Priority	Done
Do visa stuff	High	√
Check website stats	Low	√
Check the hub (Horizons Unlimited Website)	Med	√
Book accommodation in Prague	Med	√
Book flights from Prague	High	√
Book Karlovy Vary accommodation	Med	√
Book Crispy Crumblov accommodation	High	√
Sort out photo and blog software	Low	√
Translator	Low	√
Blog - update profile and do map	Low	√
www.stantours.com	High	√
Web contacts for countries - recommendations, routes, where we stay	Med	√
Enrol with Medicare (oz NHS)	Med	√
Put Facebook link on website	Low	√
WHO/Nomad - what other jabs - rabies/malaria and http://www.travax.nhs.uk/	Low	√
Sort out general vehicle insurance	High	√
Holiday contract	Low	√
Hotels in Russia and Ukraine and Kazakhstan etc	Med	√
Sartech beacon	Med	√
Check out http://www.celestial.com.kg/about_us/introduction.shtml	Low	√
Get contact details for all off-road mags, newspapers, travel mags etc	Med	√
Go through equipment list and order	Med	√
Russian book	Med	√
Print out travel insurance cert	Low	√

Task	Priority	Done
Enter emergency details on World Nomads site	Low	√
Check out Pauls docs (daily check list-car info sheet)	Low	√
Check eBay iridium 9505 (reminder in email)	Med	√
Carnet - sort out with RAC and bank	High	√
Car docs legalised (FCO legalised site)	High	√
Email sponsors for high res stickers	Med	√
Join TL owner club	Med	√
EU car insurance quotes for E	High	√
Speak to William re stickers and business cards/postcards	Med	√
Cambodian Visa	High	√
Will	Med	√
First Aid kit	Med	√
Put all docs and medical stuff on net in Hotmail place	Low	√
Register beacon	Med	√
Move equipment downstairs	Low	√
Delete all crap/big emails and unsubscribe from them	Low	√
Check out all purchased equipment	Low	√
Get all tools and stuff together	Med	√
Emergency rescue plan	Med	√
Sponsors update	Med	√
Take USB flash memory with med details on it	Med	√
Med support no.	Med	√
Do logo	Med	√
Get duct tape	Med	√
Speak to Stan Tours re hotel accommodation	High	√

Task	Priority	Done
Script for Anna and everyone to translate	Med	
Blood groups and vaccinations book updated	Med	√
SORN for tax disk	Med	√
Driving licence cover	Med	√
iPod and Nanos for kids	Low	√
Emergency contact details in all passports	Low	√
Packs for Roger for flat including locksmith no.	Low	√
Pack for Shameen	Low	√
Details to John Roake	Low	√
Get currency	Low	√
Go through manual	Low	X
Re-do - advanced print, First Direct	High	√
Eirene write up vehicle notes	Med	√
Eirene marriage cert	Med	√
Eirene embassy notes	Med	√
All emergency numbers	Low	
Print out embassy numbers	Low	√
Measure vehicle and put up sticker	Low	√
Join International Police Org	Low	√
Western Europe Lonely Planet	High	√
Get kids' blood pressure	High	√
Cancel Home Contents policy	High	√
Arrange car shampoo	High	√
WD-40 - winch	High	√
Get two more wolf boxes	High	√
Get list of antibiotics and what they do	High	√
Freezer bags	High	√
Sort out compressor problem	High	√

Task	Priority	Done
Email Paul re knocking, leaking diff box and locking wheel nuts	High	√
Double side pads for alarm sensor	High	√
Buy wallet	High	√
Jerry can filter	High	√
Break bleed bottle	High	√
Calculator	High	√
Soft cooler bag	High	√
Hydrated food	High	√
E sort out car notes	High	√
Do personal Tax Return	High	√
Join blood care foundation	High	
Money bags	High	√
Go through camping stuff for items to take	High	√
Pack clothes bags	High	√
Cooker + spares cylinders	High	√
Plastic wrap for roofbox stuff	High	√
Bubble wrap	High	√
French accommodation	High	√
Big padlock for roof	High	√
Nigel re do car pic	High	√
Collect toy from Neil's mum's	High	X
Hay fever tablets	High	√
2 x 2m padlock cables - for 2 x wolf boxes	High	√
Sellotape for keys and padlock	High	√
Stickers for boxes	High	√
Eye wash	High	√
Mosquito nets - chase up	High	√
Oil - speak to Footloose - is it semi-synthetic - they've given us 15/40 DC Three	High	

Task	Priority	Done
Find car manual and European map	High	√
Update Garmin	High	√
Toilet rolls, nappies, tampons	High	√
Laptop - back up, pack bag/synch everything	High	√
Print out translation stuff and laminate	High	√
Check radios and walkie talkies	High	√
Scan visas in passports and email to Hotmail	High	√
Dongle/paying-in slips for Shameen	High	√
Pay VAT and tell Shameen	High	√
Label all plugs	High	√
CDs & DVDs - blank	High	√
Folders for docs	High	√
2 AA batteries	High	√
4 plugs	High	√
Download radio programme	High	
Micropore water stuff	High	
Credit card holder for health cards etc	High	√
Dashboard wipes	High	√
Washing soap	High	√
Coke	High	√
Mark up plates and cups	High	
Get all books downstairs	High	√
Clear Ziploc bags for washing stuff	High	√
Hand gel cleaning	High	√
Nappy sacks (300)	High	√
Sort out wireless connection on laptop	High	√
Check out passport photographs - do I need some	High	√
Actimin probiotic mints	High	√
Email everyone Shameen's details	High	√
Canesten	High	√

Task	Priority	Done
Nintendo DS games	High	√
Tamagochi	High	
CD holder	High	
Mach 3	High	√

APPENDIX D:
PRE-DEPARTURE COSTS

Date	Payee	Item	Category	Cost
07/01/08	Chemist High St Caterham	Photos kids and Eirene	Document Costs	£20.00
07/01/08	Booth	Me photos	Document Costs	£8.00
07/01/08	National Map Centre	Travel books and maps	Books	£19.99
08/01/08	National Map Centre	Travel books and maps	Books	£45.48
09/01/08	Books Etc	Travel books	Books	£31.98
07/01/08	Kingfisher Pub Chertsey	Booze	Misc Expenses	£15.00
09/01/08	Easy Internet Solutions	Domain name www.drive-to-oz.com	Misc Expenses	£10.56
10/01/08	Train Companies	Train tickets to Grantham	Misc Expenses	£144.00
10/01/08	Dinner	Grantham	Misc Expenses	£16.35
10/01/08	Taxi	Grantham	Misc Expenses	£60.00
10/01/08	Stu Sibbick	Tube tickets	Misc Expenses	£20.00
14/01/08	National Map Centre	Maps	Books	£34.47
15/01/08	Adventure First Aid (Deposit)	First Aid course	Courses	£42.00

Date	Payee	Item	Category	Cost
19/01/08	Trade Car Group	Car	Car Costs	£9,500.00
20/01/08	RAC	International driving permits	Car Costs	£13.00
21/01/08	Railways	Return to Peterborough	Misc Expenses	£25.10
21/01/08	IPS	Emily passport	Document Costs	£46.00
25/01/08	Matt Savage @ Viair	Compressor	Equipment	£119.51
26/01/08	Easyjet	Return flights from Prague	Misc Expenses	£231.21
30/01/08	Easy Internet Solutions	Bandwidth increase	Misc Expenses	£35.25
03/02/08	Amazon	Sahara Overland	Books	£14.92
05/02/08	Footloose	Advance on vehicle work	Car Costs	£3,000.00
04/02/08	Specialist Leisure	Winch	Car Costs	£600.00
29/01/08	Anna	Russian lessons	Courses	£30.00
05/02/08	Anna	Russian lessons	Courses	£30.00
05/02/08	Click2Add	Haynes Manual for car	Car Costs	£20.00
06/02/08	Taxi	Taxi and train to Ukraine and Russian Embassy	Misc Expenses	£20.00

Date	Payee	Item	Category	Cost
12/02/08	World Nomads	Travel insurance	Insurances	£407.74
14/02/08	Wilderness Expertise	First Aid training	Courses	£300.00
14/02/08	Mobell Ltd	Satellite phone	Equipment	£517.00
12/02/08	Anna	Russian lessons	Courses	£30.00
18/02/08	Sartech	Personal locator beacon	Equipment	£232.00
21/02/08	Nature Pure Online	Water purifier	Equipment	£100.00
25/02/08	Australian Embassy	ETA	Document Costs	£32.07
29/02/08	Footloose	Car	Car Costs	£7,000.00
25/02/08	Doctors' Surgery	Hep B	Medical	£90.00
10/03/08	Remote Medical Support	Card	Medical	£79.70
09/03/08	Click2Add	Landcruiser owner's manual	Car Costs	£20.00
09/03/08	Amazon	Wilderness Medical Society: Practice Guidelines for Wilderness Emergency Care	Medical	£6.48

Date	Payee	Item	Category	Cost
10/03/08	Campbell Irvine	Fire and Theft from 1/7	Car Costs	£808.92
10/03/08	Batteriescenter (Espow International Ltd)	Laptop battery	Equipment	£59.01
11/03/08		Duct tape	Medical	£12.00
20/03/08	Destination Russia	Russia invite	Document Costs	£66.56
20/03/08	NHS	Rabies	Medical	£475.00
24/03/08	ex-med.co.uk	Medical Equip/stethoscope/burns/eye bath	Medical	£41.36
30/03/08	Halford and Homebase	Car tools, spares and rucksacks	Car Costs	£155.00
30/03/08	Footloose	Car	Car Costs	£7,000.00
30/03/08	Post Office	VEL	Car Costs	£115.00
26/03/08	Dr Taylor	Dentist	Medical	£66.45
01/04/08	Nomad Travel	Jap Encephalitis	Medical	£225.00
11/03/08	Nomad Travel	Jap Encephalitis	Medical	£225.00
04/03/08	Nomad Travel	Jap Encephalitis	Medical	£225.00
03/03/08	Moorings Med Centre	Hep B	Medical	£90.00
02/04/08	Fairalls	Secure cable	Car Costs	£15.17
11/04/08	Creative Watch Company	Medical Tags	Medical	£70.00

Date	Payee	Item	Category	Cost
18/04/08	Robert Dyas	Secure cable, wedge and plug	Car Costs	£50.00
14/04/08	Best Priced Brands	iPod Nano x 2 + Nintendo	Misc Expenses	£314.00
13/04/08	Photobox	Business cards	Misc Expenses	£40.00
19/04/08	memorybits. co.uk	3 x memory cards for camera	Misc Expenses	£44.50
19/04/08	Maplin	SW radio and 2 x personal radios	Misc Expenses	£69.98
19/04/08	Viking	Petrol book and bubble wrap	Misc Expenses	£20.07
20/04/08	Expedition Foods Online	Dehydrated food	Misc Expenses	£100.35
20/04/08	Wiggle	Cooker	Misc Expenses	£66.98
15/04/08	Dr Taylor	Dentist	Medical	£250.00
20/04/08	Adventure First Aid	First Aid course	Courses	£63.00
22/04/08	Nomad Travel	Medicine	Medical	£700.00
22/04/08	Wanderlust	Maps	Misc Expenses	£25.00
24/04/08	Footloose	Additional work	Car Costs	£1,111.00

Total: £35,472.16

Appendix E: Vehicle Checks

Task	Notes	Frequency (check)
Check Water	50/50 Mix (antifreeze/water)	Daily
Engine Oil (Yellow dipstick)	Change at 5,000k - black and sludgy not good	Daily
Gearbox Oil (Red dipstick)	Keep an eye on - do not overfill - ATF Gearbox Oil	Weekly
Air Filter	Compressor round it to remove dust	Regular
Brake Fluid		Daily
Power Steering		Daily
Fan Belt	Should go 90°	Daily
Tyres	Feel around and check for tracking problems - set pressure cold. 30 psi Europe - 35 psi at back - dirt road 15-20 percent drop. Change tyres front to back occasionally (spare tyres for punctures)	Daily
Lights	Clean	Daily
Wheel Nuts	Lubricate	Weekly
Roof rack allen key	Tighten	Weekly
Diff 80/90	Rear and Front	Monthly
Transfer Box 75/90	Mid - check if it pours out	Monthly
Prop Shaft	Grease (6 nipples to do)	Weekly
Wheel Balancing	Wheel balancing - run it 5 times and then measure and do it and then don't do it again	

APPENDIX F: PRE-DEPARTURE DOMESTIC TASKS

Item	Detail	Date
Water	23/3 - sent to work. 25/3 - Cancelled	25/03/08
Electricity	23/3 - Pin ordered. 25/3 - cancelled - send meter reading on 29/4	25/03/08
Gas	23/3 - Pin ordered. 25/3 - cancelled - send meter reading on 29/4	25/03/08
Council Tax	17095143 tel. 0845940 0160 www.croydon.gov.uk/onlineaccounts. 23/03 - all done	23/03/08
AA	E needs to speak	24/03/08
Broadband	23/3 - sent to work. 24/3 - cancelled and complaint email sent	24/03/08
Home Contents	24/3 - sent to work	
Home Telephone	23/3 - sent to work. 24/3 - cancelled and complaint email sent	24/03/08
TV Licence	E needs to speak	06/04/08
Lovefilm	23/3 - cancelled	23/03/08
Post Office Re-direct	24/3 - completed online but failed for both - call from work. 25/3 - get E to do	24/03/08
Time Out	24/3 - emailed	24/03/08
Boxing Monthly	24/3 - emailed	24/03/08
Men's Fitness	24/3 - emailed/ 25/3 - cancelled	25/03/08
Sky Digital	24/3 - phone - cancelled	24/03/08

Item	Detail	Date
LA Leisure	24/3 - sent to work. 25/3 - cancelled - one more payment then cancel DD. Ref PS2004	25/03/08
AXA Health Care	23/3 - cancelled from 23/4 - Steven Hennessey called for me. Spoke to Pam and 3 kids all cancelled from 23/4. E needs to speak	
St John's School M	E needs to speak	
St John's Maintena nce Fund	E needs to speak	
Lloyds Bank	24/3 - letter sent	
First Direct Bank	24/3 - secure message sent	24/03/08
Alliance and Leicester	24/3 - done	24/03/08
Halifax Bank (flat)	Don't tell them	
West Bromwich	E needs to speak	24/03/08
Premium Bonds	24/3 - letter sent	24/03/08
Egg	24/3 - done	24/03/08
Swiftcover Car Insurance	26/3 - canx - don't have new card details.	25/03/08

APPENDIX G:
SPONSORSHIP REQUESTS

Date	Company	Pos.	Notes
13/01/08	Blacks		
13/01/08	Roofbox	Y	Superb - excellent Roofbox
13/01/08	Maglite		
13/01/08	Leatherman		
13/01/08	Knives/Maglites etc		
13/01/08	Jessops		
13/01/08	Outdoorgear		
13/01/08	Medical Training		
13/01/08	Garmin Satnav		
13/01/08	Hapag Lloyd		
13/01/08	Nomad Travel		
13/01/08	The North Face		
13/01/08	Hitch and Hike		
13/01/08	Books etc		
13/01/08	Eurotunnel	Y	Free passage over
13/01/08	Field and Trek		
13/01/08	Millets		
13/01/08	P & O		
13/01/08	Quantas		
13/01/08	BA		
13/01/08	Emirates		
13/01/08	Singapore Airlines		
13/01/08	Berghaus		
13/01/08	Bushbaby	Y	Brilliant baby carriers
13/01/08	Malaysia Airlines		
13/01/08	Toyota		

Date	Company	Pos.	Notes
13/01/08	Ren Business Software	Y	Misc equipment
13/01/08	Superwinch		
13/01/08	Midland Radio		
13/01/08	BF Goodrich		
13/01/08	Halfords		
13/01/08	Maplin		
13/01/08	Mothercare		
13/01/08	Buffwear	Y	Lots of Buff gear
13/01/08	Trafalgar Insurance	Y	Free insurance
13/01/08	Books etc		
13/01/08	Dixons		
13/01/08	PC World		
13/01/08	Orange		
13/01/2018	Jepson Photography	Y	Free photography
13/01/08	Easyjet	Y	Return flights from Prague
13/01/08	Vodaphone		
13/01/08	Virgin		
13/01/08	T-Mobile		
13/01/08	Nokia		
13/01/08	Carphone Warehouse		
13/01/08	o2		
15/01/08	Amazon		
13/01/08	First Direct	Y	No Charges
15/01/08	National Map Centre		
15/01/08	Tooled Up		
15/01/08	Virgin Airlines		
18/01/08	RAC		
18/01/08	EHS Consulting	Y	Misc equipment
18/01/08	Shell		

Date	Company	Pos.	Notes
18/01/08	Mobil		
18/01/08	Texaco		
18/01/08	BP		
18/01/08	Conoco		
18/01/08	Total		
18/01/08	Gulf		
18/01/08	Wipac.com	Y	Spotlights
18/01/08	rcohs.com		
18/01/08	sartech.com	Y	EPIRB at cost
20/01/08	Autotrader		
20/01/08	arb.com.au		
20/01/08	mattsavage.com	Y	Air compressor
20/01/08	autolok.co.uk		
20/01/08	Sainsburys		
20/01/08	Tesco		
20/01/08	Asda		
20/01/08	Marks and Spencer		
20/01/08	British American Tobacco		
20/01/08	Topgear		
21/01/08	4x4touring-gear.com/		
21/01/08	Specialist-leisure.co.uk	Y	Discounted winch
21/01/08	challenger4x4theshop.co.uk/		
21/01/08	hilton.co.uk		
21/01/08	marriott.co.uk		
21/01/08	novotel.com/Novotel/index.html		
21/01/08	campanile.com/en/default.aspx		
21/01/08	accorhotels.com/gb/home/index.shtml		

Date	Company	Pos.	Notes
21/01/08	Sony		
21/01/08	Nintendo		
21/01/08	BigYellow		
21/01/08	Access self-storage		
21/01/08	Safestore		
21/01/08	Storageking		
21/01/08	Spacemaker		
21/01/08	Shurgard		
21/01/08	Apple		
21/01/08	Harrods		
21/01/08	Debenhams		
21/01/08	Thermarest		
21/01/08	Optima		
21/01/08	outdoorworld		
21/01/08	outdoorgb		
21/01/08	Costwold Outdoor		
21/01/08	Mountain Warehouse		
21/01/08	Snugpak		
21/01/08	GearZone		
21/01/08	Vango		
21/01/08	Outdoor action		
21/01/08	tents and camping.co.uk		
21/01/08	gooutdoors		
21/01/08	europerformance		
21/01/08	proven-products		
21/01/08	koni-shock-absorbers		
21/01/08	Camskill		
21/01/08	Paddock Spares		
21/01/08	Car Performance Parts		
21/01/08	Arbil 4x4		
21/01/08	Famour 4		

Date	Company	Pos.	Notes
21/01/08	Rebel 4x4		
21/01/08	Electric Winches		
21/01/08	offroadmdg		
21/01/08	Mobell		Gave deal on Contract notice
21/01/08	orbit		
21/01/08	g-comm		
21/01/08	Adam Phones		
21/01/08	Telemar		
21/01/08	Hire-a-Phone		
21/01/08	Cellhire		
03/02/08	The AA		
03/03/08	Footloose 4x4	Y	Free training

APPENDIX H: SPONSORS

Company	Nature of Business	Website
Footloose 4x4	4x4 Expedition Vehicle Preparation	www.footloose4x4.com
Easyjet	British low-cost carrier airline operating domestic and international scheduled services on over 820 routes in more than 30 countries	www.easyjet.com
Matt Savage Compressors	Compressors and Recovery Equipment	www.mattsavage.com
First Direct Bank	First Direct is a telephone and internet-based retail bank	www.firstdirect.com
Wipac	Leaders in Vehicle Lighting Design	www.wipac.com
Buffwear	Multi-Functional Headwear	www.buffwear.co.uk
Jepson Photography	Photographers	www.jepsonphotography.co.uk
Ren Business Software	Database Design	
Trafalgar	Risk Insurance for Businesses	www.trafalgar.uk.com
Sartech Search	Search and Rescue beacons	www.sartech.com
Brightive	Smarter Project Delivery	www.brightive.net
Bush Baby	Specialise in designing front (baby carriers) and back carriers (baby backpacks), accessories	www.bush-baby.com

Company	Nature of Business	Website
	and toddlers outdoor clothing	
Roofbox	Travel in safety, comfort and style	www.roofbox.co.uk
Specialist Leisure	Winches and other 4x4 Equipment	www.specialist-leisure.co.uk

APPENDIX J: ENDORSEMENTS

"Best of luck with the trip Graham and achieving something I never have - taking children!" **Sir Ranulph Fiennes - OBE Adventurer**

"Everyone here at Leicester City would like to wish Graham, Eirene and their family all the best for this epic journey. There will no doubt be plenty of ups and downs on the way - but I am sure you will stay strong and reach your destination. It's a fantastic cause and one that is obviously very close to my heart. Good luck and safe journey." **Ian Holloway - Leicester City Manager**

"A journey of flight is as old and primeval as life itself. But a journey of rescue is something uniquely Human. Good Luck Graham, Eirene and the crew, with your amazing journey, I know you'll make it." **Daniel Moylan - Lone Wolf Transglobal**

"We want you to know that we are proud of your initiative and kind intentions. We want to support you in your endeavours! Good luck and let us know if there is anything we can do to help out. We appreciate you! Best wishes." **Lance Armstrong—The Lance Armstrong Foundation**

"I hope it's warmer out there than it is here!" **Glen Hoddle - Former England Manager**

"Wishing you all the luck in the world on your mad trip—you will certainly feel the miles. You can hear it now—"Dad, are we nearly there yet?" - well hum no! Wrap fish in foil and cook it on the engine block and don't drink the water. And remember, eat Marmite and the mozzies won't bother you. Best wishes." **Si and Dave - The Hairy Bikers**

APPENDIX K: THE VEHICLE

Metallic Green 2001 Toyota Land Cruiser Amazon 4.2 litre Turbo Diesel GX

- Extra fuel tank (capacity = 96 litre main tank + 55 litre auxiliary + 2 x 20 litre jerry cans = 191 litres/42 gallons)
- Patriot roof rack
- Roofbox from The Roofbox Company
- Fitted raised air intake/snorkel
- Bullbars
- 6 x B F Goodrich All Terrain tyres with steel rims
- 2 x 20 litre water cans with mountings
- Driving lamps and roof lamps from Wipac
- Raised suspension Old Man Emu Springs
- Under bodyguard
- Warn 9500 lb winch from Specialist Leisure
- Fitted cargo net in rear of vehicle
- Duel jerry can holder
- Compressor from Matt Savage
- Water purification system
- Invertor (3 pin electric socket!)
- Life hammer and fire extinguisher
- Hi-Lift jack including jack points
- Sand plates
- Roof ladder
- Comedy air horn
- 8 Wolf boxes for storage
- Radio with iPod connection
- Spares kit
- Puncture repair kit

- Winch kit
- 4 x iPod Nanos (one emergency back-up) and Nintendo DS
- Garmin 350c Satellite Navigation System

Vehicle prepared by Paul Marsh @ Footloose4x4

APPENDIX L: MEDIA LINKS

The Daily Telegraph

Daily Mail

Drive

APPENDIX M: PICTURES

Author with former England Manager Glen Hoddle

Some of the tools and equipment for the car

We found our car!

Lapping up the media attention

© Nigel Jepson Photography 2018

© Nigel Jepson Photography 2018

We raised money through donations from friends, family and stranger for Macmillan Cancer Support

Hannah's job - removing stones from the tires

Trying to pretend I'm a mechanic, France

Anna the donkey, France

Thiepval Memorial, France

Châteaux de la Roche, France

Precious moments - Abigail, France

Auschwitz II–Birkenau, Poland

Auschwitz II–Birkenau, Poland – the kids sensed it

Shadows of our former selves

The daily "getting out of the car and into the accommodation " manoeuvre

Paying homage to Buddha Abigail, Switzerland

The Landcruiser in Switzerland. "Scatter my ashes here" Eirene said

Still in my "taking pictures of the car everywhere" phase

Piazza San Marco, Venice. I wasn't smiling at the prices

Rialto Bridge, Venice

More worshipping from Hannah, Croatia

Tired legs in Dubrovnik, Croatia

Hannah having some time on her own, Croatia

Post wrap party after dropping Emily on her head

She hasn't changed. Dubrovnik, Croatia

Sunset in Croatia

Tunnel of Hope, Sarajevo

Kazakhstan not quite how Borat portrayed it

Kyrgyzstan looking not very Eastern Bloc

On the Silk Road Kazakhstan

Traditional local tourist clothing, Kyrgyzstan

Bird's Nest Stadium, Beijing

Great Wall of China

The interest in the children in China was phenomenal – this was in the Forbidden City, Beijing

Landslides were very common in China

Laos was my favourite country

Laos looking like I hoped it would

Love a good waterfall, Laos

Hard to believe but we are literally in a minefield in Laos

Go and play but watch out for the snakes, Laos

Swimming in Laos

With hindsight I should've maybe helped ahead of taking a picture

Bridge over the River Kwai, Thailand

Paradise in Thailand

Gorgeous Thailand

Another empty beach, Thailand

Always a threat

Hannah and I almost stood on this Monocled Cobra. Later we discovered it was exceptionally venomous.

James Bond Island (The Man With The Golden Gun)

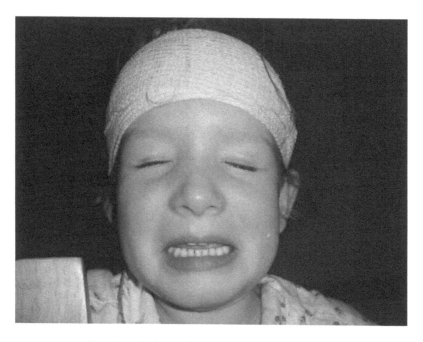

Another slight mishap with Emily in Thailand

What a find - Buffalo Bay Vacation Club, Ko Phayam island, Thailand

Ranong, Thailand near an old POW camp

My Buddhist mate, Thailand

Another Emily accident – helped by mum, photographed by dad, Singapore.

Modelling on the Beach, Australia

Modelling on the Beach 2, Australia

Too cool for school, Australia

3 sisters at the 12 Apostles

Another milestone - Sydney Opera House, Australia

It'll be fine Eirene, what's the worst that could happen? Rented car, Australia

On a bright desert highway, Australia

These buggers nip!

The BA Captain asked Hannah and me to bring her home

Talent for happiness? Peter Culshaw reports from this year's Carnival in Brazil telegraph.co.uk/audiofile

Are we there yet? No, just another 21,000 miles to go

by Stephen Adams

The family and their trusty car

Graham and Eirwen Nainwith gave up the daily commute to London and instead drove their young family all the way to Au

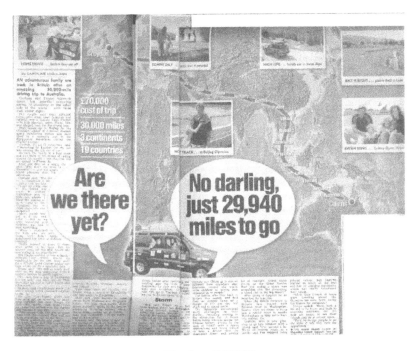

The Sun 27/02/09

WE LOVE OUR... LAND CRUISER
Graham and Eirene Naismith, Surrey

'Are we nearly there yet?' It's a question Graham and Eirene Naismith will no doubt get used to, as they embark on a 16,800 mile (27,037km) journey from their home in Croydon to Cairns, Australia with their children Hannah, six, Emily, four, and Abigail, one. The incentive? To raise money for Macmillan Cancer Support, get out of a work rut and enjoy a bit of family bonding.

It was Eirene who decided a Toyota Land Cruiser would be the perfect choice. 'It's very reliable, has a great average fuel consumption, is less noisy than other 4x4s and, most importantly, there's lots of space for everyone,' says Graham. He's well prepared for technical difficulties, having collected a veritable warehouse of spare parts and brushed up on car mechanics. 'A few months ago I couldn't even change an oil filter,' he admits. 'Now I can strip down the engine and put it back together in my sleep.'

So is he worried about keeping the kids entertained? 'Not really. We're hoping they'll be absorbed by the landscape and the different cultures they'll encounter... but we've bought a Nintendo and an iPod, just in case!'

PHOTOGRAPHY JOE MCGORTY

Toyota Magazine Summer 2008

Article © We Are Sunday Ltd 2018
Picture © www.joemcgorty.com 2018

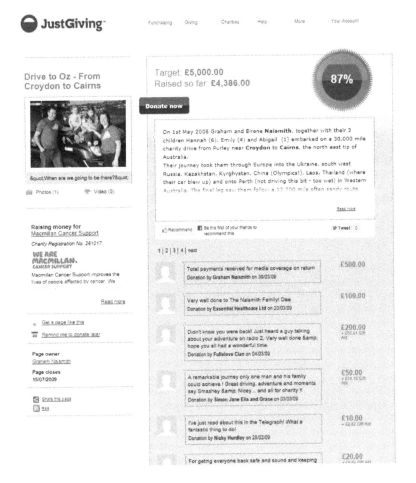

Including Gift Aid, over £5k raised for Macmillan Cancer Support

485

ABOUT THE AUTHOR

Graham Naismith lives in Tunbridge Wells with his now teenage girls where he works as an IT contractor. He still travels and still dreams. If you're reading this and thinking about doing it, do it.

He can be contacted on info@drive-to-oz.com or via Twitter @grahamnaismith.

The oldest website on the internet is at drive-to-oz.com

Lightning Source UK Ltd.
Milton Keynes UK
UKHW020924310319
340205UK00003B/3/P